Wildlife Conservation Policy

A Reader

Valerius Geist &
Ian McTaggart-Cowan,
Editors

Detselig Enterprises Ltd.
Calgary, Alberta, Canada

CANADIAN CATALOGUING IN PUBLICATION DATA

Main entry under title:
Wildlife conservation policy

Includes bibliographical references.
ISBN 1-55059-114-2

1. Wildlife conservation. 2. Wildlife management. I. Geist, Valerius, 1938- II. McTaggart-Cowan, Ian, 1910-

QL82.W54 1995 639.9 C95-910583-2

210-1220 Kensington Rd. N.W.
Calgary, Alberta T2N 3P5
Canada

Cover design by Bill Matheson.

Detselig Enterprises Ltd. appreciates the financial assistance received for its 1995 publishing program from the Department of Canadian Heritage, and the Alberta Foundation for the Arts, a beneficiary of the Lottery Fund of the Government of Alberta.

Printed in Canada ISBN 1-55059-114-2 SAN 115-0324

Contents

An Introduction

Valerius Geist

This is a reader on wildlife conservation policy; this is not a text. It aims to bring some understanding to the obscure, but vitally important, area of conservation *policy*; it discusses what we in the conservation community need to uphold and defend if wildlife is to thrive, if biodiversity is to be maintained, if natural renewable resources, of which wildlife is a part, are to be used in a sustainable fashion. In this, the North American system of wildlife conservation and management holds important lessons.

The authors of these chapters comprise scholars and practitioners. Their contributions were retained in the style they were submitted, as the differences in style are not arbitrary. Students of policy must face up to notable differences in presentation from different professions and interest groups; knowing how to communicate in science papers is not enough.

This reader focuses on an ongoing, but ancient, struggle between public and private ownership of wildlife. Historically, wildlife has been a pawn in the eternal battle between the rich and powerful and the not-so-wealthy of modest political power. Today's tensions arise not only from private interests gaining on public ones in the area of wildlife conservation and the negative consequences that entails, but also from the inadequate application of available knowledge to decisions on this matter. Beware: these pages are not free of controversy.

A number of fundamental policies have made North American wildlife conservation a great conservation success, reaped rich economic rewards from wildlife, and have shaped much of our way of life into one of high quality. These policies defeated Hardin's (1968) "Tragedy of the Commons"[1] that a century ago devastated North American wildlife. From that carnage arose a system of sustained resource devel-

[1] This denotes the consequence when all help themselves selfishly from a common resource until the resource ceases to exist, e.g. the overgrazing of the British Commons by peasants putting in mor and more livestock in the absence of an authority regulating how many cattle the land could support. The Tragedy of the Commons became a catch-phrase after Garrett Hardin wrote his famous essay on that topic in 1968.

opment in which wildlife not merely survived, but grew and prospered for over 70 years. It is also a noteworthy example of how the private sector can create great wealth and employment from a publicly owned and managed resource, and how the power of market forces can be turned to the benefit of wildlife. This system arose from common continental policies spanning two nations, the United States of America and the Dominion of Canada, with pluralistic, capitalistic societies, in which big game, for instance, is outnumbered by guns, people, and livestock. Sustainable development with the maintenance of biodiversity is today's Holy Grail of international resource conservation (Daly and Cobb 1989; Brown 1992; Bonner 1993; Schaller 1993; Wilson 1993). However, North America's success in achieving these goals is not well appreciated. Wildlife conservation here is an exemplary system of "sustainable development," and despite some shortcomings, is one of the great cultural achievements of North America (Geist 1988, 1989, 1993, 1994), the greatest environmental success story of the 20th century.

These fruitful conservation policies are under sustained attack by sectorial vested interests that, in various guises, are trying to make wildlife marketable private property, and enlarge allodial rights.[2] That would deprive the public of wildlife and make it an economic hostage as well. These interests are labelled as "alternative agriculture," or are promoted as "sustainable development" in which wildlife is exploited privately for trophy hunting, luxury products, and eco-tourism (Bonner 1993). There is a crisis in conservation. It is not being recognized for what it is by a good many who have the most to lose, the wildlife profession included. The crisis resides in the current dismantling of policies and laws that have nurtured, protected, and restored wildlife continent-wide during the last 70 years. Who shall own and benefit from wildlife has been a central question to the long struggle. At work are historic forces that, should we allow them to go unchecked, will once again see wildlife a hostage of private ownership, as it has been all too frequently in the past. Policies that legalize trafficking in dead wildlife and paid hunting are diametrically opposed to the policies proven successful in wildlife conservation in North America.

---

[2] the claim, based on Saxon Common Law, that the sovereign has no authority over private property and the owner residing thereon. The Romans called a Germanic freehold of land an allodium, the holder of which had no obligation to the sovereign. This notion played an important role in the American revolution when it was used to dismiss the claims of the British crown of sovereignty over American lands and landed immigrants. Some of Jefferson's writings deal with this and the distinctions between Saxon and British Common Law. A rancher claiming that he is the one and only decision maker on his land invokes allodial rights.

Much more is now at stake than the conservation achievements of three generations of North Americans, or its orderly evolution toward maintaining unspoiled native wildlife as a joint venture by North Americans from diverse backgrounds and cultures. The regression in laws and policies alluded to, if rectified, would merely return us to conditions of a decade ago. Efforts to return to North America the legislative foundation it once had detract from urgent efforts to safeguard wildlife globally and, somehow, see it through the difficult times that lie but a few decades in the future. Human population growth, as predicted by the "doomsday equation," would reaching infinity in about AD 2026 (von Foerster et al. 1960). Even though von Foerster et al. (1960) wrote tongue-in-cheek, their estimates of human population proved conservative; we are 500 million people ahead of schedule – and growing exponentially (Umpleby 1987). While we may now have little control over that process, the biota[3] we manage to conserve for the time after the predicted human population crisis could have a lasting, beneficial effect. We must now address multiple strategies by which to safeguard wildlife predicated on the assumption that enough social turmoil will face us in the future that all thoughts about wildlife and environment will be pushed aside by much more desperate concerns. How does one then save wildlife for a new beginning after the human population crisis is history?

Even if we ignore the human population issue, there are still issues of massive global pollution that need to be addressed, our global warming, universal habitat destruction, and burnout by ultraviolet-B radiation due to ozone depletion. Yet, is it not futile to move on these, when the very legislative framework supporting wildlife conservation is being destroyed? To understand North American wildlife management, one must know the "root" policies that made it possible. This requires less an understanding of science than of history. What we must defend is not only native wildlife and their habitats, but the legal basis that allows us to defend native wildlife and their habitats as well as a public consensus favorable to wildlife. Not an easy matter, if Henry Ford's quip, recorded in the *Chicago Tribune* in 1916, that "History is more or less bunk" has currency, for nobody can defend what they neither understand nor care about. What needs understanding are the policies, historically unique, that shaped the rise and growth of North America's system of wildlife and nature conservation. They allowed wildlife to recover, despite the wide availability of firearms. Despite its recovery, with about 3.6 billion head of livestock in the U.S. and Canada (Pimentel et al. 1980) and about 270 million people, the 30 million head of big game (after Schmidt and Gilbert 1978) amount to less than 0.5%

[3] a term denoting the whole of the living beings, plants, animals, protists on a given piece of land.

of the large mammal biomass[4] in North America. This figure is a good proxy for just how much "life" we have granted to wildlife on this continent. It is this amount, which contains virtually all the biodiversity, that is now subject to takeover and manipulation by private interests under the guise of "alternative agriculture."

In the struggle to understand under what conditions wildlife can thrive, one cannot emphasize enough a favorable public consensus, at least in a society armed to its teeth such as ours, and able to travel and trade freely. We in North America cannot afford to loose that good will towards wildlife, and trade it for the public hatred and antagonism towards wildlife that was Europe's historic lot. Access to wildlife makes all the difference. No matter what the economic equation, if the public does not have access to wildlife and enjoy a proprietary right, if wildlife slips into the control of the ruling elite, then history teaches that wildlife will be persecuted as a symbol of the hated elite (Stahl 1979).

Note for instance the attachment to wildlife by the French culture in North America, as exemplified by the popularity and deep, innovative involvement in management, research, and education by the *Fédération Québécoise de la Faune* (Quebec Wildlife Federation), as discussed in this book by Professor Yves Jean.

The successes of wildlife conservation in South Africa, based on private ownership of largely restored big game herds, have been pronounced as exemplary and worthy of imitation (Thomson 1992). However, South Africa's success is not built on stable social foundations. It is predicated on the presence of a police state in which a small minority of citizens owns the land and wildlife and has the right to bear arms. One cannot transplant policies willy-nilly between societies. Consider: what would happen to South Africa's wildlife if every citizen in good standing could buy firearms to his heart's content as we can in North America?

The policies that succeeded in returning wildlife to our continent may be universal, as they are similar to those of native people, as depicted in Harvey Feit's (1987) studies of Labrador Cree management of moose. We meet the same policies again in the chapter by Norman Simmons and Gladys Netro about native land claims and wildlife management in Canada's North (see also Dueck 1990), and they are central to recent success in wildlife conservation in Zimbabwe as discussed here by Douglas Crowe (see also Parker and Amin 1983; Bonner 1993).

As indicated in my chapter, North American policies of wildlife management arose from a continental, cooperative effort between the

[4] the measurable mass of all living beings on a given piece of ground.

United States and the Dominion of Canada between 1906 and 1921 to safeguard renewable resources. It was based on U.S. President Theodore Roosevelt's Doctrine of Conservation, in which he made common cause with Canada's Prime Minister Sir Wilfred Laurier (Smith and Witty 1970, 1972). Consequently the laws of both countries reflect the same basic policies. The urgency to restore decimated stocks of wildlife and save species teetering at the brink of extinction made the restoration of wildlife the primary goal at which policies and laws were directed. There was little debate in Canada's Commission on Conservation (1911-1919) about how to make wildlife useful, but there was no doubt that wildlife, once abundant, was to serve as an economic resource. The commissioners would have been comfortable with Leopold's (1933:3) view of game management as "the art of making land produce sustained annual crops of wild game for recreational use." There was then no confusion about the goals of wildlife management, as discussed by Douglas Crowe in this book, whether to conserve unadulterated native wildlife or husband it in agricultural fashion for productivity and harvest. However, note Professor Bob Hudson's paper to the contrary.

As discussed below, a central dilemma of North American wildlife management is the role of wildlife as a public resource on private land (Leopold 1933). That private persons should bear any real burden of public wildlife is unacceptable and requires relief, no matter how cloudy the legal definition of ownership of wildlife (see Clayjohn et al. v. Petra et al. No. 93-CV-0223-B, 06/08/94, U.S. District Court, Wyoming). How to best achieve this goal, how to make private landowners conserve wildlife and their habitat, are pertinent questions. These and other questions pertaining to economics are addressed by Rasker and Freese in this book. See also how a large international initiative, The North American Waterfowl Management Plan involving landowners, was structured to conserve waterfowl and habitat in the chapter by McKeating, Shandruk, and Trottier. Something can be done with an international migratory bird treaty, good will, and some money.

Of the policies expressed in North American wildlife law (Lund 1980; Bean 1983), I isolated five key, **enabling** policies affecting wildlife. These are discussed in greater detail in my chapter on North American wildlife management. Briefly they are: (1) Wildlife is a public resource and may be held privately only in trust for the public. (2) Markets in dead wildlife and parts and products from all vulnerable wildlife (big game, upland game, waterfowl, shore birds, song birds) are disallowed, that is, excluded from the marketplace, excepting furs. (3) Allocation of surplus wildlife for consumption is by law and settled annually after public input and debate. (4) Wildlife may be killed only for cause, that is for food, fur, in self-defence, or if it damages private property. (5) Wildlife is recognized as an international resource to be managed co-operatively by sovereign states under treaties. Two additional policies, important, but not crucial, and to this day only partially realized, are that all "outdoor" resources are an integral whole, and that science should be used as a tool to discharge policy (Leopold 1933). In all this, North Americans were decades ahead of their time.

There were powerful motives to adopt these policies. Wildlife had been destroyed almost continent-wide at the turn of the 20th century. The "Tragedy of the Commons" had run its full course (Hardin 1968), and Adam Smith's "unseen hand" had created the foreseeable havoc. George Catlin, living as a painter among western tribes in the early 19th century, foresaw the demise of the buffalo and of the native people clearly. He correctly identified the uncontrolled markets in wildlife as the cause of the impending demise (Catlin 1841). It was not public ownership of wildlife that led to the "tragedy," as wrongly attributed by *The Economist* (Oct. 22, 1988, p. 21, see Geist 1989), but lack of controls and the lack of will to control (Mathissen 1959). That was proven only too vividly by the subsequent success of North America's system of wildlife management, which rose phoenix-like from the ashes of our dead wildlife.

Unfortunately, the fruitful policies noted above also carried seeds of destruction within. One destructive element is the unexamined faith in science as the fundament of natural resource management and the consequent lack of emphasis on history, humanities, and literature in the training of North American wildlife managers. Within the wildlife profession there arose science-based wildlife managers, technically capable, but remarkably ill-informed about conservation policy, how it arose, how it is transmuted, and the all-too-human factors as agents of change. Some wildlife professionals made common cause with those who began dismantling our system of wildlife conservation. Of this there was little danger until public wildlife again became abundant and valuable, stimulating the appetite of those powerful enough to abrogate it for personal use. That only repeats what has happened often in the history of wildlife conservation: the rich and powerful expropriating wildlife from the public for their very private enjoyment and profit (Geist 1988).

An undue emphasis on science results in the common confusion of strategy and tactics. Science, essential at the tactical level, is of less use at the strategic level, as strategy and the objectives it pursues deal largely in cultural values, not laws of nature. Yet both levels are important in wildlife management. The deeper tragedy resides in misconceptions about science. When the founding fathers of North American wildlife conservation embraced science, they were aware of the great ignorance about the species of plants and animals on this continent. Knowing more about these, surely, could not but lead to better decisions about how to use them for our collective benefit. This was not an idle dream, but the informed hope of an elite endowed with a classical education, and a deeply ingrained optimism about progress and national destiny. That elite, because it was grounded in classical education, understood policy and strategy only too well, but worried over its ignorance of nature. That ignorance had to be, and was, rectified. However, we have lost sight of the strategic level in the process, because our education for wildlife managers removes them from the classics and humanities. With the birth of the wildlife profession, which can be dated by Aldo Leopold's 1933 book on wildlife management, there arose a system of training, research, and teaching that embraced science, and rightly so, but it overlooked or took for granted policies that were crucial to sound wildlife management. That worked well enough as long as wildlife populations were being restored on this continent, and wildlife was not abundant. But with wildlife becoming a wealth-creating resource (Geist 1994), the challenge to public ownership of wildlife was inevitable. Wildlife managers in North America were poorly prepared for that day.

Scientists, by their very nature, are not "professionals" in the classical sense of the term. They are, in rather important aspects, quite the opposite. An engineer or architect, both members of professions recognized in law, are nurtured during university training in the understanding that a *service* will be performed for the public, that to *design* is to compromise continually (in the choice of materials, costs, expertise, and wishes of clients), that working with those of different professions is a normal part of one's work, and that legal liability and accountability in the courts are also part of normal work. What "public" does a scientist service, besides a handful of colleagues doing research on the same topic? Are scientists trained in the art of compromise? (How can one compromise in testing hypotheses?) When are scientists brought into court and made accountable for their work? When do they serve a client? While team-research has become much more fashionable in the past decade in sciences, *interdisciplinary* research remains a conundrum in science. While our training of scientists does produce good technical researchers, it does not equip scientists in training with much understanding, or respect, for scholarship in the liberal arts, history, or law. Moreover, such training, in emphasizing current publications, obliterates an appreciation of the writings from the past, and thus any historic dimensions to their science. The mass-training of scientists tends to be long on technique, but short on analysis and scholarship. Little wonder that The Wildlife Society's *Journal of Wildlife Management* is not about management. It's a misnomer. It is a journal of wildlife *science*, for its contributions to management are rare, and almost totally wanting at the policy level. Nor is the *Wildlife Society Bulletin* a "professional" outlet, but merely an academic journal for short papers in wildlife science. That may change, however, and one may hope that it does.

A problem that scientists have difficulties with is segregating the scientifically possible from the culturally acceptable. I was unaware of this distinction when, enamored with Dasmann's and Mossman's (1965) book on game ranching, I embraced the idea, only to discover years later why it was utterly unacceptable for reasons outside science (Geist 1985, 1988). The average North American graduate from a wildlife management program, without knowledge about how our system of wildlife management came about, without an understanding of market forces, cut off from foreign systems of wildlife management by language barriers and oblivious of their successes, failures, or reason for existence, is left institutionally poorly prepared to defend wildlife. History is a vaccine against bad ideas. Unfortunately, current problems arise largely from a recycling of bad ideas from the past. Therefore, whatever our wildlife managers can gather in defence of wildlife is based on their own wits and intuitions, which, fortunately, are by no means trivial. They tend to be aware of and uneasy about deficits in their understanding of social institutions, and express this as the need to understand human behavior, or the human element in wildlife management, or the need for involvement by social scientists. One gains the impression that sitting down to a "scientific" observation of hunters would suffice. Unfortunately, it does not. Such studies reveal little about social institutions, though much about compliance with wildlife laws – or the lack thereof. Unfortunately, environmental movements, generally ahead of wildlife managers in their understanding of policy, usually fail to see wildlife management as part of the struggle for a healthy environment. Yet some wildlife managers and conservationists have rebelled against this institutionalized insensitivity to history and culture as, for instance, reflected by the contributors to Alex Hawley's (1993) *Commercialization and Wildlife Management*, or by Ted Kerasote (1993) in *Bloodties*, or Jim Posewitz (1994) in *Beyond Fair Chase* – to mention a few.

Having said what I did, I must emphasize nevertheless that when science is being used in decision making it must be of a quality to survive court challenges, that is hostile cross-examination in public by skilled lawyers. Real-life science that matters is scrutinized much more thoroughly than during peer review for publication in academic journals.

What then is policy?

Policies are value propositions that are translated into law and give guidance in the interpretation of laws, be it in the regulations or in court proceedings enforcing the laws. Policies are statements about actions. They are rooted in powerful, urgent historical events; they reflect on community ethics and leadership as David Neave (1993) clearly identified. Policies reflect different wishes by different communities. Here native people and their political aspirations are relevant. Policies derive their importance from the acuity of the problem they redress, their breadth of application, the court decisions upholding them, and the dominance they achieve in public perception. Gilbert (1993) makes the point that policies are frequently enacted in response to crises. I concur, even though academic studies of this show a very complex process in which agency agendas have a high profile (Seidenfeld 1992). Gilbert (1993) is probably also correct in concluding that policies are not enacted with a clear vision for the future in mind, but from a need to create short-term relief from intolerable situations. All this is not science, but much more important and immediate at the personal level, for court decisions can and do result in the loss of liberty and wealth by individuals transgressing game laws based on policies accepted by a community.

Leopold (1933:406) called policy "the plan of administration adopted by government"; in discussion he treats policies as ideas to be formulated into law (therefore, **not** a plan; he might have meant "manner," not "plan" in the current sense of the word). His three point "An American Game Policy" expresses **intent** only in points 2 and 3; collectively they are propositions, not a "plan." He urged that policy be derived experimentally and that such be based on an impartial search for facts (science). Robinson and Bolen (1989) treat policy as the intent of law as set out in regulations.

The authors of the "Guidelines for Wildlife Policy in Canada" treat policy as the grand product of their deliberations for desirable conditions. It is an interesting document as it highlights not only a vision of what wildlife management might mean, but also failures in dealing with policy. Its history is not relevant, but its manner of generation is. Its intentions are not as powerful as the root policies of North American conservation listed above, because it is a consensus of what is **currently** politically feasible. It is not the projection of an ideal to be achieved and defended. Also, it lacks roots, because it says little about Canada's active and admirable past in wildlife conservation. It fails to acknowledge the real success of wildlife conservation on this continent. Worse still, it treats today's wildlife as a "gift of God," and not the consequence of successful management. Thus it belittles the great achievements and sacrifices of two generations of North Americans and moves wildlife onto slippery legal ground. What was done to wildlife by whom, to what end and effect, not only allocates credit or blame, but has legal implications, as can be seen from Tilleman's paper in this volume. Note that he discusses real biology in developing legal theory, exposing an opportunity for fruitful dialogue between science and law. Far from standing in splendid isolation, biological theory can be crucially important to the generation of law. Tilleman (1991) asked for a constitutional amendment in Canada reflecting public sentiments for an "interminable right to clean air, pure water, healthy soils and protection of other natural resources, and that environmental assessments of the same be based on a holistic and comprehensive approach."

The paper by William Threlfall deals with the history of wildlife in Great Britain. At first reading one may be overwhelmed by detail, but it is detail pertinent to an understanding how systems of wildlife management arise and evolve. Roman, Celtic, Germanic, and Norman law shaped the legal system of Britain and continue in Canadian and American law. This makes the example of Britain more pertinent to us than, say, the German system of wildlife management. Here Quebec makes an exception, as its wildlife laws are affected by its French heritage as discussed by Yves Jean in this volume.

If one reads about the history of wildlife management in other countries, one would see parallels with Threlfall's account. Invariably, wildlife winds up as the property of the social elite, and much of wildlife management is generated from a struggle between the public disenfranchised from wildlife, but normally carrying the costs of maintaining wildlife, and the rich and powerful that reap benefits and enjoyment from wildlife. Blinding passions and irrational actions are the hallmark of this struggle, with the elite often using brute force and vile cruelty against the public to maintain control. Commoners, incensed about the inequities, fought back tit for tat. Wildlife was – and still is – the hapless victim of this struggle (Zimmermann 1843; Franz 1926; Ausser 1947; Stahl 1979; Lund 1980; Roedle 1971).

Few subjects teach more about man's cruelty to man than the history of wildlife management. The fierce passions surrounding wildlife possession and hunting which can make transgressors indifferent to the cruellest of fates should they be caught, and have made wildlife a prime target for retribution against the rich and mighty (Stahl 1979), led to the near-extermination of wildlife with every revolution in Europe (Ausser 1947:54; Stahl 1979), and made demands for access to wildlife and the bearing of arms a key demand of revolutionaries for centuries (Zimmermann 1843; Franz 1926; Lund 1980). This passion is one reason for the great dangers faced by wildlife law enforcement officers, who in the United States are about eight times as likely to be assaulted as police officers and twice as likely to be killed on the job. It is reflected in the poacher wars by which German hunting laws were shaped (Geist, this volume), in the shoot-to-kill orders under which game guardians in Zimbabwe operate, protecting the last of the rhinos from poachers, or in the vandalizing of New Zealand deer farms by individuals aggrieved over loss of access to land on which they hunted (Massey 1986). Bloody wars between hordes of armed poachers (over

300 armed poachers, on occasion, operating as a unit) and foresters led the Archbishop of Salzburg, Johan Ernst Graf von Tun, to order in 1709 the extermination of the last of Austria's ibex (Ausser 1947:75). The fierce passions associated with the ownership or taking of wildlife must never be underestimated – nor the ingenuity and determination of the rich and powerful to wrestle the ownership of wildlife from the public. Beware: history teaches that they have succeeded often in this ancient struggle (Geist 1988).

As to the behavior of civil servants in contact with the powerful, please be aware that the sociologist Beryl L. Crowe (1969) made this an explicit warning for scientists to heed: she wrote as follows about the behavior of bureaucracies (the "watchers" hired by the public to guard the public's interest):

> *Our best empirical answer to the question . . . Who shall watch the watchers themselves? – have shown fairly conclusively . . . that the decisions, orders, hearings and press releases of the custodians of the commons . . . give the large, but unorganized groups in American society symbolic satisfaction and assurances. Yet, the actual day-to-day decisions and operations of these administrative agencies contribute, foster, aid and indeed legitimate the special claims of a small but highly organized groups to differential access to tangible resources which are extracted from the commons. This has been so well documented in the social sciences that the best answer to the question of who watches over the custodians of the commons is the regulated interests that make intrusion on the commons.*

For informative case histories see Serber (1981). Therefore, public wildlife managers may turn into defenders and guarantors of special privileges granted to the affluent (Fitzhugh 1989), just as foresters, paid by the public to guard the public interest, have become the chief spokesmen for and defenders of the timber industry.

Private ownership or control of wildlife has had positive consequences. In the late 19th century the plains bison was saved by a handful of entrepreneurs, who turned the bison over to public ownership when private herds increased and a market for bison failed to materialize. Many landowners are exemplary guardians of wildlife on their land. However, they are mortals and if their land changes hands so may the fate of wildlife. That is, there is no guarantee of continuity of conservation, one reason why, ultimately, wildlife conservation has to rely on public ownership for continuity. Another factor is the deliberate domestication of private wildlife so it may satisfy the whims of the owner or the market place. In the long run it precludes effective wildlife conservation as wildlife becomes a commodity ranched for every whim of the marketplace, whose infrastructure offers gold-plated opportunities to launder public wildlife by criminals. Public wildlife cannot co-exist with stocks of private wildlife destined for the market after death. Ironically, expenditures for recreation based on living wildlife (currently about $65 billion in the U.S. and Canada) are by a magnitude greater than such based on dead wildlife (about $5-8 billion globally) and provide much employment in the service and manufacturing industry (Geist 1993, 1994). The market as such is not a villain, but it becomes a villain if made to reward the death of wildlife. How economics pertaining to wildlife can be perceived is discussed by Ray Rasker and Curt Freese in some detail in this book. They cover a vitally important subject that is much in need of study by wildlife managers.

History teaches that capricious events greatly affect wildlife. When the potato was introduced to Europe it made obsolete the forests of old oak and beech trees that hitherto were the source of mast to fatten pigs for bacon, an essential winter staple. Now forests could be converted to wood production and the old mast trees could be cut down. Wildlife abundance and quality plummeted in Europe with the loss of these open, highly productive old forests of mast-bearing trees (Plochmann 1979). Or, note the near collapse of red fish populations along the southern coastlines of the United States when a Cajun cook in New Orleans made "blackened red fish" a rage with trendy urbanites. The spread of exotic plants and animals is unpredictable and creates unforeseen dilemmas as discussed by Jim Teer (this volume).

A policy question of concern in Canada is: What would happen if native people were granted greater **legal** controls over the conservation and disposition of wildlife? If this would give native people some real power over wildlife's fate and make them publicly accountable for their decisions, it would probably be the best thing we could do for wildlife. It might even be a step toward reversing current conditions where wildlife has scant protection from such destroyers as modern agriculture, forestry, and transportation. In the Northwest Territories of Canada, where native people gained de facto control over wildlife, they are exemplary managers (Dueck 1990).

A vital but poorly understood part of wildlife management is law enforcement, discussed here by Thomas Striegler. However, which laws are the most likely to be obeyed? The contrast between what North Americans and Germans did (Geist, this volume) should be cause for reflection. History suggests that laws are obeyed that coincide with the wishes of the majority, and that are perceived as just. The cheapest manner of law enforcement is for the public to police themselves. That can only happen when all have a stake in the matter being policed, such as *de facto* ownership of wildlife and an effective say in its management.

Validity of information is always a concern, and in science we normally rely on peer-reviewed papers to curb inaccuracies and trivia. It's far from being a rigorous process, one not free of abuse through sheer human weakness. Its essence is reviews by peers unknown to the author. While information in a refereed journal has status, it pales besides good investigative journalism or examinations in courts of law. A report published by an investigative reporter seeks not only to expose valid information, it tries to allocate blame. As a result, it is subject to court challenges by those blamed. The report must consequently be one that can survive unscathed the court process of hostile public challenge by the very best legal minds as guided by the best technical expertise money can buy. That process is a much harder method of ferreting out the truth than any peer-review process in academia.

To formulate policy, a broad understanding of many concerns is required. However, this is opposed by the jargon in which scholarly and professional disciplines communicate. How does one, as a scientist writing for fellow-scientists, reference matter pertaining to law enforcement? I have excellent videotapes on investigations pertaining to wildlife law enforcement, showing evidence that was used in court. How does one cite it? Do I cite court transcripts for evidence? This is just a tiny part of the problem of communication facing a scientist who crosses disciplinary borders. Wildlife policy simply cannot be based on science alone, but on an interdisciplinary winnowing of information, some of which may strike us, the wildlife biologists and professionals, as peculiar in style and content.

What crises will shape wildlife conservation policies in the future? A number of issues are already on the horizon, such as the challenge to the notion of "wilderness" and "natural" (Wagner and Kay 1993), which will have profound consequences on how we will manage public lands in the future. Cowan (this volume) shows that in the past the continent was much affected ecologically by native people and what we saw as "wilderness" was already a biota much shaped by the intelligent mind and skilled hands of aboriginal Americans. We are likely to shift from "wilderness values" and "let nature be" policies to managing for biodiversity; national parks will be much affected.

The economic decline of the West and the slide in importance of extractive industries is likely to see the land converted more and more to public ownership, giving rise to a "buffalo commons," as its proponents Frank and Deborah Popper (1991) have named it. It's an intriguing idea to recreate a "frontier," and a profitable one at that, very well argued and one deserving attention. In the greater scope their proposal is one of "rehabilitation," of ecological restoration, of putting biodiversity back onto degraded landscapes, of consciously returning the earth's surface to productivity from degradation. A tangible example of this is the restructuring of strip mines in the West into bighorn sheep habitat (MacCullough and Geist 1991). Ozone depletion will almost certainly drive conservation "under cover" into a Noah's Ark approach to conservation, till the ozone blanket has reconstituted. Large areas of land

and water face "burnout," so that biota to be protected, let alone our food production, will shift under some sort of cover and controlled indoor environments (Geist in press). Not low-tech, but high-tech will be the near future of conservation. As mentioned earlier, a similar approach may have to be taken with increasing population turmoil during the global world population crisis.

More immediate, rapid action may soon have to be taken to halt the spread of livestock diseases in wild native mammals from game farms and infected livestock. The fate of tuberculosis in wild and domestic animals in New Zealand is briefly discussed in my main chapter. We may face elk and deer herds in North America infected with livestock diseases. What then?

Hunting is in decline, while the proponents of wildlife as an aesthetics rather than as a tangible resource are gaining ground. That opens the way for easy transfer of ownership of wildlife from the public to the private domain, as well as the loss of freedom to own arms. There is the rise to power of native movements and their striving towards self-government. With their close cultural link to wildlife, this may well be a positive development in conservation – provided wildlife remains in public ownership.

The plunder of public wildlife by organized crime in order to satisfy "conspicuous consumption" via luxury markets in urban centres, mainly in developed countries, but also in such rapidly growing economies as China. Reverence for natural life is not as highly developed in many nations. There are other developments that will affect policy, such as the rise of the "Quality Deer Management" movement in the southern States. It may slip into managing for trophies and the concomitant problems that generates for conservation. The blessing of the growing numbers of introduced exotics, particularly in the southern states, is yet to make itself felt. It will. The costs and benefits of "urban wildlife" will become more prominent as cities become larger still, and some species find here a secure basis for living. Biology and law will have to find an accommodation in taxonomy and formal names as legal entities (Geist 1992). The Chinese curse "May you live in interesting times" appears to be upon us.

Acknowledgements

This book arose from a conference held May 2-5 1990 at the University of Calgary on the future of wildlife. This is not a proceedings volume since a number of speakers did not submit a paper, though their contribution remains captured on videotape, and their views are included in some fashion in these pages.

References

Ausser, C. 1947. *Der Alpensteinbock.* Universum Verlag, Vienna, 243 pp.

Bean, M. J. 1983. *The Evolution of National Wildlife Law.* Praeger, Westport. 448 pp.

Bonner, R. 1993. *At the Hand of Man.* A. Knopf, New York. 329 pp.

Brown, L. (ed.) 1992. *State of the World 1992.* Norton, NY. 256 pp.

Catlin, G. 1841. *Letters and Notes on the Manner, Customs and Conditions of the North American Indians, Written during Eight Year's Travel among the Wildest Tribes of Indians in North America.* Wildey and Putman, New York. ??pp.

Crowe, B. L. 1969. The tragedy of the commons revisited. *Science* 166: 1103-1107.

Dasmann, R. F. 1964. *African Game Ranching.* Pergamon Press & Macmillan Co., London & New York, 75 pp.

Daly, H. E. and Cobb, J.B., Jr. 1989. *For the Common Good.* Beacon, Boston, Mass. 482 pp.

Dueck, H. A. 1990. Carnivore conservation and interagency cooperation: A proposal for the Canadian Rockies. Masters Degree Project, Faculty of Environmental Design, University of Calgary, Calgary. 151 pp.

Feit, H. A. 1987. North American Native hunting and management of moose populations. *Swedish Wildl. Res. Suppl.* 1: 25-42.

Fitzhugh, E.L. 1989. Innovation of the private lands wildlife management programme: A history of fee hunting in California. *Transactions Western Section Wildlife Society* 25: 49-59.

Foerster, H. von, Mora, P. M. and Amiot, L. W. 1960. Doomsday: Friday, 13 November, A.D. 2026. *Science* 132: 1291-1295.

Franz, G. 1926. *Der Deutsche Bauernkrieg 1525.* Deutsche Buch Gemeinschaft, Berlin. 363 pp.

Geist, V. 1988. How markets in wildlife meat and parts, and the sale of hunting privileges, jeopardize wildlife conservation. *Conserv. Biol.* 2(1): 1-12.

—— 1989. Legal trafficking and paid hunting threaten conservation. *Trans. 54th N. A. Wildl. & Nat. Res. Conf.* pp. 171-177

—— 1991. Deer ranching for products and paid hunting: Threat to conservation and biodiversity by luxury markets. pp. 554-561, in R. D. Brown (ed.), *The Biology of Deer.* Springer Verlag, New York.

—— 1992. Endangered species and the law. *Nature* 357: 247-276.

—— 1993. Great achievements, great expectations: Success of North American wildlife management. pp. 47-72 in Hawley, A. W. L. (ed.), *Commercialization and Wildlife Management: Dancing with the Devil.* Krieger Publishing Co., Malabar, Florida.

—— 1994. Wildlife conservation as wealth. *Nature* (London) 368: 491-492.

——. 1995. Noah's Ark II: Rescuing species and ecosystems. pp. 93-102 in Norton, B. G., Hutchins, M., Stevens, E. F. and Maple, T. L. (eds.) *Ethics on the Ark: Zoos, Animal Welfare, and Wildlife Conservation.* Smithsonian Inst. Washington, DC.

Gilbert, F. F. 1993. The vision: Wildlife management in North America. pp. 23-33 in Hawley, A. W. L. (ed.), *Commercialization and Wildlife Management: Dancing with the Devil.* Krieger Publishing Co., Malabar, Florida.

Hardin, G. 1968. The tragedy of the commons. *Science* 162: 1243- 1248.

Hawley, A. W. L. (ed.) 1993. *Commercialization and Wildlife Management: Dancing with the Devil.* Krieger Publishing Co., Malabar, Florida. 124 pp.

Kay, C. E. (in press). Aboriginal overkill: The role of native Americans in structuring western ecosystems. *Human Nature*

Kerasote, T. 1993. *Bloodties.* Random House, New York. 277 pp.

Leopold, A. 1933. *Game Management.* Univ. Wisconsin Press, Madison. 481 pp.

Lund, T. A. 1980. *American Wildlife Law.* Univ. California Press, Berkeley. 179 pp.

MacCallum, N. B. and Geist, V. 1992. Mountain restoration: Soil and surface habitat. *Geo Journal* 27(1): 23-46.

Massey, W. 1986. Escape! The crisis faced by Robbie and Barbara Oldeman. *The Deer Farmer,* Sept.: 6-10.

Mathissen, P. 1959. *Wildlife in America.* Viking, New York. 304 pp.

Neave, D. J. 1993. Who is accountable: The ethics of conservation. pp. 85-101. in Hawley, A. W. L. (ed.), *Commercialization and Wildlife Management: Dancing with the Devil.* Krieger Publishing Co. Malabar, Florida.

Parker, I. and Amin, M. 1983. *Ivory Crisis.* Chatto & Windus, London.

Pimentel, D., Oltenacu, P.A., Nesheim, M.C., Krummel, J., Allen, M.S. and Chick, S. 1980. The potential for grass-fed livestock: Resource constraints. *Science* 207: 843-848.

Plochmann, R. 1979. Mensch und Wald. pp. 157-197 in H. Stern (ed.), *Rettet den Wald,* Kindler Verlag, Munich.

Popper, F. J. and Popper, D. E. 1991. The reinvention of the American frontier. *The Amicus Journal,* Summer: 4-7.

Posewitz, J. 1994. *Beyond Fair Chase.* Falcon Press, Helena, Montana. 118 pp.

Roedle, J. 1971. *Wenn die Hirsche roehren.* Kosmos, Fraencksche Verlagshandlung, Stuttgart, 80 pp.

Serber, D. 1981. The masking of social reality: Ethnographic field work in the bureaucracy. pp. 77-87 in Messerschmidt, D. A. (ed.), *Anthropologists at Home in North America.* Cambridge University Press, New York.

Schaller, G. 1993. *The Last Panda.* Univ. Chicago Press, Chicago. 280 pp.

Schmidt, J. L. and Gilbert, D. L. (eds.) 1980. *Big Game of North America.* Stackpole Books, Harrisburg, Pa. 494 pp.

Seidenfled, M. 1992. A civic republican justification for the bureaucratic state. *Harvard Law Review* 105(7): 1511-1577.

Smith, R. C. and Witty, D. R. 1970, 1972. Conservation, resources and environment. An exposition and critical evaluation of the commission of conservation, Canada. part 1. *Plan Canada* 11(1): 55-71, part 2 11(3): 199-216.

Stahl, D. 1979. *Wild, Lebendige Umwelt.* Alber, Freiburg. 349 pp.

Tilleman, W. A. 1991. We need an environmental amendment. *Policy Options* 12(1): 18-20.

Thomson, R. 1992. *The Wildlife Game.* Nyala Wildlife Publication Trust. Westville, South Africa. 292 pp.

Umpleby, S. A. 1987. World population: Still ahead of schedule. *Science* 235: 1555-56.

Wagner, F. H. and Kay, C. E. 1993. "Natural" and "healthy" ecosystems: Are U.S. national parks providing them? pp. 257-270 in McDonnell, M. J. and S. T. Pickett (eds.), *Humans as Components of Ecosystems.* Springer-Verlag, NY.

Wilson, E. O. 1993. *The Diversity of Life.* Norton, New York. 424 pp.

Zimmermann, W. 1843. *Der grosse Deutsche Bauernkrieg.* (republished by Dietz Verlag, Berlin). 815 pp.

Editor's Note:
Conservation and Wildlife Management in Britain

To study man's inhumanity to man, study wildlife management of the past. Wildlife, throughout history, has been torn between private and public ownership, each side passionately and doggedly fighting for what it considers to be its rights. The taking of wildlife, normally, is associated with intoxicating excitement. That maybe an echo from our long evolutionary past as hunters, and even the viewing of wildlife ignites passions. People are plain fascinated by wildlife – as are wolves that view prey. No matter what origin, these passions are a fact in wildlife conservation, and a prohibition on the taking of wildlife is likely to be as enforceable as celibacy. Professor Threlfall's detailed account of the history of wildlife management in Great Britain reflects this factor. One encounters parallels on the continent of Europe. However, British records are better, for, while Britain was not spared civil war since the Norman conquest, it was spared the many terrible continental wars that destroyed records and archives, or the massive revolutions such as the 16th century peasant wars in Germany or the French Revolution. Still, following the civil wars in Britain there was massive destruction of wildlife as the population helped itself in the moments of opportunity. This happened after every war and revolution on the continent. Compared to Britain, the continental history of wildlife management is replete with greater violence and extremes. The peasant wars led to the slaughter of nobility and clergy and the razing of their castles, monasteries, and churches. Nobility responded with massive retribution that cleared the countryside of peasants and deeply impoverished the land; most castles were never rebuilt due to poverty and remain as ruins to this day. These uprisings originated in good part from demands for access to wildlife, fish, and forests – as did the poaching wars Professor Threlfall describes. While wildlife suffers as a pawn of social struggles, it is also victim (rarely a beneficiary) of the many technological changes that shape the economy and public life, of whims of fashion in politics, and of traditions too dear to let go. Science by itself is not enough for wildlife conservation. The continent contributed early major treaties on wildlife ecology, management, and conservation which are considered brilliant to this day, such as the book on falconry and ornithology by the Hohenstaufen Emperor Frederick II (1194-1250), or the handbooks on wildlife management by Doebel (1739) and Flemming (1749). These laid the foundation for the scholarly traditions in continental wildlife management, with worthy successors in the 19th and 20th century, such as Ferdinant von Raesfeld, Franz Vogt, Walter Frevert, and Professor Hans Stubbe. The history of wildlife conservation in Britain is important as North Americans, while retaining British common-law, deviated strongly from British traditions in wildlife management. A science-based wildlife biology is currently establishing a precarious foothold in Europe, a sign of the unsettled nature of wildlife conservation in modern Europe and the influence of North American ideas on conservation.

Professor Threlfall is a biologist with a Canadian university.

Conservation and Wildlife Management in Britain

William Threlfall

A visitor's first impressions of Britain are that it is a land of contrasts, with a patchwork of fields, hedges, woodlands, and wild open upland areas, all intermingling with large conurbations. Rivers, streams, lakes, ponds, reservoirs, and canals are also apparent. Both the flora and fauna are rich. The attitudes of people on this densely populated island toward conservation and the countryside itself have changed greatly during the past 50 years (Allen 1987; M.G. Morris 1987; P.A. Morris 1987; Poore 1987; Prestt 1987; Sheail 1987; Smith 1987; Stamp 1969).

Why Conserve the Countryside and its Wildlife?

Reasons for conserving the countryside and its wildlife fall into two categories, namely, the ethical and the utilitarian. Ethical values, or arguments, espouse the idea of man's stewardship of nature. It is now recognized that man is a part of nature, and not divorced from it, with the "Land Ethic" of Leopold (1970:239, 240) expressing this truism as follows:

> *All ethics so far evolved rest upon a single premise; that the individual is a member of a community of interdependent parts. . . . In short, a land ethic changes the role of Homo sapiens from conqueror of the land community to plain member and citizen of it. It implies respect for his fellow-members, and also respect for the community as such.*

The utilitarian reasons for conservation include aesthetics, which are yet again difficult to define. However, during the past 30 years increasingly large numbers of people (Green 1981) have obtained pleasure and enjoyment from non-consumptive uses of the countryside, such as bird-watching. Cultural, scientific, and ecological values may also be used to build a case for countryside and wildlife protection. Scientific and ecological values are closely related and are concerned with areas such as the conservation of species and habitats, the gene pool, and the ecological balance of the planet. Never before in history have humans had the ability to alter and manipulate the environment, both for good and bad, as they do at present. Conservation may be undertaken for purely material or commercial (including recreational) reasons, and it is here that it is easiest to justify the expenditure of money in conservation efforts. These conservation values parallel closely the wildlife values noted by Bailey (1984), who notes that negative values must also be considered when conserving wildlife. These negative values include wildlife damage to property and crops, and the costs of controlling, mitigating, and rectifying the damage.

Conservation consists of the planned and wise use of natural resources, in such a way that the productivity of habitats is maintained. This is a dynamic process that is strongly influenced by practices and attitudes of the past. In no case is the latter statement more true than in Britain. To some people, conservation means the preservation and protection of environmental features thought to be of amenity value, including man-made objects such as buildings, yet others believe that it is the maintenance of a clean, livable environment, free of pollution (Green 1981). The prime concern of people today, with regard to the environment and conservation, is the burgeoning, seemingly unstoppable, population explosion and its effect on natural resources (both renewable and non-renewable; Warren and Goldsmith 1983), pollution, aesthetic heritage, and nature. As the population grows we are seeing depletion of non-renewable resources, increasing pollution, and degradation and destruction of habitats and whole ecosystems. Concerns over wildlife and its future have increased during the past several decades, with wildlife conservation having become recognized as an integral part of land use, which competes with, or may complement, agriculture, forestry, industrial and urban development, and recreation. In assessing the potential wildlife conservation value of an area, it is necessary to formulate a series of criteria to be followed in reaching a decision. Margules and Usher (1981) recognized three groups of criteria to be used in conservation evaluations. The first, concerned with diversity and area, can be assessed by a site visit. The second set of criteria require the acquisition of a database in a larger area, with regard to subjects such as naturalness, representativeness, and rarity. Finally, before any decision to conserve an area is taken, notice should be taken of its past history (Sheail 1983), work performed at ecologically similar sites, its potential value, and its fragility. After the biological criteria have been assessed, political concerns may then be considered. Politics has given rise to many countryside conflicts (Lowe et al. 1986) as it relates to the relationship between farming, forestry, and conservation. There can be no doubt that as closer ties develop within the European Economic Community, and with the extension of laws and/or agricultural policies to cover the whole of the Common Market area, conflicts will continue to arise. The use of legislation in wildlife conservation is decried by many people (Mabey 1980) yet in certain circumstances it is essential to conserve habitats and prevent overexploitation, or even extinction, of certain wildlife populations and species.

What is Wildlife and Wildlife Management?

The term "wildlife" has different meanings for different people, but is usually applied to those free-ranging vertebrates that are not domesticated, or have escaped from the constraints of man. Further, it is often used to designate those fish, birds, and mammals that are hunted by man (Threlfall 1989). Bailey (1984) uses a somewhat more restrictive definition in which he includes all free-ranging vertebrate animals in the naturally associated environments that have determined their evolution. This concept excludes those animals that have been introduced into an area, as well as feral animals. Even more difficult to define is the term "game animal," which is usually taken to mean an animal that is taken under pursuit or hunting for food or sport. McKelvie (1985) notes that the term "game" can have a narrower, more precise and legislated meaning, and first appeared in British law in an Act of 1389. The passage of the word into British law has led to many anomalies, particularly as defined by the 1831 Game Act (for example, red grouse and pheasants are game birds, yet the capercaillie is not, because it was extinct in Britain at the time the act was passed. It was subsequently reintroduced and is now hunted. Further, snipe and woodcock are not classed as game birds even though a game licence is required to hunt them. Certain species of fish such as trout and salmon are regarded as game, yet the laws that govern their exploitation differ throughout the country. Mills 1971, 1989). This paper will concentrate on certain species of birds and mammals, perhaps reinforcing the thoughts of McClanahan (1990) that the majority of conservationists are fish bigots.

Wildlife management is the art of producing populations of wildlife that may be harvested within defined limits and without destroying either the wildlife population or its habitat (Leopold 1948). This discipline is one of three areas fundamental to any conservation project: the scientific, socio-economic, and management sectors (Bailey 1984). Wildlife management itself draws on a variety of other professions to supply the diversity of information needed to arrive at rational management decisions, such as ecology, hydrology, forestry, meteorology, vertebrate behavior and physiology, and agriculture. Management of wildlife occurs worldwide, yet in many cases there appears to be little interchange of ideas among workers on the different continents (Dagg undated), a situation that is to be deplored in this age of rapid and easy communication. Part of the reason for the apparent lack of exchange may lie in the very different systems of wildlife ownership in the various countries, such as a public, government-controlled resource in North America, as opposed to a private system in Britain supported by individuals, non-government organizations (NGOs), and occasional government money. The principles underlying the North American system are fully developed in the seminal work of Leopold (1948), who applies biological principles to the management of wildlife as a renewable crop. In the past the manipulation and management of wildlife populations occurred only if the economic returns warranted the expenditure. With the growth of the conservation movement this is no longer true. Manipulations of populations include reductions in the number of a given species due to it being a pest, and the enhancement of numbers of a species that will provide cultural benefits (from aesthetic to research) to man. The manipulation of the population of some species is undertaken to provide a constant supply of individuals or material resources by stabilizing the population (Wood 1983).

The Landscape of Britain and the Effects of Humans

Little, if any, part of the landscape of Britain is untouched, or uninfluenced, by humans. Stamp (1949) discusses the geological structure of the country, and how the landforms in the various regions have given rise to widely different scenery, such as limestone, volcanics, and glaciated areas. Ratcliffe (1984) noted that "the culminating effect of a human population of 54 millions on an island measuring only 230,000 km^2 has been to leave very little truly natural vegetation, i.e. that unmodified by man's activity." There is a plethora of works that attest to this fact (Baker and Harley 1973; Edlin 1972; Millward and Robinson 1977; Rackham 1976, 1986; Stamp 1962, 1964; Woodell 1985). The vast majority of changes seen in the vegetation of Britain have been wrought by humans, but it should not be forgotten that climate also plays a role in determining the climax vegetation[1] in an area, and that over a period of thousands of years both climate and climax vegetation may change (Pennington 1974). The early human history in Britain is discussed by Hawkes and Hawkes (1958). In Palaeolithic times, before 8000 B.C., humans lived by hunting, fishing, and food gathering, and had little effect on their environment. Even in Mesolithic times, 8000-3250 B.C., the small population of humans on the island practised a shifting culture, and while not strictly nomadic, no permanent settlements were established. There is evidence that at this time humans were living in the north of England, Scotland, and Ireland, and there are the first signs of temporary woodland clearances, such as in Dartmoor. The red deer was almost certainly the subsistence animal at this point in time. The Neolithic period, 3250-1700 B.C., saw great cultural changes, with much forest clearance, the development of primitive arable farming, and the

---

1 a common ecological term denoting the last plant community in a succession of plant communities. "Old-growth forest" is a climax community; the shrubs and herbs following in the wake of a forest fire are the beginning of a succession of plant communities that culminates in the climax vegetation.

growth of cereals, usually on high ground (Dimbleby 1984; Roberts 1978). In the Lake District of northwestern England, Pearsall (1965) noted that a long-continued climax of predominantly oak and alder woodlands, which showed little human interference, gave way in the Neolithic and Bronze Age to a slow replacement by "grasslands." Sheep may also have been introduced to Britain at this time and the red deer lost its importance as a subsistence animal.

The Bronze Age, 1700-500 B.C., saw the development of metallurgical skills. However, stone and wooden implements were still used, including a primitive wooden plough. Further forest clearance occurred, with humans moving to lower ground in the Midlands. Fowler (1983) gives a thorough account of farming in prehistoric Britain, and notes that both pastoral and arable farming were undertaken. Tubbs (1986), in describing the settlement of the New Forest, indicates that the first significant clearances there probably began in the middle or late Bronze Age, with a progressive expansion of heathland, at the expense of the woodland, for several centuries.

The Iron Age, 500 B.C.-A.D. 43, saw the establishment of a variety of settlements, from farms to hamlets to hilltop forts. The development of the iron plough made the intensification of arable farming possible, resulting in soil movement. The process of soil degradation, which started as early as the Mesolithic, continued apace. Land was given over to grazing for cattle and sheep, and further forest clearance undoubtedly occurred.

During the Roman Invasion and Occupation, A.D. 43-410, towns sprang up, as did a well-developed road system (Hodder 1978). There was a further loss of forests, and arable farming dominated the southern parts of Britain (Dimbleby 1984). Much of the forest loss may be related to the proliferation of villas, each with its own extensive field system and bathhouse. To heat the latter would require approximately 20 hectares of continuously producing coppice woodland.[2] The Roman influence on the woodlands of the north and west of England were less dramatic.

The Dark Ages (or Anglo-Saxon Period, A.D. 410-1066, when the country was dominated by Germanic tribes [Jones 1978]), saw the establishment of many towns and villages that are still extant. The arrival and settlement of the Scandinavians placed further stresses on the environment. It is of interest that many Viking names reflect much about the countryside, although literal translations are often queried or can be interpreted several ways. Some words of Saxon or Norse origin

[2] a European woodland affected by repeated cutting and much shaped by human hand, and in a shrubby, low-growth state.

of this type include: Frith = woodland; Had-, Hat-, Hed-, Heath- = heath, heather; Lea, -leigh, -ley, -low = forest, wood, glade, clearing; Med-, -mede = meadow; Thwaite, -thwaite = clearing, meadow. The Saxon landscape shows many large earthworks such as Offa's Dyke, and a continued destruction of the forests. The regeneration of woodland and its uses in Anglo-Saxon times are discussed by Hooke (1989), who suggests that hunting and the use of woods as game reserves before the 11th century were far more extensive than previously realized. Anglo-Saxon kings supposedly reserved tracts of forest for hunting, although there are doubts about the truth of this assertion and the customary forest laws that were supposed to exist before the Norman Conquest (Cross 1928). It is also at this time that the principle of common lands may have become established (Hoskins and Stamp 1964). During the Dark Ages there was a movement of people from higher ground to the heavier, richer lowlands and valleys. The reasons for the migration are unclear, but may be related to the loss of soil fertility in the higher reaches after hundreds of years of cultivation, or to the development of ploughs and other tools that could be used to till the heavier soils. The mould-board plough, possibly a Roman invention, and ridge-and-furrow ploughing appeared in England, but Wales, Ireland, and Scotland (Celtic Britain) lagged far behind. In those countries, monasteries exerted a great influence on the people who often located their houses around them, resulting in fewer villages in the countryside. Farms, when built away from the monasteries, were usually in enclosures.

The Norman Conquest (A.D. 1066) and early Middle Ages saw even more marked changes in the countryside, with the building of castles, monasteries, villages, and roads (Darby 1973; Dodgshon 1978). The monasteries continued to wield great power and control much land. With the accession of William I (the Conquerer) the word "Forest" acquired a legal meaning (Hooke 1989; Rackham 1986), and came to mean large, unfenced tracts of land on which deer were protected by special bylaws. Only the king, and those to whom he gave the right, could hunt deer in the Forest (or Chase). A Forest was usually composed of trees, shrubs, and rough-grazing areas. The word first appears in the Domesday Book. Just before the Magna Carta was signed, 143 Forests were known to exist in England. The king might own the land on which the Forest stood, or just run deer on other people's land where he hunted. During the next couple of hundred years successive Norman kings enforced strictly a set of repressive Forest Laws, and spread Royal Forests throughout the whole realm. Degradation of the land continued, and heather became the dominant plant in upland areas. William I surveyed England, with the exception of some parts of the north, and the results appeared in the Domesday Book, A.D. 1086 (Darby 1973). The survey covered a large variety of topics, including names of property holders, property held, its dimensions, ploughing capacity, number of agricultural workers employed, their mills, fishponds, other amenities, and total value in pounds. At the time of the survey the population of England was about 1.5 million, and rose to 4.5 million by A.D. 1300. The majority of the southern and central parts of England were well populated in the early Middle Ages, with little chance of further exploitation or expansion of farmland. Growth did occur with expansion into less favorable wastelands, forests, and fens. The main farming practice at the time was based on the open field system, with two or three large fields situated around a village. Each farmer was given a strip, or strips, of land to cultivate by the ridge and furrow method of ploughing. This methodology was used commonly throughout the 12th and 13th centuries. Once again, changes to the system occurred more slowly in Wales, Ireland, and Scotland.

Early in the 14th century the Black Death (bubonic plague) decimated Britain, with some 33-50% of the population dying in the years 1348-1350 (Bowsky 1971; Gasquet 1908; Shrewsbury 1970). This resulted in the mass desertion of some 2000 villages. Other epidemics occurred in 1361, 1369, and 1374. Adding to the misery and depopulation were weather-related famines (1315-1317, 1321) when little or no corn grew. Between 1450 and 1520 the wool trade began to flourish and large numbers of sheep were raised to supply wool to a variety of centres, including Flanders and Italy. Monasteries were heavily involved in the trade, and many people were dispossessed to leave the land for sheep grazing. The dispossessed usually moved to urban areas where they led a life of squalor. Farming thus returned to the pastoral from the arable, with great vegetational damage being caused by overgrazing of large flocks of sheep.

After 1485, when Henry Tudor (later Henry VII) defeated Richard III at Bosworth Field in Leicestershire, three centuries of dramatic changes occurred in the landscape. One of the major changes involved the enclosure of fields (Chapman 1987; Scrutton 1887; Turner 1980, 1984; Yelling 1977). In the early 16th century Henry VIII began his onslaught on the church, which included the dissolution of monasteries. Some of the released land reverted to the Crown, but much was given to a new breed of landed gentry. This led to the construction of many country houses with landscaped parklands (parts of the Royal Forests often being enclosed). After the Act of Union between England and Wales (1536), more country houses were built, in styles that were less defensive than formerly, with beautiful formal gardens or parklands (Jacques 1983; Jarrett 1978; Petzsch 1971; Pragnell 1984; Watkin 1982). Villages were also rebuilt, often in local stone (Brunskill 1981). From the Middle Ages on, the lifestyle of the people living in the country houses was more than comfortable, with much game being eaten (Girouard 1987).

Industrial enterprises were moving from small scale operations to large, with ever larger foundries demanding fuel, and thus decimating the woodlands even further. However, in the 1600s many trees were planted and coppices were managed. As the population grew, so did trade, towns, transportation, and communications systems. These changes occurred at a faster rate in England than in the rest of Britain. Enclosure, mentioned earlier, led to many tenant farmers being evicted by wealthy landowners, and to the Highland Clearances in the early 1800s. By the mid-16th century, only in the Midlands was farming still on unenclosed strips, and by the 18th century only a "mopping-up" job remained for the Parliamentary Commission (Chapman 1987; Turner 1984; Yelling 1977). Between 1750 and 1780, two hundred Acts of Parliament enclosed three million acres of strips.

As farmland became increasingly scarce, the Fenland of eastern England was drained to become some of the richest agricultural land in the country. An area that was rich in fish, fowl, and fur became the source of market garden products, potatoes, and cereals. The Romans tried to drain the fens, but it was the efforts of a Dutchman, Cornelius Vermuyden, that made the dream a reality (Millward and Robinson 1977). This is considered by many to be the single greatest environmental change and engineering achievement of the 17th century in Britain. The Fenland was reduced from 3380 km^2 in 1630 to 10 km^2 in 1984. Rivers were also harnessed to provide power for industry, only to be replaced at a later date by steam. The period 1760 to 1840 saw the heyday of the Canal Age in Britain. Canals were built in many parts of the country and used for the transportation of bulk commodities, such as coal. The canals also provided a whole series of new habitats and niches ready for exploitation by a variety of wildlife.

Despite all the changes that had occurred in the lowland areas of Britain, little effort had been made to improve the upland areas, even as late as the 18th century. The soil in the upland regions may have become depleted early in human occupation of the island. Water drains rapidly through the soil, quickly leaching out nutrients, thus making it unresponsive to improvement for agricultural purposes. This does not mean that there have been no attempts to improve uplands. One of the best known success stories in this area is that of the reclamation of Exmoor by John Knight. In 1818 the Midlands ironmaster acquired an estate of 15 000 acres, from some 25 000 acres that had been secured for enclosure by an Act of Parliament in 1815. It is recorded that 25 000 sheep, from 50 parishes, were grazing on the moor in 1816. John, and his son Frederick, built a 29 mile long stone wall around their property, and established 15 farms (Millward and Robinson 1977). The land was drained, ploughed, and limed, with shelterbelts of conifers being planted, as well as hazel, beech, and sycamore (Orwin and Sellick 1970).

The result was rich, productive farmland, compared with the barren bleakness of Dartmoor, which lies at much the same height as Exmoor. A similar success was achieved in Wales by Thomas Johnes, who transformed the Ystwyth Valley, which had been devastated by lead mining, into "one of the wonders of Wales" (Clarke et al. 1980). His major action consisted of planting over four million trees, mostly larch but also some deciduous species such as oak and beech.

In Scotland, the transition from subsistence arable farming to pastoral use caused great conflict. Sheep rearing was more profitable and less labor intensive than arable farming, and resulted in the Highland Clearances. A few landlords were sympathetic toward their tenants, for example Sir John Sinclair of Thurso Castle, who tried to resettle anyone he displaced into coastal villages.

In Ireland, attempts to improve uplands ranged from the establishment of fine estates, kept in order by numerous laborers, to absentee landlords who did nothing to reclaim bog and mountain land. Tenants on the unimproved land had no security of tenure and were frequently evicted. The evicted generally moved to towns, or became squatters on common land. As few of the landless were able to find jobs, emigration reached great proportions by the end of the 18th century.

The Industrial Revolution began in the 1700s with a change from an agrarian/hand craft society to one dominated by industry and machine manufacturing. In the 1840s road and railway systems were well established, and there was an influx of people into the urban areas from the countryside. The town dwellers usually worked in the factories that were the lifeblood of the economy and lived in slums. Mining for commodities such as coal was also despoiling much of the countryside, such as in Wigan in the northwest of England.

As the foregoing discussion shows, by 1700 the original vegetation of the country had been mostly destroyed or modified by anthropogenic[3] influences. Since 1700 many distinctive semi-natural vegetation types have decreased, and losses have increased rapidly since 1940-1950. Agriculture now affects about 80% of Britain's surface, obviously affecting the amount of natural vegetation that remains. Ratcliffe (1984) discusses recent changes in British vegetation, and notes those factors, such as pollution, recreational pressures, and urban-industrial growth that have affected and continue to affect the vegetation. Few species of vascular plants[4] (19) have become extinct in the past 300 years, but many species have become rare. Forest cover in Britain was reduced to 5.4%

[3] influences relating to the origin and development of humanity, either individually or ethnically.

[4] common botanical term for plants that have tissues for internal fluid circulation.

by 1924 but has increased to almost 10%, due mainly to the planting of alien conifers in upland areas. Only 300 000 hectares of ancient, semi-natural broad-leaved woodland (1.3% of land area of Britain) remain today. In the period since 1930 some 46% of this vegetation type has been destroyed, to be replaced in some cases by conifers.

A feature of the British landscape that may have become more common and extensive after enclosure is the hedgerow. Hedges indisputably added to the richness of the flora and fauna of the country, but they are being destroyed at an ever-increasing rate. It has been estimated that in 1946-47 some 500 000 miles of hedge existed in England and Wales, but by 1974 about 140 000 miles had been removed. All but 20 000 miles was destroyed for agricultural reasons. Since 1974 the loss has continued, with 190 000 miles (22%; 2600-4000 miles of hedge per year) being destroyed (Muir and Muir 1987). Much of the removal has resulted from an increase in field size during the period from 1945 to 1983. There can be no doubt about the use of hedgerows by wildlife (Best 1983), and the necessity of preserving them if we are to maintain the diversity and abundance of the flora and fauna of the countryside.

In addition to direct changes wrought by humans, we are now seeing changes brought about by pollution resulting from increased industrialization and use of herbicides and pesticides (Mellanby 1967). People utilizing the countryside in increasing numbers for non-consumptive purposes are also having a deleterious effect on the countryside and its wildlife (Bracey 1972). Changes continue to occur in the countryside (Lockhart and Ilbery 1987), with much concern being expressed about the future (Blacksell and Gilg 1981; Green 1975). Major changes in agricultural practices have resulted in much of the destruction of the island's natural vegetation. Green (1975) addresses some of the conflicts between agriculture and conservation of the countryside, and notes that great efforts have been made to demonstrate that agricultural practices can be made compatible with, or accommodate, other interests. However, the approaches used fail to recognize that fundamental ecological differences exist between the two types of land use. The same author (Green 1989) addresses the substantial environmental impacts that agriculture has imposed on the countryside since World War II, and shows that subsidized farming is now producing food supplies to a level where surpluses exist. The time might be appropriate to switch state support from farming to environmental management. How this might be achieved, and the strategy/strategies to be used, are the subjects of intense debate among environmentalists. The conflict between agriculture and conservation is not a problem unique to Britain but is of worldwide interest and concern (Hawkes 1978).

Changes are being made in upland areas that will further erode their utility, for example, moor-draining (Stewart and Lance 1983) and upland afforestation[5] (Goldsmith and Wood 1983). Miller and Watson (1983) discuss the uses and future of heather moorlands, while Watkins (1987) is optimistic about the future and management of woodlands in the rural landscape, and concludes that the total area of woodland in Britain will increase until the end of the century, albeit mostly in the form of conifers. Peterken (1983) is equally optimistic and feels that by the year 2050 woodland may be double its present extent. Britain is the most poorly wooded country in Europe (9% of land surface, as compared to 20-40% in many European countries). It is suggested that in the Highlands as much as 40% of the land might eventually be wooded, almost exclusively by conifers.

Borrowing from the United States, the British Government in 1949 established a National Parks System. The parks designated under this scheme, however, do not conform to the IUCN definition of National Parks, although they were created for the same purposes. MacEwen and MacEwen (1982, 1983) cast a somewhat jaundiced eye on the system as it now stands, with the observation that only 26.9% of land in areas designated as National Parks is under public or semi-public ownership and only 1.16% is actually owned by the National Park Authorities. For the system to become workable and to allow for implementation of sound conservation strategies, it is essential that parks acquire ownership of the land. In this way extensive areas of natural beauty can be made available to the public for non-consumptive purposes, and the existing semi-natural vegetation systems, and attendant fauna they contain, can be properly managed.

Mammalian and Avian Faunas of Britain

In addition to causing changes in the flora of Britain, humans have had a tremendous impact on its fauna (Edlin 1952; Hawksworth 1974; Perry 1978). Human history is well known, and human relations with the environment have been documented, studied, and discussed at length (Fleure and Davies 1970). Mammals and birds have been an important source of food and other basic requirements of life since humans first lived in Britain. They have been used as a source of sport and have long appeared in the literature and art of the country (Goodfellow 1983; Harting 1864; Phipson 1883). The early history of mammals in Britain is relatively well known, due the great number of fossil finds that have been made (Bramwell et al. 1990; Currant 1989; Hooker 1989; Kurten 1968; Savage 1989). Data on game animals for recent centuries can be gleaned from often meticulously kept estate game records. The history of the present mammalian fauna can be related to the great glaciations or Ice Ages (Matthews 1968).

---

[5] replanting, a forest in the process of being created by human hands.

The last glaciation ended about 20 000 B.P. (before the present), at which time Britain was connected to Europe, allowing a relatively free movement of animals. The climate at first was cool, resulting in a tundra-like ecosystem inhabited by herds of reindeer. As the climate ameliorated, with warm summers, horses became the dominant large mammals. The tundra vegetation gave way to birch, then pine, and finally hazel, with concomitant changes in the fauna. The final separation from Europe came about 5000 B.C., at which time the mammalian fauna was much like that of the present. By the Stone Age Britain was populated by a small number of humans (300 to 400), who relied on hunting and food gathering for their subsistence (Perry 1978). By the Mesolithic the population may have risen to 3000 or 4000. Suggestions have been made that the subsistence animal for these people was the red deer, which may have been domesticated. Corbet (1974), using the data of Harting (1880), discusses the distribution of mammals in Britain in historic times. He notes that no species of mammal has become extinct in Britain since the wolf was exterminated in the 18th century. In 1974 the mammalian fauna comprised 56 species, of which 14 were introduced. During the years, ranges of various species have changed, either as a result of persecution or artificial extension. The only mammal to be deliberately eradicated was the muskrat, which was originally introduced to be farmed for pelts in the 1920s, but escaped and became feral. Environmental damage can be caused by these animals so eradication campaigns were started in the 1930s, with a successful conclusion in 1939 (Gosling and Baker 1989). Red and roe deer populations are now quite high, after progressive reductions until the end of the 18th century. The declines were most probably related to loss of woodland habitat; deer were absent from lowland areas, except for parks (Prior 1968; Putman 1988; Rackham 1980; Whitehead 1964).

Six species of large mammals have become extinct in Britain in the last 2000 years. The wolf disappeared from England in the 1500s, from Scotland in 1743, and from Ireland in 1770. The status of the brown bear in Britain is a more contentious issue, but Harting (1880) suggests it was extinct by the 10th century. The beaver, which was a source of both fur and food, survived until the 10th or 12th centuries in Wales and Scotland. Deforestation of lowland riverbanks, coupled with hunting, undoubtedly caused the demise of this animal. Further, flooding of agricultural land by dam construction would not be tolerated. Wild boars survived in England until the 17th century, at which time parks had been established for their protection. This animal was well regarded as a food and Henry III, in 1251, ordered 200 wild swine from the Forest of Dean as part of his Christmas dinner. Reindeer may have survived until the 12th century in northern Scotland, while the date of extinction of aurochs (or urus) is uncertain. It is of interest that several herds of semi-wild white cattle have survived from the Middle Ages (Hall and Hall 1988; Whitehead 1953) until the present.

As a general statement it appears that carnivores have been exterminated, or their numbers drastically reduced, while herbivores, both wild and domestic, have been introduced or maintained as a source of food or for amenity reasons (Edlin 1952).

The origin and history of the avifauna[6] of Britain are less well known than those of the mammals. Harrison (1980) described a Pleistocene bird assemblage from caves in Devon, and more recently Harrison (1988) described the avifauna as it presently stands, the end result of thousands of years of shifting populations that were affected by both climate and humans. The literature on the birds of Britain is extensive (see Miller 1986), with works varying from species lists/descriptions such as Yarrell (1871-85), to the birds of specific habitats and their origins (Simms 1971; Yapp 1962). Bird habitats are well known (Fuller 1982), as are the birds found therein (for example, Prater 1981). The British Trust for Ornithology has been responsible for the collection of data that has resulted in our present knowledge of both wintering and breeding bird populations in the country (Lack 1986; Sharrock 1976). Numerous monographs have been produced that deal with individual species, or groups of species (such as Brown 1976), while the relationships between humans and birds have been explored by workers such as Murton (Murton 1971). The wealth of data on birds has been collected for several reasons, namely, they are important as game and food, they may pose problems as pest species to agriculture, and most importantly they are the objects of study and recreation for thousands of people. Bird populations at the present time are probably larger than they were in the Middle Ages (Nicholson 1988), but they are also subjected to more deleterious factors than ever before. Herbicides, pesticides, and other pollution, coupled with changes in agricultural practices, all exert a toll, while alterations in species composition might be expected where the environment is being manipulated, for example, the change from broad-leaved deciduous forests to large stands of a single species of conifer. Williamson (1972) discusses this latter point and suggests that with proper management, and at a minimal economic cost, the original woodland avifauna will be able to adapt to the radical transformation of forest cover.

British Game Laws

Any understanding of the present-day game management system in Britain is predicated on a knowledge of the Game Laws. Animals have been hunted in Britain since Palaeolithic times, with few restrictions. No

---

[6] a term denoting bird life.

person could own a wild animal (*ferae naturae*), and anything that was caught or killed belonged to the captor or hunter. Under Roman Law game was considered *res nullius*, and belonged to whoever killed it, regardless of where it was killed. The first laws relating to control of game were supposedly those of Ine, King of Wessex, who enacted Forest Laws in 693, while the laws of Hywel Dda, which covered many types of wildlife, date back to the 10th century. The game law of King Canute (1016) prevented people from hunting on the king's land on the pain of death. In Scotland numerous laws were passed in medieval times to protect deer, wild fowl, and hawks (Edlin 1952). The theme running through these laws, which were almost certainly forged by the Normans, is that property in wild creatures could be reserved by the king. He alone could own wild animals, and could give others permission to hunt them. He would be unable to hunt throughout the whole of his kingdom, and consequently gave the right to hunt to the nobility and clergy. This ultimately resulted in sporting rights passing to landowners. Prior to the Norman Invasion, Britain had been oriented toward Scandinavia with regards to its laws and outlook. After the conquest, however, the orientation was toward Europe with changes occurring in both the game laws and hunting methods. The Forest Laws enacted by the Normans were supposedly draconian, although this fact is disputed (Rackham 1986). William I enforced the laws that were based on the European Code, with punishments that ranged from death to mutilation. Brander (1971) quotes the following as an example of a savage penalty: "Whoever shall kill a stag, a wild boar, or even a hare, shall have his eyes torn out." It is now suggested that fines, or imprisonment, were the norm. Forests may well have been useful to monarchs as a source of food, but they were also the source of much income from the granting of rights to pasture and cut wood. It should be noted that Forests were not hunting preserves, and the king could not visit or use all those within his domain. Animals were killed by professional hunters and delivered to the Court as required. Rackham (1986) notes the numbers of animals taken for the Christmas Feast of Henry III, in 1215, including 430 red deer, 200 fallow deer, 200 roe deer, 200 wild swine, 1300 hares, 450 rabbits, 2100 partridges, 290 pheasants, and 395 swans. Succeeding Norman kings made full use of the laws. Henry I expanded his forest continually under a "Charter of the Forests," which stated "I retain by the common consent of my barons my forests as my fathers had theirs." The charter was relinquished in 1136 by his successor Stephen.

Under Richard I and John, the Forest Laws were administered by wardens, under a justice. In effect a civil service developed to enforce laws, collect fines, and perform other related duties; and as in modern-day politics, bribery and graft thrived. John was constantly trying to undermine the power of the barons. In 1215 they rose in revolt and the king sealed the Magna Carta which confirmed their feudal rights. A new civil war erupted, during which John died. Until this time, the clergy were subject only to ecclesiastical law and not common law. Abbots and bishops hunted, hawked, and fought, just as the knights and barons. In 1184, however, the clergy were made subject to Forest Laws, and fines replaced the existing brutal penalties for commoners. Grievances against the Forest Laws gradually increased until the barons forced William of Pembroke, the regent for Henry III, to issue a Forest Charter (Charta Forestae) in the king's name in 1216. The barbaric Norman Code was softened, with the new charter stating "10. No man shall from henceforth lose either life or member for killing of our Deer; but if any man be taken and convicted for taking of our Venison, he shall make a grievous fine, if he hath anything whereof; . . ." (Walsh 1983). Rights to hunt "Beasts of Venery" (hart, hind, hare, bear, and wolf) were only granted outside Royal Forests, while the right to hunt "Beasts of Chase" (fallow deer, roe deer, fox, and marten) were granted within the forests (Brander 1971). Grants of warren allowed the awardee to hunt foxes, wild cats, badgers, and otters in the forests. Barons were allowed to empark parts of the Royal Forests and often lured deer into the walled-off areas. The English Parliament, in 1293, in an effort to stem an activity that was to become increasingly important in later centuries, namely poaching, decreed that no actions were to be taken against officials (foresters, parkers, warreners) who killed poachers who resisted arrest (McCall 1979). The nobility continued to obtain concessions from weak monarchs and a share of what had previously been the Royal Prerogative. In 1381 a Peasant's Revolt followed the imposition of an unpopular poll tax. The problem was exacerbated by the fact that the people of the time were desperately poor, and in need of food, and they were unhappy with the virtually exclusive privilege of the rich to hunt. After the revolt, in 1389, Richard II decreed that the pursuit of game would be lawful only for those "qualified" by land ownership. Sharpe (1984) reports that the act declared "no manner of artificer, laborer, nor any other layman, which hath not lands or tenements to the value of x 1s [40s] by year" would be allowed to keep hunting dogs or equipment to take game. This edict was in response to a petition about commoners hunting where they shouldn't with greyhounds, on religious holidays when they should have been in church. New legislation continued in this vein with the right to hunt game being vested only in men of landed property. Poaching by the poor continued apace, with small landholders and tenant farmers taking game on the land they owned or rented, as did laborers.

In 1603 a law was passed that prohibited the sale of hares, pheasants, and partridges in an attempt to stem poaching. In the years 1642 to 1660 the English Civil War took place, the Parliamentary Forces were victorious, Charles I was executed, and a Commonwealth was established. The Long Parliament assumed responsibility for the Royal Forests and repealed many of the Forest Laws. Poaching went unchecked and many walls around the parks were destroyed. With the restoration of the monarchy, in 1671 Charles II instituted a "gentleman's game privilege" based on a high land "qualification." Kirby (1933) and Munsche (1981) note that only four classes of people, making up a minute proportion of the population, were allowed to shoot or otherwise kill game. The four classes were: (1) persons who had lands, tenements, or other estate of inheritance of value of £100 p.a.; (2) persons with copyhold or leasehold (for 99 years or longer) with a value of £150 p.a.; (3) the son and heir apparent of an esquire, or other person of higher degree; and (4) owners and keepers of forests, parks, chases, or warrens, stocked with deer or conies (rabbits) for their own use. The act did not specifically state who could hunt game, but in effect meant that only the landed gentry would be in a position to hunt. Lords of the manor, not below the degree of Esquire, were empowered to appoint gamekeepers who could seize dogs, guns, and other hunting equipment from the "unqualified." The gamekeepers with their new powers were much resented as they were able to search "suspect" homes for hunting gear. These actions set the basic law of the game system for the next 160 years, which authority fought to maintain. Over the next 20 years heavier and heavier fines were imposed for poaching. The aristocracy, whose control of the government was assured after the revolution of 1688, proceeded to pass regulations and penalties that effectively superseded the earlier game laws, without repealing them. Gamekeepers were given almost unlimited powers by acts in 1691 and 1693 to resist and oppose deer and night poachers, and were indemnified from prosecution if the offender was killed. In 1721-1723 a few individuals (at most 60), known as the Waltham gang and modelled on the followers of Robin Hood, conducted a series of poaching raids for deer, and damaged property and trees in Farnham and Waltham Chase. The poachers either blackened their faces or wore a mask. Some were caught after the first raid, and were jailed, fined, pilloried, or acquitted. Further acts followed, some of which seemed to be motivated by direct class hatred, and included the theft of a shipment of French wine intended for the Prince of Wales, and murder. Many were caught, with some being executed for murder, while others were transported for deer-stealing and assault (Rogers 1974). In 1723 the notorious "Black Act" was passed, which provided capital punishment for not only poaching "blacks," but also for more than 200 other offenses. The act was supposed to be a temporary measure limited to three years, but it was regularly renewed until it became permanent in 1758. Hopkins (1985) discusses the poaching wars that continued for the next 200 years and notes that 1770 saw the enactment of the Night Poaching Act. Persons caught poaching, armed or unarmed, between an hour after dark and an hour before sunrise were dealt with in summary proceedings before a single magistrate. A first offence merited not less than three months imprisonment, while a second offence resulted in a public whipping and not less than six months in prison. The act was amended in 1773 to permit a fine for the first-time offender. Tobias (1979), in discussing the layer upon layer of game laws, points out the iniquitous nature of law enforcement. Severe laws were enforced by a justice of the peace, usually a member of the local landed gentry, who had a vested interest in protecting the rights of property that the offender had violated. As noted by Tobias (1979), justices often had more freedom of action to punish poachers than most other offenders. One writer in discussing poaching noted "This offence, thus aggravated, I have ranked under the present head, because the only rational footing, upon which we can consider it as a crime, is, that in low and indigent persons it promotes idleness, and takes them away from their proper employments and callings; which is an offence against the public police and economy of the commonwealth" (Blackstone 1773). Munsche (1977) discussed the game laws in Wiltshire, and their enforcement between 1750 and 1800. He noted that "qualified" sportsmen constituted less than 0.5% of the population, and that they appointed some 200 working gamekeepers. The farmers were up in arms due to the increase in game such as hares, which were destroying their crops, and they resented the damage caused by the hunters. The illicit trade in game flourished, especially in London, with poachers in Wiltshire supplying many of the animals sold. It is evident that poaching was the major rural "crime" at that time. Bovill (1963) gives an eloquent account of country life in the years 1780-1830, including the sporting activities of gentlemen and the poaching war.

The game laws continued to expand during the next 100 years, with layers and layers of new regulations being added to further obscure an already confused system. In 1800 any person who was found at large after dark could be classified as a "rogue or vagabond" if they were armed with a net or any weapon to kill game. The penalties for the infraction included whipping, imprisonment for two years, or impression into the army or navy. Gamekeepers and manorial servants were empowered to seize suspects without warrant, and in 1803 it became a capital offence to forcibly resist arrest (Ellenborough's Act). The sale of game had been prohibited in the early 17th century, a fact that was much resented by the ever-increasing urban middle class. Poaching supplied a lucrative and expanding trade in game in the early 19th century (Kirby 1941). London was the centre of the traffic with game being sold openly in the markets, and inns and taverns serving game as part of their normal fare. The market was often glutted due to the vast amounts of game being poached by organized gangs. One wholesaler in Leadenhall market testified that he handled over 19 000 head of game in one year. The rise in gang poaching led to a number of game battles between the landed gentry and the poachers. The escalating violence resulted in the Night Poaching Act (1816), which introduced transportation for seven years if the poacher was armed with a net or stick with the intent to take game or rabbits. At this time it was illegal to sell game. In 1818 the Bankes' Act made it equally illegal to buy game, with a fine of £5 per head of game bought. The informer received half of any fines collected. Gamekeepers were the front line defence against poachers, but the methods they often employed can only be described as cruel and unusual. Spring-guns and man-traps were used to incapacitate, or kill, poachers. These barbaric methods were made unlawful in game preserves in 1827 (Lord Suffield's Bill). The Night Poaching Act was amended in 1828, replacing impressment into the Armed Forces by transportation for up to 14 years for poaching gangs of three or more, only one of whom need be armed. Lone poachers were transported for seven years for a third offence. A major change occurred in 1831 when the Game Reform Bill eliminated "qualification" of any sort as a requirement to take game. Game shooting was open to any person who purchased a Game Certificate. Trading in game also became legal with the purchase of a Game Dealer's licence. Poaching during daylight hours netted a fine of £5, but transportation remained for night poaching. Poaching also reached unprecedented levels at this time (Jones 1979). It was established that game is the property of the owner of the land, **not** its occupier. This led to problems for tenant farmers, who were unable to kill the increasing numbers of rabbits and hares on their farms because the owners retained the right to kill the game themselves (Kirby 1932). Attacks on the game laws continued through the 1840s. As a result of a motion by John Bright, a Member of Parliament and mill-owner, a select committee on the game laws was set up in 1846. After numerous hearings and much testimony, no action was taken. In 1862 the passage of the Poaching Prevention Act drew the police more firmly into the poaching war. The police were given unprecedented powers of search on the highways. They could stop and search carts and people they suspected were coming from preserves, which led to many unlawful arrests. It should be noted that the majority of poachers were working people, not indigents, male, and in their 20s. Females were usually more active as carriers and sellers. No legislative actions were taken over the next several years despite the testimony presented to a select committee on the game laws in 1873. This included representations from Scottish farmers who were angry over the amount of damage being caused to their crops by deer and grouse. Finally, in 1880, after Gladstone's Liberals had gained a landslide victory at the polls, the Ground Game Act was passed. This act gave tenant farmers the "inalienable and concurrent right," with the landowners, to shoot hares and rabbits that were destroying their crops. The act was little loved by the landowners and was fiercely resisted in the House of Lords. It did, however, have the effect of reducing sympathy for the poacher (Emsley 1987). Porter (1986) feels that benefits accrued by farmers as a result of the passage of the act have probably been overestimated, and notes that in Devonshire the act was restrictively interpreted.

In the late 1800s the ever-burgeoning urban population began to take a greater interest in both wild animals and the countryside, often making their views known to political figures through organizations such as the Royal Society for the Prevention of Cruelty to Animals (Harrison 1973). Access to the countryside by urbanites was fiercely resisted, as evidenced by the rejection (for the second time) of the Access to Mountains Bill (James Bryce 1889) after representations from owners of grouse moors. Efforts continued over the next several years to make the countryside more accessible, particularly to non-consumptive users. Resistance to such use of the land was demonstrated in 1932, when a force of gamekeepers and police met hikers who were undertaking an organized "mass trespass" over Kinder Scout grouse moors. Five hikers were ultimately imprisoned. The situation since that time has greatly improved.

The game laws are still in a state of some confusion, with little effort having been made to rationalize or consolidate them. Poaching is still covered by the earlier laws, with additions being made in 1960 (Game Laws [Amendment] Act), 1963 (Deer Act), and 1968 (Firearms Act). Laws against poaching are concerned with criminal trespass and possessing the equipment for poaching, not theft. Although sporting rights are conceived as property, the owner of land or sporting rights does not own wild creatures until they are dead, or in his/her power.

Hunting and Hunting Methods

An understanding of the present-day game management system revolves around a knowledge of hunting techniques and technology. The reasons for hunting are many and varied, with the activity being rationalized in all sorts of ways, such as hunting is a part of the nation's heritage and is thus worthy of preservation on the basis of tradition alone (Thomas 1983).

In Anglo-Saxon times game was driven along hayes (funnel-shaped hedges) to the hunters who killed them with bows and arrows. Wounded animals such as stags or boars were hunted down with dogs. With the arrival of the Normans hunting became *par force*. This involved finding deer tracks or droppings (fewmets) early in the morning, and following them to the animal's resting place with a dog (usually a lymer or bloodhound). Mounted hunters were there summoned by three long blasts on a horn, and the animal was chased with other dogs. The use of horns became ritualized with different sounds being used in different stages of the hunt. This style of hunting continued for several centuries with the main weapons used being swords, knives, bayonets, and bows and arrows (Blackmore 1971). Slings, snares, and various types of nets were also used. It is of interest that animals were not hunted year round, but were protected in those months in which they were breeding, the so-called "fence months" first mentioned in the reign of Henry I. Thiebaux (1967), in writing about the medieval chase, notes that hunting was supposedly good for moral improvement, provided exercise, and was perhaps a surrogate for war. The French literature from this period stresses the pleasure, profits, and nobility of the hunt, as well as the importance of technical skills and ceremony. Falconry was common from the 1200s until the 1600s, and still survives as a sport today (Cade 1982; Cummins 1988; Salvin and Brodrick 1855). Falconry may well have led to the preservation of birds of prey for several centuries due to their usefulness. Different species of falcons and hawks were used by different strata of society, as noted by Berners (1486). Hunting methods are well represented in the art of the times (Baillie-Grohman 1925), including such exotic practices as heron-hawking, fox-tossing, and hare-hunting with leopards. Baillie-Grohman (1925) also lists some of the enormous "bags" taken by royalty, for example that of Elector John George I of Saxony (reigned 1611-1656) who counted amongst his trophies 35 421 red deer, 11 489 roe deer, 31 902 wild boar, and 19 015 foxes. Crossbows were widely used in hunting. Queen Elizabeth I hunted deer with this weapon. Bows gradually gave way to guns in the 1500s, although many techniques were used at that time. At first birds were shot on the ground, often after being stalked with a stalking horse, ox, or dummy.[7] Flintlock fowling pieces made wing shooting possible, with 1686 being the earliest reference to this style of shooting in Britain. Over the years the guns became more accurate and their range was extended (Brander 1971). Guns were initially handmade, but with the coming of the Industrial Revolution, mass production started. Further refinements led to the hunting weapons of today such as rifles and shotguns.

Dogs were used widely in hunting, with many varieties being bred for the different types of hunting over the centuries. Similarly, horses were selected and bred for hunting.

The British were slow to take to, and make, firearms, and only in the 17th century did they introduce a form of flintlock. Guns were used in the first instance to fill the pantry or pot, and were not considered sporting weapons. Many birds were still being taken by the use of dogs, nets and kite-hawks, or free-flying falcons. In the 1600s the stag was the main quarry of the aristocracy, while the hare was hunted by squires and farmers (Trench 1973). Forests were rapidly disappearing, deer

7 i.e., blinds and decoys.

numbers were down, and by the end of the century the fox was starting to have sporting qualities. Fox hunting was slow and methodical in the early years of the 18th century. The hunt started at dawn with the fox hounds walking the animal to death over a period of several hours. More frequently the fox went to earth, was dug up, and then killed. The hunter generally followed the dogs on horseback. The development of fox hunting as a sport in Britain is detailed by Carr (1976) and Itzkowitz (1977).

It should not be forgotten that other forms of hunting were undertaken in the 18th century, with shooting over dogs becoming popular, and almost universal by the turn of the century.

The development of fox hunting led to certain individuals, who acquired the title Master of the Foxhounds, keeping packs of dogs that were used in the hunt. One of the notable things about the fox hunt was that anyone could legally follow the hounds. This type of hunt was not for the dashing, active young aristocrats, who found it boring. However, enclosure resulted in dramatic changes in the hunt. Hedges and fences presented barriers to the passage of horsemen and dogs, resulting in the breeding of faster, stronger animals, which in turn made the hunt faster. The young, landed gentry now participated. Leicestershire became the centre of this new style of hunting, and particularly the region of Melton-Mowbray, where some people hunted for six days each week. The best known and most prestigious hunt was the Quorn Hunt, whose membership included the nobility (Nimrod 1901). In addition to the above, "provincial" hunts were run by country gentlemen, and many classes of people participated. Both foxes, which ran fast and straight, and hares, which required greater skill to follow, were hunted. Eventually this style of hunting became so popular and encompassed people from so many walks of life that shooting became the snob-sport.

Fox hunting was also extremely expensive for the Master of the Foxhounds. In 1825 it cost at least £1935 to hunt in a provincial four days a week (Trench 1973). In the shires the cost could run as high as £4000-£6000. By the 1830s an agricultural depression set in, and prosperous landowners became less common. They were replaced by small tenant farmers who did not participate in the hunt. The main proponents of the hunt then became industrialists, businessmen, professionals, army officers, and a number of foreign nationals. In the 1850s females were hunting alongside the men. The heyday of this sport occurred between 1815 and 1870. Despite this, the number of packs of harriers in the country usually exceeded that of foxhounds.

As travel became easier it also became possible to move game over large distances without it spoiling. This resulted in large quantities of wildlife, including wildfowl, being killed for the table. Ducks were caught by the thousand, using traps and decoys, especially in East

Anglia. Up to 250 ducks per day could be caught in one trap, but this pales by comparison with one decoy in Holland that in 1784 accounted for 67 000 ducks. In the early 1800s red grouse were still being shot over pointers. Some of the first records of these birds being driven to the guns are from 1805 on the Yorkshire moors. Game was finally being affected by hunting and the bustard was extirpated from East Anglia in 1838. Complaints in 1841 about a lack of grey partridges to shoot implicated not hunting but agricultural practices. Copper sulphate was used as a fungicide on wheat, which killed the birds when they ate it. Furthermore, the farmers were destroying the turf banks where the birds could breed.

Scotland was being used more and more by sportsmen from all over Britain by the mid-1800s, and particularly after 1848 when Queen Victoria and Prince Albert moved to Balmoral Castle. Interesting accounts of the Victorian Era and countryside may be seen in Carr (1981), Mingay (1981), and Thompson (1981). Sheep that had caused the Highland Clearances were now themselves displaced by red deer and red grouse. The 1850s saw the advent of the breech-loading shotgun, and by the 1860s the shooting of driven game became popular. English guns were now among the best made in the world, and included Purdey, Holland and Holland, Webley, and Scott. The 1880s saw the start of the Edwardian Era, during which time "weekend" (Thursday-Tuesday) shooting parties reported some record game bags. The Maharajah of Lahore, Prince Duleep Singh, in 1876, killed 789 partridges with 1000 cartridges at his Elvenden Estate in Norfolk, and shot 2350 birds in 9 days. He also shot 440 red grouse in one day at Grandtully, an estate he rented in Perthshire (Alexander and Anand 1980). This record was eclipsed by Lord Walsingham, in 1888, who shot 1070 red grouse on Blubberhouse Moor in one day. At Elveden the average seasonal bag was 10 000 pheasants, 10 000 grey partridges, 3000 hares, and 70 000 rabbits. Blackmore (1971) listed the total kills of the Marquis of Ripon, who had a fanatical interest in shooting. From 1867 until his death in 1923, the Marquis shot 556 813 animals, including 97 503 red grouse, 124 193 grey partridge, 241 234 pheasants, 31 934 hares, and 40 138 rabbits. MacIntyre (1950) records much more modest bags during the same time period (60-75 brace of red grouse per day) in the Scottish Highlands. With the changes in shooting habits, the evolution of hunting dogs continued, resulting in better retrievers. Throughout the reign of Edward VII, class barriers remained rigid. However, a few types of hunting such as hare coursing remained unaffected by social structures. Deer stalking was practised, but this sport was only for the most physically fit. Live pigeon shooting, considered by many to be a most unsavory sport, was gradually replaced by clay-pigeon shooting.

At the turn of the century game was becoming scarce because of overexploitation, changing agricultural practices, and an increasing human population. In 1756 the population of Britain stood at 6 million, by 1911 it had risen to 42 million, most of which lived in towns. It was recognized that game needed to be preserved, and "vermin" killed, but the public seemed largely unconcerned. Only rabbits seemed to be thriving and formed the basis of an industry. The First World War brought an end to hunting as it had been known for the previous several decades. Horses were expropriated for use by the cavalry, and packs of hounds were destroyed. Shooting was only for food and not for sport. Attempts to preserve game ceased, and poaching once again became rampant. The gap that had always existed between the people living in rural areas and towns became larger, and vocal anti-hunting groups were formed in the urban areas. This resulted in the formation of the British Field Sports Society, in 1930, to represent and safeguard field sports interests. It was also to counter the increasing calls for legislation against field sports (Rogers et al. 1985). The changes continued after the Second World War. No part of the country is now beyond reach, and the numbers of guns owned by the public has increased. This resulted in legislation being passed that required all shotguns to be registered. Many thousands of people now hunt in Britain, with several NGOs such as The British Association for Shooting and Conservation controlling the behavior of participants in the sport. A variety of field sports are now available to the public, in large part as a result of the redistribution of wealth since the First World War, and the commercialization of many estates. The number of relatively wealthy people in Britain has risen over the years, but the number of landed gentry with hereditary rights to land and sporting rights has fallen. Taxes reduce disposable unearned income to a point where the gentry cannot afford to pay wages for staff, or forego shooting and fishing rents. It is almost impossible to make farming pay, and death duties have done away with the operation of primogeniture (Longrigg 1977). Institutions are now buying up sporting rights either as an investment, or for fringe benefits for their employees (Blacksell and Gilg 1981).

Wildlife Management in Britain

Management in the past consisted of game preservation with three main facets: the breeding of game, destruction of vermin, and concentration of game in protected areas (Munsche 1981). Little evidence exists of game management prior to the 1600s. Rabbits had been protected since the Middle Ages (Sheail 1971), as had deer which were enclosed in parks. By the 1600s hares were also being kept in warrens. By the early 1700s the elements of game preservation (management) were well established, but implementation was sporadic and uneven throughout the country. In certain instances conflicts arose between the sportsmen and those who were managing their stocks. For example, hares from the surrounding countryside would run to the managed warrens when they were being hunted.

Early attempts to rear and release pheasants and grey partridges were unsuccessful as the birds produced were "tame" and little use for sport. Gradually this practice gained acceptance, especially the planting of coverts with game at times when large bags were the order of the day. The rearing of these birds became systematic in 1750s and 1760s when eggs obtained from the wild were hatched in pheasanteries. By the 1770s crops such as buckwheat were being planted to attract game, especially pheasants, into an area and to keep it there. Hares were also protected, warrens were established, hedge trimming was restricted, and payment was made for hares to be placed in the warren.

Hunting seasons were set in 1762, and by 1776 they existed in the form we see at the present time. Some preserves were fenced, but fenced or not it was not possible for the gentry to hunt where they wished. Lords of manors tried both persuasion and warnings to dissuade illegal hunting. Even in the late 1800s game preservation was not always viewed favorably as can be seen in the following extract from a letter to Prince Duleep Singh from Queen Victoria (Alexander and Anand 1980: 129):

> *One thing especially, I have for some time wished to mention to you, as it is unpopular in the country, and what I myself, particularly dislike, viz. the great extent to which you preserve game – It is very expensive, & is much disliked for many reasons in the Country.*

Vermin control was practised until the middle years of this century (Anon 1945; MacIntyre 1952; Vesey-Fitzgerald 1946). Animals that have been considered to be vermin over the years have ranged from birds of prey, owls, corvids, foxes, badgers, stoats, weasels, squirrels, and rats, to hedgehogs (Cresswell et al. 1989; Gurnell 1987; Neal 1986; Vesey-Fitzgerald, 1946). Further, the animals that are considered "pests" will change over time (Jones 1972).

Gamekeepers became increasingly important figures in the management of estates, and in the production of game. Numerous works have been written on their craft and duties (Parker 1952; Virgoe and Yaxley 1986). The number of gamekeepers increased during the 1800s to about 15 000 in 1871. This figure reached a high of approximately 22 500 in 1910, dropping off to about 5000 in 1971. Thompson (1981) noted that gamekeepers were unevenly distributed throughout the country. In 1911 there were 20 to 30 per 10 000 population in some rural counties, but only 1 or 2 per 10 000 population in the highly industrialized and urbanized counties. The present-day gamekeeper has far more duties than in the past, and many are working at the position only part time. Skills expected of a gamekeeper are the ability to (1) shoot game and kill vermin, (2) raise pheasants, and (3) train dogs. The duties will of course vary from county to county, with a Scottish Highlands keeper obviously having many duties different from those of a keeper in the south of England. In advertising for gamekeepers the apprehension of poachers was rarely mentioned. This profession was never particularly lucrative, remuneration varying from very poor to adequate.

The management of game and countryside conservation is now shared, co-operatively and not antagonistically, between government agencies and NGOs that are supported by the public (Usher 1989). Included among the former is the Nature Conservancy, and the latter the Royal Society for the Protection of Birds, the Royal Society for Nature Conservation, and the National Trust. Sheail (1986) suggests that agricultural historians might also become more involved in nature conservation by offering advice to the conservation movement. It is also important to realize that while managing terrestrial systems we disregard aquatic systems at our peril. The proper management of water is often critical to wildlife management objectives. Eaton (1989) discusses man-made changes in British freshwaters, and suggests that ecological studies will make a great contribution to several areas of water management in the future.

Lowe (1983), in discussing the evolution of nature conservation in Britain, lists four phases of development: the natural history/humanitarian period (1830-90), the preservation period (1890-1940), the scientific period (1910-1970), and the popular/political period (1960-present day). Each period has contributed certain values to the movement, which in their totality and if used wisely will help us manage our wildlife and countryside in the future. It is essential to realize that many organizations that are now helping to make management decisions have political influence (Lowe and Goyder 1983), and pressure groups can influence legislation on moral issues (Pym 1972). Hunting is one area in which there is a constant battle and into which politics have intruded (Thomas 1983).

We are now in a management era (Blunden and Curry 1985), which started with the passage of the Countryside Act 1968, and the establishment of the Countryside Commission. The Wildlife and Countryside Act 1981 has led to increased tension between conservation groups and the National Farmers Union/Country Landowners Association (NFU/CLA). The latter coalition has a close and long-standing relationship with several ministries, and as a result is able to exert more influence than the former. This gives the impression, perhaps erroneous, that management decisions governing conservation are unduly influenced by the NFU/CLA because of their economic importance.

Finally, one of the major changes seen in management strategies during the past several years, and one that will become increasingly important, is the management for biodiversity rather than for a small number of selected species (Westman 1990).

History and/or Management of Selected Species

Modern British game hunting concentrates on birds, mainly pheasants, red grouse, and grey partridges. Few species of mammals are the objects of the chase. Only hares and deer are considered game, although legally deer are not game. However, a Game Licence is needed to hunt them.

Rabbits were introduced to Britain (Lever 1977; Veale 1957), and have been reared for a variety of purposes (meat, skin, fur, hunting) over the past several centuries. They are also the subject of many folktales (Purchase 1982). Sheail (1971) notes the numbers killed each month on Ashburnham Estate, Sussex. Monthly totals varied from 590 to 1695 in 1874, and 236 to 1209 in 1877. He also details figures on another estate where numbers varied from 944 in 1850-51, to 128 in 1852-53, with a peak of 6629 in 1869-70, followed by a downward trend to 4332 in 1878-79. Warrens of vast size existed elsewhere until the mid-1800s. Thetford Warren covered 3000 acres, and in the period 1855-60 averaged 28 886 rabbits per year. The importance of the rabbit to the economy of medieval East Anglia was outlined by Bailey (1988). Sheail (1978) discussed rabbits and agriculture in post-medieval England and suggests that rabbit warrens may have represented the optimal use of very light soils. Crompton and Sheail (1975) present a case study of the use and management of Lakenheath Warren, which was still producing rabbits until 1940-41. The rabbit flourished until 1953 when myxomatosis was discovered in animals in Kent. The disease spread rapidly and within a few years had destroyed over 99% of the population, estimated at some 60-100 million individuals after World War Two. The population of resistant individuals is growing once again.

Otters were hunted from the 13th century on, and were declared a pest in 1566 due to their predilection for fish being raised for food in fish ponds (Chanin 1985). Their numbers declined dramatically due to persecution throughout the 18th and 19th centuries. The population recovered during the First World War, but dropped once again due to intensive hunting in the 1920s and 1930s. A catastrophic fall in numbers occurred throughout most of the country starting in 1957-58. Numbers now appear to be rising from a 1977-79 low. This is a case where good water management may aid in the recovery (Jefferies 1989).

The brown hare is much larger than the rabbit (up to 7 pounds in weight). Corbet and Southern (1977), Evans and Thomson (1972), MacPherson (1896), and Tegner (1969) discuss the biology of this animal.

Hares have always been common on the drier, arable lowlands of south and east England, as well as in northeastern Scotland. In Norman times they were hunted by dogs that relied on scent to track them. In medieval times they were held in great esteem. Berners (1486) called them the "Kyng of Venery." Minor gentry and the clergy hunted them in the 17th and 18th centuries, by which time their population was beginning to be enclosed. Coursing became popular (Richardson 1896), with warrens guaranteeing the continuance of the sport. Populations of this animal may reach high numbers, at which time they begin to cause problems. This often results in a February hunt (Gibbons 1896; Lascelles 1896; Longman 1896) in many parts of the country. Large-scale hunts were common until the 1960s but are now less frequent. Europeans are more interested in this animal than the British, and farm owners are able to capitalize on this by leasing their shooting rights to interested parties. Since the 1960s there has been a decline in populations. The Game Conservancy set up a three year Hare Research Project in 1980, supported by the government and NGOs, to study populations and discover the reasons for the decline. Two projects were undertaken, one to study a local population, the other a broader study of several populations in several areas, each with its own farming and game management scheme. It was shown that a mixture of woodland, hedgerows, and crops were preferred habitat for this animal. Modern agricultural practices, with large fields, less hedgerows, and general tidiness are thus mitigating against hares. The fox was found to be its chief predator.

Deer have been hunted since humans reached Britain. The hunt for these animals was first formalized and ritualized by the Normans. They have appeared consistently in the game laws, and most recently in several post-war acts culminating in the Deer Act 1963. Six species with well established populations are now living in Britain. The red and roe deer are native, with fallow, sika, muntjac, and Chinese water deer having been introduced (Prior 1983). Populations in the past were probably controlled by predators, but have now risen due to the lack of predators and widespread afforestation. Basic differences exist in red deer hunting in England and Scotland. In England horses and deerhounds are used, in Scotland deer are stalked and shot (Eltringham 1984). Forestry and management for deer are inextricably entwined. Forest management practices affect deer and vice versa. The forester should attempt to reduce deer damage, keep the population of deer healthy, and make the presence of deer in the forest an economic asset (Prior 1983). Proper management should allow a crop to be harvested annually. This will provide for sport, venison, surplus animals to be sold as stock for parks, and nature recreation. The venison from deer shot in Britain is sold largely in Europe, with a market developing in the Far East for a variety of "deer parts" that are used widely in medicine (Kong and But 1985). Models have been developed for the efficient exploitation of deer (for example, Putman 1985), and in the future this renewable resource will continue to be harvested (see Fennessy and Drew 1985). There can be no doubt that deer stalking and rearing and leasing of hunting rights are economically worthwhile (Nahlik 1974). The integration of timber production and deer harvesting has the potential for producing economic returns far into the future. Eltringham (1984) examines the sources from which income may be derived and notes that approximately £1.5 million was obtained for 1000 tonnes of dressed carcasses in 1977. To comply with European Economic Community regulations, the deer carcass must be processed immediately, and cooled to 1°C within 10 hours if the venison is for human consumption. Culling of red deer in the Scottish Highlands presents some problems when trying to stick within the above bounds. Here the animals live on the open hillsides, rather than in woodland areas, often far from where they can be properly processed. In this operation profits are minimal. In England and Wales some 17 000 animals, from a population of 70 000 (red, roe, fallow, sika), are culled annually, with a further 4000 to 5000 being poached. In an effort to determine the technical feasibility of managing domesticated red deer an experiment was performed on the Glensaugh Experimental Farm, in the foothills of the Grampians. Economic aspects were not considered but the experiment did show the practicability of deer farming.

The majority of birds that are shot for sport are edible, and while much is known of the biology of many species, many data are anecdotal (see Kirkman and Hutchinson 1936). It is only in the past several years that good, sound, scientific data have started to accumulate on the game birds of Britain (for example, Hill and Robertson 1988; Hudson and Rands 1988; Potts 1986). Game birds (Galliformes) constitute the majority of birds shot, with some 6 million pheasants, 500 000 grey partridges, and 215 000 red grouse being taken annually (Medway 1980 *fide* Eltringham 1984). Most are shot on estates that are stocked and/or managed, but much "rough shooting" also occurs at the present time. The latter appellation refers to areas where game birds are harvested without the aid of a gamekeeper. To shoot game birds usually requires the ownership of sporting rights, or membership in a syndicate that holds such rights. Other birds that are shot but not considered to be gamebirds are wildfowl (average annual bag 200 000), woodpigeons (2.25 million), and woodcock (71 000).

The exact date when the pheasant was introduced to England is somewhat uncertain (Lever 1977), but the species was well established by the 15th century. Today it is the premier game bird, and is shot in numbers that far exceed the former staple of British game birds, the grey partridge. The Game Conservancy, established in 1970 as a management and research body, has been instrumental in producing superb data on the ecology, general biology, and management of this species (Hill and Robertson 1988). The pheasant is quite catholic in its choice of habitat, but thrives best in East Anglia and less well in the northwest of England. Unlike many other game bird species, the numbers shot have risen in recent years (67 per km^2 in 1961; 107 in 1985), rather than declined. Hill and Robertson (1988), after discussing the general biology of the bird and its unusual breeding and mating system (territorial harem defence polygyny), turn to management and the techniques used for rearing pheasants for release into the wild. An open-field rearing system, using bantams or other hens, may be used and is a long-established system. A second method involves the use of movable pens, resulting in fewer problems with predators, but more with parasites and diseases. Intensive methods are now used, with incubators and brooders making it possible to raise huge numbers of chicks. The number now reared and released may exceed 10 million annually. The number of hand-reared birds released has risen from 53 per km^2 (1961) to 180 (1985). The number shot is increasing at the same rate as the number released, suggesting that wild stocks are not increasing.

The chicks are released into the wild in July and August just prior to the hunting season (starts in November). Occasionally birds will be released in spring in an effort to increase the breeding stock, although this practise is unusual in Britain. The greatest loss of chicks occurs between release and the start of the hunt, with fox predation causing the greatest losses (Robertson 1988). It was found that habitat cover, amount and height, was of critical importance when considering predation. Data suggest that surviving cocks contribute little to natural productivity. Hand-reared females are more susceptible to predation, rearing only one quarter the number of broods fledged by wild birds. There does appear to be a relationship between shooting success and numbers of birds released. The greater the number released the greater the bag. Where only wild birds are present the number shot per hectare is usually low. If supplemented by small numbers of reared birds and woodlands/coppices, the number does increase. Wild bird shoots are now uncommon. Active management is an essential part of the pheasant hunt in this day and age. The number of birds shot in an area will depend on the policies of the estate owner. The proportion of birds shot may increase as the population rises, with the age/sex composition of the bag varying as the circumstances change. Generally the number of birds shot "levels-off" when the population exceeds 200 birds per km^2, and a normal seasonal bag would be about 70% of the autumn population. It is obviously desirable to determine the Maximum Sustainable Yield (MSY) of the population in an area before harvesting, although Larkin (1977) had problems with the MSY concept as it relates to fish. There is no doubt that rearing and release result in greater numbers of birds being shot, with Hill and Robertson (1988) demonstrating that with no rearing/release the numbers shot would drop from the approximately 107 per km^2 (in 1985) to 12 (in about 8 years).

The value of woodlands and coverts to pheasant management was recognized over 80 years ago. Young broad-leaved plantations are more attractive than older ones, and particularly coniferous stands. Mixed farming is important in presenting a series of habitats for the birds, and is more desirable than the present-day practice of monoculture in large fields. Management prescriptions today mirror those of yesteryear. Hedgerows may not be important in the management of this species, as they are with many other species, as evidenced by the birds thriving in the Fenland of East Anglia.

Woodland management is a long term process, not particularly conducive to raising pheasants in a short time span. Other quicker methods may be used as a substitute for woodland management, or as a stopgap measure until woodland/coppices are available for the birds. Game crops, such as kale, mustard and fodder radish, maize, millet, and sunflowers, in half hectare blocks, will provide cover and food for birds. "Instant" spinneys may be developed as may new woodlands while older woods are properly managed.

The future of the pheasant as a gamebird will depend on continued rearing, habitat manipulation, and woodland management. Small woods, less than a hectare in area, are more desirable than large woodlands. The smaller blocks of trees provide more "edge habitats" where the cocks can establish territories and are good for cover and holding birds. In this age of managing for biodiversity, other species of wildlife will also benefit from the above scheme.

The grey partridge (as opposed to the French or red-legged partridge, which was introduced to England [Lever 1977]) used to be one of the most commonly hunted game birds. In the 1880s some classic partridge manors were producing daily bags in excess of 500 brace. During the past few decades there has been a dramatic decline in the annual bag of the species throughout its range (Potts 1986). The mean annual pre-1940 (or predecline) bag in Britain was about 2 million, with a decline to about 100 000 in recent years. Potts (1986) investigated the species for the Game Conservancy, and concluded that herbicides, sprayed on crops to eliminate weeds, affected chick survival and allowed increased nest predation by reducing nest cover. These factors would account for much of the decline noted. The most critical factor in the equation appeared to be early chick mortality. Herbicides and pesticides have long been known to have deleterious effects on wildlife (Moore 1965; Sheail 1985). In this instance the herbicides also decimate the populations of invertebrates that are essential for the survival of partridge chicks in their first few days. The problem may be mitigated by not spraying the outer 6 m of the field margin, and compensating farmers for lost crops. The original reason for not spraying the margins of fields was to conserve plants that were becoming rare. The ideal situation would involve not spraying a 12 m band around the field, including headlands. To prevent weeds gradually spreading into the crops a metre-wide sterile strip could be made between the sprayed and unsprayed areas. The cost of production of wild birds would be about £16 per bird shot, as compared to £12 for reared birds.

Future management will depend on the provision of suitable habitat, including open countryside, few trees, and cereal crops. Good quality nesting cover is essential in the form of linear habitat (hedgerows) that is about half a metre above the field surface, contains long, dead grass from the previous year, and few trees (Potts 1986; Rands 1986). This habitat, except in wet areas, would support about one nest every 200 m. Chick mortality would have to be reduced, as mentioned earlier, and nest predation would have to be controlled (Tapper et al. 1982). It is suggested that production of wild birds is more desirable than trying to maintain or increase populations through releases. Other species of wildlife such as butterflies would benefit from the management policies outlined.

The epitome of the sporting life of the rich, in the eyes of many people, is the annual red grouse shoot on the moors of northern England and Scotland. This species became a fashionable quarry in the early 19th century, when birds were shot over pointers. The change to driving birds to sportsmen in butts occurred in the 1860s. As more people participated in the sport, moorland management improved, with gamekeepers being responsible for things such as stock sizes and heather burning. By the early 1900s grouse hunting reached its heyday. Present trends are such that upland landowners are now letting some, or all, of their land to game syndicates who wish to pursue this prey. This offsets the cost of their own sport, or helps with the finances of the estate or farm.

The biology and behavior of red grouse has received much attention over the years, starting with the work of the Committee of Inquiry on Grouse Disease (Leslie and Shipley 1912), and leading to the works of Watson and his colleagues (Hudson 1986a; Hudson and Watson 1985; Jenkins et al. 1963; Watson and Jenkins 1964). The population of these birds shows cyclic fluctuations (Williams 1985), as is typical of species in the Family Tetraonidae (Watson and Moss 1979). This makes the production of a harvestable surplus each year much less precise than for pheasants or grey partridges. The reasons for the cycles are as yet unknown, although many hypotheses have been proposed and predictive models developed (Hudson and Watson 1985; Potts et al. 1984; Watson et al. 1984).

The habitat and food requirements of the species are well known (Miller and Watson 1978; Moss and Miller 1976; Moss et al. 1988; Savory 1978). They feed primarily on heather, which restricts their distribution to the moorlands of Britain (about 1.5 million hectares). Management for grouse requires proper maintenance of heather on the moorlands and the provision of a mixture of heather of different ages. Quality of food is just as important as the quantity available. The moorland flora is a successional stage developed after the destruction of upland forests, and unless it is maintained by regular burning (see Darling and Boyd 1969), or other practices, it will eventually revert to woodland.

Survival and production of grouse is intimately tied to predation by foxes and crows, and the effects of parasites. Hudson (1986b) found that female grouse treated with an anthelmintic (a vermifuge) against the round worm *Trichostronyylus tenuis* showed a significantly increased production of young.

Unlike the pheasant and grey partridge, red grouse are not reared and released, because although they are easy to rear they do not thrive on release. Red grouse bags have declined in Scotland to approximately 20% of previous levels. The reasons for this decline are the subject of study. It is still possible to return a profit on investment in this species in England, but less so in Scotland (the return is about £35 per brace shot. A well managed English moor of 1620 hectares will produce about 1000 brace per annum, with a value of £35 000 [Hudson and Watson 1985]).

Other game birds worthy of mention are the red-legged partridge, ptarmigan, capercaillie, and black grouse. The red-legged partridge was introduced some 300 years ago (Lever 1977), and has become well established in parts of southern and eastern England. The bird was little liked on its introduction, particularly in areas where the grey partridge was plentiful, and gamekeepers even went to the trouble of destroying its nests and eggs. As the number of grey partridges declines more hunters are relying on the red-legged partridge as a source of sport. About 800 000 birds are released annually, an action that has helped to maintain, and perhaps increase, the wild population that has been in decline since the 1970s. It seems likely that the species would fail to survive in England without an annual "topping-up." Many aspects of the biology of the species are similar to those of the grey partridge, but differences do occur in the breeding strategy (chicks are able to survive on vegetable matter soon after hatching and do not rely heavily on insects). In the management of the species, unsprayed headlands assume some importance.

One of the least-known gamebirds in Britain is the ptarmigan (Bannerman 1963), which is usually found in the Highlands of Scotland at heights over 2000 feet. This is a circumpolar (Holarctic) species found as far down as sea level in some parts of its range such as Scandinavia. Watson (1972) studied its behavior, and described population changes on a 500 hectare estate in the Cairngorms (Watson 1965). He noted that predation was the only important form of adult mortality, and more recently he (Watson 1987) described the weight and sexual cycle of the species. It is unlikely that hunting has any effect on this species.

The largest of the grouse, the capercaillie, is at home in the northern coniferous forests. The capercaillie became extinct in Britain after the destruction of the Forest of Caledon in the late 1700s, but was successfully reintroduced in the 19th century, and is now well established (Lever 1977). Its future depends on the provision of suitable habitat, including mixed stands of trees of varying ages, with undergrowth. The modern forestry practice of growing even-aged stands of softwoods (usually a monoculture system of Sitka spruce) is not conducive to capercaillie management. Fires, integrated with a cutting program, will produce suitable "edge zones" for this species in such a woodland.

A further species of tetraonid, formerly common in many parts of Britain but showing a rapid decline, is the black grouse. Bags of 250 or more per day were being taken in the 1860s, yet the population is now confined to the west country, parts of northwest England, Wales, and Scotland (Grove et al. 1988; Johnstone 1969). Scotland is the last remaining stronghold for the species in Britain. It may well be the place where its future lies, if there is a change in farming and forestry practices that are destroying the birds' preferred habitat (Parr and Watson 1988). Large scale afforestation may have helped reestablish stocks (and those of the capercaillie), but recent practices are mitigating against continued gains. Much research remains to be performed on this species (Robel 1969). Few hunters will make the black grouse their sole quarry, and hunting pressure on the species is low. These birds are difficult to drive, and many hunters achieve bags of several brace by shooting over setters.

The snipe and woodcock are considered by many sportsmen to be game birds, even though their close season protection lies not in the game laws, but in the general wild bird laws, of which the Wildlife and Countryside Act 1981 is the most recent. Both species are hunted widely, with the best sport being had in late autumn (snipe) or early winter (woodcock). In both cases habitat management is critical to maintain numbers. Artificial bogs, or managed natural bogs, are necessary for snipe, preferably with open areas and short vegetation, interspersed with longer vegetation for cover, while woodcock require shrubby daytime cover, near damp pastures and meadows where they can feed at night. The area must also be relatively quiet. During Victorian and Edwardian times some estates maintained shoots specifically for woodcock.

The final group of birds are the wildfowl, which use both aquatic and terrestrial habitats. Humans have and will continue to influence wildfowl in many ways, including losses and threats to habitats (drainage for agriculture, coastal reclamation, estuarine barrages, and reservoirs). Pollution of several kinds, including agrochemicals (that affect water bodies causing eutrophication[8]), sewage, industrial waste, oil, lead poisoning (from shotgun pellets and fishing weights) take their toll (Owen et al. 1986). The populations of several species of geese have risen dramatically during the past 20 years, which is leading to conflicts between farmers and conservationists where geese are damaging crops (Jalil and Patterson 1989; Patterson et al. 1989). The problems are generally local in nature, and it is suggested that compensation be paid for crop losses, although the farmers would in many cases prefer to cull the geese. As in North America, habitats are being created and improved throughout the country, where management may be undertaken to maintain stocks. Wildfowling is a sport enjoyed by people of all ages and socio-economic groups. It is suggested that of 850 000 shotgun owners, 160 000 participate in the sport. The majority (75%) of ducks are shot on inland waters, mallard forming the bulk of the bag (60%). On inland waters conflicts may occur as a result of their being used for other recreational purposes. The hunter may put other people at risk, but the recreational users may disturb the wildfowl. Some disturbances are of short duration and may have indirect effects (cause habitat changes), or direct effects (displace birds). The possibility of permanent damage must be assessed, however, when recreational uses are suggestion for areas that are used heavily by wildfowl.

No game licence is required to hunt wildfowl, which are covered by the Wildlife and Countryside Act 1981. In law three groups of wildfowl are recognized, namely, those that are fully protected, those that can be taken in the open season, and those that can be sold dead (between 1 September and 28 February). Bans and restraints on hunting may be imposed, if necessary, by the Secretary of State for the Environment. The management of this resource has been extremely successful, but continued gains depend on the maintenance of habitats and provision of new reserves.

The Future

The world is changing more rapidly now than ever before. New technologies are helping improve the quality of our lives, but it is becoming increasingly difficult to predict what kind of world we will face 20 years from now. Development in both the industrialized world and the developing world must become more rational and efficient,

---

[8] a technical term denoting the silting in, stagnation, and slow death of a lake in transition to becoming swamp and finally land.

with less waste of natural resources (terrestrial, freshwater, marine), and less pollution. Failing this, we may well finish up with a world like that described in the prophetic book by Wylie (1972), or that depicted in the movie *Soylent Green.*

The present British system of privately controlled land and waters will continue, although the owners themselves may change with the break-up of estates, and a new class of wealthy people emerging. It may also be that institutions (especially financial) and the government will acquire more land, and thus be in a position to exert a greater influence on its development and use. There will be no change to what Crutchfield and Pontecorvo (1969), in discussing the Pacific salmon fisheries, called an "open access resource."

Coles (1968), and many other British hunters, prefer the present system and decry the concept of an open access resource. Coles (1968:18, 21) expressed his feelings in the following way:

> *I would think the overall density of game in Great Britain is still probably higher than anywhere in the world. This is mainly because our laws state that the right to shoot game belongs to the man who owns the land – though he can of course let these rights to someone else if he wants to. This means that every shoot – large or small – can be cared for like a man's garden. . . . Personally I would rather try and improve the sport on a small rented farm, than share a thousand square miles of free shooting with a thousand other shooters.*

As an expatriate Briton I still find the North American system to be fairer to the greatest number of people who wish to avail themselves of game. I would suggest that every effort be made to ensure that the present system of publicly owned, properly managed resources be maintained, and that privatization of the lands and their living resources be resisted.

A further trend that we are seeing, and that will be of greater significance over the coming years, is that of non-consumptive use of wildlife. Wildlife managers must become aware of this fact and devise policies that will cater to all sections of the public (Gilbert and Dodds 1987). In Britain I feel that hunting will continue, but at a lower level. As the degradation and destruction of wildlife habitat continue in Europe, hunters from the Continent will turn increasingly to Britain for their sport. Hares are highly prized on the Continent but not in Britain, where many landowners consider them to be pests. These same landowners will, however, let their property to Europeans who are willing to pay for the privilege of shooting the animals. Sale of game will almost certainly remain legal, but pressure from animal rights groups might ultimately cause a re-evaluation of this policy.

While more intensive wildlife management seems unlikely there may be a change in emphasis, with management for biodiversity becoming more important. For wildlife to survive in its present numbers, or increase, it is essential that a closer integration between farming, forestry, and game policies develop. Research will become ever more important, and will make use of modern technologies such as computer modelling (Starfield and Bleloch 1986).

Overall, I feel that in Britain the future for wildlife (or game) is good, as long as the public maintains its interest in the natural world, and is willing to press both the Government and NGOs to take action to conserve the countryside before it is too late.

References

Alexander, M. and Anand, S. 1980. *Queen Victoria's Maharajah Duleep Singh 1838-93*. Weidenfeld & Nicolson, London, 326 pp.

Allen, D. E. 1987. Changing attitudes to nature conservation: The botanical perspective. *Biological Journal Linnean Society (London)* 32: 203-212.

Anon. 1945. *The control of vermin*. Gilbertson and Page Ltd., Hertford, 66 pp.

Bailey, J. A. 1984. *Principles of Wildlife Management*. John Wiley & Sons Inc., New York, 373 pp.

Bailey, M. 1988. The rabbit and the medieval East Anglian economy. *Agricultural History Review* 36: 1-20.

Baillie-Grohman, W. A. [1925] *Sport in Art: An Iconography of Sport During Four Hundred Years from the Beginning of the Fifteenth to the End of the Eighteenth Centuries.* Benjamin Blom Inc., New York, 422 pp. (reissued 1969)

Baker, A. R. H. and Harley, J. B. 1973. *Man Made the Land: Essays in English Historical Geography*. Rowman and Littlefield, Totowa, 208 pp.

Bannerman, D. A. 1963. *The Birds of the British Isles.* Volume 12. Oliver and Boyd, Edinburgh, 443 pp.

Berners, J. [1486] *The Boke of Saint Albans.* Theatrum Orbis Terrarium Ltd., Amsterdam. (facsimile edition 1969)

Best, L. B. 1983. Bird use of fencerows: Implications of contemporary fencerow management practices. *Wildlife Society Bulletin* 11: 343-347.

Blackmore, H. L. 1971. *Hunting Weapons.* Walker and Company, New York, 401 pp.

Blacksell, M. and Gilg, A. W. 1981. *The Countryside: Planning and Change.* George Allen & Unwin Ltd., London, 262 pp.

Blackstone, W. 1773. *Commentaries on the Laws of England.* Book the fourth. 5th ed. Printed for John Exshaw et al., Dublin, 436 pp. + appendix and index.

Blunden, J. and Curry, N. (eds.) 1985. *The Changing Countryside.* Croom Helm Ltd., London, 269 pp.

Bovill, E. W. 1963. *English Country Life 1780-1830*. Oxford University Press, London, 266 pp.

Bowsky, W. M. (ed.) 1971. *The Black Death. A Turning Point in History?* Holt, Rinehart & Winston, New York, 128 pp.

Bracey, H. E. 1972. *People and the Countryside*. Routledge & Kegan Paul Ltd., London, 310 pp.

Bramwell, D., Yalden, D. W. and Yalden, P. E. 1990. Ossom's Eyrie Cave: An archaeological contribution to the recent history of vertebrates in Britain. *Zoological Journal Linnean Society (London)* 98: 1-25.

Brander, M. 1971. *Hunting and Shooting*. G. P. Putnam's Sons, New York, 255 pp.

Brown, L. 1976. *British Birds of Prey: A Study of Britain's 24 Diurnal Raptors*. Collins, London, 400 pp.

Brunskill, R. W. 1981. *Traditional Buildings of Britain: An Introduction to Vernacular Architecture*. Victor Gollancz Ltd., London, 160 pp.

Cade, T. J. 1982. *The Falcons of the World*. Comstock/Cornell University Press, Ithaca, 192 pp.

Carr, R. 1976. *English Fox Hunting: A History*. Weidenfeld & Nicolson, London, 273 pp.

—— 1981. Country sports. pp. 475-487 in G. E. Mingay (ed.), *The Victorian Countryside*, Volume 2, Routledge & Kegan Paul Ltd., London.

Chanin, P. 1985. *The Natural History of Otters*. Croom Helm Ltd., London, 179 pp.

Chapman, J. 1987. The extent and nature of Parliamentary enclosure. *Agricultural History Review* 35: 25-35.

Clarke, P., Jackman, B. and Mercer, D. 1980. *Book of the Countryside: Including One Thousand Days Out in Great Britain and Ireland*. Macdonald General Books, London, 350 pp.

Coles, C. L. 1968. *Game Conservation in a Changing Countryside*. Museum Press, London, 192 pp.

Corbet, G. B. 1974. The distribution of mammals in historic times. pp. 179-202 in D. L. Hawksworth (ed.), *The Changing Flora and Fauna of Britain*, Academic Press, London.

Corbet, G. B. and Southern, H. N. (eds.) 1977. *The Handbook of British Mammals*. Blackwell Scientific Publications, London, 520 pp.

Creswell, P., Harris, S., Bunce, R. G. M. and Jefferies, D. J. 1989. The badger (*Meles meles*) in Britain: Present status and future population changes. *Biological Journal Linnean Society (London)* 38: 91-101.

Crompton, G. and Sheail, J. 1975. The historical ecology of Lakenheath warren in Suffolk, England: A case study. *Biological Conservation* 8: 299-313.

Cross, A. L. 1928. *Eighteenth Century Documents Relating to the Royal Forests, the Sheriffs and smuggling*. Macmillan & Company Ltd., London, 328 pp.

Crutchfield, J. A. and Pontecorvo, G. 1969. *The Pacific Salmon Fisheries*. Johns Hopkins Press, Baltimore, 220 pp.

Cummins, J. 1988. *The Hound and the Hawk: The Art of Medieval Hunting*. St. Martin's Press, New York, 306 pp.

Currant, A. 1989. The Quaternary origins of the modern British mammal fauna. *Biological Journal Linnean Society (London)* 38: 23-30.

Dagg, A. I. (not dated) *Wildlife Management in Europe*. Otter Press, Waterloo, 324 pp.

Darby, H. C. 1973. *A New Historical Geography of England*. University Press, Cambridge, 767 pp.

Darling, F. F. and Boyd, J. M. 1969. *The Highlands and Islands*. Collins, London, 336 pp.

Dimbleby, G. W. 1984. Anthropogenic changes from Neolithic through medieval times. *New Phytologist* 98: 57-72.

Dodgshon, R. A. 1978. The early Middle Ages, 1066-1350. pp. 81-117 in R. A. Dodgshon and R. A. Butlin (eds.), *An Historical Geography of England and Wales*, Academic Press, London.

Eaton, J. W. 1989. Ecological aspects of water management in Britain. *Journal of Applied Ecology* 26: 835-849.

Edlin, H. L. 1952. *The Changing Wild Life of Britain*. B. T. Batsford Ltd., London, 184 pp.

—— 1972. *Trees, Woods and Man*. Collins, London, 272 pp.

Eltringham, S. K. 1984. *Wildlife Resources and Economic Development*. John Wiley & Sons Inc., New York, 325 pp.

Emsley, C. 1987. *Crime and Society in England, 1750-1900*. Longman Group UK Ltd., Harlow, 257 pp.

Evans, G. E. and Thomson, D. 1972. *The Leaping Hare*. Faber and Faber Ltd., London, 262 pp.

Fennessy, P. F. and Drew, K. R. (eds.) 1985. Biology of deer production. *Roy Society of New Zealand Bulletin* 22.

Fleure, H. J. and Davies, M. 1970. *A Natural History of Man in Britain: Conceived as a Study of Changing Relations Between Men and Environments*. Collins, London, 320 pp.

Fowler, P. J. 1983. *The Farming of Prehistoric Britain*. University Press, Cambridge, 246 pp.

Fuller, R. J. 1982. *Bird Habitats in Britain*. T. & A. D. Poyser Ltd., Calton, 320 pp.

Gasquet, F. A. 1908. *The Black Death of 1348 and 1349*. George Bell and Sons, London, 272 pp.

Gibbons, J. S. [1896]. Harriers. pp. 191-228 in *The Hare*. Ashford Press Publishing, Shedfield. (reprinted 1986)

Gilbert, F. F. and Dodds, D. G. 1987. *The Philosophy and Practice of Wildlife Management*. Robert E. Kreiger Publ. Co., Malabar, 279 pp.

Girouard, M. 1987. *A Country House Companion*. Yale University Press, New Haven, 192 pp.

Goldsmith, F. B. and Wood, J. B. 1983. Ecological effects of upland afforestation. pp. 287-311 in A. Warren and F. B. Goldsmith (eds.), *Conservation in Perspective*, John Wiley & Sons Ltd., Chichester.

Goodfellow, P. 1983. *Shakespeare's Birds*. The Overlook Press, Woodstock, 96 pp.

Gosling, L. M. and Baker, S. J. 1989. The eradication of muskrats and coypus from Britain. *Biological Journal Linnean Society (London)* 38: 39-51.

Green, B. 1981. *Countryside Conservation: The Protection and Management of Amenity Ecosystems*. George Allen & Unwin Ltd., London, 249 pp.

Green, B. H. 1975. The future of the British countryside. *Landscape Planning* 2: 179-195.

—— 1989. Agricultural impacts on the rural environment. *Journal of Applied Ecology* 26: 793-802.

Grove, S. J., Hope Jones, P., Malkinson, A. R., Thomas, D. M. and Williams, I. 1988. Black grouse in Wales, spring 1986. *British Birds* 81: 2-9.

Gurnell, J. 1987. *The Natural History of Squirrels*. Christopher Helm, London, 201 pp.

Hall, S. J. G. and Hall, J. C. 1988. Inbreeding and population dynamics of the Chillingham cattle (*Bos taurus*). *Journal of Zoology*, London 216: 479-493.

Harrison, B. 1973. Animals and the state in nineteenth-century England. *English Historical Review* 88: 786-820.

Harrison, C. J. O. 1980. Pleistocene bird remains from Tornewton Cave and the Brixham Windmill Hill Cave in south Devon. *Bulletin British Museum Natural History (Geology)* 33: 91-100.

—— 1988. *The History of the Birds of Britain*. Collins, London, 224 pp.

Harting, J. E. [1864] *The Ornithology of Shakespeare: Critically Examined, Explained and Illustrated*. Unwin Brothers Limited, Old Woking. (facsmile edition 1978)

—— 1880. *British Animals Extinct Within Historic Times, with Some Account of British Wild White Cattle*. Trubner & Co., London, 258 pp.

Hawkes, J. and Hawkes, C. 1958. *Prehistoric Britain*. Penguin Books Ltd., Harmondsworth, 176 pp.

Hawkes, J. G. 1978. *Conservation and Agriculture*. Allanheld, Osmun & Co. Publ. Inc., Montclair, 284 pp.

Hawksworth, D. L. (ed.) 1974. *The Changing Flora and Fauna of Britain*. Academic Press, London, 461 pp.

Hill, D. and Robertson, P. 1988. *The Pheasant: Ecology, Management and Conservation*. BSP Professional Books, Oxford, 281 pp.

Hodder, I. 1978. The human geography of Roman Britain. pp. 29-55 in R. A. Dodgshon and R. A. Butlin (eds.), *An Historical Geography of England and Wales,* Academic Press, London.

Hooke, D. 1989. Pre-conquest woodland: Its distribution and usage. *Agricultural History Review* 37: 113-129.

Hooker, J. J. 1989. British mammals in the Tertiary period. *Biological Journal of the Linnean Society (London)* 38: 9-21.

Hopkins, H. 1985. *The Long Affray: The Poaching Wars, 1760-1914.* Secker and Warburg, London, 344 pp.

Hoskins, W. G. and Stamp, L. D. 1964. *The Common Lands of England & Wales.* Collins, London, 366 pp.

Hudson, P. and Watson, A. 1985. The red grouse. *Biologist* 32: 13-18.

Hudson, P. J. 1986a. *Red Grouse: The Biology and Management of a Wild Gamebird.* The Game Conservancy, Fordingbridge.

—— 1986b. The effect of a parasitic nematode on the breeding production of red grouse. *Journal of Animal Ecology* 55: 85-92.

Hudson, P. J. and Rands, M. R. W. 1988. *Ecology and Management of Gamebirds.* BSP Professional Books, Oxford, 263 pp.

Itzkowitz, B. C. 1977. *Peculiar Privilege: A Social History of English Foxhunting 1753-1885.* The Harvester Press Ltd., Hassocks, 248 pp.

Jacques, D. 1983. *Georgian Gardens: The Reign of Nature.* B. T. Batsford Ltd., London, 240 pp.

Jalil, S. A. and Patterson, I. J. 1989. Effect of simulated goose grazing on yield of autumn-sown barley in north-east Scotland. *Journal of Applied Ecology* 26: 897-912.

Jarrett, D. 1978. *The English Landscape Garden.* Academy Editions, London, 144 pp.

Jefferies, D. J. 1989. The changing otter population of Britain 1700-1989. *Biological Journal Linnean Society (London)* 38: 61-69.

Jenkins, D., Watson, A. and Miller, G. R. 1963. Population studies on red grouse, *Lagopus lagopus scoticus* (Lath.) in north-east Scotland. *Journal of Animal Ecology* 32: 317-376.

Johnstone, G. W. 1969. Ecology, dispersion and arena behaviour of black grouse *Lyrurus tetrix* (L.) in Glen Dye, N.E. Scotland. Unpublished Ph.D. thesis, Univ. of Aberdeen.

Jones, D. J. V. 1979. The poacher: A study in Victorian crime and protest. *Historical Journal* 22: 825-860.

Jones, E. L. 1972. The bird pests of British agriculture in recent centuries. *Agricultural History Review* 20: 107-125.

Jones, G. R. J. 1978. Celts, Saxons and Scandinavians. pp. 57-79 in R. A. Dodgshon and R. A. Butlin (eds.), *An Historical Geography of England and Wales,* Academic Press, London.

Kirby, C. 1932. The attack on the English game laws in the forties. *Journal of Modern History* 4: 18-37.

—— 1933. The English game law system. *American Historical Review* 38: 240-262.

—— 1941. English game law reform. pp. 345-380 in *Essays in Modern English History, in Honor of Wilbur Cortez Abbott*. Kennikat Press, Port Washington.

Kirkman, F. B. and Hutchinson, H. G. (eds.) 1936. *British Sporting Birds*. T. C. & E. C. Jack Ltd., London, 428 pp.

Kong, Y. C. and But, P. P. H. 1985. Deer – the ultimate medicinal animal (antler and deer parts in medicine). In Biology of deer production, eds. P. F. Fennessy and K. R. Drew. *Royal Society New Zealand Bulletin* 22:311-324.

Kurten, B. 1968. *Pleistocene Mammals of Europe*. Weidenfeld & Nicolson, London, 317 pp.

Lack, P. 1986. *The Atlas of Wintering Birds in Britain and Ireland*. T. & A. D. Poyser Ltd., Calton, 447 pp.

Larkin, P. A. 1977. An epitaph for the concept of Maximum Sustained Yield. *Transactions American Fisheries Society* 106: 1-11.

Lascelles, G. [1896]. Shooting the hare. pp. 85-108 in *The Hare*. Ashford Press Publishing, Shedfield. (reprinted 1986)

Leopold, A. 1948. *Game Management*. Charles Scribner's Sons, New York, 481 pp.

—— 1970. *A Sand County Almanac, with Essays on Conservation from Round River*. Sierra Club, San Francisco, & Ballantine Books Inc., New York, 295 pp.

Leslie, A. S. and Shipley, A. E. (eds.) 1912. *The Grouse in Health and in Disease: Being the Popular Edition of the Report of the Committee of Inquiry on Grouse Disease*. Smith, Elder and Co., London, 472 pp.

Lever, C. 1977. *The Naturalized Animals of the British Isles*. Hutchinson & Co. Ltd., London, 600 pp.

Lockhart, D. and Ilbery, B. (eds.) 1987. *The Future of the British Rural Landscape*. Geo Books, Norwich, 223 pp.

Longman, G. M. [1896] Beagling. pp. 179-190 in *The Hare*. Ashford Press Publishing, Shedfield. (reprinted 1986)

Longrigg, R. 1977. *The English Squire and His Sport*. Michael Joseph Ltd., London, 302 pp.

Lowe, P., Cox, G., MacEwen, M., O'Riordan, T. and Winter, M. 1986. *Countryside Conflicts: The Politics of Farming, Forestry and Conservation*. Gower Publ. Co. Ltd., Aldershot, 378 pp.

Lowe, P. and Goyder, J. 1983. *Environmental Groups in Politics*. George Allen & Unwin Ltd., London, 208 pp.

Lowe, P. D. 1983. Values and institutions in the history of British nature conservation. pp. 329-352 in A. Warren and F. B. Goldsmith (eds.), *Conservation in perspective*, John Wiley & Sons Ltd., Chichester.

Mabey, R. 1980. *The Common Ground: A Place for Nature in Britain's Future?* Hutchinson & Co. Ltd., London, 280 pp.

MacEwen, A. and MacEwen, M. 1982. *National Parks: Conservation or Cosmetics?* George Allen & Unwin Ltd., London, 314 pp.

—— and —— 1983. National parks: A cosmetic conservation system. pp. 391-409 in A. Warren and F. B. Goldsmith (eds.), *Conservation in perspective,* John Wiley & Sons Ltd., Chichester.

MacIntyre, D. 1950. *Wild Life of the Highlands: Shooting, Fishing, Natural History and Legend.* The Batchworth Press, London, 254 pp.

—— 1952. Trapping & vermin. pp. 136-157 in E. Parker (ed.), *The Lonsdale Keeper's Book,* Seeley Service & Co. Ltd., London.

MacPherson, H. A. [1896] Natural history of the hare. pp. 3-82 in *The Hare.* Ashford Press Publishing, Shedfield. (reprinted 1986)

Margules, C. and Usher, M. B. 1981. Criteria used in assessing wildlife conservation potential: A review. *Biological Conservation* 21: 79-109.

Matthews, L. H. 1968. *British Mammals.* Collins, London, 410 pp.

McCall, A. 1979. *The Medieval Underworld.* Hamish Hamilton Ltd., London, 319 pp.

McClanahan, T. R. 1990. Are conservationists fish bigots? *BioScience* 40: 2.

McKelvie, C. L. 1985. *A Future for Game?* George Allen & Unwin Ltd., London, 228 pp.

Mellanby, K. 1967. *Pesticides and Pollution.* Collins, London, 221 pp.

Miller, G. R. and Watson, A. 1978. Territories and the food plant of individual red grouse. 1. Territory size, number of mates and brood size compared with the abundance, production and diversity of heather. *Journal of Animal Ecology* 47: 293-305.

—— and —— 1983. Heather moorland in northern Britain. pp. 101-117 in A. Warren and F. B. Goldsmith (eds.), *Conservation in Perspective,* John Wiley & Sons Ltd., Chichester.

Miller, M. A. 1986. *Birds: A Guide to the Literature.* Garland Publ. Inc., New York, 887 pp.

Mills, D. 1971. *Salmon and Trout: A Resource, its Ecology, Conservation and Management.* Oliver and Boyd, Edinburgh, 351 pp.

—— 1989. *Ecology and Management of Atlantic Salmon.* Chapman & Hall Ltd., London, 351 pp.

Millward, R. and Robinson, A. 1977. *Landscapes of Britain.* David & Charles Ltd., Newton Abbot, 112 pp.

Mingay, G. E. 1981. *The Victorian Countryside.* Volume 2. Routledge & Kegan Paul Ltd., London.

Moore, N. W. 1965. Pesticides and birds – a review of the situation in Great Britain in 1965. *Bird Study* 12: 222-254.

Morris, M. G. 1987. Changing attitudes to nature conservation: The entomological perspective. *Biological Journal Linnean Society (London)* 32: 213-223.

Morris, P. A. 1987. Changing attitudes towards British mammals. *Biological Journal Linnean Society (London)* 32: 225-233.

Moss, R. and Miller, G. R. 1976. Production, dieback and grazing of heather (*Calluna vulgaris*) in relation to numbers of red grouse (*Lagopus l. scoticus*) and mountain hares (*Lepus timidus*) in north-east Scotland. *Journal of Applied Ecology* 13: 369-377.

Moss, R., Watson, A. and Parr, R. 1988. Mate choice by hen red grouse *Lagopus lagopus* with an excess of cocks – role of territory size and food quality. *Ibis* 130: 545-552.

Muir, R. and Muir, N. 1987. *Hedgerows: Their History and Wildlife.* Michael Joseph Ltd., London, 250 pp.

Munsche, P. B. 1977. The game laws in Wiltshire 1750-1800. pp. 210-228 in J. S. Cockburn (ed.), *Crime in England 1550-1800*, University Press, Princeton.

—— 1981. *Gentlemen and Poachers*. The English Game Laws 1671-1831. University Press, Cambridge, 255 pp.

Murton, R. K. 1971. *Man and Birds.* Collins, London, 364 pp.

Nahlik, A. J. de 1974. *Deer Management: Improved Herds for Greater Profit.* David & Charles Ltd., Newton Abbot, 250 pp.

Neal, E. 1986. *The Natural History of Badgers.* Croom Helm Ltd., London, 238 pp.

Nicholson, E. M. 1988. The bird population of Great Britain. *British Birds* 81: 613-624.

Nimrod 1901. *The Life of a Sportsman.* Downey and Co. Ltd., London, 401 pp.

Orwin, C. S. and Sellick, R. J. 1970. *The Reclamation of Exmoor Forest.* David & Charles Ltd., Newton Abbot, 312 pp.

Owen, M., Atkinson-Willes, G. L. and Salmon, D. G. 1986. *Wildfowl in Great Britain.* 2nd edn. University Press, Cambridge, 613 pp.

Parker, E. (ed.) 1952. *The Lonsdale Keeper's Book.* Seeley Service & Co. Ltd., London, 256 pp.

Parr, R. and Watson, A. 1988. Habitat preferences of black-grouse on moorland-dominated ground in north-east Scotland. *Ardea.* 76: 175-180.

Patterson, I. J., Jalil, S. A. and East, M. L. 1989. Damage to winter cereals by greylag and pink-footed geese in north-east Scotland. *Journal of Applied Ecology* 26: 879-895.

Pearsall, W. H. 1965. *Mountains and Moorlands.* Collins, London, 312 pp.

Pennington, W. 1974. *The History of British Vegetation.* The English Universities Press Ltd., London, 152 pp.

Perry, R. 1978. *Wildlife in Britain and Ireland.* Croom Helm Ltd., London, 253 pp.

Peterken, G. F. 1983. Woodland conservation in Britain. pp. 83-100 in A. Warren and F. B. Goldsmith (eds.), *Conservation in Perspective,* John Wiley & Sons Ltd., Chichester.

Petzsch, H. 1971. *Architecture in Scotland.* Longman Group Ltd., London, 146 pp.

Phipson, E. 1883. *The Animal-lore of Shakespeare's Time Including Quadrupeds, Birds, Reptiles, Fish and Insects.* Kegan Paul, Trench & Co., London, 476 pp.

Poore, M. E. 1987. Changing attitudes in nature conservation: The Nature Conservancy and Nature Conservancy Council. *Biological Journal Linnean Society (London)* 32: 179-187.

Porter, J. H. 1986. Tenant right: Devonshire and the 1880 Ground Game Act. *Agricultural History Review* 34: 188-197.

Potts, G. R. 1986. *The Partridge: Pesticides, Predation and Conservation.* Collins, London, 274 pp.

Potts, G. R., Tapper, S. C. and Hudson, P. J. 1984. Population fluctuations in the red grouse: Analysis of bag records and a simulation model. *Journal of Animal Ecology* 53: 21-36.

Pragnell, H. 1984. *The Styles of English Architecture.* B. T. Batsford Ltd., London, 176 pp.

Prater, A. J. 1981. *Estuary Birds of Britain and Ireland.* T. & A. D. Poyser Ltd., Calton, 440 pp.

Prestt, I. 1987. Changing attitudes to nature conservation: The ornithological perspective. *Biological Journal Linnean Society (London)* 32: 197-202.

Prior, R. 1968. *The Roe Deer of Cranborne Chase.* An ecological survey. Oxford University Press, London, 222 pp.

—— 1983. *Trees & Deer.* B. T. Batsford Ltd., London, 208 pp.

Purchase, B. 1982. *The Rabbit and the Hare.* John Wiley & Sons Canada Ltd., Toronto, 143 pp.

Putman, R. 1988. *The Natural History of Deer.* Cornell University Press, Ithaca, 191 pp.

Putman, R. J. 1985. Efficient exploitation of natural populations of fallow deer: A management model. In Biology of deer production, eds. P.F. Fennessy and K.R. Drew. *Royal Society New Zealand Bulletin* 22, pp. 339-342.

Pym, B. A. 1972. Pressure groups on moral issues. *Political Quarterly* 43: 317-327.

Rackham, O. 1976. *Trees and Woodland in the British Landscape.* J. M. Dent & Sons Ltd., London, 204 pp.

—— 1980. *Ancient Woodland: Its History, Vegetation and Uses in England.* Edward Arnold Ltd., London, 402 pp.

—— 1986. *The History of the Countryside.* J. M. Dent & Sons Ltd., London, 445 pp.

Rands, R. W. 1986. Effect of hedgerow characteristics on partridge breeding densities. *Journal of Applied Ecology* 23: 479-487.

Ratcliffe, D. A. 1984. Post-medieval and recent changes in British vegetation: The culmination of human influence. *New Phytologist* 98: 73-100.

Richardson, C. [1896] Coursing the hare. pp. 111-176 in *The Hare.* Ashford Press Publishing, Shedfield. (reprinted 1986)

Robel, R. J. 1969. Movements and flock stratification within a population of blackcocks in Scotland. *Journal of Animal Ecology* 38: 755-763.

Roberts, B. K. 1978. Perspectives on prehistory. pp. 1-27 in R. A. Dodgshon and R. A. Butlin (eds.), *An Historical Geography of England and Wales,* Academic Press, London.

Robertson, P. A. 1988. Survival of released pheasants, *Phasianus colchicus,* in Ireland. *Journal of Zoology,* London 214: 683-695.

Rogers, A., Blunden, J. and Curry, N. 1985. *The Countryside Handbook.* Croom Helm Ltd., London, 98 pp.

Rogers, P. 1974. The Waltham Blacks and the Black Act. *Historical Journal* 17: 465-486.

Salvin, F. H. and Brodrick, W. [1855] *Falconry in the British Isles.* Thames Valley Press, Maidenhead, 147 pp. (reissued 1971)

Savage, R. J. 1989. British mammals of the Mesozoic Era. *Biological Journal Linnean Society (London)* 38: 3-7.

Savory, C. J. 1978. Food consumption of red grouse in relation to the age and productivity of heather. *Journal of Animal Ecology* 47: 269-282.

Scrutton, T. E. [1887] *Commons and Common Fields, or the History and Policy of the Laws Relating to Commons and Enclosures in England.* Lenox Hill Pub. & Dist. Co. (Burt Franklin), New York, 180 pp. (reprinted 1971)

Sharpe, J. A. 1984. *Crime in Early Modern England 1550-1750.* Longman Group Ltd., London, 230 pp.

Sharrock, J. T. R. 1976. *The Atlas of Breeding Birds in Britain and Ireland.* British Trust for Ornithology, Tring, 477 pp.

Sheail, J. 1971. *Rabbits and Their History.* David & Charles Ltd., Newton Abbot, 226 pp.

—— 1978. Rabbits and agriculture in post-medieval England. *Journal of Historical Geography* 4: 343-355.

—— 1983. The historical perspective. pp. 315-328 in A. Warren and F. B. Goldsmith (eds.), *Conservation in Perspective,* John Wiley & Sons Ltd., Chichester.

—— 1985. *Pesticides and Nature Conservation: The British Experience 1950-1975.* Oxford University Press, New York, 276 pp.

—— 1986. Nature conservation and the agricultural historian. *Agricultural History Review* 34: 1-11.

—— 1987. From preservation to conservation: Wildlife and the environment, 1900-1950. *Biological Journal Linnean Society (London)* 32: 171-177.

Shrewsbury, J. F. D. 1970. *A History of Bubonic Plague in the British Isles.* University Press, Cambridge, 661 pp.

Simms, E. 1971. *Woodland Birds.* Collins, London, 391 pp.

Smith, A. E. 1987. The Nature Conservation Trust movement. *Biological Journal Linnean Society (London)* 32: 189-196.

Snow, D. W. (ed.) 1971. *The Status of Birds in Britain and Ireland.* Blackwell Scientific Publications, Oxford, 333 pp.

Stamp, L. D. 1949. *Britain's Structure and Scenery.* Collins, London, 255 pp.

—— 1962. *The Land of Britain: Its Use and Misuse.* Longmans, Green & Co. Ltd., London, with Geographical Publications Ltd., London, 546 pp.

—— 1964. *Man and the Land.* Collins, London, 272 pp.

Stamp, [L.] D. 1969. *Nature Conservation in Britain.* Collins, London, 273 pp.

Starfield, A. M. and Bleloch, A. L. 1986. *Building Models for Conservation and Wildlife Management.* Macmillan Publishing Co., New York, 253 pp.

Stewart, A. J. A. and Lance, A. N. 1983. Moor-draining: A review of impacts on land use. *Journal of Environmental Management* 17: 81-99.

Tapper, S. C., Green, R. E. and Rands, M. R. W. 1982. Effects of mammalian predators on partridge populations. *Mammal Review* 12: 159-167.

Tegner, H. 1969. *Wild Hares.* John Baker Ltd., London, 107 pp.

Thiebaux, M. 1967. The mediaeval chase. *Speculum* 42: 260-274.

Thomas, R. H. 1983. *The Politics of Hunting.* Gower Publishing Co. Ltd., Aldershot, 313 pp.

Thompson, F. M. L. 1981. Landowners and the rural community. pp. 457-474 in G. E. Mingay (ed.), *The Victorian Countryside.* Volume 2, Routledge & Kegan Paul Ltd., London.

Threlfall, W. 1989. Use and abuse of wildlife in research. pp. 155-167 in T. I. Hughes (ed.), *Bio-Ethics '89. A report of the proceedings of an international symposium on the control and use of animals in scientific research,* Published by the Animal Welfare Foundation of Canada, Cobourg, Ontario.

Tobias, J. J. 1979. *Crime and Police in England 1700-1900.* Gill & Macmillan Ltd., Dublin, 194 pp.

Trench, C. C. 1973. Nineteenth-century hunting. *History Today* 23: 572-580.

Tubbs, C. 1986. *The New Forest.* Collins, London, 300 pp.

Turner, M. 1980. *English Parliamentary Enclosure: Its Historical Geography and Economic History.* Wm. Dawson & Sons Ltd., Folkestone, with Archon Books, The Shoe String Press Inc., Hamden, 247 pp.

—— 1984. The landscape of parliamentary enclosure. pp. 132-166 in M. Reed (ed.), *Discovering Past Landscapes,* Croom Helm Ltd., London.

Usher, M. B. 1989. Scientific aspects of nature conservation in the United Kingdom. *Journal of Applied Ecology* 26: 813-824.

Veale, E. M. 1957. The rabbit in England. *Agricultural History Review* 5: 85-90.

Vesey-Fitzgerald, B. 1946. *British Game*. Collins, London, 240 pp.

Virgoe, N. and Yaxley, S. 1986. *The Banville Diaries: Journals of a Norfolk Gamekeeper 1822-44*. Collins, London, 224 pp.

Walsh, E. G. 1983. *The Poachers Companion*. The Boydell Press, Woodbridge, 265 pp.

Warren, A. and Goldsmith, F. B. (eds.) 1983. *Conservation in Perspective*. John Wiley & Sons Ltd., Chichester, 474 pp.

Watkin, D. 1982. *The English Vision: The Picturesque in Architecture, Landscape and Garden Design*. Harper & Row, Publ. Inc., New York, 227 pp.

Watkins, C. 1987. The future of woodlands in the rural landscape. pp. 71-96 in D. Lockhart and B. Ilbery (eds.), *The Future of the British Rural Landscape*, Geo Books, Norwich.

Watson, A. 1965. A population study of ptarmigan (*Lagopus mutus*) in Scotland. *Journal of Animal Ecology* 34: 135-172.

—— 1972. The behaviour of the ptarmigan. *British Birds* 65: 6-26, 93-117.

—— 1987. Weight and sexual cycle of Scottish rock ptarmigan. *Ornis Scandinavica* 18: 231-232.

Watson, A. and Jenkins, D. 1964. Notes on the behaviour of the red grouse. *British Birds* 57: 137-170.

Watson, A. and Moss, R. 1979. Population cycles in the Tetraonidae. *Ornis Fennica* 56: 87-109.

Watson, A., Moss, R., Parr, R., Trenholm, I. B. and Robertson, A. 1988. Preventing a population decline of red grouse (*Lagopus lagopus scoticus*) by manipulating density. *Experientia* 44: 274-275.

Watson, A., Moss, R., Rothery, P. and Parr, R. 1984. Demographic causes and predictive models of population fluctuations in red grouse. *Journal of Animal Ecology* 53: 639-662.

Westman, W. E. 1990. Managing for biodiversity: Unresolved science and policy questions. *BioScience* 40: 26-33.

Whitehead, G. K. 1953. *The Ancient White Cattle of Britain and Their Descendants*. Faber & Faber Ltd., London, 174 pp.

—— 1964. *The Deer of Great Britain and Ireland: An Account of Their History, Status and Distribution*. Routledge & Kegan Paul Ltd., London, 597 pp.

Williams, J. 1985. Statistical analysis of fluctuations in red grouse bag data. *Oecologia* 65: 269-272.

Williamson, K. 1972. The conservation of bird life in the new coniferous forests. *Forestry* 45: 87-100.

Wood, T. B. 1983. The conservation and management of animal populations. pp. 119-139 in A. Warren and F. B. Goldsmith (eds.), *Conservation in Perspective,* John Wiley & Sons Ltd., Chichester.

Woodell, S. R. J. (ed.) 1985. *The English Landscape: Past, Present, and Future.* Wolfson College Lectures 1983. Oxford University Press, Oxford, 240 pp.

Wylie, P. 1972. *The End of the Dream.* Doubleday and Co. Inc., Garden City, 264 pp.

Yapp, W. B. 1962. *Birds and Woods.* Oxford University Press, London, 308 pp.

Yarrell, W. 1871-1885. *A History of British Birds.* John van Voorst, London. Vol. 1, 646 pp.; Vol. 2, 494 pp.; Vol. 3, 684 pp.; Vol. 4, 531 pp.

Yelling, J. A. 1977. *Common Field and Enclosure in England 1450-1850.* Archon Books, The Shoe String Press, Inc., Hamden, 255 pp.

Editors Note:
North American Policies of Wildlife Conservation

Whatever its shortcomings, North America's system of wildlife conservation is the 20th century's greatest environmental success story. It is based on public ownership of wildlife, the prohibition of trafficking in vulnerable wildlife, the allocation of surplus wildlife by law, the prohibition of frivolous killing, the joint management of migratory wildlife by sovereign states, and the use of science as a basis for management. It returned North America's wildlife from the edge of extinction, and made it a source of wealth: in 1991 it generated in the United States alone $59 billion or $16 305/mile^2. This economy creates wealth through deliberate inefficiencies in the viewing and taking of wildlife, and maximizes the net benefit of wildlife to society. This is done by private enterprise from a publicly managed resource, a rare example of *sustainable development*, a defeat of the "Tragedy of the Commons." It illustrates the crucial distinction between markets based on *dead* versus *living* wildlife, how local empowerment protects wildlife, how armed citizens are a prerequisite to wildlife harvest. Affluent land owners, aided by agricultural bureaucracies, are now dismantling this system to gain private control of wildlife, so as to commercialize wildlife and hunting. This serves neither wildlife nor the public as good conservation laws are revoked and civic liberties are eroded, while diseases, genetic pollution, competition with exotics, and illegal killing put in jeopardy wildlife, native people, livestock, public health, and a job-intensive service and manufacturing industry based on *access to living* wildlife. Due to Pleistocene extinctions, North America has a young fauna, whose old survivors are poor competitors and its Siberian immigrants are susceptible to diseases and parasites. Effective policing of markets in wildlife is precluded by problems of scale, high costs, and the inherent inefficiency of policing. International debate about wildlife economics focuses on luxury markets in wildlife, or on tourism by the affluent, both poor long term policies which trivializes wildlife as playthings of the rich, and ignore the powerful North American model based on *local*, populist self-interest. Where tried, such ideas as empowering native people are a conservation success.

North American Policies of Wildlife Conservation

Valerius Geist

Introduction

The entry of Captain Harry Moses at the head of M Troop, 1st United States Cavalry, into Yellowstone National Park, 17 August 1886 (Hampton 1971), marks the beginning of modern North American wildlife management. Captain Moses replaced the capable but unfortunate Superintendent D.W. Wear, and took over the administration of the park in the name of the army. It was the beginning of the end for the "Tragedy of the Commons" that decimated North America's wildlife. It was also the beginning of a process that, three decades later, saw the implementation, as continental policies, of what the army learned in protecting wildlife under its care. These lessons, along with others, absorbed by the watchful mind of a congressman destined to become president, Theodore Roosevelt, were ably formulated and implemented as a conservation doctrine; it made wildlife conservation a success and a rare example of sustainable development. Wildlife recovered; there are more than 30 million big game animals north of Mexico (after Schmidt and Gilbert 1978). This happened despite the ready availability of firearms, which today outnumber big game 8 to 1, despite a human population that outnumbers big game 9 to 1, and despite an aggressive agricultural industry whose livestock outnumber big game at least 120 to 1 (Pimentel et al. 1980).

Our current system of wildlife conservation is rooted in the destruction of wildlife a century ago by settlers and traders, by markets in eastern cities, by railways linking loci of wildlife production and consumption, by guns that permitted safe and convenient slaughter, and by the skilled implementation of military policy to destroy native people through the destruction of wildlife. This was done by Generals Tecumseh Sherman and Phil Sheridan shortly after the Civil War, when the army in the west faced Indian warriors they could not defeat in battle. Consequently, the generals embarked on a policy of depriving the Indians of sustenance (Ambrose 1975). All this destroyed wildlife in less than two decades after the Civil War (Hornaday 1913; Mathissen 1959; Roe 1970).

In Canada, despite transportation routes kept underdeveloped by Hudson Bay Company policy, fur traders, settlers, and natives eliminated wildlife just the same. The excellent historical work on the fate of buffalo by Roe (1970) serves as a proxy for wildlife's fate. The wildlife of the far North, despite market hunters supplying various gold-rushes, was less damaged, judging from the accounts of Max Hinsche (1989) who travelled through the Yukon Territory in 1934. Had there been better transportation to serve southern markets, northern wildlife might not have survived. Nevertheless, comparing my experience with Hinsche's when travelling the same routes in the 1970s, the depletion of wildlife was painfully obvious to me.

A cornerstone of conservation was the establishment of national parks, beginning in 1872 with Yellowstone National Park. With wildlife destruction proceeding rapidly, General Sheridan appears to have had second thoughts, for he sent his cavalry into Yellowstone to protect the park and its wildlife. The army ably administered the national parks for 32 years and probably saved these institutions of American culture (Hampton 1971). The national parks were enhanced by national forests under President Theodore Roosevelt, and later, by other forms of protected public land. Canada's system of protected lands developed in parallel (Hewitt 1921).

North Americans had indulged in an unprecedented orgy of wildlife destruction (Hornaday 1913; Hewitt 1921; McHugh 1972; Roe 1970). Native people played a long, unhappy role in this tragedy. Calvin Martin (1978) argues that their ready destruction of wildlife beginning in the 16th century leads back to a breakdown in cultural values, and a change in perception of wildlife. Co-existence with wildlife was based on the notion of reciprocity, which to violate invited retribution from wildlife, in the form of diseases inflicted on offending people. The terrible suffering caused by diseases (of European origin) on natives, and the helplessness of traditional shaman, led to reprisal on wildlife for what was felt to be excessive retribution. Martin argues that it permitted the ready killing, even extermination of wildlife, which had been unthinkable under earlier conditions. As discussed below, natives are currently excellent managers of wildlife, but they are noticeably absent from the 20th century activities in North America to restore wildlife. In good part this is a reflection on their need to restore themselves after their demise.

In the 19th century, excesses in luxury consumption, abuse of wildlife, and the rapid decline of species generated determined attempts to save what could be saved. Market hunting and conspicuous consumption of wildlife were much discredited by the turn of the century (Hornaday 1913; Leopold 1933; Roe 1970). The U.S. Cavalry, protecting national parks, put in place policies that were destined to become universal with the acceptance of resource conservation, spearheaded by President Theodore Roosevelt with Gifford Pinchot. Their counterparts were the Canadian Prime Minister Sir Wilfred Laurier and Sir Clifford Sifton. Commissions of Conservation worked in close cooperation on both sides of the border, giving rise to the first international wildlife treaties (1911 Marine Mammal Treaty; 1916 Migratory Bird Treaty), and to policies that shaped the wildlife conservation laws of both countries.

Policies that Worked

Modern North America's wildlife conservation is based on five primary and enabling policies that support the superstructure of laws, regulations, beliefs, and attitudes that support management. These are:

(1) The public ownership of wildlife *de jure* and (normally) *de facto*. The sovereign grants or withholds ownership; wildlife may be held privately only in trust for the public (Lund 1980; Bean 1983:12-17, 76; Chandler 1985:2-4). That maintains the genetic integrity of native species, for it reduces the risk of private owners breeding freaks or hybridizing native species, which in turn could escape to genetically pollute wild stocks. It thus prevents the domestication of wildlife. It also prevents the spread of livestock diseases into wildlife populations, protecting thereby not only wildlife, but also livestock, native people, and the public. This policy precluded widespread ownership of native species and avoided many conservation problems (Geist 1988a, 1989, 1991).

(2) The elimination of trafficking in the meat, parts, and products of game animals, shore birds, and song birds, that is, of wildlife that was highly vulnerable to exploitation, while retaining markets in furs of the less vulnerable fur-bearers. History demonstrated how quickly a price on dead wildlife could decimate stocks, while viable populations of fur-bearers could be retained (Hewitt 1921; Mathissen 1959). Only services focusing on living vulnerable wildlife could henceforth be sold. The distinction between markets in dead wildlife as opposed to markets on living wildlife is crucial.

This policy is probably the most important one in protecting wildlife, as it precludes the market, the occident's most powerful institution, from rewarding the killing of wildlife. There is a long history to this, beginning in 1886 when the U.S. cavalry prohibited the sale of fish and in 1887 the import of game meat into Yellowstone National Park (Hampton 1971:83, 92). In 1911 New York prohibited sale of game and by 1915, 47 from 48 U.S. states had passed similar laws (Vreeland 1916:98). Canada began to follow the U.S. lead by 1920 (Hewitt 1921:331). Since then, U.S. federal trade prohibitions were placed into various acts and treaties (Bean 1983:105, 106-115, 239-277; Lyster 1985:26, 57 & footnote p. 78, 87).

(3) The law allocates surpluses in wildlife for consumption. This is settled annually after public input (Hornaday 1913; Hewitt 1921; Lund 1980; Bean 1983). Wildlife, surplus to healthy populations, is thus allocated not by the market, or land ownership, or special privileges, or birth right – excepting aboriginal people. That creates an opportunity for all citizens in good standing to participate in the management and harvest of wildlife. Limits were legislated regarding the duration of hunting season, the localities open to hunting, the species, sex, and numbers of wildlife that could be taken, and the gear allowable for hunting (Allen 1962). Allocation of surplus wildlife by law makes every citizen a *de jure* "shareholder" in wildlife in North America, and a *de facto* shareholder in most jurisdictions. It generates a sense of proprietorship in those who regularly avail themselves of their allocation of wildlife.

Annual public consultation, followed by debate in the legislatures, keep wildlife management decisions largely rational, but not universally satisfying. Decisions will reflect, of necessity, local views. These, invariably, offend some groups or individuals holding different positions. Such controversies are exemplified by the "buck law" (Allen 1972), predator control (Leopold 1933), and reintroductions of predators (Di Silvestro 1985). The quality of decisions depends not only on science, or on an enlightened public, but also on the political power of many special interest groups and the vested interests of bureaucracies. The system is characterized by an ongoing review and redefinition of values, aims, policies, and decisions, often by acrimonious disputes over positions that cannot be commensurated (Wellman 1992). This is an inescapable by-product of a democratic system of government.

(4) Wildlife may be killed only for cause, that is for food, fur, in self-defence, or if it damages private property. The U.S. congress in 1874 passes a bill against "useless" slaughter of buffalo; in 1877 Florida prohibited wanton destruction of bird eggs and young (Mathissen 1959:282). Geer v. Connecticut (1896) affirmed the sovereign's right to affix conditions to the killing of game which would remain with the game even after killed (Bean 1983:16-17). The Migratory Bird Convention of 1916, Article 7, stipulates conditions for permission to kill birds that do agricultural damage (Hewitt 1921:273). Killing wildlife and leaving it is wanton waste, a felony in the U.S.

This policy is the least visible one. It prohibits the waste of wildlife once such is killed and recognizes subsistence hunting as a priority. On sport or trophy hunting, both unpopular with the American public (MacDonald 1987), this policy is ambiguous. Lund (1980:1) is explicit: American wildlife management arose due to those that exploited wildlife for entertainment, the sportsmen. Aldo Leopold (1933) made recreational hunting an integral part of his definition of game management.

The literature preceding his work (for example, Commission on Conservation 1910-1919, Hewitt 1921) emphasizes that it would be better to sell wildlife for "sport" than to slaughter it for sale. That is, it has been historically recognized that restrained hunting for sport, which confers desirable social qualities to the hunter, is a worthy goal. In the words of Theodore Roosevelt, as quoted on the dust jacket of the 7th (1977) edition of the Boon and Crockett Club's *North American Big Game*: "The chase is among the best of all national pastimes: it cultivates that vigorous manliness for the lack of which in a nation, as in an individual, the possession of no other qualities can possibly atone."

(5) Wildlife is an international resource to be managed co-operatively by sovereign states. This led to international wildlife treaties on marine mammals and migratory birds (Hewitt 1921; Hayden 1942).

Two additional policies, important, but not crucially so, and to this day only partially realized, were that all "outdoor" resources are an integral whole, and that science should be used as a tool to discharge policy. This is the Roosevelt Doctrine (Leopold 1933:17-18). The former policy foreshadowed what is currently called "ecosystem management"; the second policy led to the creation of a new profession, the wildlife manager. In all this, North Americans were decades ahead of their time.

In practice, these policies made the killing of wildlife an economic liability. Not only is it costly to legally kill wildlife, but it must not be abandoned under penalty of law. To hunt or observe native wildlife requires unrecoverable investment in equipment, effort, and time. That has deterrent value. However, it also generates requests for services and goods by millions of wildlife users (Filion et al. 1993; Geist 1994).

From the outset, legislatures granted some exceptions to these basic policies. Texas gave *de facto* control over wildlife to landowners with a stiff trespass act, allowing allocation of wildlife by the market, thereby denying many *de jure* shareholders in wildlife access to their resource. In the Northwest Territories of Canada the sale of wildlife meat remained legal. There were special case exceptions added in other provinces and states.

There is now evidence that the fundamental policies of North America's system of wildlife conservation are also fundamental to some aboriginal systems of wildlife management. That is, our system of wildlife management has "tribal" qualities. Feit's (1987) anthropological research on wildlife management by James Bay Crees showed that wildlife is effectively managed by band-elders on designated territories; allocation of wildlife to individual hunters is by tribal convention through the elders; wildlife is not killed frivolously, but strictly for sustenance; there is no sale of wildlife. In recent years the cooperative management of caribou in the Northwest Territories largely by natives has been a conservation success (Dueck 1990), as has been the return of wildlife to tribal control in several African states (Bonner 1993).

North American wildlife management is currently under attack by animal rights advocates (Regan 1983:353), by agricultural bureaucracies bent on game ranching (Geist 1988a, 1992), and even by a faction of affluent hunters supporting allodial rights (Hargrove 1989:57-63). The achievements of our system of wildlife conservation are largely ignored. Years of legislative neglect and regionalism have made it vulnerable. Thus a 1989 survey of game ranching legislation (Ervin et al. 1992:244-252), showed discrepancies and contradictions between states and provinces in wildlife legislation, with some having no legal definition of wildlife or even a clear legal authority over wildlife.

Allodial Rights

Wildlife in North America is *de facto* and *de jure* a public resource, a point of ongoing contention to vested interests, eager to privatize wildlife. This view of some landowners goes back to old Germanic law via the American Revolution. Thomas Jefferson, looking for a legal precedent to contest the Crown's claim to unoccupied land, dismissed the oppressive Norman common law as imposed on Anglo-Saxon England by conquest in 1066, in favor of the earlier Germanic common law with its concept of "freeman." Such a man was free to bear arms, free to exploit unclaimed commons, and held land free of binding obligations to the sovereign by virtue of *allodial rights (allodium,* the Roman term for the Germanic estates held free of obligations). Jefferson linked this with Lock's view that property is owned by the citizen due to his labor, not by the grace of a sovereign. The claim by the British king to land beyond the frontier became thus conveniently unacceptable, justifying the expansion westward by American settlers (Hargrove 1989:57-67), and wildlife, no longer property of the king, again became property of whoever reduced it to possession by his labor. Jefferson may have given only an intellectual justification to prevailing practices: in British North America, without his justification of "allodial behavior," wildlife exploitation, as exemplified by the fate of the bison (Roe 1971), was also unchecked.

Allodial rights are central to the conflicts over legalized trafficking in dead wildlife and the sale of hunting privileges. Some landowners are currently before the courts attempting to gain *de facto,* if not *de jure* control of public wildlife. This process has happened repeatedly in European history (Geist 1988a). It has the support of the agricultural bureaucracies in Canada and the U.S. Some have pointed out how this threatens North America's system of conservation (Swenson 1983; a, b, 1986, 1988a; Struzik 1987; Kruckenberg 1987; Cowan 1987). Undaunted, the vested interests foresee raising captive wildlife in an agricultural mode for slaughter, sale, and consumption; others promote the sale of trophies or sport hunting. This version of "wildlife management" has been advanced as global solution to "sustainable development" (Bonner 1993).

The concern over wildlife on private land is old (Leopold 1933:208), and has spawned legitimate fears by wildlife managers for the fate of wildlife. The solution commonly perceived is to make the presence of public wildlife profitable to landowners in the hope that habitat for wildlife is maintained where otherwise such might be destroyed in favor of other economic uses. Also, wildlife management on private lands, so some managers hoped, would be less shackled by scrutiny and interference by a public "uninformed" about wildlife management. That is, wildlife management on private land can be more "creative," less subject to public scrutiny and political interference.

Unfortunately, this "creative" management leads to "improvements" such as the management for "trophies." This has included in the past introduction of non-local native stocks for a desired improvement in the phenotypic development or performance of local populations (Beninde 1937; Draskovich 1959; Etling 1985), the introduction of exotics to improve the offerings to a clientele of hunters but at the expense of native species (White 1986; Brothers and Ray 1975), the "eugenic culling" or removal of individuals that did not fit a perceived ideal (von Raesfeld and Frevert 1954), risking the selection of "beautiful" but ill-adapted males (Frevert 1957), to the inadvertent introduction of diseases (Frevert 1957), to the elimination of predators (Frevert 1957), and to habitat improvements and artificial feeding, creating in essence luxury-type populations (A. and J. von Bayern 1977), the individuals of which may be very susceptible during even slight food shortages (Vogt 1948). That is, trophy management has little to do with the maintenance of biodiversity, or the genetic integrity of native adaptations and the transmission of such from generation to generation within the managed populations.

The history of extending special hunting privileges in return for habitat improvements is discussed by Lee Fitzhugh (1989) for California. The allocation of hunting rights by the marketplace becomes an inescapable part of such programs. That in turn emphasizes hunting as an elitist activity and, as expected, generates "politics of envy." This is fuelled by public perceptions of unfair favors being granted to landowners at the expense of wildlife and the public, such as extended hunting seasons, the hunting of wildlife during vulnerable periods such as during the rut in deer, the luring of public wildlife onto private land where it is taken for profit, the taking of unearned wildlife where it is migratory, the abuse of wildlife hidden from sight on private property, and the unfair financial subsidies landowners receive from the public purse when administrative costs of cooperative programs on private land are paid for by the state. In addition there is legitimate concern (see Crowe 1969) that state employees become captives of landowner interests and, though paid by the public, actually work against the public interest. If successful, such programs make wildlife *de facto* private property. That extending privileges to the wealthy fuels bitter acrimony should surprise no one familiar with the long history of European wildlife management (Stahl 1979).

Research into wildlife economics shows that *de facto* public ownership of wildlife, linked to allocation of surplus wildlife by law (not by the market), with enforced prohibition against frivolous killings and limitations placed on the means of taking or observing wildlife, leads to high economic returns (Filion et al. 1983; 1993; 1991 National Survey of Fishing, Hunting, and Wildlife-Associated Recreation, U.S. Fish & Wildlife Service, Washington, DC). The $59 billion expended in the U.S. in 1991 on wildlife-associated recreation (U.S. Fish & Wildlife Service National Survey, 1993) translates into $16 295 per square mile. The wildlife based economic activity in Wyoming in 1985 was about a billion dollars. Since that was based largely on big game, this amounts to about $1000 per head of big game (*Proc. of the Privatization of Wildlife and Public Lands Access Symposium,* Wyoming Game and Fish Department, Casper, Wyoming, 1987, pp. 3-9 & 25-29). Calculated more conservatively on the basis of one-time spending, the restitution value to Wyoming of a grizzly bear in 1992 was $25 000, of an elk $4000, of a deer $2500, of a cottontail rabbit $53 (1993 Annual Report, Wyoming Game & Fish Dept., Cheyenne, WY, p. 120).

Wildlife is paying its way in North America. "Privatizing America's West" as advocated by *The Economist* (22 Oct. 1988:21) would lead not only to poor conservation practices, but also to a loss in economic activity due to loss in public participation. To be effective in wildlife conservation we must know the kinds of economic models that foster conservation and which do not. The conventional economic model aims at efficiency of production and export. Yet wildlife economics teach that wealth is generated by the obverse, by the inefficiency of consuming wildlife, such as making every consumer buy the appropriate equipment to obtain, process, and store the quarry, travel to and from the hunting or fishing grounds, and often legislating the hiring of guides in pursuit of wildlife. Even wildlife viewing is made inefficient by a prohibition on ownership of native wildlife, so that those wanting to observe native wildlife cannot do so by caging it for private enjoyment, but must equip themselves and travel to where such wildlife resides. Inefficient consumption and viewing must be management's goal.

Campaigns to turn public wildlife over to private control aim at the abolition of policies that successfully conserved North America's wildlife for the past 70 years. This has now affected Canadian and U.S. wildlife legislation (a, 1988a, 1990). In particular, it led to legal holding of large numbers of wildlife for private gain, exposing these to genetic manipulation and thus degradation of their adaptations or genetic pollution (see below).

Achievements of North American Conservation

The primary policies protecting wildlife brought about many successes, including:

(1) *The recovery of wildlife,* which had been decimated over most of the southern and central parts of the continent (Hornaday 1913; Hewitt 1921; Mathissen 1957). This new conservation system returned endangered species from the edge of extinction (Drabelle 1985:150, 388-562) and allowed wildlife to rise to modest abundance: the number of wild large mammals in the U.S. and Canada rose to over 30 million by the late 1970s (after Schmidt and Gilbert 1980; Kallman et al. 1987), more than three times their number in 1958 (Highsmith et al. 1962:160-162). This happened despite more than 3000 million head of livestock (Pimentel et al. 1980), about 270 million people and some 200 million firearms in private hands, and much poaching. Bison, musk oxen, pronghorned bucks, elk, and wood duck returned from the edge of extinction; most big game species increased. No longer are wild large mammals regarded by the public as so many dollars on the hooves, nor are song and shore birds regarded as luxury food in restaurants, as described in Ranhofer's (1893) treatise on the culinary arts as practised at Delmonico's in New York. Data on wildlife biomass are limited and subject to many variables, but in well managed North American jurisdictions, *The Economist* not withstanding, wildlife biomass appears to exceed that found in Texas, or Germany (Geist 1988a). While its emphasis on "charismatic mega species" may be questioned, the preservation of large areas of habitat for such also allowed less conspicuous forms to thrive. Far from being a "Tragedy of the Commons," as claimed by *The Economist* (Oct. 22, 1988, p. 21), North American wildlife management reversed "The Tragedy" (Geist 1989). A historic review of legislation protecting wildlife is given by Gilbert and Dodds (1992; Gilbert 1993).

(2) *Economic gain.* The recovery of wildlife led to a large, labor-intensive service and manufacturing industry based on living wildlife (Filion et al. 1983, 1993; Bailey 1984:37; Johnson and Lidner 1986; Kruckenberg 1987; Lueck 1989; Geist 1994; 1985 & 1991 National Survey of Fishing, Hunting, and Wildlife-Associated Recreation, U.S. Fish & Wildlife Service, Washington, DC). Wildlife is managed for many uses, including subsistence, sport hunting, and tourism, yet the safeguarding

of wildlife takes precedence over use (Bean 1983). The economic returns, no matter how computed, are high; our system of wildlife conservation maximizes net benefits to society (Lueck 1989). It shows how restraints, intelligently and sternly applied to Adam Smith's "unseen hand" by political consent, generate wealth and jobs in the private sector from a publicly owned and managed resource.

The elimination of wildlife markets increased the economic return from wildlife. This is at least twice that of the German wildlife management system based on private control of wildlife; the number of jobs created is about three-fold (Geist 1988a:Table 1). The total expenditures on fishing, hunting and wildlife related recreation is in the U.S. and Canada combined about $67 billion per annum (1993). By comparison, the world market in *dead wildlife* (venison, tusks, horns, pelts, etc., legal and illegal) is only $5-8 billion, an order of magnitude less than the U.S. market alone based on living wildlife (*Traffic USA*, World Wildlife Fund-USA, Washington, DC).

West Germany gets about half the monetary value from wildlife compared to Wyoming or Wisconsin (see Geist 1988a). The German figures come from Wiese (1986). Expenditure per hunter in West Germany is almost $2500; it is about $860 per resident hunter in Wyoming. West Germany paid out about $68 million in wildlife damages (Wyoming paid out $0.3 million). Tourist hunters are not encouraged in Germany. There were some 2300 non-residents among 265 000 hunters in Germany (Wiese 1986:84-106), and 248 000 among 478 000 in Wyoming (Kruckenberg 1987). Non-consumptive expenditures tend to be three or four times hunting expenditures in Canada (Filion et al. 1983), but are not considered by the Germans, as tourism there is not wildlife related as it often is in America. German wildlife is crepuscular or nocturnal, particularly where well managed (in overpopulated areas roe deer become diurnal; Schaefer 1982). Canadian data indicate that the manufacturing sector's benefits are larger than those of the service sector (Filion et al. 1983). In Europe, 1000 hunters generate 16 jobs (Wiese 1986:103); in Alberta the number of jobs generated is at least 58 (based on 11% of 2.23 million citizens being hunters, and 14 192 jobs). The figures of Filion et al. (1983) suggest about 38 100 full-time wage earning jobs, plus some 6000 jobs such as those of working owner, partner, or family helper, per billion dollars (Canadian) of wildlife related expenditures. As predicted by Jacob's (1984) concept of import replacement, New Zealand's early success in deer ranching led to deer ranching in Germany, where it pitted conservation against agricultural interests (Ueckermann and Hansen 1983). This led to losses for deer ranchers in New Zealand (Bryant 1986).

Wildlife economics in North America are based on legislated inefficiency in harvesting and viewing wildlife. Conventional economics brings the resource to the consumer, North American wildlife economics brings the consumer to the resource, while the means and amounts of consumption are limited by law. The hunter and fisher must observe bag, time and equipment limits, while the viewer may enjoy native wildlife in the free state, but may not keep it privately for pleasure nor interfere with it. Wealth is created by the many who are lured to living wildlife, and who generate diverse local market demands. These demands foster many innovative, competitive producers and distributors of goods and services.

(3) *The profession of wildlife management.* A system of management and conservation arose, based on state employed wildlife managers responsible to elected representatives at the state, provincial, and federal levels. In support, there grew institutions of teaching and research, and a society to advance the new profession of wildlife management. The profession provides refereed journals, accreditation, and representatives to bodies dealing with conservation (see *Wildlife Society Bulletin* 15[1] 1987). North America set the model for others, as evidenced in the creation of National Parks, the introduction of university curricula and research in wildlife biology in Europe, and the current rise of a science-based wildlife profession in Europe.

(4) *Public involvement with wildlife.* A large number of conservation societies arose that fostered interest in wildlife, and united at the federal, provincial, or state levels to give political expression to their views. The continental scope is illustrated by societies common to the U.S. and Canada. With a population of 400 000, Wyoming has 104 conservation societies. Canada has some 360 registered conservation groups, 100 of which are represented by the Canadian Nature Federation. There are societies to raise funds for elk, bighorns, grizzlies, turkeys, ruffed grouse, and waterfowl, to regulate trophy competitions, restore habitat, and play watchdog on governments.

(5) *Taxes for wildlife,* a policy which was adopted in 1930 by the American Game Conference (Gilbert 1993). Americans taxed themselves variously on behalf of wildlife (Migratory Bird Hunting Stamp Act 1934; Pitman-Robertson, Dingell-Johnson, and Fish and Wildlife Conservation Acts of 1980; Drabelle 1985b). Canadians pay for wildlife from general taxation, or special funds created from license sales (such as Alberta's Bucks for Wildlife Fund).

(6) *Habitat conservation.* North Americans created an extensive system of protected areas for wildlife such as national parks (Hampton 1971), wildlife refuges (Drabelle 1985a), and ecological reserves, and made wildlife an object of management on public lands. Societies formed that acquire land for wildlife or to protect habitat, such as Habitat Canada and the Nature Conservancy. They encourage private landowners to preserve wildlife habitat. The Armed Forces continued

their traditional role as protectors of wildlife (Hampton 1971) on military reservations, giving formal conservation responsibilities to officers. New programs arose to create wildlife habitat on agricultural land, such as the Conservation Reserve Program in the U.S. Gilbert and Dodds (1992) review various U.S. legislative initiatives to conserve habitat.

(7) *International treaties*. North Americans negotiated international treaties to protect wildlife, beginning with the 1911 Fur Seal Treaty (Weber 1985). Better known is the Convention for the Protection of Migratory Birds (1916) between Great Britain and the U.S. (Hewitt 1921; Chandler 1985); to this day, nothing quite comparable exists in Europe. Unfortunately, the Fur Seal Treaty is under attack by the Humane Society of America, and the fur seal may again be subject to sealing on the high seas.

(8) *Large predators*. North Americans preserved large predators, which is a great achievement compared with Europe. We have viable populations of cougars (Hornocker and Quigley 1987), wolves, black bears (Raybourne 1987), grizzly, and polar bears. Great public concern surrounds grizzly bears in Yellowstone National Park (Craighead 1979; Knight and Eberhardt 1984; Povilitis 1985, 1986), and the re-introduction of wolves is being contemplated in Wyoming, or encouraged in Wisconsin (see *Wisconsin Natural Resources* 1987 Supplement 4(3):38).

(9) *Management for non-game species*. The policy that the out-of-doors is an integral whole is becoming reality. An endangered species act and programs by wildlife agencies for urban wildlife are turning resources and attention to the need to protect ecosystems. The old growth forest controversy, symbolized by the spotted owl, is a case in point (Thomas et al. 1990), but the move to include non-game species under the umbrella of wildlife conservation has a long history (Gilbert 1993).

(10) *Law enforcement*. North Americans developed an inexpensive, civil, and fairly effective system of wildlife protection that allowed wildlife to recover, despite much opportunity for illegal killing and ready access by the public to firearms. This can hardly be grasped without a comparison to the German system of policing for wildlife.

Germany, with a retail market in venison, is thorough in wildlife protection. From the outset, the ownership of firearms is highly restricted in Germany. German law (Bundesjagdgesetz 28. 9. 1976, # 25) makes every lessee or owner of a hunting territory a deputized policeman responsible for wildlife protection. The law allows him to use firearms in protection against armed poachers. It allows him to shoot to kill in cases of justifiable doubt to his security (Nuesslein 1983:53-56). Figures for the former West Germany may be of interest: there were about 65 000 lessees or owners of hunting territories, that is 65 000 armed wildlife protectors for about 91 000 square miles of land open to hunting (23.574 million hectares [Wiese 1986: 84] divided into 40 000 hunting territories). In addition there were some 1000 professional hunters (Wiese 1986:405) employed full time to manage and protect hunting leases of clients, and on state land about 5000 foresters were charged with the duty of wildlife protection. Moreover, any one of the remaining 195 000 of Germany's registered hunters could be so deputized (Nuesslein 1983:55-56). The foresters and professional hunters not only carry long-arms (much more effective than regular police weapons), but may be accompanied by dogs. All wildlife protectors are allowed to carry concealed hand guns. In addition, regular police forces are responsible for wildlife protection. Together with stiff food protection laws, there are food inspectors with policing powers to control the flow of wildlife from kill to the retail market, and stiff gun control laws (Nuesslein 1983; Balse 1968; Wiese 1986), Germany has succeeded in keeping wildlife and a retail market in venison.

The costs of wildlife protection in Germany are beyond calculation. Surveillance alone is at least 300-fold greater than in Alberta, and while most is done by unpaid deputies, there are still about 40 times more publicly employed wildlife protectors and about 10 times more who are paid privately. By comparison, in the province of Alberta, my home, 109 unarmed wardens guard wildlife on 255 285 square miles of land.

Policing on behalf of wildlife is costly as shown by the unsuccessful anti-wildlife trafficking Operation Falcon (McKay's 1987). It would have been safer for falcons and cheaper for taxpayers had there been no "loophole" to sell falcons legally. The difficulties of wildlife law enforcement are well described by Reisner (1991) in his account of undercover operations.

Legal trafficking in wildlife removes the most important protection from wildlife, the absence of a market. The criminal element takes advantage of the legal trade in wildlife parts. Difficult as it is now to apprehend wildlife law violators, the situation becomes hopeless with a multiplicity of retail outlets and processing facilities to launder illegal wildlife. A study by Boxall and Smith (1987) shows that only about 1% of wildlife violations are reported; only 1 in 5 are successfully prosecuted. Doubling policing efforts would thus result in an 0.4% conviction rate. With illegal kills of the same order as legal kills (Spalding 1987; Boxall and Smith 1987), any encouragement to kill wildlife illegally for profit undermines all efforts to save common, let alone rare, species. Investigative reporting uncovered a growing black market in "wildlife medicines" in North America (Cowan 1987; Poten 1992).

The Tragedy of the Commons Misused

The Economist (22 Oct. 1988:21-24) in an unsigned essay on wildlife economics in the U.S., equates "public ownership" with "The Tragedy of the Commons" (Hardin 1968). This is confusion. It leads to the expedient view that, since wildlife in public ownership cannot be managed "properly," it should be turned over to private ownership for management and profit (Roseborough 1986). Few confusions could be more damaging to wildlife conservation, here or abroad. Historically, private ownership of wildlife has not been to the benefit of wildlife, nor of the public.

The Economist, in addition to the above confusion, assumed, falsely, that wildlife in North America is treated currently as a classical "commons," that is, as a commons without control over stake-holder access. It is not, nor has it been treated as such for over 70 years (Geist 1988a). *The Economist* also ignored that in the 19th century, a true "Tragedy of the Commons" was acted out on North America's wildlife, remorselessly, and that this did lead to the expected tragedy: species, once abundant, were exterminated or reduced to tiny remnants as market hunters, free from control, killed for profit (see Hornaday 1913, Hewitt 1921, Mathissen 1959, Hampton 1971, Lund 1980; and reports by the Canadian Commission on Conservation, 1910-1919). The "wildlife commons" was a consequence of more than public ownership: it was maintained by a conviction in the superabundance of nature, and by an abhorrence for controls over private initiative (Smith and Witty 1970, 1972). The destruction of wildlife was also encouraged by a military policy to subdue western Indian tribes: as long as the U.S. Army could protect the expanding railways, market hunters could be relied on to destroy the big game (Ambrose 1975).

It is in response to the destruction of wildlife by unfettered private exploitation that North America's system of wildlife management took its shape at the beginning of this century. Effective controls were placed over the exploitation of public resources, terminating plunder and reversing the tragedy. Garret Hardin's (1968) notion of the "Tragedy of the Commons," followed by Beryl Crowe's (1969) response "The Tragedy of the Commons Revisited," deserves critical attention from those interested in wildlife conservation lest it be misused. Hardin illustrated his idea with an old system of pasturing in Great Britain. Each village held piece of ground in common ownership, on which villagers grazed their stock. The "commons" was the last vestige of land not claimed by the feudal system in personal ownership by nobility, to be given to his vassals in return for loyalty and service.

The essence of the tragedy lies in each herder perceiving that adding one more cow to the commons gives him a benefit of 1, and distributes the cost among all herders (n), so that the cost to each is only 1/n. His gain is much greater than his neighbors' individual losses. Since each economically rational herder thinks so, and adds another cow, and another, etc., the commons becomes overgrazed. Predictably, all lose out. Adam Smith's "unseen hand" and laissez-faire, lead not to an increase in the public good, but to public disaster. The essence of the tragedy is uncontrolled access to a public good, not the ownership of that good by the public, as proclaimed by *The Economist*.

The "Tragedy of the Commons" would hardly deserve attention, were it not an example of the use of inaccurate technical concepts in political battles to influence decisions without recourse to the necessary disinterested research. It shows how shoddy scholarship shapes perceptions. While *The Economist* is at least visible, there is a large amount of "grey literature" on this subject. Internal government briefings and some public papers show shoddy research. Secrecy, deliberate distortions of public input processes as disclosed by the Ombudsman of the province of Alberta, damaging legislation written and passed in haste as happened in 1988 in Saskatchewan, and silence by professionals or by university professors caught in conflicts of interest, are all part of the scene.

The Economist deflected attention from the vibrant, wealth- and employment-creating manufacturing and service industry that has been generated from America's wildlife. The alternative, private exploitation of wildlife, catering to a small, wealthy elite or to luxury markets, generates much lower economic returns by comparison (Eltringham 1984; Geist 1988a). Also, *The Economist* ignores the fact that wildlife management is primarily concerned with conservation, not profit, and that conservation in Europe has a poor record compared to North America (Geist 1988a).

Dangers to North American Large Mammals

Game Ranching

Agricultural interests in Canada, with support from New Zealand deer ranching interests, aim to create a venison market in North America, take advantage of Oriental markets in wildlife parts and of a fraction of America's public disaffected with western medicine, to which parts of dead wildlife may be sold as folk medicine (Hughes 1986). The New Zealand interests hope to extend the marketing period for venison by having deer farms in both hemispheres, and thus having two non-synchronous reproductive seasons. Wildlife is to be ranched in agricultural fashion (Bannerman and Blaxter 1969; Yerex 1979) and sold widely in retail outlets. Oriental markets currently pay well for the velvet antlers, tails, and sex organs of deer (Struzik 1991), and the gall bladders, paws, claws, teeth, and milk of bears. Even "Bear ranching" was researched in Canada at public expense (*The Asian-Albertan Exchange Newsletter* 2[3], 1985). The Alberta 1984 Wildlife Act stipulates that the government will sell black bears, even the rare grizzly bear, to interested parties for commercial purposes. Carefully negotiated conservation agreements within Canada, such as the "Guidelines for Wildlife Policy in Canada," have not been barriers to such legislation. The legislation allowing game ranching in Saskatchewan and Alberta is not only a cavalier treatment of conservation, but virtually designed to spread genetic pollution and wildlife-born diseases; it is a breach of the "Guidelines for Wildlife Policy in Canada," as well as the "World Conservation Strategy," to which Canada is a signatory.

Moreover, game ranching has led to the legalization of trafficking in dead wildlife. This removes the most important protection that wildlife has had, allowing criminals to launder public wildlife through legal channels (Poten 1991). Also, ranchers in the U.S. have been found capturing public elk for sale to game ranchers (Brinkley 1994). Hunting ranches allocate wildlife by the market and encourage, for profit's sake, frivolous killing. All this is antithetical to the primary policies upholding North American wildlife conservation. In response to the bad news emanating from investigations of game ranches, various states and provinces have quickly shifted game ranching to agricultural control. Was this done to restrict public scrutiny?

The treatment of ranched wildlife can be all too often brutal, and may include de-antlering deer without anaesthesia by sawing off the velvet antlers while the animal is held in a chute (Struzik 1990). Game ranchers are reluctant to have de-antlering photographed or filmed. Much wildlife dies unaccountably on game ranches (Lanka et al. 1990).

Market Hunting

In parallel to game ranching, some native groups in the U.S. and Canada want to kill wildlife and retail its meat and parts (Geist 1988a). In Canada, land-claim settlements agreed to in principle by the federal cabinet in 1988 would enshrine in the constitution the right of natives to freely kill and sell wildlife. In Labrador, the George River caribou herd is currently subject to a commercial harvest project that ultimately aims at a continental retail market in venison. These caribou are to be "domesticated," so I heard proclaimed at a conference on northern development. Klein (1980) reviewed the damaging consequences of domestication for stocks of wild reindeer. These include the destruction by herders of wild reindeer because they maintain a reservoir of wolves, are carriers of parasites, and are a nuisance in luring domestic stock away or interfering occasionally with the breeding process.

These game-marketing ventures may come to naught due to heavy metal pollution of the caribou in areas with heavy acid rain precipitation, and due to the escape of reportable diseases from ranched into wild populations.

Hunting Ranches

One form of "game ranching" currently practised in the U.S. on private land is the raising of native or exotic big game for sale to affluent hunters for the killing or for trophies (White 1986; Roseborough 1986). For obvious reasons we know little about management practices on these private ranches. However, the German system of wildlife management is *de facto* game ranching of this type. Its consequences are well recorded: it favors game over non-game species, exterminates large predators, and severely culls small ones. It promotes agricultural-type habitat manipulation, introductions of non-native species and strains, and genetic manipulation of wildlife (Beninde 1937; Draskovich 1951; Frevert 1957; Stahl 1979; Nuesslein 1983; Eggeling 1983). While delivering only fair wildlife production and economic return (Geist 1988a), the German wildlife management system is a mediocre conservation system, and reflects a history of autocratic rule (Stahl 1979). It has lost support among the German public (*Der Spiegel* 1983, 37[4]91-100, 37[4]102-105) and is struggling to adjust as hunting in Europe becomes less popular (Schroeder 1986). Because of its close association with an elite and the perception that hunting is a frivolous pastime of the affluent, it cannot protect wildlife against local economic interests. Recently, in southern Germany, in a choice between removing domestic sheep from state forests or removing chamois and roe deer, the vote was cast to eliminate the wild ungulates (Hesper 1988). Nevertheless, Germany retains self-sustaining game populations, a significant success even though it falls short of the American success in conservation.

In view of the above it is noteworthy that private wildlife management continues to find appeal among some North American wildlife managers (Brothers and Ray 1975; White 1986; Fitzhugh 1989). Claims by trophy ranchers, by African-style game ranchers and by various schemes to farm and market dead wildlife (Bonner 1993), that they act in the interest of conservation are false or, at best, ambiguous (Ehrenfeld 1974, 1981; Pruitt 1985; a, 1988a; MacNab 1991). The trapping for sale of reef fish in the southern U.S. has become a controversy due to its devastating effects on the stocks (Poveromo 1990). In addition, genetic pollution, the unmanageable disease hazards and the lack of continuity of ownership, and thus management practices all mitigate against the claim by private game ranches that they practice "conservation".

Consequences of Commerce in Dead Wildlife

Commerce in dead wildlife and in hunting have consequences:

Destruction of proven conservation policies and laws

The marketing of dead wildlife and of hunting opportunities can operate only if the virtually continent-wide prohibition on the private ownership of large stocks of native wildlife is removed. The same applies to trafficking in wildlife, to allocation for consumption of wildlife by law, and to controls on frivolous killing of wildlife (Geist 1985a, 1988a, 1991).

The ban on private ownership of large stocks of native and exotic wildlife protects native wildlife, livestock, and the public against the spread of reportable diseases, and protects wildlife against genetic pollution and extinction by competition from, and hybridization with, feral exotics (see below). Historically, the allure of wildlife was so irresistible (Stahl 1979) that throughout Western history the powerful have repeatedly abrogated wildlife from public to private use. It happened in New Zealand in 1977 (Caughley 1983:151-165), in Texas in 1925 with the passage of strong trespass legislation, in Norway in 1899 (Swenson 1983), in England certainly by A.D. 1066, when William the Conqueror introduced to Britain the Norman Law, in the Frankish kingdoms in the 7th century A.D., with the Merovingians taking advantage of a loophole in Roman law (Plochmann 1979:161-162). That expropriation of public wildlife ushered in more than a millennium of tragedy for Europe's commoners and wildlife alike (Franz 1926; Roedel 1971: 64-78; Stahl 1979: 223-26, 152-156; Lund 1980: 3-17; Hart-Davis 1978). Is the current attempt in North America by rich landowners to gain private control over wildlife not the beginning of that historically common expropriation? The parallels with Europe are striking (Gilbert 1993).

The ban on markets in dead wildlife, enacted between 1911 and 1921 in the U.S. and by Canada, denies a retail outlet to illegally killed wildlife. For a venison industry to thrive, retail outlets and unencumbered free trade in wildlife parts are, of course, essential. For criminal elements to profit from public wildlife, an infrastructure of retail outlets, distributors, and processors is also essential. Note, the wish of game ranchers to abolish laws against trafficking contradicts, of course, the fundamental interests of "shooting ranches," since the stocks of the latter, in nations awash with firearms, are threatened by commercial poaching.

The policy against frivolous killing is eroded by the notion that hunting is killing for "sport," fun, or entertainment and that wildlife is consequently a "recreational" resource. Hunting has therefore been attacked as a frivolous blood-sport, as an unworthy exercise of needless destruction and cruelty, and as a degradation of those that hunt (Amory 1974). Current public views do not support killing wildlife for sport, much encouraged by an article in *The Economist* (22 Oct. 1988:21), but do support such killing for food (MacDonald 1987).

Policing Costs

Policing the retail sales of wildlife against entry of illegally killed public wildlife is bound to be futile. The policing of a North American market in dead wildlife must founder on a problem of scale: a continental population of large wild mammals of 30 million is faced by about 270 million humans and in excess of 200 million firearms in private hands.

The size of the existing illegal market in wildlife is difficult to determine. Indications are that it is huge – the value of confiscated illegal wildlife at the borders of the U.S. exceeds $100 million annually; a random check in 1983 by the Fish and Wildlife Service on 50 shipping containers crossing the border revealed 30 with concealed, illegal wildlife (800 000 such containers cross the border annually; Kosloff and Trexler 1987).

Germany has a retail trade in venison and a fairly effective system of wildlife policing. However, that system is so large and costly, so limiting of civil liberties taken for granted in North America, as to be an unrealistic example to follow. The criminal element in North America, which already has generated a thriving black market in wildlife parts (Cowan 1987; Struzik 1990; Reisner 1991; Poten 1991), is very large compared to the amount of wildlife available. Difficult as it is now to apprehend wildlife law violators, the situation becomes hopeless with a multiplicity of retail outlets and facilities to launder illegal wildlife. A study by Boxall and Smith (1987) shows that only about 1% of wildlife violations are reported; only 1 in 5 are successfully prosecuted. Doubling policing efforts would thus result in an 0.4% conviction rate. With illegal kills of the same order as legal kills (Spalding 1987; Boxall and Smith 1987), any encouragement to kill wildlife illegally for profit undermines all efforts at conservation. A price on dead wildlife not only places public wildlife at risk, but also public guardians of wildlife (see National Geographic Society, TV Series "Wildlife Wars USA", 1991; Poten 1991; Williams 1992).

Genetic Pollution

Game ranching, regardless of type, is a threat to the genetic integrity of wildlife. Genetic pollution is extinction by degree, the destruction of adaptation by the intrusion of foreign hereditary factors (Geist 1988b). Between 1989 and 1992, game ranchers in Colorado reported the escape of 231 elk and red deer of which 52, including 31 red deer were never recaptured (Brinkley 1994). Between 1992 and 1994, hybrids of elk and red deer were being shot in Colorado, Wyoming, and Montana. In short, the expected (Geist 1986) genetic demise of the American elk has begun.

However, genetic pollution arises not only inadvertently, but also deliberately, in part for dubious reasons, that is, hybridizing in order to escape formal taxonomic designation under the law: if the law recognizes *Cervus elaphus nelsoni* and *C. e. roosevelti*, then a cross of these is neither and outside the law. This argument, fortunately, failed when tested in Alberta. It does, however, alert to the fact that formal taxonomic names must not be placed lightly into legislation (Geist 1992).

Selective breeding or hybridization for tractability or body conformation destroys the adaptations of the species. That such stock can be permanently kept behind fences is not born out by experience, here (Lanka et al. 1990; Brinkley 1994) or abroad (Massey 1986b; Rennie 1986). While hybrids can readily survive in captivity where food and security are assured, that need not be the case for free-living hybrids exposed to predators.

Genetic pollution to foster antler growth is already reality for white-tailed deer (Odocoileus virginianus) in the U.S. (Etling 1985). In Colorado, escaped mouflons (*Ovis musimon*) may have hybridized with bighorn sheep (*Ovis canadensis*) in a national park. This herd is slated for elimination at great public expense. In Oregon, mouflons that escaped to a former bighorn sheep range have precluded the re-introduction of bighorns (Lanka et al. 1990). In Europe, escaped sika deer (*Cervus nippon*) have hybridized so extensively with red deer that the red deer may already be lost as a species (Harrington 1973; Lowe and Gardiner 1975; Bartos et al. 1981; Bartos, in press; Geist 1988b). According to Tuercke and Tomiczek (1982: 57-60), mouflon stocks on mainland Europe were much hybridized with domestic sheep for the purpose of increasing trophy size. Many (failed) attempts were made to "upgrade" European roe deer (*Capreolus capreolus*) with Siberian roe deer (*C. pygargus*; Stubbe and Passarge 1979: 29-30). In Canada, reindeer farming has resulted in some mixing of domestic Siberian reindeer with barrenground caribou (Struzik 1990).

Genetic pollution essentially disrupts the integrity of a time-tested co-adapted gene complex, as Turcek (1951) illustrated for crosses of ibex (*Capra ibex*) with domestic goats (*C. hircus*) and Nubian ibex (*C. nubiana*). The timing of breeding seasons was disrupted and resulted in births during the cold months, followed by the extinction of the hybrid population through high neonatal mortality. Crosses of Siberian roe bucks and European roe deer females lead to birth complications due to larger than normal fawns (Turcek 1951; Stubbe and Passarge 1979). European wild boar (*Sus scrofa*) appear to have various admixtures of domestic pig, recognizable by the presence of spotted individuals. Spotting is associated with decreased survival, lower oxygen-binding capacity in the blood, decreased thermoregulatory ability, and poorer development of the underwool (Briedermann 1986:94). Our work with the behavior of mule deer/white-tailed deer hybrids showed that the anti-predator strategies of the hybrids is totally disrupted. In addition, the ability of the hybrids to run is impaired by a variety of inefficiencies not found in the comparable gait of the parent species; stotting,[1] a speciality of the mule deer, was not witnessed even in 7/8 mule deer by 1/8 white-tailed deer hybrids (Lingle 1989, 1992, 1993).

Since game ranching depends on "improved" varieties of wildlife, and since escapes are inevitable, it can be safely predicted that the hybridization of elk and red deer, bighorns and Asiatic sheep, American-type moose with European-type moose, white-tailed deer from various regions, and mule deer and black-tailed deer is likely to occur, or has happened already. Game ranches are trying to breed "super elk" with appropriate "trophies" for sale to wealthy hunters.

Diseases and Competition

An extensive review of existing information on this topic by Lanka et al. (1990), was submitted to court in Wyoming and withstood lengthy cross-examination (Dorrance v. McCarthy et al. No. C90-0110-J, 1991; ibid. civic actions 6244/6245, 1990; J. Dorrance III Application: see ruling 26 Feb. 1993 by Game & Fish Commission). It showed that our current technical knowledge cannot reliably detect reportable diseases in wildlife, that quarantine procedures are inadequate to stop many diseases, that import and export regulations are flouted by a criminal element, that even a few undetected diseased animals pose major risks, that escapes by ranched wildlife are frequent and inevitable, that recapture is difficult or impossible, that ranched wildlife is sold illegally and moved untested for disease, and that the stresses of captivity are expected to be greater for wild than for domestic animals. We see this expectation confirmed in the severe effects of livestock diseases on wild ungulates, even in tropical species, the very ones that ought to be most resistant to diseases (see Hibbler 1981; Kistner et al. 1982). In addition, North American species of post-glacial Siberian origin are expected to be very sensitive to diseases of southern relatives (Geist 1985b, 1986, 1988; 1991; Foreyt 1989; Onderka and Wishart 1988; Onderka et al. 1988). Ranched wildlife poses, therefore, an unmanageable risk to native wildlife, livestock, native people, and to public health (see *The Lancet*, Nov. 16, 1991:1243). A USDA assessment of bovine Tb (Anon. 1992b) concluded similarly. Moving wildlife in commerce risks the transfer of diseases between livestock, wildlife and humans (Holmes 1982; Smith 1982; Tessaro 1986; Samuel 1987; Lanka et al. 1990). Elk in Yellowstone got bovine brucellosis (*Brucella abortus*; Rush 1932; Honess and Winter 1956; Thorne et al. 1979). Swine brucellosis (*Brucella suis* biotype 4)

[1] the high, pogo-stick-like bounding of fleeing mule deer (and some antelope, fallow deer, and occasionally mountain sheep).

spread from domestic reindeer in Alaska and Canada to caribou, grizzly bears, wolves, Arctic foxes, dogs, and native people (Meyer 1966; Neiland et al. 1968; Neiland 1975; Broughton et al. 1970; Tessaro and Forbes 1986; Gates 1984). Bovine Tb spread from cattle to bison in Bison National Park (Tessaro 1986), and, along with bovine brucellosis, infected bison in Wood Buffalo National Park (Tessaro et al. 1990). *Elaphostrongylus cervi*, a parasitic nematode of brain and muscle tissue, may have been introduced with European reindeer (*Rangifer tarandus* spp.) to Newfoundland from where it spread to native caribou (Lankester and Northcott 1979) and possibly to moose (*Alces alces*; Lankester 1987). Reindeer may have also introduced *E. cervi* to mainland caribou (Lankester and Fong 1989). Game ranching forms a "disease bridge" between livestock, wildlife and humans.

Yet disease control is more than science. In a lucrative market criminal elements will trade wildlife irrespective of testing, some operators will flout rules even in the absence of financial constraints, and innocent mishaps will occur, particularly in a mature industry with large numbers of operators and captive wildlife. Technical excellence does not make up for poor policies (Dr. P. Dratch 1993, Wildlife Forensic Centre, Oregon).

Bovine Tuberculosis

Two diseases, Bovine Tuberculosis (Tb) and Transmissible Spongiform Encephalopathy (TSE) are good examples of concern. Bovine Tb is the object of erradication campaigns in the U.S. and Canada. A Tb-free status for the cattle industry, besides reducing health risks, saves veterinary cost for the producer and opens up additional markets. Ranched wildlife infected with Tb is likely to escape and infect free-living populations and livestock. That would do more than risk the health of wild animals: the mere perception of Tb infected big game as a hazard to ranching and public health would make them targets for eradication.

TSE became famous as the "mad cow" disease that led to the destruction of over 130 000 cattle in Great Britain. A human form of TSE is the dreaded Creutzfeld-Jakob-Disease. TSE is known mainly from domestic animals, but in North America it is also found in free-living cervids, the source of ranched deer.

Bovine Tuberculosis is not a new disease. Early this century, in the former Buffalo National Park, Alberta, bovine Tb spread from cattle to bison and infected 6 percent of the elk and moose (*Alces alces*), and one percent of the mule deer (*Odocoileus hemionus*; Tessaro 1986). Tb is now well established in Canada's northern bison (Connelly et al. 1990). In the U.S. confined elk were involved earlier in Tb outbreaks (Stumpf 1982, 1992a, b; Essey 1992; Thone et al. 1992).

In January 1992, a free-living elk with Tb-like lesions was killed by a hunter near Rossburn, Manitoba, 5 miles south of Riding Mountain National Park (RMNP), and confirmed for bovine Tb on June 16. The elk was shot in the vicinity of a cattle herd depopulated for Tb in November 1991 (H. Hristienok, Big Game Coordinator, Aug. 14, 1992, letter to farmers). Two wolves (*Canis lupus*) with Tb were found in Riding Mountain National Park (Carbyn 1982, & personal communication 1991). In December 1993, Montana Game and Fish officals found Tb in a mule deer near a Tb infected elk ranch in southern Montana (*Billings Gazette*, 2 June/94).

In the U.S.S.R., where deer farming is old and widespread (Stubbe 1973), the problem of Tb on deer farms is old and widespread; some 116 Tb strains have been identified in Asian wapiti (Fedoseev et al. 1982; Remenstrova et al. 1983; Lunitsyn et al. 1990). Tb is a problem in China with farmed sika deer (*Cervus nippon*), sambar (*Rusa unicolor*), and fallow deer (Wu 1986; Shyu et al. 1988). Bovine Tb has appeared in ranched fallow deer in Australia (Robinson et al. 1989), Denmark (Joergensen et al. 1988; Vigh-Larsen 1992), Taiwan (Wu 1986), in several U.S states, and in British Columbia.

Denmark, free of bovine Tb since 1959, discovered Tb in farmed fallow deer. By 1991 some 1600 deer were eliminated in 7 herds; 2 herds are now Tb-free, 5 held under observation; Tb spread to cattle (*Wild Und Hund* 91/29 Jan. 1989 pp. 20-21; Vigh-Larsen 1992). A Tb outbreak in 1985 in Great Britain followed the import of infected red and fallow deer from Hungary; deer farmers demanded public compensation and better tests (Stuart et al. 1988; *Wild Und Hund* 92/30 July 1989, pp. 18-19). In Ireland 5 of 130 free-living red deer had bovine Tb, and in Great Britain's Weltshire and Dorset counties 7 of 450 culled red deer (Stuart et al. 1988); more Tb infected red deer were found subsequently in both countries (Grange et al. 1990; Philip 1989). Deer might have been infected with Tb from infected badgers (*Meles meles;* Clifton-Hadley and Wilesmith 1991; Zuckerman 1980; Little et al. 1982a, b; Hewson and Simpson 1987).

Stress increases the susceptibility of deer to Tb (Griffin 1989; Buchan and Griffin 1990). Tb appears with high stocking rates of captive deer (Clifton-Hadley and Wilesmith 1991), and may appear in zoos (Kollias 1978; Stuart 1988; USDA 1992). Free-living deer of several species show low prevalence of bovine Tb in England, Hawaii, and Europe (Clifton-Hadley and Wilesmith 1991). Free-living red deer in England and Scotland are not uncommonly infected with avian Tb (Munroe and Hunter 1983; Stuart et al. 1988), as are ranched elk in Washington (Merritt 1992).

Historically, bovine Tb has been difficult to detect in deer (Fedoseev et al. 1982; de Lisle et al. 1985; Beatson 1985; Tessaro 1986; Stuart et al. 1988; McKeating and Lehner 1988; Griffith 1988; Fleetwood et al. 1988; Philip 1989; Buchan and Griffin 1990; Thone 1992; Lanka et al. 1992); it survives quarantine and lays dormant in tested animals (Silberman 1978; Stuart et al. 1988; Lanka et al. 1990); it is difficult to detect in stressed deer (Corrin et al. 1987); animals with advanced Tb may not respond to skin tests (Miller et al. 1991; Bringans 1992; Lanka et al. 1992) and viral diseases may suppress the immune response (Thone 1992). Moreover, common disinfectants used to decontaminate facilities will not destroy Tb bacilli (Thone 1992). Herds in New Zealand (Beatson 1986), Europe (Stewart et al. 1988), and the U.S. (Merritt 1992) tested negative for Tb shortly before Tb erupted. The "index" elk in Alberta reputedly tested twice negatively for Tb. A Montana rancher complained about the testing: "We done it and done it. You'd think some of our elk are drug addicts; they've got so many puncture holes in them."

Tb in the red deer species is more acute than in cattle; its first sign may be sudden death. Elk or red deer with advanced Tb may look normal (Fedoseev et al. 1982; Miller et al. 1991; Bringans 1992); a Tb infected elk was treated mistakenly for actinomycosis for weeks in Alberta (Fanning and Edwards 1991). Tb is more common in old elk than in young, and affects bulls more often than cows (Rementsova et al. 1983; Miller et al. 1991). In red deer, Tb lesions up to 20 cm in diameter break out in the lymphatic, respiratory and digestive systems, as contagious running sores on the exterior of the body, and rarely in liver and intestines; it may affect the pleura and serous coat of the intestines, and the mesenteries (Fedoseev et al. 1982; Baetson 1985; Stuart et al. 1988; Philip 1989; Buchan and Griffin 1990; Thone et al. 1992). At an advanced stage of Tb red deer show wasting and have visible abscesses that drain to the outside (Bringans 1992). Some Tb infected wild red deer observed in New Zealand had open sinuses draining from the pleural cavity and the submandibular, prescapular and popliteal lymph nodes. Tb may be spread among deer via the respiratory tract and via contact with contagious body fluids and feed; the bacterium may be shed with feces, urine, saliva and pus. Under ideal conditions, Mycobacterium may survive in the environment for two years, though normally it survives only weeks because of susceptibility to sunlight, ultraviolet radiation, desiccation, and high temperatures (Wray 1975; Duffield and Young 1984; Grange and Collins 1987). In infected free-living deer in New Zealand, without veterinary interference, Tb spread within the bodies of deer with age. This would insure the spread of contagious body fluids on pastures.

Elk groom themselves by working saliva with their tongue into their fur. Elk familiar with one another groom one another, normally where the partner cannot reach (neck, head, withers, croup). Bulls and cows during courtship lick one another extensively, and bulls in rut spray their underside copiously with urine. Contagious cow elk could have their hair contaminated by Tb bacteria from saliva and pus, and bulls by contagious urine as well. Handling the contaminated hair of a living or dead elk could be dangerous, because it contaminates the hands and the meat with Tb bacteria, and because dried, contagious mucous particles could become airborne from the hair and be inhaled.

A comparison of dates marking the beginning of deer ranching and the outbreak of bovine Tb suggests that Tb follows with a lag time of 5-10 years when captive herds multiply (Clifton-Hadley and Wilesmith 1991). Deer ranching grew rapidly since 1985 in North America (Anon. 1992b). It was thus not surprising that multiple bovine Tb epidemics struck game ranches by 1990 (Miller and Thorne 1993).

Legislation, such as the 1990 Alberta Bill 31, enabling game ranching, ignores our technical inabilities to control wildlife diseases (Lanka et al. 1990). This was soon shown by multiple outbreaks of bovine Tb, which in 1990 led to the largest and most expensive disease control operation in Canada:

(1) In April 1990, 380 fallow deer in two herds were destroyed in British Columbia due to an outbreak of Tb; 13 showed Tb lesions, including 3 deer imported from Oregon and one from New York. Faulty records did not allow complete tracing of Tb. The trend to put game ranching from the strict control of Game Departments to state or provincial agriculture departments, will insure this state of affairs will continue.

(2) Between Jan. 1991 and Feb. 1992, seven Ontario red deer farms were hit by Tb; 1300 red deer depopulated. 6000 red deer imported from New Zealand (NZ) in the preceeding 3 years, despite widepread Tb in NZ and inadequacies of testing (a NZ source reports about 10 000 red deer imported into Canada). All imports had tested Tb free. In addition, the foreign muscle worm (*Elaphostrongylus cervi*) was discovered in imported red deer (Nov. 19), 90 of which, all suspected carriers, escaped in transit (Dec.9). After one of these escapes, 7 were captured, the rest were shot (Dec. 18). An independent outbreak of Tb in Ontario led to the depopulation of an entire game ranch, at a cost of $2 million in public funds.

(3) 1990. A massive Tb outbreak on elk ranches in Alberta and Saskatchewan was traced to elk imported from the U.S.; it occupied up to 52 veterinarians and technicians in Alberta. From infected ranched elk, Tb crossed to people, cattle, a bison, and a pig. Workers, technicians, and inspectors in a rendering plant handling elk carcasses tested positive for bovine Tb (Fanning and Edwards 1991); they had been assured by Agriculture Canada that there was no danger. Wildlife technicians in an Alberta government research facility, who took precautions against infection when handling dead elk, still tested positive for Tb. A

veterinarian who administered to sick elk became infected with Tb. From 412 persons who were in contact with diseased elk, 20% tested positive for Tb, and 36 people were placed under medical care. Alberta government veterinarians, meat inspectors, rendering plant and abattoir workers expressed public concern about bovine Tb, and refuse to handle elk – dead or alive.

About 2600 elk in herds infected with Tb have been killed in Alberta in the 1990-93 epidemic, and over $16 million in public funds has been paid in compensation to elk ranchers. By contrast, between 1980-1990, about $2.5 million was paid in compensation to cattle ranchers for the destruction of their Tb-infected cattle. An additional $250 000 per month was being spent in operating funds to stem the epidemic.

Compensation for affected elk ranchers was not fixed as was the case for cattle ranchers which were limited by law to $1500 per head in compensation. It was set in early December 1990 at $15 000 per elk by Agriculture Canada, but was dropped to $7000 for a female and $3500 for a male after public protests. A Dec. 1/91 auction, at which prices up to $16 400 per elk were paid, was dismissed by Agriculture Canada due to irregularities. Game ranchers then clamored for public elk from Canada's national parks for compensation.

In addition to the millions of dollars in compensation, and the unknown veterinary costs, this epidemic cost Canadian cattle producers the Tb-free status expected at the end of 1989 (Tessaro et al. 1990). Based on 1978 study: brucellosis & Tb-free status would save Canada's livestock industry $1 billion over 20 years (Annon 1989). Tb transmitted from captive deer to cattle led to the downgrading of the Tb-free status for cattle in the state of New York on August 16/92 (*Federal Register* 57[137]:31429-30) and August 20 in Pennsylvania (*Federal Register* 57[162]:37686-87); cattle producers in Virginia moved that deer ranching be abolished in the state.

Since many elk are tame in national parks, the spectre of Tb infected elk mixing with visitors on lawns, picnic grounds, golf courses, promenades, etc. is now a distinct possibility. It might have consequences for the tourist industry. Should wild elk in western North America become infected with Tb, they would also pose a risk to hunters and to the hundreds of millions of dollars in economic gains generated from elk.

Game ranches form a bridge for the transmission of livestock diseases between captive and wild populations. Over 120 elk from Tb infected ranches in Alberta and Montana alone are known to have escaped or were inadvertently released into the wild. Investigations by law enforcement officers have uncovered many irregularities in record keeping and illegal transport of elk, putting in doubt the efficacy of regulations controlling game farms. Thus Colorado investigated 30 elk ranches in 1993 and found 215 violations (Brinkley 1994).

Consider what happened with the spread of bovine Tb in New Zealand. Bovine Tb struck the fledgling deer farming industry in New Zealand in 1978 (Beatson 1985). A voluntary Tb control scheme (August 1985), and a compulsory one (January 1990) reduced the incidence of Tb in farmed deer (Bringans 1992; Hutching 1992a), which stabilized since 1988 at 260-270 deer herds diagnosed with Tb per annum and under movement control (Carter 1992, 1993); this number is expected to rise (Livingstone 1993). This did not prevent Tb from emerging as a major threat to New Zealand's European and U.S. export markets in beef, dairy, and deer products (Buddle 1992).

By 1980 the number of cattle herds under Tb movement control had declined sharply, but then the trend reversed and numbers have risen steadily (Buddle 1992; Livingstone 1993), even though Tb on deer farms declined to 4-5% of the more than 6000 farmed deer herds (Carter 1992, 1993). By 1990 there were 6 Tb infected free-ranging herds of red deer (with a prevalence of up to 30 percent), and 2 free-living Tb infected fallow deer herds (with a prevalence of 2 percent). Epidemiology suggests that infected captive red deer repeatedly passed on Tb to brush-tailed possums (*Trichosurus vulpecula*) and to cattle (Beatson 1985; Livingstone 1990; deLisle et al. 1990; O'Neil 1990; Pickett 1993; & correspondence); Tb infected wildlife continues to pass on Tb to captive deer and cattle (Carter 1993; Livingstone 1993). A preliminary study showed a high rate of Tb in feral ferrets within a Tb endemic area (van Reenen 1992). Areas with endemic Tb, and control areas surrounding these, cover 28% of New Zealand (Buddle 1992). The market in live deer declined, and with the loss of income, compliance with the mandatory Tb testing program has also declined (Hutching 1992b; Carter 1993); two large venison exporters, Venison New Zealand and Fortex went under in 1994.

Tb herd tests are expensive; 410 000 deer were tested in 1992 (Carter 1993); compensation for cattle producers is to be abolished by July 1995 (Livingstone 1993). Some deer farmers have abandoned deer farming and a few have opened the gates and (illegally) let out their deer (Stevenson 1992). While possums were thought to be the major agent in spreading Tb, the high rate of Tb in deer and ferrets, and the high infectivity of deer (Hutching 1992a) has given rise to concerns. So have deer fences in disrepair, poor compliance with deer farming regulations, the inability by inspectors to police the industry, and the escape or release of deer, in particular such as appeared on dairy pastures. Eradicating released deer has proven costly and ineffective (Stevenson 1992). A small proportion of the 300 cases of Tb in humans is due to bovine Tb (Buddle 1992). The ability of New Zealand to control

Tb is in doubt (Buddle 1992), The much praised BTB test developed in NZ for deer, to the dismay of NZ researchers, has been found wanting by a (still secret) study by Agriculture Canada (*The Deer Farmer*, Dec. 1993, "Tb test questioned"). NZ veterinarians face unexplained Tb occurrences (Carter 1993). It is considered technically impossible to eradicate Tb from NZ free-living wildlife in the 5 large areas in which Tb is now endemic in wildlife; Tb control is very expensive (Livingstone 1993).

Transmissible Spongiform Encephalopathy

This is a fatal, incurable brain degeneration that breaks out after a long latency period, up to 30 years after oral infection in humans (Brown 1990; Davanipour 1991). TSE is named scrapie in sheep, Bovine Spongiform Encephalopathy (BSE) in cattle, Chronic Wasting Disease (CWD) in elk and mule deer (Williams and Young 1980, 1982, 1992), and Transmissible Mink Encephalopathy (TME) in mink (Marsh et al. 1991). In humans TSE has several variants, all transmissible: Creutzfeld-Jakob-Disease (CJD), Gerstmann-Streussler-Scheinker-Syndrome (GSS), and kuru. This gives the impression of many types of TSE, but note Paul Brown's (1990:38) comment: "The separation of transmissible spongiform encephalopathies into veterinary and human categories is fundamentally artificial, as they all result from the same pathological process, involving the transformation of a normal host-encoded protein into amyloid fibrils that accumulate in and eventually destroy the brain."

TSE is a troubling disease, particularly when found in free-living elk, mule deer (Williams and Young 1992), and white-tailed deer (T. Thorne, Wyoming Game and Fish, 1993), the legal (and illegal) source of ranched cervids. Canada imported thousands of elk from the western U.S., 820 in 1989 alone (Dr. Maria Koller, Agriculture Canada Veterinarian, *The Ottawa Citizen*, 26 Sept. 1990). Technical reviews of TSE preclude the need for a detailed review here (Lehr 1979; Weissmann 1989; Kimberlin 1990; Brown 1990: Paine 1990; Stoeber 1990; Truyen and Kaaden 1990; Collee 1990; Bastian 1991; Diringer 1990, 1991; Pruisner et al. 1991; Herbst and Moeller 1992).

Uncertainties about public health issues combine with a number of troubling factors: (1) a nearly indestructible infectious agent that is next to impossible to remove during food processing (Taylor 1989, 1991; Brown et al. 1990; Brown and Gajdusek 1991); (2) the oral transmission of TSE to many species, primates included; (3) the long latency periods (Diringer 1990); (4) the multiplicity of routes of transmission (*Der Spiegel* No. 23: 208, 6/6/1994); (5) the rapid appearance of BSE in Ireland, the Channel Islands, Iceland, Oman, Switzerland, France (Herbst 1991), and Germany; (6) the unpredictable changes in pathogenicity in passage between species; (7) the lack of an immune response; (8) the difficulties in detecting TSE post- and ante-mortem (Williams and Young 1992); (9)

the under-reporting of CJD and GSS due to overlapping symptoms with several neurological diseases (Collinge et al. 1990; Davanipour 1991); (10) the lethal nature of TSE and resistance to therapy; (11) its rapid spread within Great Britain exceeding 130 000 dead cattle by 1994 (*Der Spiegel* No. 23: 208, 6/6/1994); and (12) the appearance of TSE as a new disease in British cats (Leggett et al. 1990; Wyatt et al. 1991), and in 5 species of captive antelopes (Kirkwood et al. 1990).

Investigative reporting (*Der Spiegel* No.32/21: 254-255, 1990; No.32/44: 164-166, 1990; No. 45/3: 189, 1991; No. 23/ 1994: 208; *Quirks and Quarks* 27th Oct. 1990, Canadian Broadcasting Corporation), revealed divergent perceptions of BSE, and showed how regulations to contain the spread of BSE were circumvented. The view of TSE in medicine (Bastian 1991), is not reassuring.

Twenty cases of TSE have now been confirmed in wild mule deer, white-tailed deer, and elk in Colorado and Wyoming, with 4 further cases pending confirmation (Williams and Young 1992; Wyoming and Colorado Dept. of Game & Fish 1993). TSE was found here first in captive cervids (Williams and Young 1980, 1982, 1992; Bahmanyar et al. 1985; Guiroy et al. 1991 a, b), however, captive white-tailed deer appeared resistant to TSE (Williams and Young 1992). TSE in elk and mule deer contains the same signature protein as scrapie (Guiroy et al. 1991 a, b) and has been transmitted via intracerebral inoculation from mule deer to other species of mammals (Williams and Young 1992). Game ranching could help distribute TSE; an elk imported into a Canadian zoo from a U.S. facility with TSE, was diagnosed with TSE (Williams and Young 1992). Escapes could spread TSE inadvertently: an elk, originally from a Wyoming game farm, escaped from a North Dakota ranch, and was shot 1992 in Alberta. In sheep scrapie is transmitted laterally through the ingestion of the expelled placenta (Dickinson et al. 1974; Diringer 1991); in captive elk and mule deer there appears to be inter- and intraspecific lateral transmission (Williams and Young 1992). American cervids could contract TSE where their ranges overlap those of domestic sheep. Deer are likely to nibble bones, a possible route of infection if the bones are from sheep that died of scrapie and contain residues of bone marrow. "Wasting disease," as used by Bringans (1987) for wapiti in New Zealand, is unrelated to TSE; it may be a nutritional deficiency disease.

TSE has not been found in Eurasian deer, which may have evolved protection against TSE due their long historic contacts with wild caprids with endemic TSE. In Britain BSE was traced epidemiologically to cattle fed on protein meal prepared from sheep cadavers (Wilesmith et al. 1991), however, in 1994 one third of all BSE infected cattle were born after the prohibition to feed cadavers to cattle, while some cattle herds fed only grass and hay developed BSE (*Der Spiegel* No. 23:208,

6/6/1994). BSE was found in a cow born after the 1988 start of the ban on protein feed from cadavers (Vet. Rec. 128:15, 1991). Scrapie has been spread experimentally to cattle only by tissue injection (Gibbs et al. 1990). Oral infection is suspected in 5 species of African antelope which died of TSE in zoos (Kirkwood et al. 1990); it spread from female to young and erupted within 2-3 years. TSE appeared in mink on a U.S. fur farm fed meat of cattle that died of "downer syndrome"; cattle inoculated with mink TSE tissue developed TSE, and the infected cattle in turn passed on TSE via inoculation and the oral route to healthy mink (Marsh et al. 1991). Scrapie and CWD were transmitted to mink (Burger and Hartsough 1965; Hanson et al. 1971; Lehr 1979; Williams and Young 1992).

In humans kuru is transmitted orally (Gajdusek 1977), but there can also be a genetic predisposition to CJD (Pruisner et al. 1991). A review by Davanipour (1991) supports the view that CJD is related to meat consumption. The milk of a patient with CJD infected experimental mice (*Der Spiegel* No. 23:208, 6/6/1994). CJD is a rare disease which appears world-wide at 1-2 cases per million of population per year (Davanipour 1991). *The Lancet* (July 7, 1990, No. 336: 21-22) suggested that CJD is under-reported in Great Britain by orders of magnitude. CJD was linked to iatrogenic infections from rabies vaccine produced from sheep brains (Arya 1990), and to injections of hormone extracts from human pituitaries (Brown 1990). Oral transmission of TSE, less effective than intracerebral inoculation, requires in large mammals from 30 to 130g of infected tissue (Diringer 1990, 1991).

The disease agent has not been found in muscle tissue, which is considered safe to eat. However, power-sawing through spinal cord, brain and marrow, and thus spraying the carcass with a film of infected neural tissue and marrow would contamination the meat with TSE. The removal of brain, spinal chord, large nerves and lymph nodes, all loci of TSE infections, is inadequate; one cannot remove large nerves and lymph nodes adequately from fresh, let alone from frozen meat. Cooking infected tissues does not remove the TSE agent; it has survived autoclaving (Collee 1990) and heating at 360° C (Brown et al. 1990). Burning, not burial of carcasses, is the only safe way to destroy the TSE agent, as it survives years of burial in soil (Brown and Gajdusek, 1991).

Other disease outbreaks and their costly consequences are described by Lanka et al. (1990); parasitologists warn of disease and parasite introductions (Holmes 1982; Samuel 1987; Samuel et al. 1992). However, agricultural bureaucracies continue to foster the spread of game ranching. Some states and provinces have disallowed game ranching, such as Newfoundland, Manitoba, Wyoming and Washington.

Inferior Competitors and Disease-prone Siberian Immigrants

North American large mammals, due to a quirk of history, are not resistant to competition from their Eurasian cousins, nor to their diseases. Post-glacial megafaunal extinctions in North America between 14 000-7000 BP removed most of the ecologically highly specialized fauna megaherbivores and their predators (Guthrie 1984, 1989), followed by a new fauna poorly adapted to North America. This fauna is a mixture of Siberian immigrants and surviving primitives. The latter are specialists in opportunistic resource exploitation and are, consequently, poor competitors for material resources; the former appear to be highly susceptible to diseases of southern relatives. As ecological generalists, they are expected to be poor competitors as well (Geist 1985a, b; 1988a, 1991).

The few survivors of the old fauna are primitive species with a preference for low fibre, high nutrient foods. They specialized as opportunists, that is, as species that avoid competition in favor of dispersal and high reproduction; they are specialists in finding and exploiting locally abundant food in ecosystems set back in their succession. They include the white-tailed (*Odocoileus virginianus*) and black-tailed deer (*O. hemionus*), pronghorned buck (*Antilocapra americana*), collared peccary (*Tayassu tajacu*), black bear (*Ursus americanus*), and coyote (*Canis latrans*).

Circumstantial evidence confirms that the herbivores among these survivors are poor competitors. They are rare in the paleontological record of the Pleistocene, but are common after megafaunal extinction; only then did the peccary extended its range northwards (Kurten and Anderson 1980). The competitive inferiority of American compared to Eurasian deer species was shown by introductions into New Zealand and Europe. In NZ, white-tailed deer are reduced to two populations, one of doubtful viability; black-tailed deer and American moose died out. The wapiti did establish itself, but spread much less than the red deer. Wapiti, white-tailed deer, and moose in NZ shrank in body and antler size; wapiti have thin, translucent skulls (Batcheler and McLennan 1977). However, the Eurasian red deer, sika deer (*Cervus nippon*), fallow deer (*Dama dama*), rusa deer (*Rusa timorensis*), and sambar (*Rusa unicolor*), are still thriving (Wodzicki 1950; Caughley 1983; Harris 1984).

In Europe, white-tailed deer have done poorly against roe deer (Bojovic and Halls 1984). Only in Finland, on agricultural land in the absence of roe deer, are they a qualified success (Nygren 1984). Elsewhere in Europe, introduced white-tails live in small, closely managed populations (Bojovic and Halls 1984).

On the eastern shores of Maryland, sika deer introduced in 1916 are out-competing and displacing white-tailed deer (Flyger 1960; Feldhamer et al. 1978; Keiper et al. 1984; Keiper 1985); sika deer are better foragers than white-tailed deer as shown in field and experimental studies (Armstrong and Harmel 1981; Feldhamer et al. 1978). In a long-term experimental study, sika deer displaced white-tailed deer within an enclosure (Armstrong and Harmel 1981; White 1986:63). Fallow deer are now established in Montana (near Sidney) and on some Gulf Islands in British Columbia (Cowan and Guiguet 1965), despite native deer.

In Texas, extensive introductions of foreign species of ungulates have been carried out. In a careful review, White (1986:56-68) points out that these are difficult to control, while on some ranches they have virtually displaced white-tailed deer. White (1986), a proponent of wildlife ranching, cautions about the introduction of exotics, pointing out that the results are unpredictable, the long-term consequences unknown, and the introduction and the spread of parasites and pathogens a dangerous reality. That exotic ungulates are introduced to the detriment of white-tailed deer has been know for some time among wildlife managers in Texas (Brothers and Ray 1975).

A growing threat to North America's unique desert bighorn sheep are the introductions of Barbary sheep (*Ammotragus lervia*) in the southern U.S. and Mexico. This is a hardy carrier of diseases with fairly rapid dispersal, a high reproductive rate, and broad food habits (Simpson et al. 1978, 1980; Seegmiller and Simpson 1979). The current evidence indicates that escaped Eurasian and North African forms from game farms readily become feral (Lanka et al. 1990), and that the American species are likely to be outcompeted.

The second group of extant North American large mammals are Siberian immigrants, including wapiti (*Cervus elaphus*), moose (*Alces alces*), caribou (*Rangifer tarandus*), bison (*Bison bison*), grizzly bear (*Ursus arctos*), wolf (*Canis lupus*), wolverine (*Gulo luscus*), and man (*Homo sapiens*). To this one may add two species formerly of Siberian origin, but which entered early in the Rancholabrean, the bighorn sheep (*Ovis canadensis*) and the mountain goat (*Oreamnos americanus*). This group, due to a long evolutionary history in the dry, cold climates of Siberia, which are inhospitable to pathogens and parasites, is vulnerable to the diseases of southern relatives. The best data for this hypothesis come from the effects of the diseases of Eurasian immigrants on American Indians (Baruzzi et al. 1977; Black et al. 1979; Neel 1979; Lightman 1979; Joralemon 1982; Dobyns 1983).

The susceptibility to diseases may have obscured the poor competitive abilities of northerners wherever they were pitted against Eurasian species. American and Siberian wapiti, released in Europe, soon became ill and fared poorly against red deer (Beninde 1937), as they did in New Zealand (Wodziki 1950). American moose brought into zoos in Europe died inexplicably soon thereafter. Siberian roe deer, introduced repeatedly into Europe, have also failed to thrive (Stubbe and Passarge 1979). Foreyt (1989) placed 6 clinically healthy domestic sheep together with 6 bighorn sheep. The first bighorn was dead in 4 days, the last in 71 days, victims of *Pasteurella hemolytica*, carried by 4 of the 6 domestic sheep. Similar experiments were conducted in Alberta on bighorns by infecting them with pathogens carried by domestic sheep and cattle (Onderka et al. 1988; Onderka and Wishart 1988). These experiments confirmed earlier conclusions about the direction of disease transfer between bighorns and livestock (Goodson 1982). Domestic sheep and cattle originate from wild ancestors adapted to warmer climates than the ancestors of bighorn sheep (Zeuner 1967; b).

These experiments illustrate what is quite likely a general problem for North American large mammals of Siberian origin. They are not adapted to deal effectively with the parasites and pathogens of relatives from southern latitudes. Siberian mammals are likely to suffer from the diseases of native American relatives, such as the effects of *Odocoileus* parasites on moose, wapiti, and caribou (Anderson 1972; Anderson and Lankaster 1974; Samuel 1979; Hibbler 1981). A consequence of introducing white-tailed deer into Europe has been the introduction of the giant liver fluke (*Fascioloides magna*) into the local faunas (see Halls 1984:558). Today this parasite is a serious problem for livestock and roe deer. Arctic wildlife now carries swine brucellosis and *E. cervi* contracted from introduced domestic reindeer as noted earlier. White (1986), however, states that bison are more, not less resistant to diseases than cattle.

What makes the American post-glacial fauna of particular zoological interest is its apparently poor adaptation to North America and poor co-adaptation to one another. This should not surprise, considering that these Siberians now often live at low latitudes. An inadequacy in adaptations is seen in the overlap of antler growth and rutting in California elk (McCullough 1969), apparently a consequence of the elk's northern origin (Geist 1982:248, 272-274). Or, note the frozen "cauliflower" ears of mule deer in the Yukon Territory of Canada, or the intolerance to the parasites of *Odocoileus* by the Siberian cervids, or the poor fit of bighorn sheep to American deserts and their struggle to survive, compared to the success of reintroduced "old Americans" such as the subgenus *Asinus* and *Equus* in the same deserts (see Bailey 1980, 1984; McCutchen 1981; Weyhausen 1984; b), or the success of desert-adapted Eurasian and African caprids (Decker 1978). None of the Siberians, excepting man, entered South America in contrast to the plains-adapted counterparts of the old fauna. North America's extant megafauna is thus unusual and of the highest cultural value, one worth guarding.

Predator Elimination

Predators face grim prospects when they are forced to prey on wildlife in private ownership; game ranching threatens predators. Ranching eliminated grizzlies and wolves from the western U.S., and currently wages prosecution – overt or covert – of mountain lions, coyotes, and eagles. In Europe reindeer herders eliminate even small predators, let alone large ones (Pruitt 1985, Klein 1980); in Africa predator control is also associated with game ranching (MacNab 1991).

Loss of Wildlife Habitat

The spread of game ranching must of necessity lead to the spread of game fences that halt migratory movements and exclude free-ranging big game from land it had previously used. Game ranching reduces the amount of habitat available to public big game (D. Rowledge, in correspondence). Fence cutting can then lead to the entry of public wildlife onto private game farms, that is, to theft of public wildlife.

Loss of Public Land

Game ranching proponents foresee the conversion of public land into large privately controlled wildlife ranches ("trophy ranches"), where ungulates, bred for trophy production, are sold to trophy hunters as happened in New Zealand (Massey 1986a). The conversion of public land to private control was an expressed goal of the Hageman bill defeated in Wyoming by public opposition. With public lands slipping into private control, less land for effective conservation remains.

Loss of Native Rights

Game ranching of an unspecified nature was also seen as a means of *de facto* eliminating native hunting rights in Canada (Kahdren 1983). Since native people have treaty hunting rights on unoccupied Crown land in Canada, it is logical to extinguish that right by claiming large areas of land as game ranches under lease.

Loss of Civic Liberties

One must point out that wildlife policies have had important implications for civic liberties, such as ownership and use of weapons (Lund 1980), freedom from categories of wildlife crime, freedom to use public lands (Caughley 1983), and freedom from personal dangers arising from irresponsible trespass protection (Geist 1988a). The ownership of weapons by the public is, historically, tied closely to the right to hunt and the abundance of wildlife. Caughley (1983) gives an excellent account of how the transfer of deer in New Zealand from public to private ownership created "poaching" as a new crime, which to control,

New Zealand foresters obtained police powers superior to those of regular policemen. Private wildlife was historically ferociously protected against poachers (Stahl 1979); in Texas men are hired to protect wildlife on private ranchers against trespassing hunters (Brothers and Ray 1975).

Decline of the Wildlife Profession

The emphasis on the use of science in the management of wildlife is a notable feature in the North American system of wildlife conservation. It gave rise to the profession of wildlife manager, to a society of wildlife professionals dedicated to wildlife conservation with a scholarly journal and a bulletin, and to university-based programs that train wildlife professionals.

This is the more remarkable if we compare the use of science in wildlife conservation, to the use of science in public policy formulation were it is virtually non-existent (Doern 1981). In part this reflects the low esteem science has in the eyes of policy makers – and the inability of senior administrators to keep pace with science. While there is, consequently, a deplorable waste of intellect in national policy formulation, that is not the case in wildlife conservation, where even basic science does contribute to management decisions.

However, the use of science in wildlife conservation is predicated on the public buying the services of wildlife biologists. When wildlife is in private hands, management is, normally, not science based, but craft based. It is then in the hands of professional hunters or foresters, as exemplified in Germany. There is, traditionally, little science in the German system of wildlife management. Each owner or lessee of a hunting reserve is a "manager." In our North American view each lessee is a layman in wildlife management. Even though each hunter in Germany has to pass an exam in wildlife management, this management is based on traditional notions as interpreted by foresters and other gifted laymen. There is, of course, little incentive by private owners of wildlife to hire wildlife biologists, who are likely to be at odds with owners about what to do. How could a biologist hired by a "hunting ranch" oppose trophy management? In Germany there is currently a modest interest in wildlife biology, but also an antipathy by hunters towards such (Schaefer 1982).

With the move to private ownership of wildlife and thus reduced scrutiny for wildlife and its managers, the position of authority currently enjoyed by wildlife biologists as a profession cannot but decline. This is currently evident in the transfer of power to police game ranching from departments of wildlife to provincial or state departments of agriculture, such as happened in Alberta, Idaho, Colorado, Kansas, and elswhere.

What Can We Do?

What are the reasons for the current assault on public wildlife? After attending over 200 public hearings, seminars, debates, conferences, and court cases on this matter in the last six years, it appears that there are several problems:

(1) The loss of value of marginal agricultural land. As the productivity of intensive agriculture increases, as new methods of growing food are exported, so traditional markets are displaced. Extensive agriculture, despite high subsidies, no longer assures landowners of a secure income. Consequently, landowners are looking to turn the amenity value of their land into cash. They are encouraged in this by a trophy-hunting cult, by affluent middle class hunters willing to pay for exclusive use of land, by hopes for a luxury market in wildlife meats and the lure of oriental markets in folk medicine. Just as the collapse of the European seal fur and declining wild fur market led to the commercial exploitation of Labrador caribou, so the declining agricultural markets are making land owners look at wildlife as a source of income.

This is, however, but part of a greater economic depression in America's West, as elegantly argued by Popper and Popper (1991). The solution to the economic plight of holders of marginal land does not lie in granting them the right to sell the land's amenity values. The solution lies with something more radical as advanced by the Poppers in their vision of a "buffalo commons." In essence it is to recreate a large wilderness for economic use, taking land out of the commodity market and placing it in the public domain. The obverse, ownership of vast tracts of land by a few controlling interests exposes the public to predatory exploitation, with wildlife conservation slated for near extinction. The lesson learned from North America's system of wildlife management is that resource allocation by law can leads to thriving economic activity – as well as excellent conservation. One can hardly do better for "Wild Life."

(2) The demand in affluent urban populations for "conspicuous consumption," using wildlife as one way to display acquired wealth. Does it surprise that the most destructive wildlife markets are the U.S., Japan, and Germany, the most affluent of developed countries? Strong international control on commerce in wildlife, with the intent of total prohibition in such trade, should be the goal. Yet humans will display. They will travel and seek to bring home mementos of their trips. Controlled, as in the case of consumptive uses of North American wildlife, it generates wealth and conservation.

Public hearings on commerce in dead wildlife and paid hunting are needed in the U. S. and Canada. This would be a good beginning – as it was some 80 years ago.

Acknowledgements

This paper is a modified and upgraded extension of my essay in *Conservation Biology* (1988, vol. 2[1]: 1-12). The paper benefited from audiovisual programs prepared on commerce in dead wildlife by the National Geographic Society and U.S. Fish and Wildlife Special Agent David L. Hall. I am grateful to colleagues, helpful reviewers, and to my wife Renate Geist who have contributed valuable criticism and information.

References

Anonymous 1989. Evaluation of brucellosis and tuberculosis in northern bison. Bison Disease Task Force. Federal Environmental Assessment Review Office, Ottawa, ON.

Anonymous 1991. Tb and deer farming: Return of the king's evil? *The Lancet* 338 (Nov. 16, 1991): 1243-1244.

Anonymous 1992a. *Game Farming in Canada: A Threat to Native Wildlife and Its Habitat.* Canadian Wildlife Federation. Ottawa, ON.

Anonymous 1992b. Assessment of risk factors for *Mycobacterium bovis* in the United States. U.S. Department of Agriculture, Centre for Epidemiology and Animal Health, Fort Collins, Colorado.

Allen, D. L. 1962. *Our Wildlife Legacy.* Revised edn. Funk & Wagnalls, New York, 422 pp.

Ambrose, S. E. 1975. *Crazy Horse and Custer.* New American Library, New York, 527 pp.

Amory, C. 1974. *Man Kind?* Harper & Row, New York, 372 pp.

Anderson, R. C. 1972. The ecological relationships of meningeal worm and native cervids in North America. *Journal of Wildlife Diseases* 8: 304-310.

Anderson, R. C. and Lankester, W. M. 1974. Infectious and parasitic diseases and arthropod pests of moose in North America. *Naturaliste Canadien* 101: 25-50.

Armstrong, W. E. and Harmel, D. E. 1981. Exotic mammals competing with the natives. *Texas Parks and Wildlife* 39: 6-7.

Arya, S. C. 1990. Prion diseases (correspondence). *The Lancet* 336: 369-370.

Bailey, J. A. 1980. Desert bighorn, forage competition and zoogeography. *Wildlife Society Bulletin* 8: 208-216.

——— 1984. Bighorn zoogeography: Response to McCutchen, Hansen and Weyhausen. *Wildlife Society Bulletin* 12: 86-89.

Bahmanyar, S., Williams, E. S., Johnson, F. B., Young, S. and Gajdusek, D. C. 1985. Amyloid plaques in spongiform encephalopathy of mule deer. *Journal of Comparative Pathology* 95(1): 1-6.

Balse, R. 1968. *Die Jaegerpruefung.* Verlag Neumann-Neudamm, Melsungen, West Germany, 575 pp.

Bannerman, M. M. and Blaxter, K. L. (eds.) 1969. *The Husbanding of Red Deer.* Rowett Res. Inst., Aberdeen, 79 pp.

Bartos, L. 1990. Sika/red deer hybridization – recognition and present status. Paper given at Intercol 90, Yokahama, 24 August 1990 (in press).

Bartos, L., Hyanek, J. and Zirovnicky, J. 1981. Hybridization between red and sika deer. I. Craniological analysis. *Zoologischer Anzeiger Jena* 207: 260-270.

Baruzzi, R. C., Marcopito, L. F., Serra, M. L. C., Souza, F. A. A. and Stabile, C. 1977. The Kren-Akorore: A recent contacted indigenous tribe. pp. 179-200 in P. Hugh-Jones (ed.), *Health and Disease in Tribal Society,* Ciba Foundation Symp. 49 (new series), Elsevier, Amsterdam.

Bastian, F. O. (ed.) 1991. *Creutzfeld-Jakob Disease and other Transmissible Spongiform Encephalopathies.* Mosby Year Book, St. Louis, MO.

Batcheler, L. C. and McLennan, M. J. 1977. Craniometric study of allometry, adaptation and hybridization of red deer (*Cervus elaphus* L.) and wapiti (*C. e. nelsoni,* Bailey) in Fjordland, New Zealand. *Proceedings New Zealand Ecological Society* 24: 57-75.

Bayern, A. von and Bayern, J. von. 1977. *Uber Rehe in einen Steirischen Gebirgsrevier.* 2nd ed. BLV. Verlags-gesellschaft, Munich, 245 pp.

Bean, M. J., 1983. *The Evolution of National Wildlife Law.* Praeger, New York, 449 pp.

Beatson, N. S. 1985. Tuberculosis in red deer in New Zealand. pp. 147-150 in Fennessy, P. F. and Drew, K. R. (eds.), *Biology of Red Deer.* Bull. 22, The Royal Soc. New Zealand.

Beninde, J. 1937. *Zur Naturgeschichte des Rothirsches.* Monographie der Saugetiere, Vol. 4, P. Schoeps, Leipzig, 223 pp.

Black, F. L., Pinnheiro, F. de P., Hierholzer, W. J. and Lee, R. V. 1979. Epidemiology of infectious disease: The example of measles. pp. 115-130 in *Health and disease in tribal societies.* Ciba Foundation Symp. 49 (new series), Elsevier-New Holland, New York.

Bojovic, D. and Halls, L. K. 1984. Central Europe. pp. 557-560 in Halls, L. K. (ed.), *The White-tailed Deer,* Harrisburg, Pa.

Bonner, R. 1993. *At the Hand of Man.* A. Knopf, New York, 329 pp.

Boxall, P. C. and Smith, L. C. 1987. *Estimates of the Illegal Harvest of Deer in Alberta: A Violation Simulation Study.* Occasional paper No. 2, Alberta Fish and Wildlife Division, Edmonton, 51 pp.

Briedermann, L. 1986. *Schwarzwild.* Verlag Neumann-Neudamm, Melsungen, 539 pp.

Bringans, M. 1987. Wapiti health. *The Deer Farmer* No. 40, November: 43-44.

Bringans, M. J. 1992. Clinical aspects of bovine tuberculosis in Cervidae with comments on the New Zealand Herd Accreditation Scheme. pp. 11-13 in Essey, M. A. (ed.), *Bovine Tuberculosis in Cervidae: Proceedings of a Symposium.* U.S. Dept. of Agriculture, Miscellaneous Publication No. 1506.

Brinkley, J. 1994. Rustlers, cross-breeding threaten wild elk. *Rocky Mountain News*, May 15: 70A.

Brother, A. and Ray, M. E. Jr. 1975. *Producing Quality Whitetails*. Wildlife Service Publication, Laredo, Texas, 244 pp.

Broughton, E., Choquette, L. P. E., Cousineau, J. G. and Miller, F. L. 1970. Brucellosis in reindeer (*R. tarandus*) and the migratory barren-ground caribou (*R. t. groenlandicus* L.), in Canada. *Canadian Journal of Zoology* 48: 1023-1027.

Brown, P. 1990. Transmissible spongiform encephalopathy in humans: Kuru, Creutzfeld-Jakob Disease and Gerstmann-Straussler-Scheinker Disease. *Canadian Journal of Veterinary Research* 54(1): 38-40.

Brown, P. and Gajdusek, C. 1991. Survival of scrapie virus after 3 years' internment. *The Lancet* 337(8736): 269-270.

Brown, P., Liberski, P. P., Wolff, A. and Gajdusek, D. C. 1990a. Resistance of scrapie infectivity to steam autoclaving after formaldehyde fixation and limited survival ashing at 360°C: Practical and theoretical implications. *Journal of Infectious Diseases* 161(3): 467-472

Brown, P., Wolff, A. and Gajdusek, D. C. 1990b. A simple and effective method for inactivating virus infectivity in formaline-fixed tissue samples from patients with Creutzfeld-Jakob disease. *Neurology* 40(6): 887-890

Bryant, R. 1986. Roger Douglas: Medicine man or Grim Reaper? *The Deer Farmer*, Jan.: 7-10.

Buchan, G. S. and Griffin, J. F. T. 1990. Tuberculosis in domesticated deer (*Cervus elaphus*): A large animal model for human tuberculosis. *Journal of Comparative Pathology* 103: 11-22.

Buddle, B. 1992. Control for Tb. *Farm Progress*, June 10: 53-54.

Burger, D. and Hartsough, G. R. 1965. Encephalopathy of mink. II Experimental and natural transmission. *Journal for Infectious Diseases* 115: 393-39

Carbyn, L. N. 1982. Incidence of disease and its potential role in the population dynamics of wolves in Riding Mountain National Park, Manitoba. pp. 106-116 in Harrington, F. and Paquet, P. (eds.), *Wolves of the World: Perspective of Behavior, Ecology and Conservation*. Noyes Publication, New Jersey.

Carter, C. E. 1992. Tuberculosis control in the New Zealand deer industry. pp. 61-65 in M. A. Essey (ed.), *Bovine Tuberculosis in Cervidae: Proceedings of a Symposium*. U.S. Dept. of Agriculture, Miscellaneous Publication No. 1506.

Carter C. E. 1993. TB control in the New Zealand deer industry: A review of progress. Proc. Deer Course for Veterinarians, Deer Branch, NZ. Vet. Assoc. July 6/93 Course # 10: 203-208.

Caughley, G. 1983. *The Deer Wars*. Heinemann Publishers, Auckland, New Zealand, 187 pp.

Chandler, W. J. 1985. Migratory bird protection and management. pp. 26-70 in Eno, A. S. and Di Silvestro, R. L. (eds.), *The Audubon Wildlife Report 1985*. National Audubon Society, New York.

Clifton-Hadley, R. S. and Wilesmith, J. W. 1991. Tuberculosis in deer: A review. *Veterinary Record* 129(1): 5-12.

Collee, J. G. 1990. Food borne illness. Bovine spongiform encephalopathy. *Lancet* 336: 1300-1303.

Colling, J., Owen, F., Poulter, M., Leach, M., Crowe, T. J., Rossor, M. N., Hardy, J., Mullan, M. J., Jonata, J. and Lantos, P. L. 1990. Prion dementia without characteristic pathology. *Lancet* 336: 7-9.

Connelly, R. G., Fuller, W., Mercredi, R., Wobeser, G. and Hubert, B. 1990. Northern diseased bison. Report No. 35, Federal Environmental Assessment Review Office, Ottawa, Ont.

Corrin, K. C., Carter, C. E., Kissling, R. C. and De Lisle, G. W. 1987. *New Zealand Veterinary Journal* 35: 204

Cowan, D. 1987. Medicine that kills. *Globe and Mail*, August 22: D5.

Craighead, F. C. 1979. *Track of the Grizzly*. Sierra Club Books, San Francisco, 261 pp.

Cumming, D. H. M. 1991. Developments in game ranching and wildlife utilization in East and southern Africa. pp. 96-108 in Renecker, L. A. and Hudson, R. J. (eds.), *Wildlife Production: Conservation and Sustainable Development*. Univ. Alaska, Fairbanks.

Dagg, A. I. 1974. *Canadian Wildlife and Man*. McLelland & Stewart, Toronto. 192 pp.

Dasmann, R. F. 1964. *African Game Ranching*. Pergamon Press, Oxford, U.K., 75 pp.

Davanipour, Z. 1991. Epidemiology. pp. 131-152 in Bastian, F. O. (ed.), *Creutzfeld-Jakob Disease and other Transmissible Spongiform Encephalopathies*. Mosby Year Book, St. Louis, MO.

Decker, E. 1978. Exotics. pp. 249-256 in Schmidt, J. L. and Gilbert, D. C. (eds.), *Big Game of North America*, Stackpole Books, Harrisburg, Pa.

de Lisle, G. W., Hansen, M., Yeats, G. F., Collins, D. M., MacKenzie, R. W. and Walker, R. 1990. The epidemiology of bovine tuberculosis in the Mackenzie basin. pp. 34-42 in Proc. *Deer Course for Veterinarians*, Deer Branch, New Zealand Veterinary Association, Auckland.

Dickinson, A. G., Stamp, J. T. and Renwick, C. C. 1974. Maternal and lateral transmission of scrapie in sheep. *Journal of Comparative Pathology* 84: 19-25.

Diringer, H. 1990. Durchbrechen von Speciesbarrieren mit unconventionellen Viren. *Bundesgesunfheitsblatt* 33(10): 435-440.

Diringer, H. 1991. Transmissible Spongiform Encephalopathy (TSE) virus-induced amyloidossis of the central nervous system (CNS). *European Journal of Epidemiology* 7(5): 562-566.

Di Silvestro, R. L. 1985. p. 131 in Eno & Di Silvestro (eds.), *Audubon Wildlife Report 1985*, National Audubon Society, Washington, DC.

Dobyns, H. F. 1983. *Their Numbers Become Thinned: Native American Population Dynamics in Eastern North America*. Univ. Tennessee Press, 378 pp.

Doern, B. G. 1981. The peripheral nature of scientific and technological controversy in federal policy formulation, Science Council of Canada, Background Study No. 46 (Supply & Services, Ottawa, 1981).

Drabelle, D. 1985a. The national wildlife refuge system. pp. 150-179 in Eno, A. S. and Di Silvestro, R. L. (eds.), *The Audubon Wildlife Report 1985*, National Audubon Society, New York.

——. 1985b. Federal funding for wildlife conservation. pp. 266-279 in Eno, A. S. and Di Silvestro, R. L. (eds.), *The Audubon Wildlife Report 1985*, National Audubon Society, New York.

Draskovich, I. 1951. *Rotwildhege*. Roehrer Verlag, Innsbruck, 103 pp.

Dueck, H. A. 1990. Carnivore conservation and interagency cooperation: A proposal for the Canadian Rockies. Masters Degree Project, Faculty of Environmental Design, University of Calgary, Calgary, 151 pp.

Duffield, B. J. and Young, D. A. 1984. Survival of *Mycobacterium bovis* in defined environmental conditions. *Veterinary Microbiology* 10: 193-197.

Eggeling, F. K. von, 1983. *Diezels Niederjagd*. 23rd edn. Paul Parey, Hamburg, 460 pp.

Ehrenfeld, D. E. 1974. Conserving the edible sea turtle: Can mariculture help? *American Scientist* 62(1): 23-31.

—— 1981. Options and limitations in the conservation of sea turtles. pp. 457-463 in Bjorndal, K. (ed.), *Biology and Conservation of Sea Turtles*, Smithsonian Inst. Press, Washington, D.C..

Eltringham, S. K. 1984. *Wildlife Resources and Economic Development*. J. Wiley & Sons, New York, 325 pp.

Eno, A. S. and Di Silvestro, R. L. (eds.) 1985. *Audubon Wildlife Report 1985*. Natl. Audubon Soc., Washington, DC. 671 pp.

Ervin, R. T., Demarais, S. and Osborn, D.A. 1992. Legal status of exotic deer throughout the United States. pp. 244-252 in Brown, R. D. (ed.), *The Biology of Deer*. Springer Verlag, New York.

Essey, M. A. 1992. Bovine tuberculosis in captive Cervidae in the United States. pp. 1-5 in Essey, M. A. (ed.) *Bovine Tuberculosis in Cervidae: Proceedings of a Symposium*. U.S. Dept. of Agriculture, Miscellaneous Publication No. 1506.

Etling, K. 1985. Can science produce a race of super bucks? *Outdoor Life*. Jan.: 2

Fanning, A. and Edwards, S. 1991. *Mycobacterium bovis* in human beings in contact with elk (*Cervus elaphus*) in Alberta, Canada. *The Lancet* 338: 1253-1255.

Fedoseev, V. S., Rubtsova, L. N., Omarbekov, E. O. and Kirilenko, N. G. 1982. Control of tuberculosis among farmed marals (*Cervus elaphus maral*). *Veterinariya* No. 4: 35-36.

Feit, H. A. 1987. North American native hunting and management of moose populations. *Swedish Wildlife Research Supplement* 1: 25-42.

Feldhamer, G. A., Chapman, J. A. and Miller, R. L. 1978. Sika deer and white-tailed deer on Maryland eastern shores. *Wildlife Society Bulletin* 6: 155-157.

Filion, F. L., James, S. W., Ducharm, J., Pepper, W., Reid, R., Boxall, P. and Teillet, D. 1983. *The importance of wildlife to Canadians*. Environment Canada. Supply & Services, Cat. No. CW66-62/1983E, 30 pp.

Fitzhugh, E. L. 1989. Innovation of the private lands wildlife management programme: A history of fee hunting in California. *Transactions Western Section Wildlife Society* 25: 49-59.

Fleetwood, A. J., Stuart, F. A., Bode, R. and Sutton, J. P. 1988. Tuberculosis in red deer. *Veterinary Record* 123(10): 279-280.

Fletcher, T. J. 1992. Bovine Tuberculosis in Cervidae: The history, current status, and accreditation program in Britain. pp. 27-29 in Essey, M. A. (ed.), *Bovine Tuberculosis in Cervidae: Proceedings of a Symposium.* U.S. Dept. of Agriculture, Miscellaneous Publication No. 1506.

Flyger, V. 1960. Sika deer on islands in Maryland and Virginia. *Journal of Mammalogy* 41: 140.

Foreyt, W. J. 1989. Fatal *Pasteurella haemolytica* pneumonia in bighorn sheep in direct contact with clinically normal domestic sheep. *American Journal of Veterinary Research* 50(3): 341-344.

Frevert, W. 1957. *Rominten*. Bayerischer Landwirtschafts Verlag Munich, (1977 ed.) 225 pp.

Gajdusek, D. C. 1977. Unconventional viruses and the origin and disappearance of Kuru. *Science* 197: 943-960.

Gates, C. C. 1984. Rangiferine brucellosis in a muskox, *Ovibos moschatus moschatus* (Zimmermann). *Journal Wildlife Diseases* 20(3): 177.

Geist, V. 1982. Adaptive behavioral strategies. pp. 219-277 in Thomas, J.W. and Toweill, D.E. (eds.), *Elk of North America*, Stackpole Books, Harrisburg Pa.

—— 1985a. Game ranching: Threat to wildlife conservation in North America. *Wildlife Society Bulletin* 13: 594-598.

—— 1985b. On Pleistocene bighorn sheep: Some problems of adaptation, and relevance to todays American megafauna. *Wildlife Society Bulletin* 13: 351-359.

—— 1986. Antlered harvest. *Harrowsmith* 70: 13-17.

—— 1988a. How markets in wildlife meat and parts, and the sale of hunting privileges, jeopardize wildlife conservation. *Conservation Biology* 2(1): 1-12.

—— 1988b. Hybridization: Extinction by default. pp. 381-383 in Trense, W. (ed.), *The Big Game of the World*, P. Parey, Berlin.

—— 1991. Deer ranching for products and paid hunting: Threat to Conservation and biodiversity by luxury markets. pp. 554-561 in Brown, R. D. (ed.), *The Biology of Deer*. Springer Verlag, New York.

—— 1992. Endangered species and the law. *Nature* 357: 247-276.

—— 1994. Wildlife conservation as wealth. *Nature* (London) 368: 491-492.

Gibbs, C. J., Jr., Sofar, J., Ceroni, M., Martino, A. di, Clark, W. W., and Hourrigan, J. L. 1990. Experimental transmission of scrapie to cattle. *The Lancet* 335: 1275.

Gilbert, F. F. 1992. The vision: Wildlife management in North America. pp. 23-33 in Hawley, A. W. L. (ed.), *Commercialization and Wildlife Management: Dancing with the Devil*. Krieger Publishing Co., Malabar, Florida.

Gilbert, F. F. and D. Dodd. 1992. *The Philosophy and Practice of Wildlife Management*. Krieger Publishing Co., Malabar, Florida.

Goodson, N. 1982. Effects of domestic sheep grazing on bighorn sheep populations: Review. *Biennial Symposium North American Wild Sheep and Goat Council* 3: 287-313.

Grange, J. M. and Collins, J. D. 1987. Bovine tubercle bacilli and disease in animals and man. *Epidemiology & Infection* 92: 221-234.

Grange, J. M., Collins, J. D., O'Reilly, L. M., Costello, E. and Yates, M. D. 1990. Identification and characteristics of *Mycobacterium bovis* isolated from cattle, badgers and deer in the Republic of Ireland. *Irish Veterinary Journal* 43(2): 33-35.

Griffin, J. F. T. 1989. Stress and immunity: A unifying concept. *Veterinary Immunology and Immunopathology* 20: 263-312.

Griffin, J. F., Buchan, G. S., Cross, J. P. and C. R. Rogers. 1992. New Testing procedures for diagnosis of tuberculosis in Cervidae. pp. 15-20 in Essey, M. A. (ed.), *Bovine Tuberculosis in Cervidae: Proceedings of a Symposium*. U.S. Dept. of Agriculture, Miscellaneous Publication No. 1506.

Griffith, L. M. 1988. Tuberculosis in red deer. *Veterinary Record* 123(5): 138.

Guiroy, D. D., Williams, E. S., Yanagihara, R. and Gajdusek, D. C. 1991a. Immunolocalization of scrapie amyloid PrP27-30 in chronic wasting disease of Rocky Mountain elk and hybrid of captive mule deer and white-tailed deer. *Neuroscience Letters* 126(2): 195-198.

Guiroy, D. D., Williams, E. S., Yanagihara, R. and Gajdusek, D. C. 1991b. Topographic distribution of scrapie amyloid-immunoreactive plaques in chronic wasting disease in captive mule deer (*Odocoileus hemionus*). *Acta Neuropathologica* 81(5): 475-478.

Guthrie, R.D. 1984. Mosaics, allochemics and nutrients. An ecological theory of Late Pleistocene megafaunal extinctions. pp. 259-298 in Martin, P. S. and Klein, R. G. (eds.), *Quaternary Extinctions*, U. of Arizona Press.

——. 1989. *Frozen Fauna of the Mammoth Steppe*. University of Chicago Press, Chicago, 323 pp.

Halls, L. K. 1984. (ed.) *White-tailed Deer Ecology and Management*. Stackpole, Harrisburg, Pa., 870 pp.

Hampton, H. D. 1971. *How the U.S. Cavalry Saved our National Parks.* Indiana Univ. Press, Bloomington, 246 pp.

Hanson, R. P., Eckroade, R. J. and Marsh, R. F. 1971. Susceptibility of mink to scrapie. *Science* 172: 859-861.

Hardin, G. 1968. The tragedy of the commons. *Science* 162: 1243-1248.

Hargrove, E. C. 1988. *Foundations of Environmental Ethics.* Prentice Hall, Englewood Cliff, New Jersey, 229 pp.

Harrington, R. 1973. Hybridization among deer and its implication to conservation. *Forestry* 30: 64-78.

Harris, L. H. 1984. New Zealand. pp. 547-556 in Halls, L.K. (ed.), *The White-tailed Deer.* Stackpole, Harrisburg, Pa.

Hart-Davis, D. 1978. *Monarchs of the Glen.* J. Cape, London, 249 pp.

Hayden, S. S. 1942. *The International Protection of Wild Life.* Columbia Univ. Press, New York, 246 pp.

Hesper, B. 1988. Gams oder Schaf – wer frisst den Bergwald? *Wild und Hund* 91 (August 12): 4-8.

Herbst, M. 1991. BSE und andere spongiforme Encephalopathien. *Der praktische Tierarzt* 6: 485-488.

Herbst, M. und Moeller, W. D. 1992. Spongiforme Encephalopathy bei Mensch und Tier. *TW Neurologie Psychiatrie* 6: 68-73.

Hewitt, C. G. 1921. *The Conservation of the Wildlife of Canada.* C. Scribner's Sons, New York, 344 pp.

Hewson, P. I. and Simpson, W. J. 1987. Tuberculosis infection in cattle and badgers in an area of Staffordshire. *Veterinary Record* 120: 252-256.

Hibler, C. P. 1981. Diseases. pp. 129-155 in Wallmo, O. C. (ed.), *Mule and Black-tailed Deer of North America.* University of Nebraska Press, Lincoln.

Hinsche, M. 1989. *Canada Wirklich Erlebt.* Teil 2. Neumann-Neudamm, Melsungen, 286 pp.

Highsmith, R. M. Jr., Jensen, J. G. and Rudd, R. D. 1962. *Conservation in the United States.* Rand McNally, Chicago.

Holmes, J. C. 1982. Impact of infectious disease agents on the population growth and geographical distribution of animals. pp. 37-51 in Anderson, R.M. and May, R.M. (eds.), *Population Biology of Infectious Diseases.* Springer Verlag, New York.

Honess R. F. and Winter, K. 1956. *Diseases of Wildlife in Wyoming. Bulletin 9.* Wyoming Game and Fish Dept., Cheyenne.

Hornaday, W. T. 1913. *Our Vanishing Wild Life.* New York Zoological Society, New York (reprinted 1970, Arno Press, New York), 411 pp.

Hornocker, M. G. and Quigley, H. 1987. Mountain lion: Pacific coast predator. pp. 177-189 in Kallman, H. (ed.), *Restoring America's Wildlife 1937-1987,* U.S. Dept. Interior, Washington DC.

Hughes, D. 1986. Long-term Korean market prospects poor. *The Deer Farmer*, July: 33-35.

Hutching, B. 1992a. Tb incidence low and falling. *The Deer Farmer*, June: 17-19.

Hutching, B. 1992b. Shaking up the shirkers. *The Deer Farmer*, Jube: 23.

Jacobs, J. 1984. *Cities and the Wealth of Nature*. Random House, New York, 257 pp.

Joergensen, J. B., Husum, P. and Soerensen, C. I. 1988. Bovin tuberkulose i en hjortefarm, *Dama dama*. *Dansk Veterinaertidsskrift* 71: 806-808.

Johnson, C. W. and Lindner, R. L. 1986. An economic valuation of South Dakota wetlands as a recreation resource for resident hunters. *Landscape Journal* 5(1): 33-38.

Joralemon, D. 1982. New World depopulation and the case of disease. *Journal of Anthropological Research* 38(1): 108-127.

Kahdren, P. 1983. Dying wilderness. *Western Canada Outdoors* 7(4): 2.

Kallman, H. (ed.) 1987. *Restoring America's Wildlife 1937-1987*, U.S. Dept. Interior, Washington, DC, 394 pp.

Keiper, R. R. 1985. Are sika deer responsible for the decline of white-tailed deer on Assateague Island, Maryland? *Wildlife Society Bulletin* 13: 144-146.

Keiper, R. R., Stephens, J. and Baldwin, D. 1984. Sex, age, and dressed weights of hunter-killed sika and white-tailed deer from Assateague Island, Maryland. *Proceedings Pennsylvania Academy of Science* 58: 101-102.

Kimberlin, R. H. 1990. Transmissible encephalopathies in animals. *Canadian Journal of Veterinary Research* 54: 30-37.

Kirkwood, J. K., Wells, G. A. H., Wilesmith, J. M., Cunningham, A. A. and Jackson, S. I. 1990. Spongiform encephalopathy in an arabian oryx (*Oryx leucoryx*) and a greater kudu (*Tragelaphus strepsiceros*). *Veterinary Record* 127(17): 418-420.

Kistner, T. P., Greer, K. R., Worley, D. E. and Brunetti, O. S. 1982. Diseases and parasites. pp. 181-271 in Thomas, J. W. and Toweill, D. E. (eds.), *Elk of North America*, Stackpole Books, Harrisburg, Pa.

Klein, D. R. 1980. Conflict between domestic reindeer and their wild counterparts: A review of Eurasian and North American experience. *Arctic* 33(4): 739-756.

Knight, R. R. and Eberhardt, L. L. 1984. Projected future abundance of Yellowstone grizzly bears. *Journal of Wildlife Management* 48: 1434-1438.

Kollias, S. V. Jr. 1978. Clinical and pathological features of Mycobacterial infections in sika and fallow deer. pp. 173- 177 in Montali, R. J. (ed.), *Mycobacterial Infections of Zoo Animals*. Smithsonian Institution Press, Washington DC.

Kosloff, L. H. and Trexler, M. C. 1987. The convention on international trade in endangered species: No carrot, but where's the stick? *Environmental Law Reporter*, 27(7): 10222-10236.

Kruckenberg, L .L. 1987. An overview of wildlife privatisation and access in Wyoming. *Proceedings Symposium on Privatisation of Wildlife*. Wyoming Wildlife Federation, Casper, WY, 9-11 Jan. 1987.

Kurten, B. and Anderson, E. 1980. *Pleistocene Mammals of North America*. Columbia Univ. Press, New York, 442 pp.

Lanka, R., Guenzel, R., Fralick, G. and Thiele, D. 1990. *Analysis and Recommendations on the Application by Mr. John T. Dorrance III to Import and Possess Native and Exotic Species*. Game Division, Wyoming Game and Fish Dept., Cheyenne, 139 pp. + appendices.

Lankester, M. W. 1987. Pests, parasites and diseases of moose (*Alces alces*) in North America. *Swedish Wildlife Research*, Suppl. 1: 461-489.

Lankester, M. W. and Fong, D. 1989. Distribution of elaphostrongyline nematodes (Metastrongyloidea: Protostrongylidae) in cervids and possible effects of moving *Rangifer* spp. into and within North America. *Alces* 25: 133-145.

Lankester, M. W. and Northcott, T. H. 1979. *Elaphostrongylus cervi* Camaron 1931 (Nematoda: Metastrongyloidea) in caribou (*Rangifer tarandus caribou*) of Newfoundland. *Canadian Journal of Zoology* 57: 1384-1392.

Leggett, M. M., Dukes, J. and Pirie, H. M. 1990. A spongiform encephalopathy in a cat. *Veterinary Record* 127: 586-588.

Lehr, C. 1979. *Die Traberkrankheit (Scrapie) der Schafe*. Doctoral Dissertation, Tieraerztliche Hochschule, Hannover, 124 pp.

Leopold, A. 1933. *Game Management*. Charles Scribner's Sons, New York, 481 pp.

Lightman, S. 1979. The responsibility of intervention in isolated societies. pp. 304-314 in *Health and Disease in Tribal Society*. Ciba Foundation Symp. 49 (new series). Elsevier-New Holland, New York.

Lingle, S. 1989. Limb coordination and body configuration in the fast gaits of white-tailed deer, mule deer and their hybrids: Adaptive significance and management implications. Masters Degree Project, Faculty of Environmental Design, Univ. Calgary, 289 pp.

Lingle, S. 1992. Escape gaits of white-tailed deer, mule deer and their hybrids: Gaits observed and patterns of limb coordination. *Behaviour* 122(3/4): 153-181.

Lingle, S. 1993. Escape gaits of white-tailed deer, mule deer and their hybrids: Body configuration, biomechanics and function. *Canadian Journal of Zoology*, 71: 708-724.

Little, T. W. A., Swan, C., Thompson, H. V. and Wilesmith, J. W. 1982a. *Mycobacterium bovis* in cattle, badgers and other mammals in an area of Dorset. *Veterinary Record* 110: 318-320.

Little, T. W. A., Naylor, P. F. and Wilesmith, J. W. 1982b. Laboratory study of Mycobacterium bovis infection in badgers and calves. *Veterinary Record* 111: 550-557.

Livingstone, P. G. 1990. Tb in New Zealand – where have we reached? Ministry of Agriculture and Fisheries, Wellington, New Zealand, unpublished conference paper, Massey Univ., 11 pp.

Livingstone, P. G. 1993. Review of the Animal Health Board five year strategy. Proc. Deer Course for Veterinarians, Deer Branch, N.Z. Vet. Assoc. July 6/93 Course #10: 209-221.

Lowe, V. P. W. and Gardiner, A. S. 1975. Hybridization between red deer (*Cervus elaphus*) and sika deer (*C. nippon*) with particular reference to stocks in N.W. England. *Journal of Zoology (London)* 177: 553-566.

Lueck, D. 1989. The economic nature of wildife law. *Journal of Legal Studies.* 18(2): 291-324.

Lunitsyn V. G., Guslavskii, I. I., Ognev, S. I., Surtaev, V. M., Khor'kov, I. A. Yuzhanov, A. Y., Nichkov, A. E. and Zhelesnova, E. 1990. BCG vaccine to control tuberculosis among farmed marals (*Cervus elaphus*). *Veterinariya* 1990 (No. 9): 31-33 (in Russian).

Lund, T. A. 1980. *American Wildlife Law.* Univ. Calif. Press, Berkeley, 179 pp.

Lyster, P. S. 1985. *International Wildlife Law.* Grotius, Cambridge, UK, 470 pp.

MacDonald, D. 1987. Hunting – an exercise in pluralistic democracy. *Wildlife Society Bulletin* 15: 463-465.

MacNab, J. 1991. Does game cropping serve conservation? A reexamination of the African data. *Canadian Journal if Zoology* 69: 2283-2290.

Marsh, R. F., Bessen, R. A., Lehmann, S. and Hartsough, G. R. 1991. Epidemiological and experimental studies on a new incident of transmissible mink encephalopathy. *Journal of General Virology* 72(3): 589-594.

Martin, C. 1978. *Keepers of the Game.* University of California Press, Berkeley, 226 pp.

Massey, W. 1986a. The Lilybank safari. *The Deer Farmer,* Jan.: 12-13.

—— 1986b. Escape! The crisis faced by Robbie and Barbara Oldeman. *The Deer Farmer,* Sept.: 6-10.

Mathissen, P. 1959. *Wildlife in America.* The Viking Press, New York, 304 pp.

McCullough, D. R. 1969. *The Tule Elk: Its History, Behaviour and Ecology.* Univ. Calif. Publications in Zool. 88, Berkeley and Los Angeles, 209 pp.

McCutchen, H. E. 1981. Desert bighorn zoogeography and adaptation in relation to historic land use. *Wildlife Society Bulletin* 9: 171-179.

McHugh, T. 1972. *The Time of the Buffalo.* E. A. Knopf, New York.

McKeating, F. J. and Lehner, R. P. 1988. Tuberculosis in red deer. *Veterinary Record* 123: 62-63.

McTaggart-Cowan, I. and Guiguet, C. J. 1965. *The Mammals of British Columbia.* 3rd edn. Provincial Museum, Victoria, B.C., 414 pp.

Merritt, S. 1992. Tb outbreak scares wildlife managers. *Wyoming Wildlife News* 1(4): 1.

Meyer, M. E. 1966. The epizoology of brucellosis and its relationship to the identification of Brucella organisms. *American Journal of Veterinary Research* 25: 553-557.

Miller, M. W. and Thorne, E. T. 1993. Captive Cervids as potential sources of disease for North America's wild cervid population: Avenues, implications and previous management. pp. 460-467 in Proceedings, 58th North American Wildlife and Natural Resources Conference.

Miller, M. W., Williams, J. M., Schiefer, T. J. and Seidel, J. W. 1991. Bovine Tuberculosis in a captive elk herd in Colorado: Epizootiology, diagnosis, and management. pp. 533-542 in *Proc. 95th Annual Meeting, U.S. Animal Health Assoc,* San Diego, CA.

Munroe, R. and Hunter, A. R. 1983. Histopathological findings in the lungs of Scottish red deer and roe deer. *Veterinary Record* 112: 194-197.

Neiland, K. A. 1975. Further observations on rangiferine brucellosis in Alaska carnivores. *Journal of Wildlife Diseases* 11: 45-53.

Neiland, K. A., King, A. J. Huntley, B. E. and Skoog, R. 1968. The diseases and parasites of Alaskan wildlife populations. Part I. Some observations on brucellosis in caribou. *Bulletin of the Wildlife Disease Association* 4: 27-37.

Neel, J. V. 1979. Health and disease in unacculturated Amerindian populations. *Ciba Foundation Symp.* 49 (new series): 155-167.

Neiland, K. A. 1975. Further observations on rangiferine brucellosis in Alaska carnivores. *Journal of Wildlife Diseases* 11: 45-53.

Neiland, K. A., King, A. J., Huntley, B. E. and Skoog, R. 1968. The diseases and parasites of Alaskan wildlife populations. Part I. Some observations on brucellosis in caribou. *Bulletin Wildlife Disease Association* 4: 27-37.

Nuesslein, F. 1983. *Jagdkunde.* 11th edn. BLV Verlags-gesellschaft, Munich, 375 pp.

Nygren, K. F. A. 1984. Finland. pp. 561-568 in Halls, L. K. (ed.), *White-tailed Deer*, Stackpole, Harrisburg, PA.

O'Neil, B. 1990. Control measures to control a tuberculosis breakdown in a deer herd. Proc. Deer Course for Veterinarians, Deer Branch, New Zealand Vet. Assoc. Auckland. pp. 43-48.

Onderka, D. K., Rawluk, S. A. and Wishart, W. D. 1988. Susceptibility of Rocky Mountain bighorn sheep and domestic sheep to pneumonia induced by bighorn and domestic livestock strains of Pasteurella haemolytica. *Canadian Journal of Veterinary Research* 52: 439-444.

Onderka, D. K. and Wishart, W. D. 1988. Experimental contact transmission of *Pasteurella haemolytica* from clinically normal domestic sheep causing pneumonia in Rocky Mountain bighorn sheep. *Journal of Wildlife Diseases* 24(4): 663-667.

Paine, S. 1990. BSE: What madness is this? *New Scientist* 126(1720): 32-34.

Pickett, K. 1993. Survivors. *The Deer Farmer,* Dec.: 41-42.

Pimentel, D., Oltenacu, P. A., Nesheim, M. C., Krummel, J., Allen, M. S. and Chick, S. 1980. The potential for grass-fed livestock: Resource constraints. *Science* 207: 843-848.

Philip, P. M. 1989. Tuberculosis in deer in Great Britain. *The State Veterinary Journal.* 43(123): 193-204.

Plochmann, R. 1979. Mensch und Wald. pp. 157-197 in Stern, H. (ed.), *Rettet den Wald,* Kindler Verlag, Munich.

Popper, F. J. and Popper, D. E. 1991. The reinvention of the American frontier. *The Amicus Journal,* Summer: 4-7.

Poveromo, G. 1990. Cages of death. *Salt Water Sportsman* 51(6): 70.

Povlitis, T. 1985. A citizens' proposal to save the Yellowstone grizzly bear. *Naturalist* 36(2): 23-31.

——. 1986. Is grizzly bear policy in Yellowstone based on false assumptions? *Wildlife Society Bulletin* 14: 88-90.

Pruisner, S. B., Torchia, M. and Westway, D. 1991. Molecular biology and genetics of prions – implications for sheep scrapie, "Mad cows" and the BSE epidemic. *The Cornell Veterinarian* 81(2): 85-101.

Pruitt, W. O. Jr. 1985. Caribou, reindeer and snow. *The Explorer Journal,* March: 30-35.

Poten, C. 1991. A shameful harvest. *National Geographic* 180(3): 106-132.

Raesfeld, F. von, and Frevert, W. 1954. *Das Deutsche Waidwerk.* P. Parey, Hamburg, 497 pp.

Ranhofer, C. 1893. *The Epicurean.* Dover edn. 1971, Dover Publications, New York, 1183 pp.

Raybourne, J. W. 1987. The black bear: Home in the highlands. pp. 105-117 in Kallman, H. (ed.), *Restoring America's Wildlife* 1937-1987, U.S. Dept. Interior, Washington DC.

Reenen, G. van, 1992. Ferreting out the truth about Tb carriers. *The Deer Farmer,* June: 27-29.

Reisner, M. 1991. *Game Wars.* Viking Penguin, New York, 294 pp.

Regan, T. 1983. *Animal Rights.* Univ. California Press, Berkeley.

Rementsova, M. M., Postricheva, O. V. and Rybalko, S. I. 1983. Brucellosis and other zoonoses associated with the farming of marals (*Cervus elaphus maral*). *Voprosy Prirodnoi Ochogovosti Boleznei* 13: 102-110.

Rennie, N. 1986. Good insurance deals are available. *The Deer Farmer,* Sept.: 11-12.

Rhyan, J. C., Saari, D. A., Williams, E. S., Miller, M. W., Davis, A. J. and Wilson, A. J. 1992. Gross and microscopic lesions of naturally occurring tuberculosis in a captive herd of wapiti (*Cervus elaphus nelsoni*) in Colorado. *Journal of Veterinary Diagnostic Investigation* 4: 428-433.

Robinson, R. C., Phillips, P. H., Stevensen, G. and Storm, P. A. 1989. An outbreak of *Mycobacterium bovis* infection in fallow deer (*Dama dama*). *Australian Veterinary Journal* 66: 195-197.

Roe, F. G. 1970. *The North American Buffalo.* 2nd edn. Toronto, University of Toronto Press.

Roedle, J. 1971. *Wenn die Hirsche roehren*. Kosmos, Fraenckscher Verlagshandlung, Stuttgart, 80 pp.

Roseborough, D. J. 1986. Wildlife as a cash crop? *The Globe and Mail*, July 17: 7A.

Rush, W. M. 1932. Bang's disease in the Yellowstone National Park buffalo and elk herds. *Journal of Mammalogy* 13: 371.

Samuel, W. M. 1979. The winter tick *Dermacentor albipictus* (Packard, 1869) on moose *Alces alces* (L.) of central Alberta. *North American moose conference workshop 1979, Proceedings* 15: 303-348.

Samuel, W. M. 1987. Moving the zoo – or – the potential introduction of a dangerous parasite into Alberta with its translocated host. pp. 85-92 in Renecker, L. A. (ed.), *Focus on a New Industry*. Proceedings, Alberta Game Growers Association Conference, Edmonton.

Samuel, W. M., Pybus, M. J., Welch, D. A. and Wilkie, C. J. 1992. Elk as potential host for meningeal worm: Implications for translocation. *Journal of Wildlife Management* 56: 629-639.

Schaefer, E. 1982. *Hegen und Ansprechen von Rehwild.* 4th edn. BLV Verlagsgesellschaft, Munich, 218 pp.

Schmidt, J. L. and Gilbert, D. L. (eds.) 1978. *Big game of North America.* Stackpole Books, Harrisburg, Pa., 494 pp.

Schroeder, W. 1986. Jagd 2000. *Die Pirsch* 38(11): 773-777.

Seegmiller, R. F. and Simpson, C. D. 1979. The Barbary sheep: Some conceptual implication of competition with desert bighorns. *Transactions Desert Bighorn Council* 23: 47-49.

Shyu, C. L., Tung, K. C., Shiau, J. R. and Wang, J. S. 1988. Studies on the diagnostic methods of tuberculosis in deer and identification of the pathogen. *Taiwan Journal of Veterinary Medicine & Animal Husbandry* No. 52: 53-61.

Silbermann, M. S. 1978. Epidemiology of tuberculosis outbreak in sitatunga antelope house at a municipal zoo. pp. 193-194 in Montali, R. J. (ed.), *Mycobacteria Infections in Zoo Animals.* Proc. International Conference on Mycobacteria in Zoo animals 1976, Washington, DC.

Simpson, C. D., Krysl, J. B., Hampy, D. B. and Gray, G. G. 1978. The Barbary sheep: A threat to desert bighorn survival. *Transasctions Desert Bighorn Council* 22: 26-31.

Simpson, C. D., Krysl, J. B. and Dickinson, T. G. 1980. Food habits of Barbary sheep in the Guadalupe Mountains, New Mexico. pp. 87-91 in Simpson, C. D. (ed.), *Proceedings Symposium Ecology and Management of Barbary sheep,* Texas Tech Univ., Lubbock.

Smith, C. E. G. 1982. Major factors in the spread of infections. *Proc. Symp. Zool. Soc.* London 50: 207-235.

Smith, R. C. and Witty, D. R. 1970, 1972. Conservation, resources and environment. An exposition and critical evaluation of the Commission of Conservation, Canada. *Plan Canada,* part 1, 11(1): 55-71, part 2, 11(3): 199-216.

Spalding, D. J. 1987. The law and the poacher. pp. 59-70 in Murray, A. (ed.), *Our Wildlife Heritage,* The Centennial Wildlife Society of British Columbia, Victoria, BC.

Stahl, D. 1979. *Wild, Lebendige Umwelt.* K. Alber, Freiburg/Munich, 349 pp.

Stevenson, P. 1992. Going ahead with hot issue. *The Deer Farmer.* May: 15-17.

Stuart, F. A. 1988. Tuberculosis in farmed red deer (Cervus elaphus). *Current Topics in Veterinary Medicine and Animal Science* 48: 101-111.

Stuart, F. A., Manser, P. A. and McIntosh, F. G. 1988. Tuberculosis in imported red deer (*Cervus elaphus*). *Veterinary Record* 122: 508-511.

Stoeber, M. 1990. Bovine Spongiforme Encephalopathie (BSE): Stand der Kenntnisse und Massnahmen. *Deutsche tieraerztliche Wochenschrift* 91: 540-544.

Struzik, E. 1987. Don't fence them in. *Nature Canada* 16(2): 15.

———. 1990. The antlers of a dilemma. *Harrowsmith* 25(4): 37-45.

———. 1991. Wild harvest. *Equinox* 10(2): 33-43.

Stubbe, C. and Passarge, H. 1979. *Rehwild.* Verlag Neumann-Neudamm, Berlin, 432 pp.

Stumpf, C. D. 1982. Epidemiological study of an outbreak of bovine Tb in confined elk herds. Proceedings, U.S. Animal Health Association. 86: 524-527.

Stumpf, C. D. 1992a. Epidemiology of an outbreak of bovine tuberculosis. pp. 31-32 in Essey, M. A. (ed.), *Bovine Tuberculosis in Cervidae: Proceedings of a Symposium.* U.S. Dept. of Agriculture, Miscellaneous Publication No. 1506.

Stumpf, C. D. 1992b. Epidemiology of bovine Tuberculosis in elk herds – 1981. pp. 33-34 in Essey, M. A. (ed.), *Bovine Tuberculosis in Cervidae: Proceedings of a Symposium.* U.S. Dept. of Agriculture, Miscellaneous Publication No. 1506.

Swenson, J. E. 1983. Free public hunting and the conservation of public wildlife resources. *Wildlife Society Bulletin* 8: 75-87.

Taylor, D. M. 1989. Scrapie agent decontamination: Implications for bovine spongiform encephalopathy. *Veterinary Record* 124: 219-292.

Taylor, K. C. 1991. The control of bovine spongiform encephalopathy in Great Britain. *Veterinary Record* 129(24): 522-526.

Tessaro, S. V. 1986. The existing and potential importance of brucellosis and tuberculosis in Canadian wildlife: A review. *Canadian Veterinary Journal* 27: 119-123

Tessaro, S. V. (1992). Bovine tuberculosis and brucellosis in animals, including man. *Alberta* 3(1): 207-224.

Tessaro, S. V. and Forbes L. B. 1986. *Brucella suis* biotype 4: A case of granulomatous nephritis in a barren ground caribou (*Rangifer tarandus groenlandicus* L.) with a review of the distribution of rangiferine brucellosis in Canada. *Journal of Wildlife Diseases* 22: 479-483.

Tessaro, S. V., Forbes, L. B. and Turcotte, C. 1990. A survey of brucellosis and tuberculosis in bison in and around Wood Buffalo National Park, Canada. *Canadian Veterinary Journal* 31: 174-180.

Thomas, J. W., Forsman, E. D., Lint, J. B., Meslow, E. C., Noon, B. R. and Verner, J. 1990. *A Conservation Strategy for the Northern Spotted Owl.* Report of the interagency committee to address the conservation of the northern spotted owl. U.S. Dept. Agric., Forest Service; U.S. Dept. Interior, Bureau of Land Management, Fish & Wildlife, National Park Service, U.S. Government Printing Office: 1990-791-171/20026), Portland, OR, 427 pp.

Thone, C. O. 1992. Pathogenesis of *Mycobacterium bovis infection.* pp. 7-10 in Essey, M. A. (ed.), *Bovine Tuberculosis in Cervidae: Proceedings of a Symposium.* U.S. Dept. of Agriculture, Miscellaneous Publication No. 1506.

Thone, C. O., Quinn, W. J., Miller, L. D., Stackhouse, L. L., Newcomb, B. F. and Ferrell, J. M.. 1992. Mycobacterium bovis infection in North American elk (*Cervus elaphus*). *Journal of Vetrinary Diagnostic Investigation* 4: 423-427.

Thorne, E. T., Morton, J. K. and Ray, W. C. 1979. Brucellosis, its effect and impact on elk in western Wyoming. pp. 212-222 in Boyed, M. S. and Hayden-Wing, L. O. (eds.), *North American Elk: Ecology, Behavior, and Management.* Univ. Wyoming, Laramie.

Truyen, U. and Kaaden, O. R. 1990. BSE, die bovine spongiforme Encephalopathie. *Tieraerztliche Praxis* 18: 463-468.

Tuerke, F. and Tomiczek, H. 1982. *Das Muffelwild.* 2nd edn. P. Parey, Hamburg, 197 pp.

Turcek, F. J. 1951. Effect of introductions on two game populations in Czechoslovakia. *Journal of Wildlife Management* 15: 113-114.

Ueckermann, E. and Hansen, P. 1983. *Das Damwild.* P. Parey, Hamburg, 336 pp.

Vigh-Larsen, F. 1992. History, current status, and accreditation program in Denmark for bovine tuberculosis in Cervidae. pp. 35-36 in Essey, M. A. (ed.), *Bovine Tuberculosis in Cervidae: Proceedings of a Symposium.* U.S. Dept. of Agriculture, Miscellaneous Publication No. 1506.

Vogt, F. 1948. *Das Rotwild.* Osterreichischer Jagd-und Fischer- eiverlag, Vienna, 207 pp.

Vreeland, F. K. 1916. Prohibition of the sale of game. pp. 93-99 in *Conservation of Fish, Birds and Game,* Commission of Conservation Canada, Toronto.

Weber, M. 1985. Marine mammal protection. pp. 180-211 in Eno, A. S. and Di Silvestro, R. L. (eds.), *The Audubon Wildlife Report 1985,* National Audubon Society, New York.

Wellman, J. D. 1992. *Wildland Recreation Policy*, Krieger Publishing Co., Malabar, Florida, 284 pp.

Weissmann, C. 1989. Sheep disease in human clothing. *Nature* 338(6213): 292-299.

Weyhausen, J. D. 1984. Comment on desert bighorn as relict: Further considerations. *Wildlife Society Bulletin* 12: 82-85.

White, R. J. 1986. *Big Game Ranching in the United States*. Wild Sheep and Goat International, Melissa, NM, 355 pp.

Wiese, M. (ed.) 1986. *DJV Handbuch, Jagd 1986*. Deutscher Jagdschutz-Verband, Germany (BR), 486 pp.

Wilesmith, J. W., Ryan, J. B. M. and Atkinson, M. J. 1991. Bovine spongiform encephalopathy: Epidemiological studies on the origin. *Veterinary Record* 128(9): 199-203.

Williams, E. S. and Young, S. 1980. Chronic wasting disease of captive mule deer: A spongiform encephalopathy. *Journal of Wildlife Diseases* 16(1): 89-98.

—— and —— 1982. Spongiform encephalopathy of Rocky Mountain elk. *Journal of Wildlife Diseases* 18(4): 465-471.

—— and —— 1992. Spongiform encephalies in Cervidae. *Rev. sci. tech. Off. int. Epiz.* 11(2): 551-567

Wilson, E. O. 1993. *The Diversity of Life*, Norton, New York, 424 pp.

Wodzicki, K. A. 1950. *Introduced Mammals in New Zealand*. Dept. Sci.& Induct. Res. Bull. No. 98, Wellington, NZ, 255 pp.

Wray, C. 1975. Survival and spread of pathogenic bacteria of veterinary importance within the environment. *Veterinary Bulletin* 45: 543-550.

Wu, Y. H. 1986. Study of Tuberculosis of deer in Taiwan. 1 Epidemiology, isolation of pathogen and Pathological changes. *Journal of the Chinese Society for Veterinary Sciences* 12: 323-329.

Wyatt, J. M., Pearson, G. R., Smerdon, T., Gruffydd-Jones, T. J. and Wells, G. A. H. 1990. Spongiform encephalopathy in a cat. *Veterinary Record* 126(20): 513.

Wyatt, J. M., Pearson, G. R., Smerdon, T. N., Gruffydd-Jones, T. J., Wells, G. A. H. and Wilesmith, J. W. 1991. Naturally occurring scrapie-like spongiform encephalopathy in five domestic cats. *Veterinary Record* 129(1): 233-236.

Yerex, D. 1979. *Deer Farming in New Zealand*. Deer Farming Division, Agricultural Promotion Associates, Wellington, NZ, 120 pp.

Zeuner, F. E. 1967. *Geschichte der Haustiere*. Translated from English by R. Ross-Rath, eds. J. Bosseneck and T. Halthenorth. Bayerischer Landwirtschaftsverlag, Munich, 448 pp.

Zuckerman, Lord. 1980. *Badgers, Cattle and Tuberculosis*. London, HMSO.

Editor's Note: The Law Relating to Ownership of Wild Animals is Rather Complicated

This paper differs in style from the preceding ones. This is an important point. The referencing system used in law is the traditional footnote system of ancient occidental scholarship, and that with good reason. In the conventional system of referencing used in science, the assumption is made that the reader, a fellow researcher, will be able to quickly look up the reference in a scientific journal. The reader of a submission to court will be the judge. His ability to hand down a decision will be much enhanced if **all** the relevant material is at hand. That is, he must be able to follow the argument closely, step by step; he does not have the time to run to a library to search out a paper, read it and second guess just exactly what the reference is all about. He needs to have not only each reference, but also an account of why it is relevant. He must not be asked to rely on authority, but requires a detailed exposition of the facts and logic to arrive at a just decision. Consequently, presentations such as scientists do in their journals are inadequate in a submission to court. This demands that when preparing material for the courts, one must have some familiarity with how to structure explanations and facts so that all may be able to follow the reasoning and the evidence closely. Consequently, in public affairs, an ability to explain clearly, without recourse to jargon or authority is an essential skill. So much for style. As to the content, it stresses how closely biology, that is science, enters into theoretical legal arguments. Moreover, here are several policy initiatives worth pursuing – as a protection of species from industrial, agricultural or planning transgressions. Since courts hand down binding decisions, some familiarity with legal matters is essential for those professing wildlife conservation.

The Law Relating to Ownership of Wild Animals is Rather Complicated[1]

William A. Tilleman

Research into wildlife law is complicated, but it is also very interesting. My professor of jurisprudence at Columbia University – a man whose intelligence gathers international respect – once stated:

> *Any judgment about how far the law should be used to protect animals requires some assessment of animal interests against human interests; here the difficulties become even greater.*[2]

How true. His comment, which could apply equally to wild or domestic animals, sets the stage for the controversy.

As an elementary student, I found great personal interest in wildlife because their guarantee of freedom always seized my jealousy.[3] As a law student, I became further interested in wildlife law because of how odd it was that law professors could only cite archaic principles when analyzing the law of wild animals (ferae *naturae*). My interest increased

---

1 For a discussion of how complicated these matters can get, see F. Lawson and B. Rudden, *The Law of Property* (2nd ed. 1982). See also L. Goodeve, *Goodeve on Personal Property* (5th ed. 1912) and J. Williams, *Law of Personal Property* (11th ed. 1881).

2 Kent R. Greenawalt, "Religious Convictions and Lawmaking," 84 *Michigan Law Review* (1985).

3 The most recurring example, for me, is sitting in my elementary classroom (bored) and seeing through the window a flight of ducks. For some reason I always envied the ducks. I wondered what river or pond they came from; where they were headed; how many times had they migrated; if they were mallards, how many were greenheads, why were the greenhead feathers iridescent; could they really fly 50 miles per hour; what did my school look like from their vantage point; was it possible (as my father claimed) that hunters could kill 5 birds in one shot (as he once did); if so, did it leave emotional scars on their adjacent survivor-friends; did wild ducks caucus and discuss these matters (in duck language); etc.?

even more when my first legal case – a criminal case – involving wildlife law, proved extremely complicated.[4]

Today we are a highly civilized people, quickly moving into the 21st century. For wildlife policy, it may serve society very well to reexamine the legal theory of wildlife. To properly understand wildlife law, the clocks must be turned back so that one sees how historical developments have shaped, or even twisted, current laws and policies.

Evolution of Wildlife Laws[5]

Early Roman Law regarded wild animals as *res nullius;* essentially, wild animals, which never had an owner, became the property of the first person to control or occupy them. The right thus belonged to individuals and therefore it was a personal right; man was in possession of the right; man controlled the right; man had to work hard for the right. Today, the governments, as sovereigns, regulate all property rights in wildlife.[6] Individuals can only legally control or occupy wild game with the permission of the government. The government is now the administrator. The government distributes possession and control of wildlife rights.

Yet, historical common law (in England) generally allocated these special rights to man, not government. Property rights, when applied to wild animals, found support in either of two fundamental principles: *ratione soli* and *ratione privilegii.*[7]

Under the first principle, *ratione soli,* the landowner had an absolute right to kill and take wild animals caught on his land. As the name suggests, *ratione soli* rested upon real property law.[8] The whole matter clearly arose as an incidental part of land ownership. As such, it could

4 It involved a rural group of hardworking people who, for religious reasons, did not believe in owning or carrying guns. These people had problems with coyotes killing their animals (coyotes have such a bad name, it seems, but this time they deserved it). In order to preserve their flocks, they asked a neighbor to hide in their buildings and shoot the coyotes. He did and was charged by the RCMP for various things (shooting out of season, etc.).

5 Required reading on the subject is found in the scholarly and comprehensive book by Michael Bean, *The Evolution of National Wildlife Law* (2nd ed. 1983); for a good historical and English common law study, cf. Tom Lund, *American Wildlife Law* (1984).

6 This regulation occurs via statutory control or via interstitial common law.

7 This is explained further in L. Goodeve, *Goodeve on Personal Property,* 2 (5th ed. 1912).

8 The development of wildlife law would have been far more fascinating had it developed out of a body of jurisprudence called natural law – but it didn't.

still have great relevance today because public lands are shrinking, absentee-ownership is increasing, "public trust" concepts are becoming legally codified[9] and, more important, where the definition of "land" is checked under *Land Titles* statutes,[10] one finds several intriguing aspects of historical jurisprudence that could protect the environment – including the wildlife resource.

Under the second principle, *ratione privilegii*, justification for killing or capturing wild game came from holding certain privileges. If an individual had a right to kill or capture wildlife, he earlier received the right (whatever right he had) through ancient traditions of the English Crown. The Crown assigned or transferred its right to allow a person to kill game on land owned or controlled by what was referred to as a government license or franchise. *Ratione privilegii* was therefore more of a "license;" as a license, it has direct relevance today[11] because modern wildlife law creates certain privileges between the licensee and the rest of society. Game killed under this right was (and still is today, if done legally) converted unconditionally to any taker with a valid hunting license. The keen reader will note at this point the emergence of a crucial "rights dichotomy" surfacing (between dead v. live wildlife). Rights change – or have the potential to change – upon the death of wildlife.[12]

Historically, for the professional or mercenary hunter, there was always some justification for maintaining absolute game ownership over the product of his efforts. The following quote explains:

> *Labor was a factor contributing to the creation of rights. . . . Game killed on the trail generally belonged to the hunter shooting it. He could dispose of it as he pleased, keeping a share, selling it, or giving permission to others to take what they wanted. It is also likely that assistance in running down the animal or helping in some way to obtain the carcass for second or third persons, demand[ed] rights on the animal.*[13]

---

9 In Canada, an example of this is the Northwest Territories' *Environmental Rights Act*.

10 The definition of land commonly includes several terms that broadly define the rights inherent with property: terms such as corporal hereditaments, incorporeal hereditaments, passageways, easements, and other legal and equitable interests relative to the "environment."

11 See *Manger v. People*, 97 Ill. 320 (1881). See also William Sigler, *Wildlife Law Enforcement*, 80-87 (1980).

12 For example, if a person accidentally kills or discovers dead wildlife, she can bring it to the attention of the Regulator who normally has the discretion to (1) formally record details of the kill, and then (2) officially give it back to the person (releasing the state's rights in the wildlife).

13 J. Reid, *Law for the Elephant: Property and Social Behavior on the Overland Trail* 142 (1980).

As far as native hunters were concerned, they normally got to keep everything. We find instruction and guidance from the philosopher Locke, who said:

> *The fruit or venison which nourishes the wild Indian, who knows no enclosure, and is still a tenant in common, must be his, and so his, i.e., a part of him, that another can no longer have any right to it, before it can do any good for the support of his life. . . . Thus this law of reasons makes the deer that Indian's who hath killed it; 'tis allowed to be his goods who hath bestowed his labour upon it, though before it was the common right of every one.*[14]

Even today, there are native Americans, aboriginal Canadians and many other people throughout the world who must feed themselves and their families from the wildlife resource.[15] In these situations, providing for human ownership of wildlife, based upon a variety of legal theories (such as property law, the law of necessity, natural laws, legal realism, etc.) is important. Rights for people who demonstrate these particular needs should never be debated.

Sustainability of populations, however, can be debated because the well-being of other humans, including *future* generations (who are unborn and cannot argue their interests), is also important. Think about it: many people today would like to have seen the passenger pigeon, the Labrador duck, the Carolina parakeet, the Townsend bunting, or other species – now extinct. These losses are a true deprivation of society's rights, *today*. Clearly, people today are justified in wanting to have argued (vicariously) in the 1800s, that excessive hunting and habitat destruction would be depriving people of their use and enjoyment of the wildlife resource 100 years later.

Problems with the Evolution of Wildlife Laws

Attempting to classify wildlife law has never been done without returning to political and social debate. Part of the reason comes from the political irresponsibility and unmanageable behavior of the animals. Their behavior is, as Herman Melville stated, "like that of a migratory fowl that in its flight never heeds when it crosses a frontier."[16] This is what sparks the interest. Wildlife, by definition, is elusive. If you want control of wildlife (whether or not you should) it has to be chased – often great distances, and caught. As a result, whenever wildlife law and

---

14 Locke, *Second Treatise of Government* at 30-31.

15 In my own family, my grandfather homesteaded the plains of northern Montana. Many times he hunted and fed his hungry family deer, antelope, and jackrabbits. This is the way things were – laws or not. No one argued with him – regulators were feeding their own families the same way.

16 H. Melville, Billy Budd and Other Tales 26 (1979).

policy is established, different political jurisdictions have a responsibility to understand and consider wildlife needs (and laws) of bordering jurisdictions. This is a shared responsibility. The international legal principle of being a "good neighbor" (which principle does exist in law) has never been required more; nor has it ever been founded on such strong ethical considerations.

Under English common law, the property rights of private individuals relative to wild animals were never absolute. In England, there were at least three qualified categories (and these arose because people established "fences" or boundaries but wildlife – by definition – are not tamed or domesticated; they do not stay in one place; they continue to cross property lines). These were the three (qualified) categories:

(1) man's limited property right by virtue of having reclaimed and industrialized the animals, by his "art, industry or education";

(2) property rights based on the inherent, natural ability of wild animals to either remain on the land, or leave as they please (in which case the right vanished); and

(3) a property right to control wild animals by hunting, taking, or training them, exclusive of other neighbors.

As these categories once again demonstrate, historical rights over wildlife were secondary to principles of land ownership. Wildlife and land ownership are so intertwined that hunting rights even became easements, restrictions, reservations, or entitlements on land. Today, many European (and North American) governments continue to emulate land title principles whenever sorting out wildlife and hunting rights. These rights, based on private property rights and whatever else *Wildlife Acts* and other related laws (such as *Criminal Codes*) so declare, are important to all of society, including landowners. The implementation of these laws create several common disputes over wild animals.[17] These disputes often become the focus of heated litigation.

Again, the earliest wildlife law principles arose in some cases (e.g., Justinian) 1400 years ago. Through the centuries, they have evolved from custom to convention, and from convention to law. Yet, writers seldom stopped to evaluate the changing mores of society, *in the context of* man's needs today, and how these needs relate to the wildlife resource, today. This evaluation is a required imperative; a vital prerequisite in diagnosing wildlife law. Like it or not, today's laws are based on early statutes (or interstitial common law), which were in turn based on complex conventions, which, in turn, were based on very early (and

[17] The parties to the disputes may include hunters v. hunters; governments v. ranchers; governments v. hunters; hunters v. landowners; landowners v. society (at large); society v. hunters (at large); etc.

mostly survival-based) customs of man. It is needless to say the ethics of human beings and our several needs vis à vis the wild creature have changed drastically. For example, early arguments supported the theory that prosperity depended upon security of property.[18] To realize this security, it was necessary for the early settlers (of North America) to deal with the wild animals and the scary environment, which presented a "frightful solitude, impenetrable forests or sterile plains, stagnant waters and impure vapours; such [was] the earth when left to itself."[19] How times have changed.

The Justification For Hunting[20] – The Chase

Ultimately, the *chase* principle is the quintessence of the whole *"man v. wildlife"* issue. The chase principle is fundamental to understanding hunting and critical to a comprehension of the *man v. animal* ethical debate. It is often the dispositive factor in deciding of property rights. It is (as lawyers call it) the *sine qua non*.

The chase is a principle that historically (and even today) has allowed society to condone, excuse, or forgive the taking or killing of wildlife. Antithetically, when the chase principle is deserted, so will society's acceptance of hunting be dropped. Hunting for sport will never survive as an activity without a fair chase.[21] Except for purposes of survival, there will be no other thread of fairness that supports, intergenerationally, the practice of sport hunting. When the chase is eliminated, sport hunting will belong to a crowd of selfish Nimrods.

According to early cases, a completed chase – such as hunting or running an animal down – gave property rights to man.[22] Today, some

---

[18] See Carol Rose, "Given-ness and Gift: Property and the Quest for Environmental Ethics," 24 *Environmental Law* 1, 2-3 (1994).

[19] Rose, id. at 2, n.3, quoting Jeremy Bentham, "Analysis of the Evils Which Result from Attacks upon Property," in *The Theory of Legislation* 70 (Oceana ed. 1975).

[20] Incidentally, there are several reasons why hunting as an activity is justified; reasons such as the tremendous funding efforts that sportsmen and women have sacrificed to contribute to the sustainability of the resource.

[21] One of our modern environmentalists, the land-ethic promoter Aldo Leopold, also enjoyed hunting. As one would expect, Leopold "learned the ethics of the chase and the value of wildlife from his father, who was a sportsman/hunter when game was plentiful in the Midwest, prior to the turn of the century. Nonetheless, [Aldo} and his brothers were schooled in hunting behaviour, restraint, moderation, and subtlety, a reverence for the species hunted." Robert A. McCabe, *Aldo Leopold: The Professor* 124 (1978).

[22] Cases such as Pierson v. Post, 3 Cai. R. 175 (N.Y. Sup. Ct. 1805); State v. Shaw, 65 N.E. 875 (1902); Dapson v. Daly, 257 Mass. 195, 153 N.E. 454 (1926).

argue this rights-based argument is vulnerable because the chase principle found justification when there was no huge disparity between the talents of man and animal. To prove the point, evolutionary thinkers believed man actually evolved from fish or animals;[23] at one point in time, arguably, there could have been complete parity in the chase (man and wildlife chasing each other). Whether or not one believes in evolution, it was historically true that early man and animals chased each other for their food. A matter of life and death.

When we consider the hunting situation today, however, we find modern apparatus very different. Scoped rifles with high velocity projectiles and modern (baited and scented) fishing gear, favor man in such a way that it more often than not leaves the fair chase question only on the minds of ethically thinking people (but no-one else). The re-institution of archery or muzzle loading is the vindication for the chase; it might also be human's apologetic response to the unfairness issue associated with modern high powered rifles, decoys, and the lack of the chase.

Even when the principle of chase found historical use, it never applied to those who hunted fish. Only in a sense of mythology could one envision chasing fish underwater. Fishermen, especially commercial fishermen, using nets or set-lines, chase nothing.[24] They sit and wait; the majority of fish silently entangle in the nets. Therefore, in most hunting or fishing situations today, there is less and less labor in the chase. Times have changed and some feel the laws have blindly and lazily proceeded in ethical ignorance. Hunting, after all, has a very special legal meaning and it must be explored.[25] When the chase principle is honored in hunting situations today, the government is bound by statutory and common law to grant ownership rights to the hunter.[26]

[23] These writers have never addressed how man (as opposed to animals) received his "conscience." This seems to be a critical oversight because the parity principle of the chase should be analyzed against the physical, mental, and even spiritual talents and characteristics of the objects being chased.

[24] This is not to deny the fact that commercial fishermen do work very hard; vis-a-vis other fishermen, the rights of hard workers increase even more.

[25] The legal (statutory) definition of the word "hunt" is still based on a question of fairness and ethics. For example, the verb "hunt," by law, contains a distinct mental element – deserving, quite frankly, of *Criminal Code* defences; in fact, "hunt" means a person – *stalks* or *pursues* or *lies in wait* or *worries* an animal. Quite clearly, the legislators expect that wild animals will be pursued in the wild; man thinks about the hunt, applies himself, sweats and struggles, burns midnight oil, and executes the hunt.

[26] Incidentally, hunters still perform the final legal act of transferring ownership: affixing a tag or mark on the animal.

Difficulties with Ownership Concepts

Today, one acquires wildlife ownership through privileges granted by the government. The wildlife resource however belongs to all people. For those property owners who misinterpret their ownership rights in this "commons" asset, their attention should turn again to the primitive Roman law, which disallowed a property right in wildlife. For example, remember the concept of *res nullius?* Again, this legal principle means certain things are never supposed to have an owner. Wild birds, fish, and wild animals belong to this category. Even the earliest common laws held that property rights were qualified with wild animals because the animals, being wild, could and would leave. When this happened, the transient property right left also. Hence, by Roman or common law,[27] "wildlife" is expected to remain autonomous, independent, and sovereign. Interestingly, this legal principle is diametrically opposite today's property law concepts (the popular axiom that possession fulfills 9/10ths of the law? Actually, if the "1/10th" prevents the absolute ownership of wild, as opposed to domestic, animals, then the theory becomes acceptable based on the old common law theory of *ratione impotentiae*).

Ownership concepts are tricky. When early man acquired rights in wildlife, initial legal writers tried to justify this, again, by calling upon property law concepts. Centuries ago it was acceptable for man to develop the land and therefore carve his ownership portion from nature, including whatever wildlife had to be taken. The contemporary view is arguably different because social needs have changed; the new push in society is to protect the environment. Principles of biodiversity encourage the equitable balance of all species in any given area; these principles also promote the right of wildlife to continue to live isolated from man. For the benefit of humans, biodiversity suggests wildlife be left alone; that there be a right of secluded reality; a sense of existence in a natural domain. From a rational perspective, man's preservation of wildlife benefits wildlife (if living is good); more significantly, biodiversity is good for present and future generations of humankind.[28] Unlike centuries past, today's environmental goals are inimical to the legal theory that man needs to advance a claim upon wildlife for the promotion of his personal property rights. Personal property, as a substantive law subject, has very little application in up-to-date wildlife issues.

---

[27] The theory of *ratione impotentiae* (by reason of inability/impotence).

[28] This is because biodiversity promotes the richness and quality of natural genetic variations, variations which exist within and between species of animals, including man. Humans prefer this genetic richness and benefit in many ways from it.

The legal argument, that "possession is 9/10ths of the law" is hard to apply to our wild animals, not to mention the balance of our world's unbridled and puzzling environment. For the environment, which encompasses and protects wildlife, scientists still have not reached consensus on major, fundamental, issues.[29] This is frustrating. Why, then, seek to "possess" something that (a) we do not understand, (b) is a resource belonging to everyone by the law of nature, (c) is something we can never accurately price or manage, (d) leads to basing our resource decisions on expert witnesses who disagree with each other, and then, (e) attempt to be ethically fair to future generations of people who will most surely value any declining resource far more than we do?

Accordingly, certain statements can soon be expected from the public regarding ownership of wildlife. First, personal property or other legal rules should only apply when those rules champion the ethics of society. Those ethics increasingly call into question the exploitation of land and habitat, with consequential negative effects on the species. The facts are: human numbers are increasing and wildlife numbers are generally decreasing. Second, hunting for sport – to survive (and it does have its benefits[30]) – must be done on the basis of a fair chase. This is to say sport hunting might require some personal introspection to dust off the ethical cobwebs. Third, those who now wish to assist in *or* detract from the preservation of wildlife must remember it is a commons resource – owned by society at large, placed in the hands of the government as trustee. Finally, we must not only remember our posterity, we must equitably forecast its resource needs.

Arguments can easily be made to encourage the passage of new wildlife laws based these premises.[31] Laws protecting wildlife are being passed worldwide. In the United States, for example, the progress is fast paced – much faster than Canada. Their *Endangered Species Act* has recently passed its 20th anniversary.[32] And the bald eagle, gray whale,

---

[29] These issues include acid rain, global warming, forest management, and several others.

[30] For example, the (U.S.) federal duck stamp sales have generated close to $500 million. The money has been used to acquire millions of acres of wetlands.

[31] For background reading, see Roger L. DiSilvestro, *The Endangered Kingdom: The Struggle to Save America's Wildlife* (1989); Peter Matthiessen, *Wildlife in America* (1987). For more assistance, reference can be made to several organizations, including the World Wildlife Fund, the Sierra Club, the Environmental Defense Fund, Defenders of Wildlife, the National Wildlife Federation, the National Audubon Society, the Wildlife Managment Institute, and several others in the United States and Canada.

[32] *Endangered Species Act of 1973*, 16 U.S.C. ss. 1531-43 (as. am.).

and peregrine show great promise of returning to healthy numbers.[33] There are other types of powerful federal legislation[34] and, although there is debate regarding the effectiveness of such laws, endangered species laws start the scheme whereby the wildlife resource is prioritized by legislators. Today, it is becoming more common for states to duplicate protection for wildlife in their own constitutions.[35] These preservation efforts exist, and are encouraging, in the international arena.[36]

Because of this progress, there is a pressing need to update wildlife legislation – particularly in Canada. This clarity of legislative position will assist jurists and legislators who at present must rely on archaic case law like *Pierson v. Post*[37] to figure out where society's priorities are *vis-à-vis* the resource. Clear legislation will also assist the hunters and fishermen to interpret those increasing occurrences when pursuit, occupation, and possession of wildlife become heated disputes (and they do).

---

[33] In fact, four species have recovered such that they no longer need the Act's protection and 17 others have been upgraded from endangered to a less serious threatened status. *U.S. Fish & Wildlife Service News, Release 94-11.*

[34] Such as the *Eagle Protection Act,* 16 U.S.C. ss. 668 (as. am. to now include the golden eagle); *Lacey Act,* 16 U.S.C. s. 701; 18 U.S.C. s. 42 (as. am.); *Migratory Bird Treaty Act,* 16 U.S.C. ss. 703 *et seq.* (as. am.); *Wild Horse and Burro Act,* 16 U.S.C. s. 1331 (as. am.); *Marine Mammal Protection Act,* 16 U.S.C. ss. 1361 *et seq.* (as. am.) and several others.

[35] Article XLI of the Constitution of Massachusetts has codified respect for the safekeeping and conservation of the wildlife resource:
Full power and authority are hereby given and granted to the general court to prescribe for wild or forest lands retained in a natural state for the preservation of wildlife and other natural resources and lands for recreational uses, such methods of taxation as will develop and conserve the forest resources, wildlife and other natural resources and the environmental benefits of recreational lands within the commonwealth.
More important, the state of New York has a "forever wild" clause in her constitution; one which is *self-executing.* This means there is no other act of the legislators required to enforce the constitutional provision. This is the essence of (Article XIV):
The lands of the state, now owned or hereafter acquired, constituting the forest preserve as now fixed by law, shall be forever kept as wild forest lands. They shall not be leased, sold or exchanged, or be taken by any corporation, public or private, nor shall the timber thereon be sold, removed or destroyed.

[36] Witness the *Convention on International Trade and Endangered Species of Wild Flora and Fauna,* 27 U.S.T., T.I.A.S. 8249; *Convention on the (High Seas),* 17 U.S.T. 5969; *Convention on Nature Protection and Wildlife Preservation in the Western Hemisphere,* 56 Stat. 1354; and several other conventions on fisheries, polar bears, ets.

[37] Referred to, *supra* note 23.

Rearranging Thoughts to a New Paradigm

Morality aside,[38] if there is a single premise upon which the modern legislative drafters are being pushed, it might be this: redefine principles of wildlife law as if wildlife received a self-reliant and independent heritage. Our society has already passed animal rights' protection statutes, some of which may go too far (man's priorities must be always sorted out). Still wildlife's inheritance (wherever it came from) and its physical creation ends up assimilating the same characteristics of humans. For example, animals breathe and drink water; they have and use the voluntary/involuntary muscle groups; wildlife has amazing maternal bonds; animals engage in planning exercises; animals seem to have certain desires shared by humans, etc. Thus, an expulsion of archaic property law principles can be encouraged – as long as it is rational. Society must decide.[39]

Historically, it seems, humans were led to draw enchanted correlations between wildlife and man – on the basis of comparing aspects of physiology. As a case in point, the function of certain wildlife suggests they possess supernatural attributes; for example, the chameleon. The chameleon's ability to change colors is astonishing.[40] Many wild animals (whales and chimpanzees, for example) possess incredible physical and emotional characteristics, such as methods of communication that approach aspects of humanness. Even at the "low" end of the scale (boars I presume), wild animals possess attributes that clearly transcend the property law definition (for example, boars wake, sleep, procreate, etc.). Perhaps these features of homo sapiens should give wildlife stronger legal rights; the argument that even *trees* should have

---

[38] Philosophically, it is important to respect wildlife *regardless* of the morals issue. This is because (1) values should be protected whether they are moral values or not; (2) promoting wildlife will generally enrich the quality of the human existence (a selfish but very important perspective; one based on morals but also on other things, e.g., values of biodiversity); (3) respecting wildlife will increase social harmony – because of the strong values held by other humans *vis-à-vis* the resource and our desire to be liked and be happy (as opposed to vice versa); (4) focusing efforts on certain wildlife, e.g., endangered species, is highly value driven (and moral based). For further reading, see Peter Carruthers, *The Animals Issue: Moral Theory in Practice* (1992). See also Tom Regan, *The Case for Animal Rights* (1984) and Peter Singer, *Practical Ethics* (1979).

[39] For further reading, see Von Ihering, *Law as a Means to an End*, 20 (1924).

[40] One is tempted to wonder if the same ability in humans would avoid problems of discrimination.

legal standing is well known and has already been made by powerful thinkers.[41]

Physiology is not the only noteworthy comparison. Some wild animals have incredible psychology and intelligence. The dolphins are the classic model (aquatic mammalian intelligence is the subject of many writings). Philosophers often seem afraid to make mammalian comparisons, but even if one switches from wildlife to a "lesser" form of nature, ants, the intelligence in these insects is *still* marvelous. A study of the battlefield of two competing ant tribes best illustrates their high degree of social structure. For example, the way ants clash with each other in battle suggests "rational" scheming and plotting. When the ant tribes enter combat, each side has "officer" ants who give orders to the "fighter" ants. When the war is over, the losing tribe of ants is "compelled by the victors to work [for the winning tribe]."[42] But if one were to argue for stronger rights for wildlife, is this rational?[43] If preservation of wildlife is good, the answer is yes. Few would argue that animals are incapable of considering issues of self-preservation – not in the perspective of heated moments of interspecies self-defense, or intraspecies rivalries. Instead, reference can be made to the fact that wildlife might feel life in their bodies; but they do not know life[44] and can not generally plan to avoid death. Animals do not comprehend the future. They do not understand the process of aging or entrapment. They cannot contemplate the possibility of acting in such a way as to cause their associates to "feel good" or satisfied. Wildlife has no ability to place a value on the preservation of their family (instinctively, however, this is often done); wildlife do not think about rejoicing with their progeny as humans do. Thus, wildlife can not make "right or wrong" decisions relative to sustainability and the future, or anything else that requires rational thought. These facts, coupled with goals of preservation, militate in favor of establishing an agent; a protector, an advocate. Ultimately, it is legislators who assume the role (and the risk) of making these decisions. But, for wildlife, an agent is necessary to make representations as legislators make vital decisions by passing laws which are critical to the sustainable future of wildlife – statutory decisions such as

---

[41] The classic statement about standing comes from Stone, *Should Trees Have Standing? Towards Legal Rights for Natural Objects*, 45 S. Cal. L. Rev. 450 (1972). For a case that developed this idea, see Mr. Justice Douglas' dissenting opinion in *Sierra Club v. Morton*, 405 U.S. 727 (U.S. Supreme Court 1972). Actually, the opinion of Blackmun, J. (who would also allow standing) is more realistic (405 U.S. 727 at 755-760).

[42] See Von Ihering, *supra* note 40.

[43] Again, see the references regarding standing at *supra* note 42.

[44] See Von Ihering, *supra* note 40.

endangered species protection, habitat preservation, prohibiting commercialism in wildlife, etc.

In short, it is analytically reasonable to better understand – and accordingly, better protect, this wildlife resource. Hence, where traditional property principles in wildlife are obsolete and illegitimate, they should be corrected (such as early concepts that man should destroy wild creatures without cause, or that, based on property concepts, man should control or keep wildlife for pleasure, or that mercenary hunters got to keep the wildlife). These concepts are based on a rationality that has generally outlived its significance by hundreds of years.[45] Conversely, early property concepts that are helpful to modern society should be safeguarded. Some of these concepts come from Roman law (Justinian) and English common law; concepts that wildlife rights are actually *privileges* maintained in common for all people, and that changing mores will see positive laws enacted to restrain unprincipled and unsporting exploitation of the resource. Indeed, the law of *ferae naturae* has other valuable applications that continue to assist us in resolving property issues such as capturing underground oil, gas, and water.[46] In fact, if any property principle, whether "old" (*res nullius*) or "new" (such as the tragedy of the commons) assists in keeping wild aspects tied to property concepts, it is good.

Admittedly, the law relating to ownership of wildlife is rather complicated. But the answers to complicated wildlife questions become easier to acknowledge as resources become harder to find.

---

[45] Assuming it was rational in the first place.

[46] By analogy, the principle of *ferae naturae* continues to solve several natural resource disputes. Cf. *Westmoreland & Cambria Natural Gas Co. V. DeWitt*, 18 A. 724 (Pa. 1889); *Trinidad Asphalt Co. v. Ambard* [1899] A.C. 594; *U Po Naing v. Burma Oil* (1929) 56 L.R. 140; *Barnard v. Monongahela Gas Co.*, 64 A. 801 (1907); *Michael Borys v. C.P. Railway*, [1953] A.C. 217.

Editor's Note:
Wildlife Management in Quebec: QF's Vision

The French culture in North America has had a close association with wildlife. The settlement of this continent is unthinkable without French explorers, without the Coureurs de Bois that scouted the land, the voyageurs that skillfully navigated its many rivers, the Métis hunters, settlers, traders, and politicians that for some time made French dominant in the centre of this continent, or the seafaring Acadians and their sad fate. The wilderness sustained these people. The cuisine of Quebec, Acadia, and Louisiana has strong, regional elements of "wild" food, a reflection of the hard life of French settlers, their ingenuity in living off a harsh land and the indomitable, life-affirming spirit of these outgoing people. To this day French North Americans have a close, "earthy" attachment of things wild. This is reflected in the sheer level of participation in hunting and fishing. Above all, the organized activities in the province of Quebec on behalf of wildlife is unmatched in North America. Civil law in Quebec is based on the Napoleonic Code. It is difficult to tell if that has anything to do with the remarkable grass root involvement with wildlife and its management. Professor Yves Jean describes here some of the current concerns and actions. It was a French Canadian prime minister, Sir Wilfred Laurier, who was instrumental in creating, with U.S. President Theodore Roosevelt, the conditions that led, before and during the First World War, to a continental set of policies and wildlife treaties that characterize the North American system of wildlife conservation to this day.

Wildlife Management in Quebec

QF's Vision

Yves Jean[1]

Introduction

Since 1945, the *Fédération québécoise de la faune* (FQF) has played a major role in wildlife conservation. Its objective has been to make as many hunters and sport fishermen as possible aware of their obligations to wildlife in Quebec. To achieve this objective, the FQF has an operating structure that reaches the majority of Quebec localities through more than 300 local affiliate associations involved in hunting, fishing, and conservation. These associations are divided into 10 regional associations throughout Quebec, with a total of more than 250 000 members. The primary objective of the FQF is to conserve wildlife and wildlife habitats. The conservation and enhancement of wildlife resources involve using these resources in a rational manner. In plain words, we must draw only on the interest, not on the capital. Wildlife management in Quebec or elsewhere must be based on this fundamental principle.

As Geist (this volume) pointed out, the North American wildlife management system is unique in that, with few exceptions, it views wildlife resources as public property. Current legislation is based on this basic principle, as we can see in Quebec's *Loi sur la conservation et la mise en valeur de la faune* (Wildlife Conservation and Enhancement Act). Note that the commercialization of game meat is prohibited.

In Quebec, regulations are based on the following, listed in order of priority: (1) protection of endangered species, (2) subsistence activities, (3) sporting activities, and (4) commercial activities.

These few basic elements are at the foundation of the philosophy underlying the positions of the Quebec wildlife users represented in this paper. We are aware that such a management philosophy is not easy to apply; one aspect of our mission is consultation and cooperation, acting as "watchdog" of the system. People should take a great part in wildlife management. A few examples of the positions of users represented by the FQF, and the reasons for these positions, will be discussed below.

---

[1]Former Vice-President, Quebec Wildlife Federation.

This paper will focus on two major themes, namely, the commercialization of wildlife and the privatization of land. To properly understand the Quebec context of land, two important events that occurred in Quebec over the past 12 years must be addressed: the disbanding of private clubs in 1978, and the trend toward privatization since 1985. The disbanding of clubs and the development of an internationally unique management system, namely the Controlled Exploitation Zones (CEZs) or *Zones d'Exploitation Contrôlées* (ZECs) are discussed later.

The second major element, privatization, follows an international trend in thinking and in management, and in this sense Quebec is no exception even in the area of wildlife management. A brief summary of the government's approach over the past five years will clarify the context. In 1985, the new government commissioned a report, known as the Leblond Report, which was to guide government policy on wildlife management. The Leblond Report, tabled in 1987, contained several recommendations specifically geared to privatizing management; that is why it is referred to as a "privatization operation."

Several of the Leblond Report's recommendations troubled us at the time. The recommendations on promoting and developing the commercialization of wildlife, and on new land distribution, caused us to express certain doubts about the future of our wildlife. The next year, the Leblond Report was followed by the Quebec Wildlife Summit, which brought together workers in the field of wildlife and representatives of various socioeconomic groups. The Summit's objective was to reach a consensus on wildlife commercialization and land privatization policies. The outcome of the Summit was the creation of sub-committees which have had some interesting results for the future of our wildlife.

Commercialization of Wildlife

Issues surrounding the commercialization of wildlife unquestionably provide striking examples of a delicate subject that has always generated intense discussion. Even though in Quebec we do not have many experiences in what we call game farming and game ranching, these issues were always important. Two specific Quebec issues were (1) the commercialization of game captured in the wild (for example, freshwater fish and caribou), and (2) domestic breeding for commercialization (for example, brook trout). Hunting and fishing associations within the FQF have always strongly opposed wildlife commercialization. The FQF has always supported subsistence activities and sport catches as the best methods of managing wildlife.

Wildlife is a traditional, and even today, a subsistence resource. It is not necessary to list the species already extinct or disappearing because of human interference, whether through intensive harvesting or habitat deterioration. However, present-day examples show us how fragile this resource is and that, without severe controls and rational management, some resources could be severely endangered.

The commercialization of wildlife is considered to be a threat to wildlife populations for two basic reasons in addition to the destruction of habitat. It easily opens the door, first to direct over-harvesting, and second to increased poaching by unscrupulous and profit-hungry individuals. It leads to over-harvesting because, in many cases, we lack knowledge about the biology of highly coveted species and set commercial quotas that are later difficult to change; in the end, socioeconomic interests take priority over sport-oriented management of the resource. We, on the other hand, believe that setting limits, controlling catches, and educating users foster flexible resource management suited to the animal populations. Commercialization generally encourages poaching, because a commercial supply involves delays and costs that poaching often bypass.

We believe that the philosophy underlying commercial harvesting differs sharply from that of sport fishing and hunting. Commercialization implies a harvest at any cost, because jobs are on the line. In most cases, governments place socioeconomic priorities ahead of sustainable resource use. It seems to be more difficult for a government to reduce commercial catch quotas than to control the regulations governing sport fishing and hunting. Furthermore, governments are obliged to compensate commercial fisheries even after they have profited from the collective heritage.

There can be subtleties to the issue. The commercialization of wildlife involving the use of entire individuals from chosen wildlife species for commercial gain differs, in our opinion, from sport hunting and fishing involving the harvesting of "by-products" of sport catches. Thus, the "recycling of wildlife by-products," which could be described as a type of commercialization, becomes an effect of rational and recreational use of the resource and not an end in itself, whereas in the case of industrialization, the objective is financial gain made by a company from the "crude" wildlife product. An example of by-product recycling would be the use of deer hides by natives. Other examples are discussed below.

Freshwater Commercial Fisheries

In Quebec, wildlife users represented within the FQF have already voiced their categorical support for banning all freshwater commercial fishing in Quebec. Why? Because evidence shows that commercial fishing in Quebec's freshwater lakes and rivers is generally harmful to fish populations and fish habitats over time, and also because sport fishing generates hundreds of millions of dollars and involves almost 1.2 million users.

Take the case of Lac St-Pierre, which is a major target in the government's annual fishing plan. Lac St-Pierre is located between the major urban centres of Quebec City and Montreal, and is frequented by almost 80% of the population within two hours driving distance. In 1987, 16 000 sport fishermen fished in this lake, and sport-related activities generated economic spinoffs of $5 million. By contrast, 42 commercial fisheries generated economic spinoffs of approximately $2.9 million.

Let us examine the demographic condition of some species, for example, the yellow sturgeon. Biologists from two departments, the *Ministère du Loisir, de la Chasse et de la Pêche* (MLCP) (Now called *Le Ministère de L'Environnement et de la Faune* [MEF]; the Wildlife Department) and the *Ministère de l'Agriculture, des Pêcheries et de l'Alimentation Québec* (MAPAQ) (Agriculture Department), agree that the yellow sturgeon population is over-exploited. The 1987-88 fishing plan announced reductions in commercial quotas, given the precarious situation of the species. The FQF clearly asked that drastic measures be taken, namely, that both types of fishing be prohibited in this waterway. For socioeconomic reasons, this action was not taken.

Perch is another example. For several years, we have witnessed a considerable decline in the size of the individuals caught, which is an indication that this species is subject to heavy catches. Experts claim that the perch population is not endangered, although they admit it is heavily used. The FQF has already pointed out that the high rate of exploitation threatens to seriously affect perch populations in the short and middle terms. A division between sport and commercial fishing was proposed, with priority to sport fishing. But what does "priority" mean, when commercial fisheries take their greatest percentage of perch during the spawning season? The FQF asked for immediate action to manage the wildlife resource by prohibiting commercial catches of this species prior to May 20. Commercial catches during the spawning period also contribute to the destruction of water plant communities in which other species spawn. Once again, the answer lies in socioeconomic imperatives. What, therefore, does the future hold for the yellow sturgeon and the perch of Lac St-Pierre, and for other aquatic species in the same predicament elsewhere in Quebec?

Caribou Slaughters

Caribou in northern Quebec are the subject of another debate in wildlife management in Quebec. High densities of caribou herds, estimated at approximately 400 000 to 600 000 head in the late 80s, as well as the mass drowning (10 000) in 1984, have led to the fear that the habitat is overpopulated and that these populations will decline. Very quickly, this fear prompted proposals for a management plan involving the commercialization of caribou meat and by-products to stabilize the herd. For several years, harvest for sport and subsistence hunting and hunting in Labrador have remained at a maximum of 30 000 caribou annually. However, the province of Newfoundland slaughters caribou of the George River herd every year for commercial sale; some of this meat is sold in Quebec. Thus, this method of management was already operating, even though the matter was still being debated.

Several groups, including the FQF and native groups, question whether we adequately understand the dynamics of these herds, the technical problems involved in marketing these products, and the effects of commercialization on the poaching of caribou and other cervid species. At that time, the FQF asked the MLCP to maintain the status quo by placing its caribou meat commercialization experiment on hold. The FQF strongly recommended more detailed studies of the herds' growth. Moreover, the FQF asked the MLCP to develop an effective management plan to promote sport and subsistence hunting. In particular, the establishment of an outfitter network involving the native community was recommended.

Some questions regarding commercialization remained unanswered. How can population densities be kept stable when, at any moment, private investors (of the about $5 million required at that time) will be obliged to adjust their quota according to caribou population levels? Data in recent years indicate that the rate of growth has declined considerably, and that the population is showing signs of faltering. Will domestic and foreign (international) commercial markets readily accept a fluctuating supply? The FQF is ready to wager that the caribou is more likely to pay the price for stable commercial markets, and not the markets for stabilization of the herds.

White-tailed Deer Enclosures

In Quebec, there are about 20 producers raising deer in captivity (50 to 200 deer). The animals are normally slaughtered for a price between $500 and $1000. What are the reasons for this game farming, when the deer population is in good health? Our position regarding the raising of game species is that we should do it only for reintroducing species that are in difficulty.

The FQF does not support the position of some organizations concerning breeding wild game on farms. The aim – to breed game as in agriculture – raises a number of problems, including tampering with the genetic integrity of wildlife, diseases, and the threat to predators. Legislation in several provinces allows this practice, but several user federations or associations are not particularly pleased with the idea.

Brook Trout Farming

For 20 years, the FQF has firmly opposed the commercialization of brook trout, maintaining that such commercialization opened the door to poaching. In several regions of Quebec, stock is regularly poached. This wildlife species is the most important in terms of sport fishing. The size of specimens has decreased significantly almost everywhere in Quebec over the past few years.

Commercial rainbow trout farming was permitted from 1960, and in the early 1960s an association was created for the commercialization of brook trout. In 1974-75, the initial move toward commercialization was broadened to include the sale of fish from ponds. In 1978, the season for pond fishing was extended to 12 months a year, no permits required. A decade later, amendments to the responsibilities involved in the commercial development of brook trout allowed the MAPAQ, Quebec's Department of Agriculture and Fisheries, to control this species for consumer use. The MCLP remained responsible for developing seeding beds and fish ponds. In the fall of 1989, a new regulation under the authority of the MAPAQ was implemented to govern the operation of brook trout aquafarms, from the processing plant to delivery to stores. This regulation put an end to the protests of groups concerned about wildlife management.

In the first operation year (1989-90), 146 general permits were issued. According to current data, the MAPAQ gave only six processing permits for brook trout. The expected production for this year is about 50 tonnes of fish. The control methods utilize a bill or label. The bill, which must be on the final product, allows the selling of live trout from a producer to a processing plant. At this time, there is only one producer using the label and consequently allowed to sell for consumer use.

The recent development of brook trout production for consumer use had to meet certain departmental objectives. The MCLP said it wanted to increase production to counter a possible invasion of the Quebec market by foreign producers, to ensure a steady, year-round supply, and to optimize the socioeconomic spinoffs associated with human consumption. However, quality and a steady supply, as well as competitive pricing, remain the chief limits to adequate commercialization.

In the most developed regions, the numbers of this species, an important symbol in Quebec, have declined considerably over the past few years. Consequently, the FQF considers it more urgent to replenish stocks in Quebec's lakes than to commercially develop the "product" without regard for the habitat or biological growing conditions of brook trout. Despite its fierce opposition, the FQF has agreed to very carefully monitor the control mechanisms involved in this commercialization.

The future of wildlife management depends on full respect for a major principle: the relentless fight against poaching. We still think that the commercialization of brook trout opens the door to this scourge and therefore conflicts with conservation objectives. Of course, we will have to wait for statistics, if any, to fix our mind on this issue.

Wildlife Lands: How Effective is Privatization?

Wildlife lands are one of the most important underpinnings of wildlife resource management. A few years ago, the government issued a document entitled "*Les réserves fauniques et les pourvoiries, des territoires en évolution*" (Wildlife Reserves and Outfitters: Expanding Sectors). The "expansion" mentioned in this document seems channelled in a single direction. The intentions it expresses clearly indicate that, in most areas protected by wildlife reserve status and not suited to development, outfitters with exclusive rights would be favored as an alternative.

The aim was to significantly increase private sector involvement, both in terms of investment and management activities. Our members do not object to a delegation of authority for management activities and equipment. However, we were wary of the haste with which the government wished to turn the controlled lands (part of the wildlife reserves) over to outfitters. The FQF always demanded certain answers to certain questions. Is the business world's concept of profitability to be applied to harvesting activities? Will the recommendations of wildlife experts be respected when they propose restrictions on catches? Will the disposal of equipment or infrastructures enable the creation of private clubs? Will accessibility, education, rates, and reservation methods remain the same? And, more particularly, will we have a guarantee concerning the perpetuation of wildlife species? It is sometimes very difficult to maintain sound wildlife management principles when financial interests are at stake. Users are waiting to see how the relation between the business people and the government develops.

Controlled Exploitation Zones (CEZs)

The other form of delegation that exists in Quebec is the CEZ. We have always maintained a clear stand in this area: if management must be delegated, the FQF considers the CEZ as the best alternative.

In 1978, a government order made the CEZs official throughout Quebec. Organized into local associations, the CEZs became hunting and fishing areas managed by independent, non-profit organizations. The challenge was met, and the public immediately became involved in the associations as members or volunteer directors. With these structures in place, we could now hope that our wildlife heritage would be saved and conserved. It was important, both for the government and the public, that the organization and cooperation of CEZs be under the authority of responsible individuals from the community, dedicated to the cause. Quebec's controlled exploitation zones now cover more than 45 000 km^2 of wildlife lands, and almost 700 km of our best salmon rivers, distributed among 72 CEZs. There are 62 hunting and fishing CEZs, 9 salmon CEZs, and one waterfowl-hunting CEZ. These lands, visited by more than 250 000 Quebeckers, stand out not only in their splendor and vastness, but especially in the development of an avant-garde management method. It is the only hunting and fishing network completely managed by member users. Thus, all users are able to become members of the CEZ they frequent, entitling them to share in decisions concerning its management.

In the beginning, the principles underlying the establishment of CEZs primarily aimed to increase their recreational use by a greater number of people, to control lands where the supply and demand for wildlife may have been unbalanced, and to provide the public with accessible lands located in relative proximity to urban centres or rural communities.

In 1990, to optimize the efforts of volunteer managers, the *Fédération québécoise des gestionnaires de ZECs,* the Department of Recreation, Game and Fish (MLCP) and the *Fondation de la faune du Québec,* signed an agreement involving a $2.5 million investment over a five-year period for the conservation and enhancement of wildlife habitat in the CEZs.

The work of volunteer managers in Quebec's 72 CEZs provides an annual saving of more than $2 million. This highly laudable gesture not only contributes to the self-sufficiency of the CEZs, but also to their growth. CEZ funds, obtained from various sources, are all reinvested in different sectors of the CEZ concerned, such as in land development, wildlife protection and conservation, roadway improvements, and construction and maintenance of reception centres.

The MCLP wanted to increase participation by the CEZs and outfitters. Our members were very clear. They demanded that the MLCP require and make public a management plan for CEZs and outfitters. The MCLP must ensure follow-up of this plan and provide the biologists required so that these managers create and follow a genuine wildlife resource management plan.

The MLCP had two objectives regarding the privatization of our wildlife heritage: (1) to ensure that the new network consisted of reserves in keeping with the new trends, and (2) that this network be substantially reduced to enable greater rationalization of government activity and increased participation by private enterprise in wildlife management. After a few years and pressure brought to bear by the FQF, the privatization operation was downsized considerably compared to the initial plans. After the aforementioned document on land development was submitted, hunting and fishing associations from every part of Quebec submitted about 500 briefs. All of these briefs opposed the initial plan to alter wildlife reserves. The Canadian Wildlife Federation also submitted a brief supporting the demands of Quebec's users.

It is appropriate to speak of "land readjustments" now – few portions of the lands (wildlife reserves) have been abandoned; instead, services have changed hands. In this respect, one positive aspect must be understood – the priority given to turning services over to non-profit organizations. The small sections of land relinquished were turned over to the CEZs, which complies with the positions of the FQF discussed previously. The latest example is a portion of the Kipawa Reserve, which was used to create the new Kipawa CEZ. The FQF is still watchful; some events can occur on a "micro-territorial" level.

The debate over the privatization of management still enables us to reopen discussion on certain questions. We can undoubtedly ask: What is the government's role in managing wildlife? What are the government's responsibilities to wildlife? Must the government's role be increasingly eliminated? Are the users the most appropriate managers of the resource, like in France? Obviously, social, political, and economic imperatives will always be with us, and will always demand consideration. Alone, the hunting and fishing industry generates economic spinoffs in Quebec in excess of 1.6 billion dollars. What strategy should we suggest to fairly distribute the weight of these imperatives, and to achieve sound management of wildlife resources? This, in our view, is the crux of the matter.

Conclusion

The topics mentioned above are the major ones in the future of wildlife management. The government must manage the resource because it is a collective right. But, at the same time, the user groups must share in wildlife management because they know the resource quite well. The wildlife users must share the cost, and I think they do, but government must make sure that the money it gets goes for wildlife purposes.

As an example, in Quebec the creation of the *Fondation de la Faune de Québec* allowed the government to preserve wildlife habitats, particularly on private lands. The FQF supported this from the beginning. For many years, the FQF has taken steps to obtain a permanent funding mechanism for the Fondation de la Faune de Québec. Members of the FQF passed a resolution at their 1986 annual meeting whereby $2, specifically earmarked to fund the *Fondation de la Faune de Québec* and not to enrich the provincial fund, would be added to and deducted from each hunting, fishing, and trapping license. In 1989, the Fondation recouped $1.7 million (85% of the revenues) and invested around $530 000 (48% of the expenses) in habitat and management projects.

The FQF also has its own foundation, the Fondation Héritage Faune (FHF). The FHF was created in 1980 and began operation in April 1987. Since that time, the FHF has given many M.Sc. scholarships of $2000 to graduate students in wildlife management, published one lithograph, and funded wildlife projects. It funded the "*Centre de production et de recherche sur la Ouananiche du lac St-Jean*" (The Ouananiche Production and Research Centre) for $10 500 over a three-year period; its objective is to restore the ouananiche population of this region. The FHF also spent $200 000 to rent 330 hectares of wet habitats on Lac St-Pierre (*Commune de la Baie de Febvre*) over a period of 21 years. The FHF acts as chief project manager, with the support of organizations like Ducks Unlimited, local corporations, and the MLCP. The annual budget of the FHF was, in the early 90s, around $180 000; from this, there was an annual revenue of $102 000, 90% of which comes from users through the Education and Security Program in Wildlife Conservation (PESCOF) courses.

The above examples show how the users invest financially in wildlife conservation. There are many other examples related to legislation and education programs, such as the habitat project of law (#15), which was incorporated in Quebec wildlife law (Chapter IV) in June 1988.

In conclusion, if we have to manage wildlife by way of privatization, we have to do it collectively (CEZs, PESCOF, foundations, etc.). We should take a closer look at joint management between government and the user groups and ask the following question: To what extent is wildlife management to be done by the government and/or by user groups?

Acknowledgements

I would like to thank the following organizations that sponsored the Calgary conference where this paper was presented: The Research and Study Commission of Quebec Wildlife Federation, the Canadian Wildlife Federation, and the Wildlife Heritage Fund. I would like to express my gratitude to Leo-Paul Quintal, Daniel Lacombe, and Daniel Vanier for their critical review of this paper and to Mrs. Lucille Gaudreault for typographical work.

Editor's Note: Yukon Land Claims and Wildlife Management: The Cutting Edge

The views of Native North Americans are vital to the conservation of wildlife, not only due to certain treaty rights, unextinguished claims to land, and aboriginal rights, but above all, to the deep cultural involvement with things wild. Slowly native people move towards self government and thus into a position of meaningful partnership in the political future of North America. This article gives some insight into the concerns of native people in the continent's North as they move towards exercising more control over things that really matter to them. Wildlife and fish are prominent in these concerns. Where native people gained political control over wildlife resources, as they did in the Northwest territories where Dr. Norman Simmons last served in the capacity of deputy minister responsible for environment, they have been exemplary guardians. May wildlife be a subject that draws us all closer together in the future.

Yukon Land Claims and Wildlife Management

The Cutting Edge

Norman M. Simmons and Gladys Netro

Perceptions of Wildlife Management – Gladys Netro

We Vuntut Gwitch'in, like other Yukon Indians, have interests in and rights to wildlife that derive from our title to lands and waters that sustain wildlife. These rights have always existed. They were not granted by government, and therefore cannot be taken away by government. Furthermore, we regard wildlife differently than governments do. We manage wildlife as communal property, which each harvesting group manages by consensus. Unlike government, we do not separate out research, management, and harvesting, or fish, migratory birds, big game, and forests, and deal with each as a compartment of renewable resource conservation (Osherenko 1988; Usher 1986). Our approach to the management of wildlife and other renewable resources is holistic rather than merely integrated (Savory 1988).

Before the days of treaties and Indian Agents, our leaders led by virtue of the fact that they had acquired the most knowledge about fish and wildlife and other resources necessary for the First Nation's well being and had demonstrated an ability to use this knowledge effectively. They led by consensus, receiving their mandate at community meetings such as those held at Klokut, near Old Crow. Even now in Old Crow, in spite of the dominant role of government in renewable resource management, the Chief gathers First Nation members together to discuss issues that affect our livelihood. Environmental concerns, including the health of wildlife populations, are central topics at these meetings. I recall that when an alarm was once raised by some First Nation members, who were finding an unusual number of dead birds after pesticide spraying near our village, the Chief led us in action that soon resulted in the termination of the spraying. He has also gained consensus to change our hunting patterns to protect breeding areas of fish and wildlife, and to change hunting and trapping areas of families to make the most of harvest while conserving the resource. All this initiative is unrelated to the centrally imposed legal requirements of government. This is our style of fish and wildlife management. An important feature is that under our system we all feel involved in the decisions that affect our lives.

Our way of fish and wildlife management changed abruptly with the advent of the gold rush in the late 1800s. The evolution of wildlife management in the Yukon then took a different path than it did in the Northwest Territories (McCandless 1985). Gold caused an avalanche of newcomers to the Yukon, with massive investment in communications, roads, and related services. Sport hunting became big business around the turn of the century. But the biggest changes came with the construction of the Alaska Highway in the early 1940s. Our influence on the management of natural resources declined sharply, and our efforts to continue our established practices were frustrated. For example, the Gwitch'in of Alaska and the Yukon faced new, uncontrollable competition for the Fortymile herd of caribou on which we always depended for food and clothing. Heavy harvests by these new hunters, who hunted from the Steese and Taylor highways (Scott et al. 1950; Davis et al. 1978) had the greatest impact on the Han Gwitch'in of Moose Hide and Eagle, Alaska. However, the effect rippled out to the Tetlit and Vuntut Gwitch'in of Fort McPherson, Northwest Territories, and Old Crow. We Vuntut Gwitch'in had always been part of a network of harvesters that included the Han and Tetlit Gwitch'in. We met annually to trade furs for basic supplies such as tea and sugar in the Blackstone area of the Yukon and to exchange information about fish and wildlife and other natural resources. The sharp decline of the Fortymile herd broke up this valuable network, and the annual meetings ended.

Since the days of the gold rush, we Gwitch'in have suffered the trauma of involuntary change and of trying to live in two different worlds: the world framed by our own culture, and the aggressively imposed world of the immigrant Canadians. Schools, laws, modern electronic communications, aircraft, roads, and Christianity have been compelling forces that have had a dramatic impact on the way we live. Our elders still urge us to cling to our culture; the new Yukoners sing the Siren's song that we must change and assimilate, or fail in this new world. Many of us did not have Ulysses' wax to plug our ears. We listened to the song and tried to change. The change has been stressful. We are only now learning how to live in both worlds at once. It is sad that it is we who are adapting to the immigrants' world; in general, they do not adapt to ours.

Once the Council of Yukon Indians was organized in 1973 as the aboriginal rights arm of the Yukon Native Brotherhood, the clash between the aboriginal system of renewable resource management and the dominant state system of the Yukon and federal governments became evident to anyone who read Yukon newspapers or listened to the radio. Conflicts over government management of traplines and fisheries have been especially bitter. It has been evident in the Yukon since the days of the Alaska Highway construction, as it is in the

Canadian provinces and the United States, that settlement and development of wild lands are givens. Society may agree to mitigate but not to eliminate impacts on natural renewable resources. It is equally evident to us that the state regards the Indian management system as transitory, and that government's role is to manage the transition (Usher 1986).

Norman Simmons

When I signed on as a Canadian Wildlife Service biologist and advisor to the Northwest Territorial Government's Game Division in 1966, I brought with me European notions of wildlife management rooted before the Norman Conquest of 1066 (McCandless 1985). These beliefs were cultivated by my American professors, who cited as their basic reference that wonderful guidebook by Aldo Leopold entitled *Game Management* (Leopold 1933). My non-native colleagues and I were comfortable with the knowledge that:

(1) Wildlife belongs to no one; it is held in trust for the people by the Crown and could be reduced to possession only with permits issued by the Crown.

(2) All citizens have equal access to wildlife on public lands.

(3) Government (the state) manages wildlife because of its sovereignty over wildlife habitat.

These teachings are in conflict with the beliefs of the aboriginal people of the North, mainly because of the Crown's role in the management of and control of access to wildlife, and the lack of consensus-building in the process that led to management decisions. However, no muscle-flexing by Inuit and First Nation or Dene individuals or organizations challenged my beliefs in the 60s, and, because I was a biologist and not a manager, I was able to vanish into the wilderness with untroubled conscience. Relations between the Canadian Wildlife Service, the Territorial Game Division, and the aboriginal people of the Territories were reasonably good, at least on the surface. Game law enforcement was relaxed because administrators of old realized the impracticality of imposing southern-style laws on native hunters and trappers. Furthermore, most active hunters and trappers who were not "status Indians" or Inuit held General Hunting Licenses (GHLs), which enabled them to hunt and fish as if they were Treaty 8 or 11 beneficiaries. Only a small part of the Territories was settled, and the fish and wildlife harvesting patterns of Dene and Inuit were little changed from the days of the Northwest Company. Because of the lack of legislation applying to Dene, Inuit, and GHL holders, law enforcement in the Northwest Territories was mainly directed at a relatively few non-native residents and at transients.

As a novice in the northern wilderness, I came to rely on an extended family of Mountain Indians out of Fort Norman to teach me how to behave in the Mackenzie Mountains. Most biologists and wildlife managers of this era and earlier similarly depended upon native people as teachers, as did the early fur traders and the gold seekers of the 18th and 19th centuries. Slowly, I learned about and developed a respect for their views of wildlife management as I accompanied them on hunts for moose and woodland caribou as part of my research.

When native political organizations became active in the early 1970s, this aboriginal system was forcefully promoted by the Dene Nation and the Inuit Tapirisat of Canada (summarized by Osherenko [1988] and Usher [1986]). I was able to maintain an academic's distance from the clash between the State and indigenous wildlife management systems (Usher 1986) until I descended from the biologist's ivory tower and became the chief wildlife manager for the Northwest Territories Government in 1975. Soon after I joined the newly formed Northwest Territories Wildlife Service, I became embroiled in a government response to a perceived decline in the Kaminuriak caribou herd that federal and territorial biologists attributed to overhunting by Inuit and Dene and to natural mortality (Simmons et al. 1979). We rejected protests by Inuit and Dene that our data were incorrect. After all, government data were gathered over a 30-year period and reports pointed convincingly to a decline. But caribou biologists themselves disagreed on the reasons for the low population estimates. Later, the Northwest Territories Wildlife Service's own biologists discovered that the native hunters were correct and that government figures had been much too low.

The positive results of this controversy over caribou management were the education of Government administrators and biologists about the advantages of co-management (Berkes et al. 1991; Osherenko 1988), and the implementation of information and education programs in the place of simple law enforcement. The co-management regime that the Kaminuriak caribou management debacle spawned, The Caribou Management Board, has been cited as one of the most successful in North America (Osherenko 1988). It brings together representatives from the Federal, Manitoba, Saskatchewan, and Northwest Territories Governments, and from Dene and Inuit communities, to manage the Beverly and Kaminuriak caribou herds.

But even in the Northwest Territoties, the full participation in the management of renewable resources by aboriginal people was not formally confirmed by the Federal government. As a matter of policy, the Territorial Government recognized Dene, Métis, and Inuit as co-managers of fish and wildlife, but legally the traditional role of the

Crown as sole trustee of renewable natural resources for all people of Canada prevailed.

The Solution: Land Claims

The current round of aboriginal rights or land claims negotiations between government and the Yukon Indian People, which began in 1986, seems to hold the most promise for reconciliation of differences between the indigenous and State systems of wildlife management. Four First Nation final Agreements, including the Vuntut Gwitch'in Final Agreement, have been ratified by the affected First Nations and approved by the Yukon Legislative Assembly. If these Agreements are passed by the parliament of Canada and become the law of the land, the system of wildlife management described in the Agreement could serve as a model for other jurisdictions in North America. It would correct some of the ills of systems now in place by taking a holistic approach to renewable resource management, by encouraging the participation of the public in management, and by confirming the right of Yukon First Nations to manage renewable resources on their own lands as set out in the Final Agreements.

In the past, treaties have been the preferred method of addressing the legal ambiguities surrounding the definition of aboriginal title. A result of the settlement of a 1973 Supreme Court of Canada decision (*Calder* v. *Attorney General of British Columbia*) was the renewal of the tradition of treaty-making in the form of comprehensive land claims. In 1973, the Minister of Indian Affairs and Northern Development announced that he was prepared to begin negotiations with the aboriginal peoples of the Canadian North (Indian Affairs and Northern Development 1987).

During subsequent land claims negotiations in the Northwest Territories and the Yukon, Government policy has reflected a willingness to decentralize and to devolve certain responsibilities to the communities in an effort to include aboriginal people in a more comprehensive public management system (Usher 1986). Some officials in the Northwest Territorial Government recommended that some elements of self-government be assumed by First Nation and Inuit organizations (Monaghan 1980).

The Inuvialuit Final Agreement, covering the western Arctic region of the Northwest Territories, was signed in 1984, making it the second comprehensive land claims agreement in the Canadian North after the James Bay and Northern Quebec Agreement of 1975 (Indian Affairs and Northern Development 1984; *Editeur officiel du Quebec* 1976). The agreement with the Tetlin Gwich'in in Fort McPherson, Northwest Territories, was signed in April 1992. An agreement was signed with the Tungavik Federation of Nunavut in the spring of 1993. The Yukon

Umbrella Final Agreement was signed in May 1993. Agreements with five First Nations, Champagne, Aishihik, Nacho Nyak Dun, Teslin Tinglit, and Vuntut Gwitch'in, were also signed in May 1993. Negotiators are optimistic that the Federal Government will soon ratify all agreements with Dene and Yukon First Nations and pass legislation needed to implement them.

Even before the agreements were signed in the Yukon, the Territorial Government had put in place certain elements of those agreements, such as the Yukon Fish and Wildlife management Board with half Government and half First Nation members, and had begun to encourage more participation by individual First Nations in wildlife management decisions. The Government was trying to treat First Nations as another level of government (H.J. Monaghan, pers. comm. 4 january, 1994). Parks Canada, the Yukon Government, and the Champagne and Aishihik First nations have signed memoranda of understanding to effect coordinated management of fish, wildlife, and their habitat in Kluane national park, thus taking steps toward the implemenetation of part of the Final Agreement.

In 1990, the Yukon Government and the First Nations received guidance and encouragement from the Supreme court of Canada in their deliberations on the role of First Nation people in fish and wildlife management. The Court accepted the defence of Ronald E. Sparrow, a Musquam Indian, that charges against him for violating the Fisheries Act in British Columbia were invalid because of Sparrow's aboriginal right to fish as guaranteed in the Constitution. In explaining its decision the Justices stated that aboriginal right to fish cannot be extinguished by the Fisheries Act, but only regulated by it. The Justices said that in regulating Government must first determine whether the legislation will result in interference with an existing aboriginal right and whether the limitation under law is unreasonable, whether it imposes undue hardship, and whether it denies aboriginal people their preferred means of exercising their right to fish. The burden of proof in such cases falls upon the Crown. Of considerable interest to the claims negotiators were the tests the Court set out for justifying limitations of the aboriginal right to fish. The Crown must determine if the objective of the law in question is valid, if it is consistent with the special trust relationship with and responsibilities of Government for aboriginals, if infringement on the aboriginal right to fish is the minimum necessary to achieve the desired management results, if compensation is available in the case of expropriation, and *if the aboriginal group in question has been consulted about conservation measures being implemented.* The aboriginal perspective of conservation objectives is a key element in the Court's elaboration of its decision. This perspective, as well as other guidelines set out in the

Sparrow decision, are honored in the Yukon Final Agreements that have been signed to date.

The process in the North is far from complete, but the options for future agreements have been narrowed as in the Innuvaliut agreement, the agreement with the Northwest Territories and Yukon First nations, and published Federal policies have set the pattern for others. Common characteristics of the agreements show that the government is willing to consider a system of preferential rights to harvest fish and wildlife on Crown lands and some exclusive rights on native-held lands, all governed by conservation, public health, and public safety. Government will agree to a special role for native people in wildlife management through institutions based on the public government model. (The replacement of this model, even at the local level, with indigenous systems of management is unlikely.) The present Federal Government has recently recognized the existing rights of First nation self government under the existing constitution.

In the Yukon, the Fish and Wildlife Management Board has been established, consisting of an equal number of government and native nominees. This Board will not replace existing government institutions, but make recommendations to the Minister regarding fish and wildlife management throughout the Yukon. At the community level, Renewable Resource Councils will have the responsibility to recommend allocation of harvesting quotas and traplines, pass bylaws, propose local regulations, report harvest levels, and serve as the window of communication between the communities, the Board, and Government. The Councils too will consist of half Government and half Yukon First Nation nominees.

Yukon First Nations are now regarded less as a special interest group and more as a distinct people with special knowledge in fish and wildlife conservation. Understandably, even with good will it is not easy for government to adapt to this fact in terms of policies and structures. For example, the Government of the Yukon has long been "adapting" by hiring qualified Yukon First Nation people. The Yukon Department of Renewable Resources and other agencies have been working with the First Nations on a renewable resource training program. Sixteen renewable resource management students graduated in 1993. Even so, at best these First Nation graduates were trained and hired to deliver newly *integrated* Government programs in renewable resource management, rather than to benefit from their distinct experiences as conservationists in the holistic sense. In the opinion of Usher (1986), they may be set up for failure, in spite of the major changes in policies and structure made by Government as a result of the aboriginal rights settlement process. "Public government institutions are not promising avenues through which to promote greater scope and authority for an indigenous management system" (Usher 1986: 125).

A Solution: The Vuntut Gwitch'in Agreement

The Vuntut Gwitch'in

The Vuntut Gwitch'in are one of three groups of Loucheux people who live in an area that stretches west 600 miles from the Mackenzie River, north to Alaska's Brooks Range, and south to latitude 65°N. Most of the Vuntut Gwitch'in now live in the village of Old Crow on the Porcupine River near the mouth of the Crow River. The village itself was not formed until the early 20th century, and permanent, sedentary town living did not commence until the early 1960s with the increase in government services in the community and a decline in the importance of trapping. Old Crow is located in an area that was known for its good fishing by the Gwitch'in who hunted and trapped in the area of the Crow Flats, about 50 miles north of the Porcupine River. The traditional meeting place of the Gwitch'in at Klokut is nearby, and the Crow Mountains just north of the river are good for caribou hunting in the fall. Acheson (1981), Slobodin (1981), and Cruikshank (1974) describe the use of the Vuntut Gwitch'in traditional territory before the village was established, the events that led to the establishment of Old Crow, and the changes in the habits of this group of Gwitch'in since the time of contact. Acheson (1981) wrote that the building of the school in Old Crow was probably the greatest single factor among several that caused people to settle yearlong in the village.

The size of the community fluctuates and is around 270 people in two categories: transient white people, mainly church and government, and Vuntut Gwitch'in First Nation members. Acheson (1981) and Cruikshank (1974) discuss the social, economic, and political situation in Old Crow, a community suffering from an inadequate economic base and increasingly reliant on government jobs and on outside resources, both material and social. The values of the renewable resource base of their economy and lifestyle has never been more appreciated by community leaders.

The Agreement

Part of the renewable resources management chapters of the Gwitch'in Final Agreement, now approved by the Yukon legislature, are already being studied by two regional governments in south America because of their attraction to the Agreement's co-management features. Co-management as used here means the sharing of power and responsibilities between Government and local resource users (Berkes et al. 1991). It means that when resources are managed locally, such as beaver or forests, most of all management becomes the responsibility of the First Nation on their land. When resource such as caribou or watersheds cannot be managed locally, resource users participate in decision making as partners with Government (Berkes et al.1991). Because of the isolation of Old Crow and the history of resource use in the northern Yukon, the application of this concept will no doubt suffer fewer conflicts than it will in the southern Yukon.

The chapter of the Final Agreement dealing with fish and wildlife management in the Vuntut Gwitch'in Traditional Territory begins with a list of objectives. These objectives stress the importance of integration of fish and wildlife management with the management of all renewable resources, and the melding of the relevant knowledge, experience, customs, and beliefs of the Vuntut Gwitch'in with those of the state-supported professional wildlife managers and scientists. This addresses one of the basic challenges to co-management, a mutual recognition of the strengths of each of the two systems of knowledge (Berkes et al. 1991). Among the objectives are acknowledgements of the need for conservation in the management of fish and wildlife, and the recognition of the needs of others to use fish and wildlife, even within the Vuntut Gwitch'in traditional territory.

These objectives introduce a system of management that is a significant compromise in light of the fact that the Vuntut Gwitch'in have never relinquished their title to the lands of their traditional territory, and that, based on this title, they have the right to manage their own resources. They argue that Section 35(1) of the Canadian Constitution Act of 1982 confirms these rights. However, recent court cases, including the Sparrow case mentioned above, appear to indicate that Government has the authority to regulate these existing aboriginal rights in order to conserve fish, wildlife, and other renewable resources and to insure public health and safety. The right to hunt and fish throughout their traditional territory, as they have hunted and fished since before the creation of the Yukon Territory, is protected until a conservation or a public health or safety need arises. Then, Section 35(3) of the Constitution Act, which states in part: "For greater certainty, in subsection (1) Treaty Rights include rights that now exist by way of land claims agreements or may be so acquired . . ." transforms these land claims agreements into constitutionally binding documents in which government's ability to regulate the use of fish and wildlife is defined.

The central Yukon Fish and Wildlife Management Board and the local Renewable Resources Council proposed in the Vuntut Gwitch'in Agreement are similar in some ways to the institutions described by Usher (1986). The major difference is that the Vuntut Gwitch'in Chief and Council and the Renewable Resources Council of government-nominated and Vuntut Gwitch'in-nominated members have more management responsibilities, and the Renewable Resources Council facilitates the integration of all renewable resource management in the traditional territory.

According to the Agreement, the Vuntut Gwitch'in First Nation may manage fish and wildlife on the lands deemed by the Final Agreement to be their own ("settlement land"), to the extent that coordination with other management agencies is considered necessary by the Board. The First Nation will also manage trapping by First Nation members. It will employ trained renewable resource specialists to carry out these management duties. When harvest seasons and quotas are required to address a conservation need, the First Nation will allocate its minimum harvest quota among its members. Many of the traditional practices of the Vuntut Gwitch'in, which are are prohibited for those people not covered by the Agreement, will be protected in the Agreement. Such practices include the free exchange of fish and wildlife amongst themselves and with other groups of First Nation people, even in the Northwest Territories, and the use of traditional harvesting methods.

Though technically an advisory body, real authority will rest with the Vuntut Gwitch'in Renewable Resources Council, which, because of a residency requirement, will most likely be made up almost entirely of First Nation members. The Council, consisting of up to six members, will be the primary instrument for renewable resource management within the traditional territory. The Renewable Resources Council will coordinate its management with the Chief and Council and Government throughout the traditional territory. It will obtain its technical support primarily from government. Central to its management responsibilities will be the proposal of fish and wildlife management plans, including harvest requirements. Of major significance is the fact that fish and wildlife management plans will be part of an overall resource management scenario, including forest, land, and watershed management, of which the Renewable Resources Council will be a major contributor.

The Vuntut Gwitch'in would like to use the Renewable Resources Council to gain influence over economic development within their traditional territory. Government and industry perceive in the Canadian North a vast natural resource base, upon which to develop a significant industrial sector. Yukon First nation and government land claims negotiators have agreed that Yukon Indian people have needs that may not necessarily be met by development of the industrial base. In fact, when considering land as wildlife habitat, the benefits derived by the Vuntut Gwitch'in from a renewable resource economy may well be much greater than those that could be derived from industrial operations (Naysmith 1971).

The entire Agreement is an acknowledgement of the Crown's ultimate responsibility for fish and wildlife for the people of Canada, a nod to the ancient European concept that no individual owns free-roaming wildlife. The Renewable Resources Council and the central Fish and Wildlife Management Board only advise the appropriate ministers of the Crown. However, it is advice with a difference. Under the Agreement, the Minister can no longer make decisions that seem to be unilateral, and then implement these decisions without explanation to the public. When the Renewable Resources Council submits a recommendation to a Minister, that Minister is given a restricted amount of time to accept or reject the recommendation. If the Minister decides to reject the Council's recommendation, the Minister must send the Council written reasons for the decision and give it an opportunity to modify its recommendations. A final rejection by the Minister must be explained publicly. The whole process must be accomplished within a set timetable, or the Council's recommendation will take effect. There is a provision for emergency action by the Minister, but even so the Council and the Wildlife Management Board will be able to involve themselves as early as a week after the action is taken and either concur with the minister's decision or recommend that the action terminate. In the Canadian system, this is a considerable restriction of the traditional powers of a Minister of the Crown.

The central, 12-member Fish and Wildlife Management Board, with half government and half Yukon First nation nominees, will look to the Renewable Resources Council for guidance in fulfilling its responsibilities. These Boards tasks will normally be focused on matters of territorial, national, or international interest, such as the management of salmon, migratory birds, and migratory barrenland caribou, and the integration of big game management in the Yukon. The Crown's relationship with the Board is governed by the same restrictions that apply to its dealings with the Renewable Resources Council.

The chapter on fish and wildlife management in the Final Agreement is woven together with chapters or sections on other renewable resources, land, finance, and government. Inseparable from the Agreement is a Government commitment to work with the Yukon First Nations in support of a college-level renewable resources training program in the Yukon. Also part of the agreement's fabric is a Fish and Wildlife Enhancement Trust. The Trust is intended to aid in the restoration, enhancement, and development of fish and wildlife habitat in the Yukon (Indian Affairs and Northern Development, 1989).

Discussion

At best, the chapter on Fish and Wildlife Management in the Vuntut Gwitch'in Traditional Territory is a compromise. In the view of the Vuntut Gwitch'in, it falls far short of their desire for self-government. However, it avoids the perils of following Berger's (1985) recommendation to Alaskans to have exclusive tribal government jurisdiction over fish and wildlife on native-owned lands and shared jurisdiction on state and federal lands. They recognize that this would lead to the illogical boundaries for managing species predicted by Osherenko (1988), making ecosystem management difficult, if not impossible. Instead, the Vuntut Gwitch'in opted for Osherenko's "co-management" approach, but with the major improvement of ecosystem management through a community-based Renewable Resources Council. The ecosystem approach of the Renewable Resource Council is followed nowhere else in North America. It does, however, incorporate the best parts of elements of established systems yet to be fully adopted in the Yukon: watershed management, forest (rather than timber) management. It will have a strong link to the communities, will grant renewable-resource users a strong voice in making management decisions that will affect their lives, and will incorporate indigenous ways of reaching collective decisions – ingredients that Osherenko (1988) considers essential to the creation of a sense of resource ownership.

The proposed co-management system could turn out to be an unwieldy bureaucracy, bogged down in endless committee meetings that consume scarce manpower in small communities. Through such a bureaucracy, the Vuntut Gwitch'in and other First Nations could lose much of the effective management capability that they had hoped to gain in their Final Agreements. However, with the imposition of training requirements for Council and Board members, and of member discipline and accountability, the result will be the formation of a strong partnership between Yukon Indians and government, two groups that need each other to protect the resources they both value.

References

Acheson, A. W. 1981. Old Crow, Yukon Territory. pp. 694-703 in Helm, J. (ed.), *Subarctic*, volume 6 of Handbook of North American Indians, ed. W.C. Sturtevant, Smithsonian Institution, Washington, D.C.

Berger, T. R. 1985. *Village Journey: The Report of the Alaskan Native Review Commission*. Hill and Wang, New York, 202 pp.

Berkes, F., George, P. and Preston, R. J. 1991. Co-management: The evolution in theory and practice of the joint administration of living resources. *Alternatives* 18(2): 12-18.

Cruikshank, J. 1974. *Through the Eyes of Strangers: A Preliminary Survey of Land Use History in the Yukon during the Late Nineteenth Century*. Report to the Yukon Territorial Government and the Yukon Archives, Government of the Yukon, Whitehorse, 152 pp.

Davis, J. L., LeResche, R. E. and Shideler, R. T. 1978. *Size, Composition, and Productivity of the Fortymile Caribou Herd*. Federal Aid in Wildlife Restoration Final Report, Alaska Department of Fish and Game, Juneau, 69 pp.

Editeur officiel du Quebec. 1976. *The James Bay and Northern Quebec Agreement.* The government of Quebec, Quebec City, 455 pp.

Fumoleau, R. 1973. *As Long as This Land Shall Last.* McClelland and Stewart, Toronto. 415 pp.

Indian Affairs and Northern Development. 1984. *The Western Arctic Claim: The Inuvialuit Final Agreement.* Minister of Supply and Services, Ottawa, 115 pp.

——— 1987. *Comprehensive Land Claims Policy.* Minister of Supply and Services, Ottawa, 26 pp.

——— 1988. *Comprehensive Land Claim Agreement in Principle Between Canada and the Dene Nation and the Metis Association of the Northwest Territories.* Minister of Supply and Services, Ottawa, 182 pp.

——— 1989. *Comprehensive Land Claim Agreement in Principle Between the Government of Canada, the Council for Yukon Indians, and the Government of the Yukon.* Minister of Supply and Services, Ottawa, 141 pp.

Leopold, A. 1933. *Game Management.* Charles Scribner's Sons, New York, 481 pp.

McCandless, R. G. 1985. *Yukon Wildlife: A Social History.* The University of Alberta Press, Edmonton, 200 pp.

Monaghan, H.J. 1980. *Renewable Resource Management in the Northwest Territories: A Proposal for Change.* Master of Natural Resources Management Practicum, Natural Resources Institute, University of Manitoba, Winnipeg, 249 pp.

Naysmith, J. K. 1971. *Canada North – Man and the Land.* Information Canada, Ottawa, 44 pp.

Osherenko, G. 1988. *Sharing Power with Native Users: Co-management Regimes for Native Wildlife.* CARC Policy Paper 5, Canadian Arctic Resources Committee, Ottawa, 58 pp.

Savory, A. 1988. *Holistic Resource Management.* Island Press, Washington, D.C., 558 pp.

Scott, R. F., Chatelaine, E. F. and Elkins, W. A. 1950. The status of the Dall sheep and caribou in Alaska. *Transactions North American Wildlife Conference* 15: 612-625.

Simmons, N., Heard, D. and Calef, G. 1979. *Kaminuriak Caribou Herd: Interjurisdictional Management Problems.* N.W.T. Wildlife Service Progress Report 2, 30 pp.

Slobodin, R. 1981. Kutchin. pp. 694-703 in Helm, J. (ed.), *Subarctic,* volume 6 in Handbook of North American Indians, ed. W.C. Sturtevant, Smithsonian Institution, Washington, D.C.

Sparrow, R. V. 1990. Canadian Native Law Reporter. 3 C.N.L.R.

Usher, P. 1986. *The Devolution of Wildlife Management and the Prospects for Wildlife Conservation in the Northwest Territories.* CARC Policy Paper 3, Canadian Arctic Resources Committee, Ottawa, 139 pp.

——— 1991. Some implications of the *Sparrow* judgement for resource conservation and management. *Alternatives* 18(2): 20-21.

Wagner, M. W. 1991. Footsteps along the road: Indian land claims and access to natural resources. *Alternatives* 18(2): 23-27.

Editor's Note: Wildlife in the Marketplace: Opportunities and Problems

Wildlife in North American society is a creator of wealth and employment. This is not widely recognized despite periodic evaluations both by the U.S. Fish & Wildlife Service and the Canadian Wildlife Service. In essence, it's presence, availability, and accessibility invites people to partake in viewing, hunting, and fishing. In so doing these users make considerable demands on goods and services, which gives rise to a widespread, job-intensive, highly innovative and diverse manufacturing and service industry. Wildlife widely available to the public thus creates economic demand. Here is a detailed discussion by two authors with training in economics about wildlife and economics.

Not everyone who is a player in wildlife conservation is also a beneficiary of the economic spin off. In particular the private land owners can be disadvantaged, and how to rectify this inequity and others is the subject of this chapter. An understanding of economics is vital to any attempt at sustainable development of a natural, renewable resource. In this our system of wildlife conservation succeeded.

Wildlife in the Marketplace

Opportunities and Problems

Ray Rasker[1] *and Curtis Freese*[2]

Introduction

"Bighorn sheep license sells for $310,000" (*Bozeman Daily Chronicle* 1994). This recent newspaper headline regarding a record auction price paid under Montana's bighorn sheep management program underscores why there is an intensifying debate concerning the application of market solutions to the management of wildlife in North America.

One of the earliest and most frequently cited calls for using the market approach as an incentive for wildlife conservation is in the "Report of the Committee on American Wildlife Policy" (Leopold 1929): "To induce wide-spread production of game on private lands there must also be the incentive of profit for the landowner." Many have endorsed this approach since then (e.g., Burger and Teer 1981, Benson 1992). Opposition to the idea, however, has been growing. Geist (1988) contends "that leasing of hunting rights to benefit private landowners has, in the long term, deleterious consequences for conservation." And in a recent article that has fanned the debate even more, Ludwig et al. (1993) conclude that "resources are inevitably overexploited, often to the point of collapse or extinction" because, in part, "wealth or the prospect of wealth generates political and social power that is used to promote unlimited exploitation of resources."

The fundamental problem and major source of disagreement is a weakness many of us share: it is tempting to look for easy solutions to complex problems. Many biologists and economists alike, having become enamored with the potential solutions offered by the free market, tend to over-simplify issues related to wildlife management. This issue is complicated by the fact that in North America we live in a mixed economy. Wildlife is a public resource, yet the habitat on which wild animals depend is often privately owned. The blend of public and private ownership makes it difficult, and at times inappropriate, to recommend a "free market" system as a means of resolving conflicts in natural resources management. In spite of difficulties inherent in a pure

[1]Resource Economist

[2]Biodiversity Consultant

market approach, economic incentive programs have been applied to the management of wild species throughout the world. Some of these have been successful in improving wildlife habitat and populations. The purpose of this paper is to address the application of market solutions to wildlife management in North America and to add some clarity to this all-too-polarized and often confusing debate. We will discuss the application of economic incentives toward the management of wildlife, the "free market" theory, and the potential for market failures. Remedies to market failure and the use of economic incentives are proposed as wildlife management tools.

We focus exclusively on economic incentives in wildlife management and habitat development. Other issues such as game ranching and the commercial trade of wildlife parts are of immediate concern but are well beyond the scope of this effort. Readers interested in these topics should begin with Geist (1985, 1988, 1989) and Lanka et al. (1990).

Privatization, Commercialization, and Economic Incentives

Because wild animals in North America are owned by the public and managed by the state, the use of economics in wildlife management will, by necessity, require a mix of private-public solutions. Because of the concern some have over the "privatization of public wildlife" (Griffith 1987), it is important to clarify some terminology, particularly the difference between "privatization" and "commercialization." In this essay the term commercialization refers to instances in which monetary gain is derived from the use of wildlife or trade in wildlife products. In particular, the focus of our discussion, and of the current debate about commercialization, regards situations in which the individual or private organization that largely controls access to land occupied by wildlife stands to profit financially from the consumptive use of wildlife. Thus, "fee hunting," where a landowner charges hunters for access to his or her land for the purpose of pursuing game, is an example of commercialization. In the strictest, legal sense of the term, what is being commercialized is access to land.

Strictly speaking, "privatization" occurs when the ownership of wildlife is transferred from the state to private individuals. Since wildlife in North America is publicly owned, there are few instances in which this has occurred legally. Presumably the ancestors of elk and bison that are now privately owned were transferred from the state many years ago. However, Benson (1992) asserts that, from a practical perspective, the presence of wildlife on private lands results in a *de facto* ownership of wildlife. Benson argues that because landowners control access to wildlife and they can profit by selling access, a profit motive ultimately determines how wildlife habitat will be managed. The fate of wild animals, therefore, can be determined largely by the land owner. Much of the current debate about commercialization and privatization centers on proposals to further strengthen the profitability of this arrangement for the private land owner.

Economic Incentives

The rationale behind enhancing profitability for the land owner is to strengthen economic incentives for wildlife management on private lands. The challenge for wildlife managers is to find ways to make incentives work for the benefit of wildlife populations and habitat. It can be argued, for example, that a private landowner who benefits financially from charging hunters a fee for land access has the "incentive" to manage the land for the benefit of wildlife. In theory, some of the proceeds of fee hunting should go back into habitat improvements. Or, at least, the farmer or rancher would be less inclined to fill in a wetland or take down a hedgerow if there are clear financial rewards for maintaining wildlife habitat. As we discuss later, although this concept is plausible in theory, there is a clear need to document whether economic incentives actually lead to measurable benefits for wildlife. More importantly, we need to better understand the biological, socio-economic, and institutional conditions that favor the operation of such incentives.

One form of economic incentive is the "perverse incentive." This exists when the financial rewards associated with resource exploitation lead to damaging results for wildlife. Perhaps the most striking example of this is the extensive over-exploitation of marine fisheries (FAO 1990, Ludwig et al. 1993). Because marine fisheries have largely been an "open access" resource, it provides a stark example of Hardin's (1968) "Tragedy of the Commons" in operation. Since, in most cases, no one owns marine fish or can strictly control access to them, a free-for-all is created whereby each person's economic self-interest is best served by taking as much as they can before the next one gets to it.

A perverse economic incentive may also operate when an individual, even though they may fully own the resource, decides that they could maximize their economic gain by harvesting and selling all of a given resource, say a stand of trees, and reinvesting the profits into something else that would yield a higher rate of return. We address this situation more fully below when we discuss discount rates. A perverse incentive also exists when commercialization favors specialization – enhancing the production of an economically valuable resource at the expense of less profitable resources, which are often non-game species (Swanson, 1992). However, wildlife habitat managed specifically for game species is better than no wildlife habitat at all, which may be the only alternative under conditions where the land is susceptible to alternative uses.

In North America, one of the most common and important examples of such specialization is displayed by state wildlife agencies in the U.S. Though various factors have influenced the evolution of state agencies, a major influence has been the user fees collected by state agencies for hunting and fishing, with the result that state agencies specialize in managing for game species. Such specialization may create two potentially perverse incentives. The first, mentioned above, may lead to decreased biodiversity on some lands because economically valuable species are favored over other species. Secondly, it may create over-dependence on the revenues generated by fees based on a few species, with the result that should one or more of these species require cuts in harvesting quotas because of population declines, the state agency may be reluctant to do so because of the resulting revenue loss.

Davis (1985) notes "The management of all wildlife lands is influenced by economics. Public land budgets are limited, forcing biologists-managers into cost analysis in order to get the most production from limited resources and leading public agencies to user fees and charges to enhance operating budgets." About 75% of the costs of wildlife management at the state level in the U.S. is from hunting-related revenues (Sparrowe 1993). The mismanagement of the black duck has been cited as an example of this perverse incentive at work in public agencies. As Gilbert and Dodds (1987:134) comment in explaining the failure to reduce bag limits despite rapidly falling black duck populations, "the black duck is a major bag species on the flyway, and management agencies derive their revenue primarily from the sale of licenses."

Thus, although the application of economic incentives often refers to private lands, market forces are also at play and have shaped, more than some would like to admit, the management of our public lands and public resources. In short, there is not a black-and-white distinction between private and public in this discussion. In contrast, in Canada, wildlife agency budgets do not directly depend on fees they collect (Neave and Goulden, 1983), though that's not to say economic activity does necessarily affect the allocation of funds for each agency.

African Elephants: A Case for Commercialization?

The success Zimbabwe and South Africa have had in expanding their elephant populations deserves mention here because it is frequently cited by proponents of commercialization in North America as an example of what market forces can do for conservation (e.g., Benson 1992). While throughout Africa elephant numbers have fallen from 1.3 million in 1979 to 650 000 in 1989, Zimbabwe's population has since 1982 increased from 47 000 to 49 000 elephants. South Africa has been able to build its elephant population from about 500 in the 19th century to its present stable numbers of about 8200 (Simmons & Kreuter 1989, Coetzee 1989).

In both Zimbabwe and South Africa some form of economic incentive is tied to the harvest of wildlife, and markets for hunting and (until 1990) ivory have given landowners and the government the incentive to manage land for the benefit of wildlife. For example, Zimbabwe's Wildlife Act of 1975 gave private land owners the right to use and profit directly from the use of wildlife on their land. As a result, wildlife use is now a major activity in the commercial farming sector, with an estimated 37 000 sq km (24% of total large-scale commercial farming land) devoted exclusively or in part to wildlife production. Sport hunting, the primary source of revenue from wildlife use, generated \$3.1 million in revenues on commercial ranches in Zimbabwe in 1990 (Bond 1993).

Under Zimbabwe's CAMPFIRE program, begun in the late 1980s, people who live on communal lands are also given the option to derive benefits from wildlife use. In 1991, 12 districts covering 30 000 sq km (18% of total communal lands area) joined the CAMPFIRE program, and 10 more were accepted into the program in 1993. Between 1989 and 1991 these first 12 districts earned over Z\$5 million from wildlife use (Bond 1993). As Bond (1993) notes, however, "In the communal sector the role of wildlife as a land use is far less certain." This is because government and district councils have not fully devolved management and revenues to communal people. For example, it is estimated that only 35% of total revenues generated by CAMPFIRE in 1989-91 were returned to participating wards and villages. In addition, wildlife-based revenues are usually invested for community infrastructure such as schools and roads, and thus the benefits are generally communal rather than individual. Bond (1993) suggests that this system places CAMPFIRE at a disadvantage when compared to the individual benefits derived from agro-pastoralism.

Kenya, where elephant hunting and ivory trade have been illegal for years, stands in sharp contrast to the success of Zimbabwe and South Africa. There, despite anti-poaching efforts, elephant populations declined from 65 000 in 1979 to 19 000 in 1989. While cause for this decline is generally attributed to poaching for the ivory trade, some find Kenya at fault for not commercializing their wildlife and thus not creating incentives for elephant protection (Simmons & Kreuter 1989).

The African elephant experiences are often held up as evidence of how commercialization and privatization of wildlife create economic incentives that benefit wildlife. However, one should be careful not to conclude that economics is all that matters – the challenge of elephant conservation is much too complex to place too much emphasis on economics as the only tool for conservation. Although it is clear that economic incentives do matter, there are obviously other social, legal, and institutional factors at work. For example, Caughley (1993) reasons that the conservation of elephants in South Africa and Zimbabwe has "little to do with private ownership but a lot to do with governmental law enforcement" because of the highly effectively wildlife law enforcement capabilities of the two countries. In fact, he goes on to suggest that the decline in elephants in Kenya occurred because, "if one ignores the economically irrelevant niceties of law, the level of actual ownership held by the people [of Kenya] over their elephants is considerably higher than it is in Zimbabwe." The people of Kenya simply exercised their free market option by converting the elephant populations into more profitable investments.

On game ranches in southern Africa, economic incentives have also led to the development of "perverse incentives." McNab (1991) warns that "At best, one can say that the conservation value of privately owned commercial ranches (in southern Africa) is very limited," because "very few of the privately owned ranches tolerate the presence of predators," and "habitats are managed in favor of commercial species (usually grassland species) to the detriment of those preferring dense thicket or forest." Rowe-Rowe (1984, in Luxmoore 1991) states that, because of the financial pressure to maximize profits, half the game farms in Natal have overstocked game with resulting habitat degradation. In other words, management for commercially valuable species can lead to a loss of biological diversity and integrity of the ecosystem (i.e., the effects of specialization mentioned above).

Commercialization of Wildlife in North America

It is tempting to conclude that the commercial system of Zimbabwe and South Africa can be effectively transferred to North America. In Oregon, for example, we have seen fee-hunting (an access fee for hunting rights on private land) serve as a powerful incentive for wildlife habitat conservation on farmland (Rasker 1989, Rasker et. al. 1991). However, there are obvious drawbacks to fee hunting, mainly because it is a system that relies on hunters to pay the bill for habitat development and assumes that landowners invest proceeds from fee leases in habitat improvements (and, it assumes that he/she has the expertise to make real improvements). Restrictions in the hunting season, often necessitated for biological reasons (e.g., a year of poor recruitment or high natural mortality) may erode the demand for hunting on private land and, in turn, the landowner's source of revenue for habitat development. Reconciling the sometimes large and often unpredictable fluctuations in wildlife populations (e.g., see Botkin 1990), which require major changes in harvest quotas, with the need for a steady and predictable income on the part of the land owner is a special challenge at the interface between ecosystems and economics.

Many authors have attempted to link financial returns from fee hunting and game ranching to conservation (see Burger & Teer 1981, Langner 1987, Schenck et. al. 1987, Teer et. al. 1983, Wesley 1987, White 1986). Steir and Bishop (1981), for example, concluded that existing policies for compensating farmers for crop damage from geese in the Horicon area of Wisconsin were ineffective and recommended that restoration of a market approach for hunting rights would "improve farmer's attitudes towards wildlife and revive the traditional partnership that existed between farmers, hunters and wildlife managers." We agree with Benson (1991), however, that "few examples exist in the US to enable a critical review of the quantity or quality of private wildlife enterprises and their contribution to wildlife conservation...."

An example of how markets for hunting rights can be developed is California's Private Lands Wildlife Management Program (PLM), which focuses largely on game animals. Under this program, agricultural landowners, after approval by the Fish and Game Commission, have authority to increase the bag limit on their land beyond those imposed on the rest of the state, and they may sell tags or permits directly to hunters (Massie 1988, Long 1987). The assumption is that the profit motive will lead landowners to increase wildlife populations at their own expense in exchange for flexibility from standard game regulations (Loomis & Fitzhugh 1989). At the time of this writing the success or failure of this program has not been clearly assessed, though as of 1993, 43 private land units totalling 556 022 acres had enrolled, and since 1984 the Department of Fish and Game estimates that PLM operators have spent $2 million on habitat improvements (Carlson, pers. comm., 1993). Fitzhugh (1989) concluded that fee hunting, especially on PLM lands, "does improve habitat for game and nongame species." Nevertheless, a rigorous evaluation of the program and its effects on wildlife habitat and diversity is lacking.

Colorado's Ranching for Wildlife Program, begun in 1986, operates on an incentive program for private land owners that is similar to California's. To be eligible for the program units must be of at least 12 000 acres (there is no minimum in California), and may consist of one ranch or two or more that have agreed to form a single management area. An evaluation of the program showed that some ranchers who participate in the program had adopted wildlife management practices, but interviews with state resource managers yielded mixed reviews regarding the adequacy of such management activities (Davis, 1993). Further, another factor that can undermine the effectiveness of such a program is that large landowners often have considerable political clout and may use this influence to circumvent the enforcement of management requirements by state wildlife personnel.

Utah also has underway a Posted Hunting Unit program that operates on largely the same profit incentive rationale for private landowners as the California and Colorado programs. Though preliminary results of the program are positive (Jense, pers. comm., 1994; Larson and Bunnell 1989), we are not aware of any rigorous assessment of the program's effects on wildlife numbers and habitat. Jordan and Workman (1989) found that in Utah less than 25% of landowners who charged a fee for hunting improved wildlife habitat or demonstrated an active interest in wildlife on their property.

Fee hunting in Texas is often pointed to as an example of the benefits of wild commercialization. As Burger and Teer (1981) note, the "leasing of land for hunting privileges in Texas . . . is the most highly developed commercial system of harvesting game animals in the continent." Texas landowners received $100-300 million from hunting leases in 1987 (Steinbach et al. 1987). The extent to which this system has benefited game species, to say nothing of other components of biological diversity, is, however, poorly understood. Though Burger and Teer (1981) state that without the lease system "many landowners would divert their range resources and management efforts to other crops," they also conclude that "few landowners invest much capital and other resources into management for wildlife." More recently, Teer (pers. comm., 1994) notes that "livestock takes second place in economic returns to the hunting lease system on great acreages west of the 100th meridian in Texas," but as of yet "there are very little data to demonstrate habitat improvement and protection of biodiversity derived from the hunting lease system."

Interest in wildlife management for profit is not limited to farms and ranchers. The southeastern division of International Paper (IP) provides an example of corporate involvement. International Paper reportedly earns 25% of its net profits from marketing recreation, including fee hunting (Anderson 1989). The company employs wildlife biologists and publishes manuals on wildlife management for their foresters (Buckner & Landers 1980). In addition to managing for game species, IP has also created habitat for bald eagles and rare woodpeckers (Anderson 1989).

Despite numerous authors lauding the benefits of economics as a tool for wildlife management, and numerous examples where incentive programs have been applied, there is ample reason to question how effective economic incentives are in leading to healthier wildlife populations. The main reason for scepticism, as the preceding examples suggest, is the scarcity of empirical evidence that economic incentives indeed lead to the maintenance or creation of wildlife habitat for the benefit of wild species.

As we warned earlier, without the proper social, legal, and institutional conditions in place, the profit motive does not necessarily clearly lead to better management of natural resources, as North America's experience with marine fisheries and Northwest forests glaringly illustrates. Add to this the concern for "perverse incentives," where landowners manage exclusively for game species with potentially adverse effects on biological diversity; the ability of some landowners to exert political pressure on fish and game agencies to avert sound management practices; and an over-reliance on what works in theory, rather than on-the-ground proof, and one can see the reason for scepticism.

Fuelling the controversy is the fact that many of us do not use the same terminology and this can lead to considerable confusion. Mention "fee-hunting" or "game ranching" as an approach to wildlife management and you are likely to be met with a variety of responses. For some, fee hunting suggests the privatization, or the *de facto* privatization of wildlife (Geist 1989, Ernst 1987, Benson 1992). Others oppose game ranching and fee-hunting due to the prospect of introducing exotic game and, as a consequence, a multitude of potential negative side effects. These include introduced diseases, competition with native species, genetic pollution, and the trade in animal parts (Geist 1988). Objections also relate to issues of land access, farmers controlling rights of way to public land (Roederer 1989, Frentzel 1986), and ranchers excluding recreationists from access to public lands on which they have a grazing privilege (Ernst 1987). To others, fee hunting, particularly in the United States, is nothing more than a landowner exercising his/her property rights (Pineo 1987, Benson 1987).

One way to add some clarity to the debate on wildlife commercialization is to briefly review how markets work and why, at times, they do not work.

Markets and Wildlife Management

We often take the market system for granted, particularly when it operates to our benefit. In principle, markets work as follows: producers and sellers compete with each other for a share of consumer expenditure and, because of this, consumers have the freedom to choose among a wide array of products and services. The end result of market competition can be efficient and effective – firms specialize, filling specific niches and thereby serving the diverse needs of consumers; economic incentives stimulate research and development which leads to new and better products; and, in an effort to sell more, deals are offered.

Will commercialization of wildlife lead to such outcomes? Will competition lead to more wildlife being "produced" and at cheaper prices? A brief review of the neoclassical theory of economics will help us address these questions.

The Theory of Competitive Markets

Economics is a study of choices by individuals or groups, which come as a result of an interplay between two forces: values and opportunities. The individual is believed to pursue satisfaction (utility) through the consumption of goods (including services and amenities). However, while the desire to consume may be insatiable, the means for consumption are limited. That is, there is a restricted set of opportunities from which the individual must choose. Goods (or resources) are limited, some are scarce and others less so, and the individual must choose among these. Moreover, an individual's ability to command scarce goods or resources is contained by income or wealth.

In its simplest terms the market encourages efficiency through specialization in the supply side of the market. An exchange economy develops such that efficient producers generate incomes which, in turn, also allows them to become consumers. In its purest form the market is thought to promote growth and efficiency without the need for central planning. The market generates information on the relative value of goods and services, expressed in terms of prices, and on the amounts of goods to be produced and consumed, all of this driven by the principle of individual choice. It is a system by which each good ends up in its highest valued use – in the hands of those willing (and able) to pay the most.

Economic Efficiency

Efficiency (or Pareto efficiency) is said to exist when the given allocation of resources is better than any other possible allocation if every individual feels it is better according to his/her own values (Arrow 1974). A trade is "efficient" if each individual is able to choose according to his or her own values in a way that makes him or her better off without making someone else worse off. Or, according to Mansfield (1979, pg. 444), "society should note any change that harms no one and improves the lot of some people. If all such changes are carried out, this situation is termed Pareto-optimal or Pareto-efficient." Under a very specific set of assumptions this form of efficiency can be achieved through the price system.

While it is possible for efficient solutions to exist in a perfectly competitive marketplace, it should not, nor is it meant to be, used as the criterion for all social well-being. The Pareto-efficiency criterion does not describe the "best" situation in terms of distributive justice. It is a criterion which takes the existing distribution of income and property rights as given. One complaint against fee hunting is that it could lead to hunters being denied access to land based on socioeconomic status (Burger & Teer 1981, Bishop 1981, Marion 1988). Marion (1988, pg. 60), for example, warns that "the wildlife resource and lower-income hunters do not necessarily benefit from [fee hunting]."

While the trade between a landowner and a pay-to-hunt customer may make both sides better off, it says nothing about the costs and benefits to those individuals not party to the transaction. Although technically the trade may be efficient as defined by economic theory, it does not imply that the full social value is reflected in the transaction. Is society better off as a result of trade (e.g., fee hunting)? We don't know, at least we cannot tell from the Pareto-efficiency criterion (Bishop 1987, Bromley 1982, Arrow 1974). With regard to equity considerations, particularly income distribution, economists have yet to develop a viable theory within the neoclassical paradigm.

Economists with a normative bent tend to argue that the market, allowed to operate as closely as possible to the dictates of theory, will result in the best possible allocation of resources. They argue that it is the restrictions placed against the market operating free and unperturbed which leads to inefficiency. Cheung (1970), Demsetz (1967) and Furubotn and Pejovich (1972) argue, for example, that the existence of common property will lead to a tragedy of the commons as described by Hardin (1968); failure to internalize the full social cost of grazing cattle on the "commons" will lead to over-exploitation. Following this theory, the extreme case argues that if only the "commons" were privately owned – if property rights were assigned and clearly defined – then the market would determine the proper distribution of resources.

If all property rights were correctly specified, and all goods and services were traded in competitive markets, then the relative value of all goods would be known. Prices would be fully determined by supply and demand factors. Inputs and resources would be allocated based on market-determined values of final outputs. Those resources not commercially traded, and therefore with no price, would not be efficiently allocated. Wildlife frequently falls into this latter category – it is typically not commercially traded.

The market also cannot fully capture non-use values of the resources, two of which are "existence values" and "option values." The "existence values" are the psychic returns associated with knowing that wildlife exists. The "option value" are returns the resource holder receives from maintaining the option of reallocating the resource to another use in some future period.

As a practical matter the application of market solutions to wildlife is at best difficult. What do we do in those frequent instances in which the price is not known? How much is a grizzly bear or a spotted owl worth? What would the price be for non-game animals, such as songbirds and rodents, animals without any conceivable market? If the market is the sole determinant of how resources are distributed, then we will value resources only on the basis of their market-derived price. In doing so, we run the danger of severely under-valuing non-market resources. As an alternative we can admit that other forms of demand also play a role in society and that these are not expressed in dollar terms (Bromley 1984). The preferences of society can also be expressed via the political process. As in economics, politics is also about choices.

Separating faith in the market from reality is a continuing dilemma for economists, and although intellectually stimulating, it has led in some instances to a dangerous over-simplification of the challenge of wildlife management. Harvard economist Thomas Shelling (1981) phrased the conflict well in an article entitled "Economic Reasoning and the Ethics of Policy";

> *Nothing distinguishes economists from other people as much as a belief in the market system, or what some call the free market system. A perennial difficulty in dealing with economics and policy is the inability of people who are not economists, and some who are, to ascertain how much of an economist's work is faith and how much is analysis and observation. How much is due to . . . observing the way markets work and judging actual outcomes, and how much is belief that the process is right and just? (p. 59)*

Most economists recognize that for various reasons, including distributive justice and potential for monopoly power, certain functions cannot be left entirely to the market. National defense, maintenance of inter-individual justice, and public works, such as education, are seen as proper and necessary functions of the state (Viner 1960).

Even in the early history of "free-market" thinking, philosophers and economists left room for the realization that society can perhaps best succeed as a mix. The market operates well in some circumstances, poorly in others. Just as the neoclassical theory teaches us the potential benefits of competitive markets, wildlife managers looking toward economics as a tool should also be aware of the possibility of market failures.

When Markets Fail

By definition, market failure occurs when incentives created in the market system fail to adequately reflect present and future preferences of consumers' or society's economic interests (Bishop 1981). Imagine a situation where a landowner in Montana charges a fee for hunting access to his/her land, which happens to be a prime elk hunting area. He/she has the good fortune that the elk are on his/her property during the hunting season, but on other ranches during the remainder of the year. This is an example where fee hunting may lead to market failure; the cost of feeding the animals throughout most of the year may be borne by someone other than the one deriving the benefits. While the elk may be a liability to one rancher (a "negative externality"), competing for pasture with his/her cattle, they are an unearned profit (a "positive externality") for another.

The problem of externalities has its roots in a lack of exclusive ownership of the resource, and of the possibility of some to act as "free riders" by deriving benefits for which they have not paid. However, even in cases where a market could be created, the costs of doing so may be prohibitive. For example, migratory waterfowl may be a cost to the farmer in Canada and a source of profits for the duck-club operator in Louisiana. There is no mechanism by which the farmer can charge for his or her share of the costs of "producing" the resource. Even if the "free-rider" in Louisiana was willing to pay, there is no market mechanism to facilitate the transaction, and if there were, the cost of carrying out the transaction could outweigh any efficiency gains made in the trade. So, not only does the possibility exist for external effects, the costs of internalizing these (the "transactions costs") may be prohibitively high.

Some non-profit wildlife organizations can help correct this form of market failure by creating a market. For example, by contributing to Ducks Unlimited, which then invests those funds to protect waterfowl nesting sites in Canada, a Louisiana duck hunter is in fact paying for some of the negative external costs borne by a wetland owner in, say, Alberta. Although they do not represent a perfect, "free" market as described by economic theory, non-profit conservation groups such as Ducks Unlimited, the Rocky Mountain Elk Foundation, and Trout Unlimited do offer a mechanism by which those willing to pay for habitat protection can do so. In a sense, these organizations at times act as the middleman between landowners and those enjoying the benefits of wildlife produced on private lands.

The Ownership of Wild Animals

Markets are more likely to operate efficiently if the goods traded are highly divisible, transferable, and absent of external effects when produced or consumed. Additionally, markets work best when entitlements to property are clearly defined and enforceable (Randall 1981, Bromley 1984). However, can migratory waterfowl, or wild deer and elk with travel patterns that cross different property boundaries, be privately owned? The fugitive nature of wildlife as a resource makes it difficult, if not impossible, to create a true market.

One way around these problems, of course, is to put a fence around the property to contain privately owned animals, as with game ranching. Although it eliminates the "fugitive" problem, it creates others, not the least of which falls more into the realm of philosophy than economics. That is, when we fence in animals do we take the "wild" out of wildlife? Of a more practical nature, fencing in game may prohibit natural migration patterns and lead to multiple changes in ecosystem structure and function.

Short-Term Profits Versus Long-Term Conservation

Other reasons why markets fail to function in society's best interest have to do with problems of imperfectly competitive markets, created, in part, by a lack of information (Runge 1984). While conservation efforts are ideally aimed at improving future as well as current conditions, economic interests usually discount future benefits and costs in favor of present consumption. Due to limited information about the future, a premium is put on the present. Thus, short-term profits may be favored over the long-term, and hence uncertain, potential profits of the future (Runge 1984, McNeely 1988, Ehrenfeld 1988, Swenson 1983). The rate at which the future economic value of a resource declines over time compared to the present value is referred to as the "discount rate."

Clark (1973a, 1973b) put the effects of private discount rates into perspective with regard to biological conservation in an analysis of the economics of killing blue whales. The policy question was whether it would be advisable, from a strictly economic point of view, to halt the harvest of these whales in order to give the population a chance to recover to levels where a sustainable harvest would be possible. The results of his analysis indicated that the rational economic decision was to harvest every blue whale as fast as possible, even to the point of extinction.

Clark concluded that in situations where the discount rates are high and growth rates are low (as with whale populations) the rational economic choice is to harvest all animals and invest the resulting revenues in areas with a higher rate of return. He emphasized that his model was not intended as a welfare model, and did not imply that extinction is socially optimal. The conclusion was that "extermination of the entire population may appear as the most attractive policy, even to an individual resource owner" when harvesters "prefer present over future revenues" (Clark 1973a, pg. 950).

Remedies Relative to Private Land

A particularly challenging task for the wildlife manager in North America is to design incentives for private landowners to manage their land for the benefit of wild animals. Unless properly compensated for the costs associated with raising wildlife, a profit-motivated land manager may be better off by reducing or even eliminating all habitat. This is especially the case when hunter trespass and liability become a significant problem (Higbee 1981, Hyde 1986, Wright & Fesenmaier 1988), when wildlife causes damage to pasture and crops (Stier & Bishop 1981, Wade 1987, Nielsen & Lytle 1985), and when the returns from farming outweigh any benefits from preserving land resources for wildlife. In the absence of incentive (or disincentive) programs, such as subsidies (or taxation), education, cost-share programs, damage compensation, farm programs and liability relief, the only option available for the landowner may be the commercialization of wildlife. Charging hunters an access fee may be the only method for some to recover the costs of having wildlife on their land.

When profit incentives offered by fee hunting and game ranching lead to market failure, however, alternatives must be explored. Concern over the expansion of fee hunting may be a symptom of a different problem: there are insufficient incentives (other than charging an access fee) for the landowner to take wildlife into consideration when land-use decisions are made.

Farmers and ranchers respond to many different incentives, of which profit may be only one. Other incentives for wildlife management may come from aesthetic appreciation, a sense of pride and public recognition for public services provided when wildlife interests are integrated into the farming or ranching operation, and the landowner's desire to hunt (Rolston 1987, Shelton 1981, Rasker 1989). Some landowners may have altruistic motives. To be practical, however, we should not expect them to maintain wildlife for free. We review below potential mechanisms for developing economic incentives for wildlife conservation.

Regulated Fee Hunting

Landowner incentive programs, such as the Private Lands Wildlife Management Program in California, have the potential to stimulate private landowner investment in wildlife and habitat conservation. The basic concept behind these programs is that a participating landowner, by agreeing to follow management guidelines specified by the state, can increase the number of game taken and/or the hunting period on his/her land and thereby earn extra income from fee-paying hunters. Two potential problems to consider in such an arrangement are the use of political influence and over-specialization for game species to the detriment of non-game species.

Similar to the above, but with considerably more state management of the fee collection and distribution system, is a variation of a system that was debated in Oregon in the late 1980s. The idea is to allow fee hunting, but that fees are collected by the state fish and game agency. In exchange, the state agency (rather than the landowner) takes over liability responsibilities, which is a major constraint to fee hunting participation. The agency also helps manage hunters (or bird watchers, for that matter). Most of the money goes back to the landowner if he/she can demonstrate visible improvements that benefit all species. If the landowner cannot demonstrate improvements in habitat, then the fish and game department applies a portion of the money to improve habitat. The remainder goes to cover liability insurance, and to compensate the landowner for allowing people to enter his/her land.

Another option is to lease the hunting rights to a hunting club, as is common in waterfowl fee hunting operations. The club can be required to carry liability insurance, post the land, and help patrol against trespassers. If the fee hunting system is to be successful, the landowner (or the state) should require that the club invest in make habitat improvements. This system could be extended to non-consumptive wildlife enthusiasts as well, such as bird watchers.

Community-Based Management Systems

The discrete nature of private land holdings may not lend itself to optimal habitat development in light of the migratory patterns and habitat needs of wildlife. Thus some form of cooperation and coordination between individual contiguous landowners may be required to fully meet the needs of wildlife. Because this involves a "community" of land owners, we refer to such systems as community-based. The Colorado Ranching for Wildlife Program provides incentives to landowners to jointly manage the land; the Eastern Slope Land Management Association in Montana and the Elk Mountain Safari operation in Wyoming (Yorks, 1989) are other examples of cooperative arrangements.

Another form of community-based land management that may use economic incentives to protect wildlife resources and other amenities is land-use zoning and regulations. These can improve conditions for wildlife, or at least mitigate the effects of development. Such zoning regulations may allow a land developer to benefit financially in return for improving wildlife habitat in one area, or for leaving valuable habitats undisturbed. For example, a landowner who wishes to subdivide his/her land may be granted extra housing density rights, and thus extra income, by agreeing to locate and cluster housing so that wildlife habitat elsewhere on his/her property is left undisturbed. Thus, the community has created a positive, private incentive for the individual landowner to protect a resource that benefits the community.

Profit-Sharing and Compensation

One of the most contentious issues in North America is the proposal to reintroduce wolves into the Greater Yellowstone ecosystem. It is a classic problem of "externalities:" the presence of wolves in and around Yellowstone National Park are a benefit to some, (e.g. wolf lovers, tourist businesses, and presumably, proponents of ecosystem management), but a cost to others (i.e., ranchers). How could such a problem be resolved using economic tools? Is there a way that landowners surrounding Yellowstone could benefit from wildlife, including predators? Some ideas that have been tried in Kenya's Amboseli National Park may hold promise for North America.

Because conflicting uses of land for wildlife and cattle threaten the integrity of the Amboseli ecosystem, a package of economic incentives has been developed. For example, cattle watering areas have been established outside the park, thereby alleviating grazing pressure within Amboseli, and local Masai landowners are compensated for wildlife that graze on their land. The Masai receive a subsidy for the development of tourist campsites and lodges, and there is a program for revenue sharing from gate receipts (Western 1993, Western 1984 in McNeely 1988). Thus, the Masai landowners are compensated for the cost of raising wildlife on their land and financial incentives are offered to help them reap part of the profits of Kenya's tourist trade.

The result is that wildlife income for the Masai has increased rapidly since the mid-1980s, elephant numbers are up, and other measures of ecosystem health in Amboseli have remained good. As Western (1993) notes, "the main reason for the increase in elephants in Amboseli . . . is the protection given by the Masai." It is estimated that the annual monetary gain to the park from the use of Masai land is $500 000. Benefits to the Masai from the park result in an income "85 percent greater than what they could obtain from livestock alone after full commercial development" (McNeely 1988). These earnings totalled over $750 000 dollars in 1990, derived primarily from concession and guide fees and from a proportion of the entrance fees. Additionally, the Masai are employed by the Park Service and by private lodges (Western, pers. comm., 1990). Notice that the compromise solution for Amboseli National Park relies on developing financial incentives, yet it does not call for the privatization of wildlife.

Just as the Masai around Amboseli now benefit from tourist dollars and thus better tolerate damage by wildlife that move in and out of the park onto their lands, so could the concept be more broadly applied in North America. Thus, ranchers living around Yellowstone National Park might be compensated for forage consumed by elk and bison that roam out of the park, or for predators that kill livestock. In an efficient market system, those that benefit from wildlife in the park, such as local motel owners, park concessionaires, and tourists, would pay local ranchers not to shoot wandering predators. The high transactions costs involved in putting "buyers" (e.g., wolf lovers) and "sellers" (e.g., predator-affected ranchers) together might make such a transaction unlikely without some form of intervention. Defenders of Wildlife, for example, has created a market mechanism to facilitate exactly this type of transaction. This group, through its Wolf Compensation Fund, uses private money to reimburse ranchers for verified losses to wolves. The group also gives monetary rewards to ranchers who have a breeding pair of wolves on their land (Hudson 1993).

Indeed, non-profit organizations like Defenders of Wildlife provide one of the more flexible and potentially creative ways for new "markets" to be created that allow consumers to make choices about how and where they "purchase" wildlife benefits.

Taxation

Another way to encourage conservation practices is through tax programs. Economists often favor tax incentives because they can be designed to work in much the same way as market prices (Bishop 1981). To illustrate how taxes can be implemented to alleviate market failures, imagine a situation where the actions of an individual result in a cost to others, such as a farmer draining a wetland valuable for waterfowl production. In order to equate social and private costs, a tax could be levied on the farmer equal to the amount of damage done to the public good, the waterfowl. Theoretically, the landowner will respond to avoid or minimize this additional cost (Bishop 1981, Savage et. al. 1974). If the tax is large enough, the price of draining the wetland may be too high and it may be more profitable to leave it intact.

From a practical standpoint taxation may be difficult to apply. Not only are politicians leery of taxation, it may also be difficult to determine the extent of the "social cost" tax equivalent. As a result, tax regulations may require a trial and error approach. Taxes also run the danger of being perceived as a penalty rather than an incentive, not always an amicable approach to enlist the cooperation of private landowners.

An interesting and promising way to encourage wildlife habitat preservation is through positive tax incentives. Conservation easements are one example. A landowner can donate a conservation easement to a charitable organization and, in return, qualify for a tax deduction (Noonan & Zagata 1982). The potential income tax savings can be substantial and complete ownership and management authority is maintained by the owner. The only limitations to land use are those which pertain to the easement and these are specifically designed for each landowner. The one strict requirement is that the land covered under the easement be used for conservation purposes (Small 1990).

Recently, in Montana, Ted Turner (of cable-television fortune) donated a substantial conservation easement to The Nature Conservancy. The easement will ban mining and timber harvesting, and prohibit sub-division of 107 000 acres of Turner's land, all within the Greater Yellowstone ecosystem. Currently The Nature Conservancy has about 150 000 acres of land in Montana under conservation easements from 35 to 40 landowners (Zackheim 1990). The Montana Land Reliance holds an additional 72 646 acres in easements, which are estimated to protect about 19 000 acres of elk habitat and offer 145 miles of river- and stream-bank protection. Easements donated to this organization in the Yellowstone ecosystem alone amount to 30 000 acres, protecting valuable wintering habitat, blue-ribbon trout streams, and preventing the common western phenomena of ranch sub-division (Wilson, pers. comm., 1990).

Green Labelling

Given the growing willingness of consumers to pay more for products whose production is environmentally benevolent, there may be ways to apply this concept to create positive economic incentives for landowners to maintain or improve wildlife habitat. Dolphin-safe tuna was one of the first applications of this concept in the area of natural resource management. The willingness of consumers to pay more for pesticide-free foods and cotton products is another expression of this idea, one with potentially far-reaching but often subtle benefits for wildlife. Forest certification programs are another recent development that could affect large acreages of wildlife habitat in North America and elsewhere (Johnson and Cabarle 1993). Under this system, forest land owners who follow good wildlife conservation practices (more broadly, environmentally and socially responsible practices) in their timber production operations are certified under an internationally recognized certification program. They can then sell their certified lumber to consumers who are willing to pay a premium for lumber produced under environmentally sound conditions. Conceivably, similar certification programs could be applied to a range of products whose production greatly affects wildlife populations and habitat, such as rice, beef and wool. Indeed, fee-paying hunters could also employ this concept by agreeing to pay a premium for hunting on private lands that have been certified as following good wildlife management practices.

Discussion and Conclusion

Two questions emerge from this review: Where and under what biological and socio-economic conditions can market mechanisms work? And, what mix of market mechanisms and government intervention work best for wildlife conservation? A simple response to either is not possible. In some instances market solutions may be the best alternative. For Zimbabwe and South Africa, commercialization of its elephant and other game populations via the granting of private management control may be effective in giving wildlife management a chance to compete with other uses of the land. It may also be that budget priorities of these countries necessitates a system by which wildlife management pays for itself. Clearly, the mix of market incentives and government intervention and regulation must be tailored to each national situation.

The apparent success some countries have had in wildlife conservation via market incentives does not imply, however, that economics needs to be the over-riding concern in the management of wildlife in North America. In some instances market incentives may indeed work to the benefit of wildlife populations, particularly if we broaden the application of these incentives through mechanisms such as community-based management, green labelling, and the development of new market places for wildlife values, such as non-profit organizations. In most, a level of government intervention will be necessary. No single mechanism will work in all instances.

The question is not whether to recommend market solutions as a tool for wildlife management. Rather, it is when, where, and how to apply them. The answer to this question requires an understanding of when and why markets fail, and of the degree of intervention required so that a "free market" approach does not ignore society's goals of social equity and biodiversity conservation. Without perfect information, when all costs to society are not accounted for by the market, and when resources are mobile and difficult to privatize, the task of the advising economist is much more complicated than dispensing market solutions as a panacea. The existence of market failure necessitates a more complex and sophisticated approach, with solutions that are socially and biologically responsible.

Some promoters of the market system are quite persuasive in extolling the virtues of private enterprise. Nevertheless, few economists ever have in mind recommending a "pure" private enterprise solution. Even the most ardent supporters of private enterprise support some form of regulation, justify certain kinds of subsidy, and even admit the need for direct governmental intervention in certain activities (Nelson 1981, Arrow 1974). We must recognize thc limitations of markets as a social institution and that to expect individuals to behave as is assumed in theory is unrealistic and ill-advised. Kellert (1981) suggests that "history is replete with examples of humans foregoing substantial material rewards because their acquisition was somehow perceived as ethically wrong or incompatible with a more desirable life-style and society." Arrow (1974) asserts that, in addition to the market, society is also governed by certain "invisible institutions": the principles of ethics and morality. In fact, Arrow argues that the price system can be attacked on the grounds that it "harnesses motives which our ethical systems frequently condemn. It makes a virtue of selfishness." Further, Bromley (1984) reminds us that "market processes are derivative of a larger social system; they do not supersede that system."

Much of this paper has focused on market failure in applying economic incentives to wildlife management. To be certain, the possibility of "government failure" is as real. Government officials operate on different sets of incentives and bureaucracies can be slow and ineffectual. Fortunately, we are not faced with an either/or decision. Wildlife management in North America will most likely always be a blend of private and public ownership of resources and a mix of market- and public-oriented management strategies. Between the extremes lie some potentially successful solutions to some of our most difficult resource management dilemmas.

A review of the literature in North America reveals a remarkable lack of rigorous research on the use and effectiveness of market forces and economic incentives in wildlife conservation. This remains a "black hole" in wildlife research in North America, in which considerable theory, rhetoric and funds have been invested, but from which little has emerged empirically to show if and how wildlife also profits from the profit incentive. Before we can go any further in recommending what may work best under a given set of conditions, much more analysis is needed of experiences to date, and more experimentation with different mechanisms is required. The field is ripe for innovative interdisciplinary thinking and research by wildlife biologists, sociologists, and economists.

Acknowledgement

The World Wildlife Fund for Nature-International and World Wildlife Fund-U.S. supported research by C. Freese that was useful in the preparation of this paper. The opinions expressed in this article are those of the authors and not necessarily those of The Wilderness Society or the World Wildlife Fund.

References

Allen, L. D. 1981. Private lands as wildlife habitat: A synthesis. pp. 153-161 in Dumke, R.T., G.V. Burger, and J.R. March (eds.), *Wildlife Management on Private Lands*. The Wildlife Society, Wicsconsin Chapter, Madison, Wisconsin.

Anderson, T. 1989. Panel discussion: Fee-based hunting and the public trust in Montana. pp. 7-14 in *Fee-Based Hunting and the Public Trust*, Proceedings of the Cinnabar Symposium, Montana State University, Bozeman, Montana.

Arrow, K. J. 1974. *The Limits of Organization,* New York, W. W. Norton.

Belt, D. C. and Vaughn, G. 1988. *Managing Your Farm for Lease Hunting and A Guide to Developing a Hunting Lease.* Extension Bulletin No. 147, Delaware Cooperative Extension, University of Delaware, Newark, Delaware.

Benson, E. D. 1992. Commercialization of wildlife: A value-added incentive for conservation. pp. 539-553 in Brown, R. D. (ed.), *The Biology of Deer.* Spinger-Verlag, New York.

Benson, E. D. 1991. Values and management of wildlife and recreation on private land in South Africa. *Wildl. Soc. Bull.* 19: 497-510.

Benson, E. D. 1987. Holistic ranch management and the ecosystem approach to wildlife conservation. pp. 67-69 in *Proceedings of the Privatization of Wildlife and Public Lands Access Symposium,* January, 1987. Wyoming Game and Fish Department, Casper, Wyoming.

Bishop, R. C. 1981. Economic considerations affecting landowner behavior. pp.73-87 in Dumke, R.T., Burger, G. V. and March, J.R. (eds.), *Wildlife Management on Private Lands.* The Wildlife Society, Wisconsin Chapter, Madison, Wisconsin.

Bishop, R. C. 1987. Economic values defined. pp. 24-33 in Decker, J. D. and Goff, G. R. (eds.), *Valuing Wildlife: Economic and Social Perspectives.* Westview Press, Boulder, Colorado.

Bond, I. 1993. *The Economics of Wildlife and Land-use in Zimbabwe: An Examination of Current Knowledge and Issues.* Project Report No. 33, WWF Multispecies Project, Harare, Zimbabwe. 42 pp.

Botkin, D. B. 1990. *Discordant Harmonies: A New Ecology for the Twenty-first Century.* Oxford University Press, New York, 241 pp.

Bozeman Daily Chronicle. March 10 1994. p. 17, Briefs: Bighorn sheep license sells for $310,000. Bozeman, Montana.

Bromley, W. D. 1982. Land and water problems: An institutional perspective. *American Journal of Agricultural Economics* 64(12): 834-844.

Bromley, W. D. 1984. Public and private interests in the federal lands: Toward conciliation. pp. 3-28 in Johnston, G. M. and Emerson, P. M. *Public Lands and the U.S. Economy: Balancing Conservation and Development.* Westview Press, Boulder, Colorado.

Brown, G., Jr. and Henry, W. 1989. The economic value of elephants. London Environmental Economics Centre, Paper 89-12.

Buckner, J. L. and Landers, J. L. 1980. *A Forester's Guide to Wildlife Management in Southern Industrial Pine Forests.* Technical Bulletin No. 10, Southlands Experiment Forest, International Paper Company, Bainbridge, Georgia.

Burger, G. V. and Teer, J. G. 1981. Economic and socioeconomic issues influencing wildlife management on private land. pp. 252-278 in Dumke, R. T., Burger, G. V. and March, J. R. (eds.), *Wildlife Management on Private Lands.* The Wildlife Society, Wisconsin Chapter, Madison, Wisconsin.

Caughley, G. 1993. Elephants and economics. *Conservation Biology* 7: 943-945.

Cheung, S. N. S. 1970. The structure of a contract and the theory of a non-exclusive resource. *J. Law and Econ.* 13: 49-70.

Child, G. 1988. Economic incentives and improved wildlife conservation in Zimbabwe. Paper presented at Workshop on Economics, IUCN General Assembly, 4-5 February 1988, Costa Rica.

Clark, C. 1973a. Profit maximization and the extinction of species. *J. Pol. Econ.* 81: 950-961.

Clark, C. 1973b. The economics of overexploitation. *Science* 181: 630-634.

Coetzee, G. 1989. Conspiracy of silence? *South African Panorama,* October: 10-14.

Cook, K. A. 1989. The 1985 Farm Act and wildlife conservation: Outlook for 1990. *Trans. N. Amer. Wildl. Nat. Res. Conf.* 54: 409-413.

Davis, R. K. 1993. A new paradigm in wildlife conservation: Using markets to produce big game hunting, improve range condition and stabilize rural incomes. Presented at 32nd Annual Meeting of Western Regional Science Association, Wailea, Maui, Hawaii. Feb. 3, 1993.

Davis, R. K. 1985. Research accomplishments in wildlife economics. *Trans. North Am. Wildl. and Nat. Resourc. Conf.* 50: 392-404.

Demsetz, H. 1967. Toward a theory of property rights. *Amer. Econ. Rev.* 57: 409-413

Ehrenfeld, D. 1988. Why put a value on biodiversity? pp. 212-216 in Wilson, E. O. (ed.), *Biodiversity.* National Academy Press, Washington, D.C.

Ernst, J. P. 1987. Privatization of wildlife resources: A question of public access. Paper presented at the South Dakota Wildlife Federation 42nd annual meeting. August 22, 1987. Pierre, South Dakota.

FAO. 1990. Review of the State of World Fishery Resources. FAO Fisheries Circular 710, Revision 7.

Fee Hunting Task Force. 1988. Report Presented to the Fish and Wildlife Commission of the State of Oregon, September, 1988, Portland, Oregon. Unpublished Manuscript.

Fitzhugh, E.L. 1989. Innovation of the private lands wildlife management program: A history of fee hunting in California. *1989 Trans. Western Section of the Wildlife Society.* 25: 49-59.

Frentzel, M. 1986. Who's keeping you off public lands? *Western Outdoors* September, Vol. 33(8): 42-44, 74-76.

Furubotn, E. and Pejovich, S. 1972. Property rights and economic theory: A survey of recent literature. *J. Econ. Lit.* 10: 1137-1162.

Geist, V. 1985. Game ranching: Threat to wildlife conservation in North America. *Wildl. Soc. Bull.* 13: 594-598.

Geist, V. 1988. How markets in wildlife meat and parts, and the sale of hunting privileges, jeopardize wildlife conservation. *Conservation Biology* 2(1): 15-26.

Geist, V. 1989. Legal trafficking and paid hunting threaten conservation. *Trans. N. Amer. Wildl. Nat. Res. Conf.* 54: 171-178.

Gilbert, F. F., and Dodds, D. G. 1987. *The Philosophy and Practice of Wildlife Management.* Krieger Publishing Co., Malabar, Florida, 279 pp.

Goldstein, J. H. 1988. The impact of federal programs and subsidies on wetlands. *Trans. N. Amer. Wildl. Nat. Res. Conf.* 53: 436-443.

Griffith, C. 1987. Turning wildlife private. *Oregon Bowhunter* July: 4-5.

Hardin, G. 1968. The tragedy of the commons. *Science* 162: 1243-1248.

Hays, R. L., Webb, R. P. and Farmer, A. H. 1989. Effects of the conservation reserve program on wildlife habitat: Results of 1988 monitoring. *Trans. N. Amer. Wildl. Nat. Res. Conf.* 54: 162-163.

Higbee, M. 1981. Farmers and wildlife: Why is there a rift and how can we bridge it? pp. 53-59 in Dumke, R.T., Burger, G. V. and March, J.R. (eds.), *Wildlife Management on Private Lands.* The Wildlife Society, Wisconsin Chapter, Madison, Wisconsin.

Hudson, W. E. (ed.) 1993. *Building Economic Incentives into the Endangered Species Act.* Defenders of Wildlife. Washington, D.C.

Hyde, O. D. 1986. Public lands, private lands and oranges. *Ambit.* March: 22-24.

Isaacs, B. and Howell, D. 1988. Opportunities for enhancing wildlife benefits through the conservation reserve program. *Trans. N. Amer. Wildl. Nat. Res. Conf.* 53: 222-231.

Jense, G. K. January 31, 1994. Personal communication.

Jordan, L. A. and Workman, J. P. 1989. Economics and management of fee hunting for deer and elk in Utah. *Wildlife Society Bulletin.* 17: 482-487.

Johnson, N. and Cabarle, B. 1993. *Surviving the Cut: Natural Forest Management in the Humid Tropics.* World Resources Institute, Washington, D.C.

Kellert, S. R. 1981. Wildlife and the private landowner. pp. 53-59 in Dumke, R.T., Burger, G. V. and March, J.R. (eds.), *Wildlife Management on Private Lands.* The Wildlife Society, Wisconsin Chapter, Madison, Wisconsin.

Knox, M. 1989. Horns of a dilemma. *Sierra.* 74(6): 58-67.

Langner, L. L. 1987. Hunter participation in access hunting. *Trans. N. Amer. Wildl. Nat. Res. Conf.* 52: 475-482.

Langner, L. L. 1989. Land-use changes and hunter participation: The case of the conservation reserve program. *Trans. N. Amer. Wildl. Nat. Res. Conf.* 54: 382-390.

Lanka, B., Guenzel, R., Fralick, G. and Thiele, D. 1990. Analysis and recommendations on the applications by Mr. John T. Dorrance III to import and poses native and exotic species. Wyoming Game and Fish Department, Cheyenne, Wyoming, 139 pp.

Larson, D. and Bunnell, D. 1993. Utah's posted hunting unit program. Presented at 2nd International Landowner/Sportsmen Relations Conference, August 14-17, 1993, Boise, Idaho.

Leopold, A. 1929. Report to the American game conference on an American game policy. *Trans. Am. Game Conf.* 17: 284-309.

Long, W. 1987. Wildlife management programs on private land in California. pp. 40-41 in Rasker, R. and Bedell, T. E. (eds.), *Developing Profitable Resource-Based Recreation on Private Land.* Proceedings of the 1987 Pacific Range Management Short Course. Oregon State University Cooperative Extension Service, Corvallis, Oregon.

Loomis, J. B. and Fitzhugh, L. 1989. Financial returns to California landowners for providing hunting access: Analysis and determinants of returns and implications to wildlife management. *Trans. N. Amer. Wildl. Nat. Res. Conf.* 54: 196-201.

Ludwig, D., Hilborn, R. and Walters, C. 1993. Uncertainty, resource exploitation, and conservation lessons from history. *Science* 260: 17, 36.

Mansfield, E. 1979. *Micro-Economics.* 3rd edition. New York, W. W. Norton.

Marion, R. W. 1988. Hunting leases for additional profits from the land. pp. 57-60 in *Proceedings of the Florida-Georgia Forest Landowner Seminar: Alternative Enterprises for Your Land.* February 27, 1988, Cooperative Extension Service, University of Florida, Gainesville, Florida.

Massie, J. D. 1988. Personal communication. California Department of Fish and Game, Wildlife Management Division, Sacramento, California.

McMeekin, D. 1990. A victory for the elephants. *Wildlife News,* African Wildlife Foundation 25(1): 1-7.

McNab, J. 1991. Does game cropping serve conservation? A reexamination of the African data. *Can. J. Zool.* 69: 2283-2290.

McNeely, J. A. 1988. *Economics and Biological Diversity: Developing and Using Economic Incentives to Conserve Biological Resources.* IUCN, Gland, Switzerland.

Miller, E. J. and Bromley, P. T. 1989. Wildlife management on conservation reserve program land: The farmer's view. *Trans. N. Amer. Wildl. Nat. Res. Conf.* 54: 377-381.

Neave, D. and Goulden, R. 1983. Provincial wildlife revenue sources-commitments. *Trans. North Am. Wildl. and Nat. Resourc. Conf.* 48: 405-412.

Nelson, R. R. 1981. Assessing private enterprise: An exegesis of tangled doctrine. *The Bell Journal of Economics* 12: 93-110.

Nielsen, D. B. and Lytle, D. D. 1985. Who gains (or loses) when big-game uses private lands? *Utah Science* Summer: 48-50.

Noonan. P. F. and Zagata, M. D. 1982. Wildlife in the market place: Using the profit motive to maintain wildlife habitat. *Wildlife Society Bulletin* 10(1): 46-49.

Pineo, D. 1987. Characteristics and general requirements for successful recreation enterprises. pp. 8-12 in Rasker, R. and Bedell, T. E. (eds.), *Developing Profitable Resource-Based Recreation on Private Land.* Proceedings of the 1987 Pacific Range Management Short Course. Oregon State University Cooperative Extension Service, Corvallis, Oregon.

Randall, A. 1981. *Resource Economics: An Economic Approach to Natural Resource and Environmental Policy.* John Wiley and Sons, New York.

Rasker, R. and Bedell, T. E. (eds.) 1987. *Developing Profitable Resource-Based Recreation on Private Land.* Proceedings of the 1987 Pacific Northwest Range Management Short Course. Oregon State University Cooperative Extension Service, Corvallis, Oregon.

Rasker, R. 1989. Agriculture and wildlife: An economic analysis of waterfowl habitat management on farms in western Oregon. Unpublished doctoral dissertation, College of Forestry, Oregon State University, Corvallis, Oregon.

Rasker, R., Johnson, R. L. and Cleaves, D. 1991. The market for waterfowl hunting on private agricultural land in western Oregon. Forest Research Laboratory, Oregon State University, Corvallis, Oregon. Research Bulletin 70, 14 pp.

Roederer, T. 1989. Access to public land: The Keystone Dialogue Project. *Trans. N. Amer. Wildl. Nat. Res. Conf.* 54: 162-163.

Rolston, H. 1987. Beauty and the beast: Aesthetic experience of wildlife. pp. 187-196 in Decker, J. D. and Goff, G. R. (eds.), *Valuing Wildlife: Economic and Social Perspectives.* Westview Press, Boulder, Colorado.

Rowe-Rowe, D. T. 1984. Game utilization on private land in Natal. Pietermaritzburg: Natal Parks, Game and Fish Preservation Board, as cited in Luxmore, A. R. 1989. Impact on conservation. pp. 413-423 in Hudson, R.J., Drew, K.R. and Baskin, L.M. (eds.), *Wildlife Production Systems: Economic Utilization of Wild Ungulates,* Cambridge Univ. Press, Cambridge.

Runge, C. F. 1984. An economist's critique of privatization. pp. 69-75 in Johnston, G. M. and Emerson, P. M. *Public Lands and the U.S. Economy: Balancing Conservation and Development.* Westview Press, Boulder, Colorado.

Sampson, N. 1986. The availability of private lands for recreation. pp. 11-12 in *Recreation on Private Lands - Issues and Opportunities.* A workshop convened by the Presidential Task Force on Recreation on Private Lands. March 10, 1986. Dirksen Senate Office Building, Washington, D.C.

Savage, T. D., Burke, M., Coupe, J. D., Duchesneau, T. D., Wihry, D. F. and Wilson, J. A. 1974. *The Economics of Environmental Improvement.* Houghton Mifflin, Boston.

Schelling, T. 1981. Economic reasoning and the ethics of policy. *The Public Interest* 63: 37-61.

Schenck, E. W., Arnold, W., Brown, E. K. and Daniel, D. J. 1987. Commercial hunting and fishing in Missouri: Management implications of fish and wildlife 'markets'. *Trans. N. Amer. Wildl. Nat. Res. Conf.* 52: 516-524.

Shelton, R. 1981. Motivating the landowner/manager to manage for wildlife. pp. 301-306 in Dumke, R. T., Burger, G. V. and March, J. R. (eds.), *Wildlife Management on Private Lands.* The Wildlife Society, Wisconsin Chapter, Madison, Wisconsin.

Simmons, T. R. and Kreuter, U. P. 1989. Herd mentality: Banning ivory sales is no way to save the elephant. *Policy Review* Fall: 46-49.

Small, S. J. 1990. *Preserving Family Lands: A Landowner's Introduction to Tax Issues and Other Considerations.* Powers and Hall Professional Corporation, Boston, Massachusetts.

Sparrowe, R. 1993. What is wise use of waterfowl populations? pp. 85-86 in Moser, M., Prentice, R. C. and Van Vessem, J. U. (eds.), *Waterfowl and Wetland Conservation in the 1990s – A Global Perspective.* IWRB Special Publication No. 26. IWRB, Slimbridge.

Steinbach, D. W., Conner, J. R., Glover, M. K. and Inglis, J. M. 1987. Economic and operational characteristics of recreational leasing in the Edwards Plateau and Rio Grande Plains in Texas. *Trans. North Am. Wildl. and Nat. Resourc. Conf.* 52: 496-515.

Stier, J. C. and Bishop, R. C. 1981. Crop depredation by waterfowl: Is compensation the solution? *Canadian Journal of Agricultural Economics* 29(July): 159-170.

Swanson, T. M. 1992. Economics of a biodiversity convention. *Ambio* 21: 250-257.

Swenson, J. E. 1983. Free public hunting and the conservation of public wildlife resources. *Wildlife Society Bulletin* 11(3): 300-303.

Teer, J. G. February 9, 1994. Personal communication.

Teer, J. G., Burger, G. V. and Deknatel, C. Y. 1983. State-supported habitat management and commercial hunting on private lands in the United States. *Trans. N. Amer. Wildl. Nat. Res. Conf.* 48: 445-456.

Viner, J. 1960. The intellectual history of laissez-faire. *Journal of Law and Economics* 3(October): 45-69.

Wade, D. A. 1987. Economics of wildlife production and damage control on private lands. pp. 154-163 in Decker, J. D. and Goff, G. R. (eds.), *Valuing Wildlife: Economic and Social Perspectives.* Westview Press, Boulder, Colorado.

Wesley, D. E. 1987. Socio-duckonomics. pp. 136-142 in Decker, J.D. and Goff, G.R. (eds.), *Valuing Wildlife: Economic and Social Perspectives.* Westview Press, Boulder, Colorado.

Western, D. 1993. Ecosystem conservation and rural development: The Amboseli case study. Prepared for the Liz Claiborne and Art Ortenberg Foundation Community Based Conservation Workshop, Arlie, Virginia, Oct. 18-22, 1993.

Western, D. 1984. Amboseli National Park: Human values and the conservation of a savanna ecosystem. pp. 160-161 in McNeely, J. A. and Miller, K. R. (eds.), *National Parks, Conservation and Development: The Role of Protected Areas in Sustaining Society.* Smithsonian Institution Press, Washington, D.C.

Western, D. June 13, 1990. Personal communication.

White, R. J. 1986. *Big Game Ranching in the United States.* Wild Sheep and Goat International, Mesilla, New Mexico.

Wilson, J. April 4, 1990. Personal communication. Montana Land Reliance, Helena, Montana.

Wright, B. A. and Fesenmaier, D. R. 1988, Modeling rural landowners' hunter access policies in east Texas, USA. *Environmental Management* 12(2): 229-36.

Zackheim, H. April 4, 1990. Personal communication. The Nature Conservancy, Helena, Montana.

Editor's Note: The North American Waterfowl Management Plan in Prairie Canada: Opportunities for the Landowner

This paper describes how, with the aid of an international migratory bird treaty, and cooperation between governments and the private sector, an excellent conservation project can be developed. The decline of waterfowl in Prairie Canada and the loss or degradation of wildlife habitat is viewed as a symptom of poor land-use practices. An innovative program of resource management is being implemented through the North American Waterfowl Management Plan (NAWMP). A variety of incentives is available to landowners to assist them to modify their land-use management techniques, thereby providing an improved approach to sustainable agriculture and wildlife. The Alberta NAWMP and the Prairie Habitat Joint Venture (PHJV) are described.

The North American Waterfowl Management Plan in Prairie Canada
Opportunities for the Landowner

Gerald McKeating, Len Shandruk, and Garry Trottier[1]

Introduction

Waterfowl are among our most valued natural resources. They are highly prized as game birds and equally valued by those who enjoy observing them. Waterfowl generate millions of dollars to the North American economy annually. Interest in this resource continues to grow rapidly.

However, waterfowl, especially ducks, are experiencing a long term downward trend in population. This is primarily attributable to changing land-use practices over the past 40 years. Upland habitat that provides important cover for waterfowl and other wildlife is being replaced by agricultural crops. Wetland drainage and clearing for agricultural expansion have reduced the amount of wetlands available for breeding waterfowl. These effects are compounded by drought, predation, hunting, and natural mortality. As a result, mallard and pintail populations are 43% and 70%, respectively, below long term (34 year) averages in Prairie Canada.

The North American Waterfowl Management Plan (NAWMP) (Environment Canada and the United States Fish and Wildlife Service 1986) is an innovative proposal to protect an integral part of the environment—our ducks, geese, and swans, while working to conserve the wider prairie environment. The United States and Canada signed an agreement in 1986 that set out the corrective action and framework for reversing the downward trend in waterfowl populations.

The NAWMP is more than a duck plan. The decline in waterfowl populations is symptomatic of a broad scale land-use problem, which not only affects all wildlife in Prairie Canada, but also the continued sustainability of agriculture and outdoor-oriented recreation and tourism.

The NAWMP involves a strategy for a series of habitat restoration activities that are beneficial to both agriculture and wildlife. The plan proposes a North American breeding population goal of 62 million

[1]Canadian Wildlife Service

ducks, including 8.7 million mallards and 6.3 million pintails. This goal reflects the average waterfowl populations of the mid-1970s, thus the objective is realistic.

The Problem

Perhaps the most important change on the land over the past 70 years has been the rate at which we are able to alter the environment around us through urbanization, modern farming, and intensive land management techniques. Many areas have been cleared or drained, rendering them unsuitable for wildlife. Cultivation right to the edge of wetlands has removed nesting cover for ducks and as a result nesting success is only about 10%, well below the level needed to sustain existing populations.

Present-day agricultural techniques are radically altering vast tracts of land in the prairies. Problems such as blowing topsoil, soil salinization, silting of water bodies, chemical pollution, and depletion of groundwater supplies are now widespread.

The wetlands being drained are not only important as waterfowl habitats; they also play an integral part in the whole prairie landscape and are vital to the long term sustenance of prairie agriculture. They help to trap snow, store the run-off, and recharge groundwater supplies. This in turn provides water for domestic and agricultural uses. Wetlands provide a valuable source of fodder for stock in dry years and also harbor many birds and insects that consume agricultural pests. Wetlands directly contribute to a higher water table, which helps to lessen soil erosion and salinization.

The loss of wetlands is closely linked to many of the severe agricultural problems that are rendering vast areas worthless for agriculture and wildlife alike. These are not just problems for farmers and land managers; they are among the most important factors in the drop in the number of waterfowl on the prairies. Many of the soil conservation problems today are the result of cultivating land of marginal value to agriculture, the same land that is of high value to wildlife.

A Solution

The retention and restoration of breeding habitat in the prairies is a first priority of the NAWMP and has led to the development of the Prairie Habitat Joint Venture (PHJV). The PHJV is a coordinated approach by the Canadian government, provincial governments, and non-government agencies with the primary task to enhance waterfowl habitat on 3.6 million hectares in Prairie Canada at a cost of $1 billion. The PHJV is an umbrella concept consisting of numerous smaller projects and programs that are incorporated into long-term implementation plans. These plans will be implemented over a 15-year period throughout the major waterfowl production areas of Alberta, Saskatchewan, and Manitoba. These plans will also create habitat for other wetland and upland wildlife including some that are rare and endangered.

The PHJV seeks to rejuvenate waterfowl and wildlife habitat by supporting sustainable development activities such as large-scale wildlife and soil and water conservation programs that will also improve economic returns to farmers. To implement this objective, an advisory board has been formed.

The PHJV Advisory Board consists of the following members: Environment Canada (Canadian Wildlife Service), Agriculture Canada (Prairie Farm Rehabilitation Administration), Government of Alberta (Department of Forestry, Lands, and Wildlife), Government of Saskatchewan (Department of Parks and Renewable Resources), Government of Manitoba (Department of Natural Resources), Delta Waterfowl and Wetlands Research Station, Ducks Unlimited Canada, and Wildlife Habitat Canada.

In each province there is a steering committee and a technical committee (Fig. 1), which guide the development of programs and plan implementation. A wide variety of other groups are also involved, including provincial agricultural agencies, municipal governments, irrigation districts, agricultural service boards, conservation districts,

Figure 1: Coordinating structure for the Prairie Habitat Joint Venture (PHJV and the North American Waterfowl Management Plan (NAWMP).

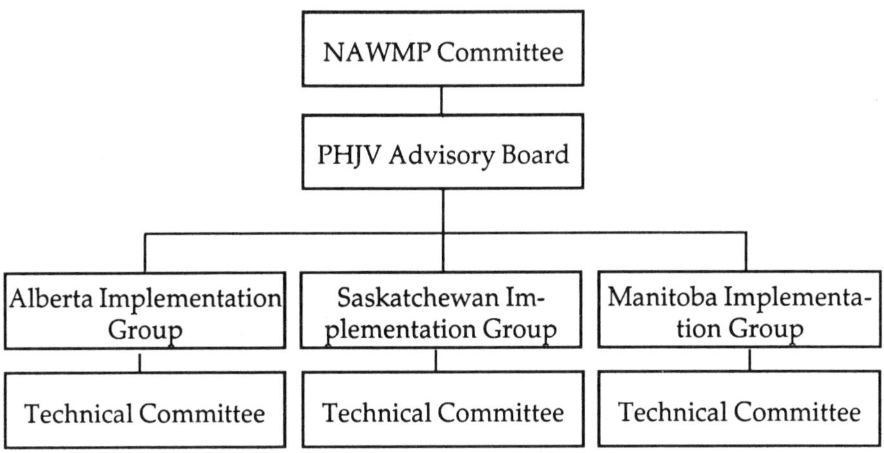

cooperating landowners, and volunteer conservation, naturalist, and fish and game groups.

The NAWMP committee members are six officials from Canada and six from the United States. They meet twice a year to provide overall program direction and revise the NAWMP.

The PHJV advisory board members are Canadian implementing agencies. The board endorses programs, arranges funding matches, evaluates programs, recommends program adjustments to implementation groups, and reports periodically on progress to the NAWMP. Its support staff carry out the work of the advisory board.

The provincial implementation group is composed of implementing agencies within a province. It approves programs, coordinates their implementation, and oversees their evaluation within a province. Its support staff carry out the work of the implementation group.

The technical committee develops work plans, makes program recommendations, and reviews/recommends a biological approach.

Program Strategy

The PHJV has four basic program components:

(1) Private and public lands in areas of high waterfowl production capability would be secured and managed intensively by wildlife agencies.

(2) Large wetland areas important to waterfowl would be protected and, where necessary, enhanced.

(3) Habitat programs are being developed that will be complementary to, and supportive of, agricultural soil and water conservation initiatives.

(4) Government policies and programs that affect land use will be reviewed with the intent of achieving both agricultural and wildlife conservation objectives, resulting in broad changes to the landscape across the prairies.

High priority areas for PHJV activity have been selected in each province based primarily on waterfowl production criteria. Program activities will be focused on those regions, but it is important to note that programs will only be undertaken in cooperation with landowners who volunteer to participate.

The key to prevention of soil and water erosion and to the recovery of migratory bird numbers is the implementation of alternative land management practices. Many such practices are already being advocated by agencies and individuals concerned about soil management on the prairies. An example is the permanent cover program being offered by the Prairie Farm Rehabilitation Administration and provincial agricultural agencies. The NAWMP builds upon such programs as well as providing a variety of incentives for the landowner. These incentives should encourage farmers to alter their land management practices. Program venture examples are illustrated in Table 1. Habitat managed under extensive programs will be largely on land owned by farmers or ranchers. Landowners are encouraged to cooperate in conservation activities that benefit the soil, water, and wildlife resources and would be offered financial incentives to do so. In the long term, sound conservation practices are expected to "pay off" as self-supporting, without the need for continued financial help to the farmer or rancher. Table 2 summarizes the acreages involved.

Table 1: Summary of upland habitat programs of the Prairie Habitat Joint Venture

CATEGORY	PROGRAM	DESCRIPTION
Intensive	Dense Nesting Cover	Establishment of appropriate perennial vegetation as nesting cover on land rented or held in fee title. Electric predator fenced, cattle fenced, or unfenced.
	Nesting structures	Nest baskets, rafts, or earth mounds in wetlands. Used where upland cover cannot be provided.
	Idle hay and pasture	Retirement of existing hay and pasture land from agricultural use. Cash rental on private or leased Crown land.
Extensive	Marginal land conversion	Lands marginal for annual crop production are converted to perennial cover (hay or pasture) and managed by the landowner jointly for agricultural and waterfowl purposes. Cash rental. Joint delivery with agriculture.

Table 1: Summary of upland habitat programs of the Prairie Habitat Joint Venture

CATEGORY	PROGRAM	DESCRIPTION
	Improved pasture management	Improve condition of perennial cover by a variety of techniques: rotational grazing, supplemental fall-seeded pasture. Cash payment to offset landowner's net costs. Joint delivery with agriculture.
	Delayed haying	Delay hay-cutting operation until July 15. Cash payment to offset reduced yield or quality costs. Adjunct to other agricultural programs.
	Green manuring	Legume seeded with an annual cereal nurse crop; legume ploughed the following summer, after nesting season. Cash payment to offset farmer's net cost. Joint delivery with agriculture possible.
	Conservation farming demonstration (extension)	Cooperative program with agriculture designed to promote conservation farming methods that have waterfowl benefits (zero-till, winter wheat, pasture management, stubble mulching).

Table 2: Habitat objectives

Type of Management	Alberta	Saskatchewan	Manitoba	Total
INTENSIVE				
Dense nesting cover *	346	54	22	422
Idle hay and pasture *	555	554		1109
Nesting structures	11 000	21 000	4000	36 000

Table 2: Habitat objectives

Type of Management	Alberta	Saskatchewan	Manitoba	Total
EXTENSIVE			,	
Marginal land conversion*	430	287	72	789
Improved pasture management*	914	1490		2404
Delayed haying *		113	29	142
Green manuring *	120	572		692
Conservation farming demonstrations *	96	1001	371	1468

* in thousands of acres

These programs have been field tested as to their acceptability at the farm gate. Some examples from southeastern Saskatchewan are briefly described below.

Fenced dense nesting cover: 500 acres secured and planted; landowner receives $30/acre/year for 10 years and the plot remains as part of the total quota acreage; plots range in size from 40 to 130 acres; accepted by 5% of landowners approached; waterfowl nesting and success increased from nil to nearly 100%.

Idle pasture: $10/acre/year incentive (licence fee); accepted by 27% of landowners approached; higher waterfowl nest density and success anticipated; habitat enhanced.

Delayed grazing: $6/acre/year licence fee; grazing not permitted until July 20; accepted by 12% of landowners approached; waterfowl nesting undisturbed, success and density increases; delayed grazing improves range productivity so stocking rate can be increased during remainder of grazing season.

Native habitat protection: $3/acre/year licence fee, in return for no draining, no burning, no breaking, no clearing, no herbicide spraying; full grazing rights allowed; accepted by 69% of landowners approached; habitat retention/protection is the primary wildlife benefit.

Hay field establishment: seed supplied free, over-delivery slip eligible for quota acreage; $20/acre/year licence fee for non-haying years; possibility of a delayed haying option.

Stubble mulching/chemical fallow: cost of chemical supply and machine rental subsidized; lower input cost to landowner anticipated; reduced soil erosion; greater soil moisture conservation through snow catchment and reduced evaporation; crop residue maintained during fallow year provides nest cover for ducks.

Salinity plantings: seed provided free to landowners; unproductive land reclaimed to hay or grazing production; provides nesting cover to waterfowl mostly on wetland margins.

Grassed waterways: seed provided free to establish 25 to 50 feet of permanent cover on waterways; reduces topsoil erosion and sediment delivered to wetlands or streams; provides minimal nest cover for waterfowl.

An innovative method for improving waterfowl nesting conditions on the agricultural landscape of Prairie Canada is intensive grazing management on native and seeded pasture land. This involves the implementation of grazing systems whereby the operator controls where and when livestock are allowed to graze. The objective is to keep grass in a vegetative state, while leaving enough leaf material to ensure adequate regrowth. The resulting healthier, taller grass provides cover for wildlife.

The fact that grazing systems can provide substantial beneficial returns to producers and to wildlife has led to inclusion of this technology as a major program activity for achieving the habitat acreage goals of the NAWMP. Fully 33% of the acreage, by far the most extensive proportion of the landscape to be affected under the PHJV, will be dedicated to grazing systems. Of this, 26% will be on private land and 7% on public grazing reserves. In total, some 914 000 acres of pasture land in Alberta and 1 490 000 in Saskatchewan will be targeted (Prairie Habitat Joint Advisory Board 1990).

Well managed grazing systems can provide substantial benefits to producers and wildlife, particularly waterfowl, as compared to a more traditional well managed season-long grazing practice. Grazing system trials conducted in Saskatchewan from 1987 to 1989 provided benefits to the producers including increased beef production per acre, extended grazing season, easier livestock handling, and improved monitoring of livestock progress (New Pasture and Grazing Technologies Project 1990).

The major advantage of grazing systems over season-long grazing is the elimination of grazing on portions of the pasture until mid-June to mid-July, thus providing undisturbed cover for nesting waterfowl. In contrast, once cattle are turned out to season-long pasture, the entire area is disturbed through grazing effects on nesting cover and by cattle presence.

A simple grazing system such as twice-over rotation grazing has potential to be one of the most cost-effective activities proposed for the PHJV. It is a fully sustainable agriculture activity, requiring minimal development costs of $7 to $10 an acre, which can potentially be recovered by the landowner within one or two years (Trottier 1990). Also, it requires no additional development and labor costs from wildlife agencies to produce ducks. If wildlife agencies cover the fencing costs to encourage producers to adopt grazing systems, then the annual cost per additional duck fledged over the 35-year life of the fencing will be approximately $0.61 (Messmer 1988). This compares with $24.05 for leased, ungrazed, fenced dense nesting cover, or to $223.00 for man-made islands (Messmer 1988).

The Grazing Trial Project was initiated by the Canadian Wildlife Service in cooperation with the Saskatchewan Department of Parks and Renewable Resources, the Saskatchewan Department of Rural Development-Extension Service, and Wildlife Habitat Canada in conjunction with the Prairie Pothole Project (Trottier 1989). Two methods of livestock grazing management are being compared on privately owned pasture land in the rural municipality of Antler. The objective is to find out which method, twice-over rotation grazing or season-long grazing, produces healthier grass cover and greater livestock gain, while raising the most ducks.

This project was designed to assist the evaluation of habitat management techniques proposed for implementation under the NAWMP. The results will provide direction on the feasibility and practicality of encouraging livestock producers to adopt rotation grazing as an alternative to the more common practice of season-long grazing.

To narrow this prairie-wide NAWMP program into a provincial focus, the Alberta plan is an excellent example. Three major areas within Alberta are targeted for program implementation: the aspen parklands, the prairies, and the Peace parklands. The major focus of the Alberta plan is in the aspen parklands in central Alberta, which comprise the most productive waterfowl habitat in Alberta. Secondary emphasis is placed on the prairies, and on the Peace parklands (Alberta Technical Committee 1989).

Major components of the Alberta plan include direct land management programs, indirect programs, protection of critical moulting and staging wetlands, crop damage amelioration, a communications program, and an evaluation and monitoring program. The land management programs propose treatment of 2.85 million acres of landscape at a total cost of $492.56 million. The total cost of all direct and indirect programs over 15 years is $590.20 million.

Within the aspen parklands the implementation plan proposes to affect 2.1 million acres over 15 years at a total cost of $329.3 million. Twenty-one management plans grouped into seven program categories are scheduled for implementation. The intensive land management programs include purchase and lease of marginal croplands and their conversion to dense nesting cover, lease and idling of tame and native grasslands, and construction and installation of nesting structures. The intensive programs will be implemented in areas of high waterfowl production capability.

Extensive land management programs involve farm demonstration and/or incentives to farmers to encourage modifications to undesirable land management practices. Programs include marginal cropland conversion to pasture or hay land, annually seeded fall pastures, grazing systems and pasture management, underseed legume, and chemical fallow/minimum tillage demonstrations. All of these conservation farming techniques will reduce wind and water erosion, improve soil moisture, fertility, and organic matter, and improve long-term productivity of crop and grazing lands. Since most of these techniques provide for more residual cover on the landscape, they will also improve upland wildlife habitat. It is anticipated that extensive programs will encourage farmer participation in these conservation farming practices and that by year 15 of the plan the total cumulative land affected by extensive programs will total 15.6 million acres.

Within the prairies, the Alberta implementation plan will treat 609 000 acres over 15 years; it proposes to treat 186 500 acres in the Peace parklands.

The implementation plan identifies several acts, policies, and procedures that are detrimental to soil, water, and waterfowl resource management. The plan proposes a more cooperative and integrated approach to development and revision of acts and policies that will promote the compatibility of agricultural and wildlife interests.

The Alberta plan, like the other plans, recognizes the necessity of crop damage amelioration as a complementary requirement to waterfowl habitat enhancement. The development of a compensation program that reimburses farmers for 80% of crop losses has been recently finalized. In addition, the plan makes recommendations for the operation of prevention programs that may include an additional 25 feeding stations, if required, to cope with increased waterfowl populations.

Complementary to the land conservation and management components of the Alberta plan are the soil and water conservation programs, which have been initiated by other land management agencies in Alberta. The Canada/Alberta Agreement on Research and Technology Transfer calls for an expenditure of $3 million over five years. The objective of this federal-provincial agricultural agreement is to develop and transfer appropriate conservation tillage and cropping technology to minimize degradation and promote economically sustainable crop production. This initiative will undoubtedly complement Alberta plan initiatives and lead to more benefits to the wildlife resource. Other initiatives such as the Canada/Alberta Soil Agreement and the Agriculture Canada (PFRA) Permanent Cover Program will promote soil and water conservation at the farm gate and through private agricultural conservation groups. These new conservation thrusts will also provide spin-off benefits to the waterfowl resource in Alberta.

Buffalo Lake Alberta First Step Project

Delivery of the NAWMP in Alberta was initiated in March 1989 with the Buffalo Lake First Step Project (Calverley 1990). This project, targeted for a 850 square km area surrounding Buffalo Lake in central Alberta, is located about 100 km south of Edmonton. The area was selected because of its high density of wetlands, low-class agricultural lands, and its previous reputation as a premier waterfowl production area. Following the NAWMP lead, the objective of the Buffalo Lake Project is to increase waterfowl recruitment in the area. Canadian and American funding sources have committed $2 million to this project. This has allowed for the implementation of four major management programs to promote soil and water conservation and increase waterfowl production.

Under the medium-term dense nesting cover program, the project has purchased 1147 acres of low-quality agricultural lands in eight separate parcels. This amounts to about 50% of our land acquisition goal for the area. Some of this acquired acreage was seeded to a grass-legume mixture in 1989, and the rest was scheduled for seeding in 1990. Other management of these parcels involves survey of boundaries, cattle fencing and/or predator fencing, and signage.

Two conservation techniques (chemical fallow and underseed legume), which will replace conventional summer fallow, are being promoted. Ten cooperators participated in the chemical fallow program, encompassing a total of 785 acres. Because of a lack of summer fallow during 1989, only two cooperators participated in the underseed legume program for a total of 180 acres. During 1990, with more production and exposure, it is anticipated that more than 2000 acres will be dedicated to conservation farming in the project area.

Another major program of this project was the construction of small nesting islands. Sites in wetlands were obtained through land acquisition, agricultural program cooperators, or other interested landowners. A total of 157 nesting islands have been constructed to date. After seeding with a grass-legume cover, these islands should provide secure nesting habitat in 1991. Through a conservation agreement with the participating landowner, the project secured an additional 885 acres of wetland habitat spread over 38 quarter sections. Other project components initiated in 1989 were an enhancement of the crop damage compensation and prevention program, development of a communication/public relations package, and a waterfowl population monitoring program within the project area.

Thus, not only have we started securing and developing wildlife habitat, we have also begun promoting sound conservation farming practices that will prevent soil erosion and provide sustainable agriculture. The experience we are gaining in delivering the Buffalo Lake Project will aid us greatly in delivering the overall NAWMP in Alberta.

Conclusion

The foregoing discussion indicates that landowners and wildlife have much to gain from this program.

The programs of the NAWMP have been designed to contribute to conservation in a number of different resource-use sectors. This system of decision making and management will provide the greatest benefits possible on a sustainable basis to both the users of the resource and to society at large.

An improved habitat and more productive landscape will replenish and stabilize waterfowl and other wildlife populations. Songbirds, wading birds, and upland game birds will have better habitat for nesting and feeding. Deer, antelope, and smaller mammals will have better escape cover and rearing areas. Endangered species of the Great Plains will have greater opportunities to expand their ranges. Improved management practices will help wetland vegetation and native grasslands recover form overgrazing.

Improved wildlife populations provide more opportunities for sportsmen and for viewing by local residents. The financial benefits of increased recreation and tourism will serve to diversify the economy.

Conservation farming programs will contribute significantly to soil and water conservation. Stabilization of the soil will decrease erosion and salinity problems. Trash cover will trap winter snow and increase soil moisture. The organic material of soils will be increased. Surface water quality and groundwater supplies will be improved. Vegetation will also trap water and help reduce the impact of flooding.

Historically, wildlife interests have expected private landowners to take on the cost of wildlife that benefits society in general. NAWMP proposes to remedy that approach and to demonstrate that through improved land-use practices wildlife can become an important crop to the landowner.

This is a plan for the present and the future. In the long term, the end result will be a healthy prairie environment.

References

Alberta Technical Committee. 1989. *N.A.W.M.P. Alberta Plan*. Edmonton, Alberta, 38 pp.

Calverley, B. K. 1990. *The Buffalo Lake Project: One Year Later*. Unpublished Annual Report. Edmonton, Alberta, 20 pp.

Environment Canada and the United States Fish and Wildlife Service. 1986. *North American Waterfowl Management Plan*. Ottawa, Ontario, 19 pp.

Messmer, T. A. 1988. *Grazing systems – Food for Thought*. Unpublished Information Note, North Dakota State University, 10 pp.

New Pastures and Grazing Technology Project. 1990. *Project summary*. Saskatchewan Agricultural Development Fund. Regina, Saskatchewan, 50 pp.

Prairie Habitat Joint Venture Advisory Board. 1990. *Prairie Habitat: A Prospectus*. Winnipeg, Manitoba, 32 pp.

Trottier, G. C. 1989. *Grazing System Trials – 1988 Annual Report*. Canadian Wildlife Service. Unpublished Report. Environment Canada, Edmonton, Alberta, 26 pp.

———. 1990. *Grazing System Trials – 1989 Annual Report*. Canadian Wildlife Service. Unpublished Report. Environment Canada, Edmonton, Alberta, 37 pp.

Editor's Note:
Wildlife Ranching: Dancing with the Devil?

Professor Robert Hudson, a proponent of wildlife ranching, explains in part why he is attracted to this idea. He also gives a glimpse into the early history of raising wildlife. Indeed, game keeping is an ancient art in the Occident and in the Orient, one reason why we are well informed about it – and very concerned about its effects on North America's fauna. In Europe due to hunting, and in China due to deer farming, the sub-specific structure and regional adaptations of deer have been lost. That is, one finds today "generic deer," hybrids of various imports and exotics. So far North America's fauna has been spared the worst genetic pollution, although there is some and traceable to the very same factors as in Europe and China: hybridization of native with exotic stock in order to achieve "better" features in the captive deer, to supply various markets. The warrior-hunter cultures of Japan and Outer Mongolia, by comparison with China's farming culture, have maintained a rich, regionally distinct wild ungulate fauna.

Wildlife Ranching

Dancing with the Devil?

R.J. Hudson

Introduction

I am neither for nor against commercialization of wildlife. I am against markets for rhino horn and consider the current international ivory ban an important emergency measure. I am against commercial hunting of wild ungulates in southern Canada but I endorse commercial harvesting of wild reindeer in the Russian Taimyr Peninsula. Significantly for this discussion, I support ranching of bison and wapiti, but not many other species, for meat production in North America. I reserve judgement on farming *Moschus* for musk, cervine deer for velvet antler, and moose for milk. I also reserve the right to change my mind on any of the above as experience unfolds. I don't consider this inconsistent or indecisive – rather, flexible and adaptive. I believe the future of wildlife depends on flexible, local, fine-tuned management.

Unless populations are irresponsibly managed or animal welfare is violated, I don't consider commercial game husbandry to be a moral issue, nor should it be contrived to be so. Moral appeals are of immense value for rallying political support, and for fund raising. However, there are many things that conservation campaigns cannot do, and ethics are too often inappropriately invoked simply to limit others from using something we want. Conservation campaigns are about as likely to save wildlife as organized religions have been in fostering world peace. They establish a general mood but are no substitute for serious negotiations. More attention must be paid to establish ground rules that align self-interest with the aims of conservation.

For 75% of Alberta that lies in the Green Zone, we have the rudiments of a system of public ownership and centralized management that sustains a rich wildlife resource and meets the public's demand for recreation. The same system does a poorer job in the 25% that lies in the White Zone where land can be cultivated from horizon to horizon and there are few incentives for farmers to do any differently. And there is little prospect that governments will ever be willing or able to devote enough fiscal resources to properly care for wildlife in the face of competing land uses. Here, some of the traditional responsibilities for management must be franchised to achieve a sustainable agriculture and to maintain wildlife habitat.

Much of the White Zone would be better under permanent pasture than exposed to erosion and laced with chemicals in crop rotations. The balance among existing land uses depends upon the relative prices and input costs of crops and livestock. Crop diversification (such as canola) shifted the balance toward cultivation. Animal diversification should shift the balance in the other direction. Although biotechnically "improved" cattle, llamas, fallow deer, and other exotic species may provide the needed incentive, there is a special appeal to adopting native species such as bison and wapiti that had been displaced from the agricultural landscape. But not everyone sees it that way, and we have been warned of "dancing with the devil" (Hawley ed. 1993). Given the seriousness of the agricultural land crisis, that is a chance I am willing to take.

The local game ranching debate has been waged for a decade. Instead of reiterating arguments, thoroughly debated by Geist (1992) and Benson (1992), I intend to review the history of game husbandry and suggest that franchising of wildlife management represents a natural adaptive response to changing pressures on resources (Hudson 1993). I argue that wildlife administrative systems should be seen as adaptive responses to different pressures and problems rather than brilliant bureaucratic creations.

The Oldest Profession

Wildlife management probably is Man's oldest profession. It differs from other human endeavors in that, because of our increasing isolation from nature, we know less rather than more with the passage of time. For our ancestors, the morality of consumptive use could never have been questioned, although there were certainly sanctions on responsible and respectful practices. The Greek goddess Artemis was a huntress as well as protectress of wildlife and punished mortals for irresponsible or cruel hunting practices. The deeper moral question of using animals could only be possible as societies became urbanized and sufficiently isolated from nature.

Such a broader morality of nature did not begin with Earth Day, 22 April 1970. The ancient Greek polis provided conditions for several schools of thought on the correct relationship between man and nature. The *Orphics* taught respect for all life similar to the principle of *Ahimsa* of the Jain religion. The Stoics saw man as part of nature, but a member with special responsibilities. These views are instantly recognizable in modern conservation.

Decentralization in the Ancient World

While these issues were debated in the cities, life went on in the countryside. The Persians maintained vast hunting reserves called *paradises* as their major conservation tool. The more democratic Greeks kept animals in smaller private reserves called *theriotrophia* (mammal feeding grounds), which suggests more intensive management. Aristotle talks about Deer Mountain in Asia Minor where animals were identified with ear notches. He obtained much of his information on animal structure and function from gamekeepers.

The practice of game husbandry was adopted by the Romans in the first century B.C., apparently in response to the declining abundance of game. These game parks were called *vivaria* or *leporia*. The latter term, derived from "hare," has been translated as "warren," but ancient writers clearly indicate that wild boars, deer, wild goats, mouflon, and even exotic antelope were also enclosed. These species were kept for the same reasons as today – amenity, sport, and meat/special products (Varro 116-27 B.C., from Hooper 1934):

> *It is reported that Quintus Fulvius Lippinus has a preserve near Torquinni of 40 iguera, in which are enclosed not only the animals I have mentioned, but also wild sheep; and an even larger one near Statonia . . . and in Transalpine Gaul, Titus Pompeius has a hunting preserve so large that he keeps about 4 square miles enclosed. . . .*
>
> *Boars, too, can be kept in a warren with very little trouble, both captives and tame animals born on the premises, and as you know, Axius, it is customary to fatten them. On the estate at Tibur the Varro bought from Piso, a trumpet sounded at regular hours and you saw boars and wild goats come for their food, which was thrown down from the exercise ground above, mast for boars and the goats vetch or something else.*
>
> *Indeed, when I was at Hortensius's place at Laurentum, I saw the thing done more in the manner of the Thracian bard. There was a wood of more than 50 acres, so our host told us, surrounded by a park wall, which he called not a leporium but a vivarium.*
>
> *There on high ground, dinner was laid, and as we were banqueting, Hortensius ordered Orpheus to be summoned. He came complete with robe and lute, and was bidden to sing. Thereupon, he blew a trumpet, and such a multitude of stags and boars and other 4-footed beasts came flooding round us that the sight seemed as beautiful to me as the hunts staged by the aediles in the Circus maximus – at least the ones without African beasts.*

Columella (A.D. 65, from Forester and Heffner 1968) devoted one chapter of his book *de Rustica* (On Agriculture) to game farming, providing detailed advice on fencing, feeding, and herd management:

The careful head of a household ought not to be content with the foods which the earth produces by its own nature, but, at the seasons of the year when the woods do not provide food, he should help the animals which he has confined with the fruits of the harvest which he has stored up, and feed them on barley or wheat-meal or beans, and especially grape husks . . . whatever costs the least.

Also, so that the wild creatures understand that provision is being made for them, it is a good plan to send among them 1 or 2 animals which have been tamed at home, and which, roaming through the whole park, may direct the hesitating creatures to the fare offered them.

Game farming was accommodated by Roman Law. The Romans classified things according to "natural laws" of ownership. Some things, by their very nature, belonged to the public (*res communes*), the state (*res publicae*), or to individuals. Some things such as wildlife or abandoned property belonged to no one (*res nullius*). They could be possessed (but not owned) by killing and retreiving or capturing and enclosing. Generally, upon escape, possession ceased. But a special provision was made for bees, deer, and other species that had a tendency to return (Gaius, from Whittuck, 1904):

For wild beasts, birds and fishes as soon as they are captured, become, by natural law, the property of the captor, but only as long as they continue in his power . . . Their natural liberty is deemed to be recovered when they have escaped from his sight, or, though they continue in his sight, when they are difficult to recapture.

In the case of those wild animals, however, which are in the habit of going away and returning, as pigeons, and bees, and deer, which habitually visit the forest and return, . . . only the cessation of the intention of returning is the termination of ownership in them is acquired by the next occupant.

Recapitulation in Europe

The disintegration of the Roman Empire after the fourth century led to a recapitulation of the pattern in the ancient world. Unbridled exploitation was halted with strong centralized administration and this, in turn, was gradually replaced with an increasingly franchised system. (Threlfall's this volume).

The disorder that followed the fall of Rome undoubtedly led to the unbridled exploitation of game. However, the negative effects of unregulated hunting were offset somewhat by the depopulation of the countryside by plague and a general movement of people to towns and cities in response to lack of security.

Order was restored around A.D. 800 with the consolidation of most of Europe under Charlemagne. Administration of wildlife was centralized and the so-called "Forest Laws" were developed as a conservation measure. To preempt aboriginal rights defined by *leges barbaratum*, the state established the equivalent of Crown lands for production forestry (*sylva*) and wildlife conservation (*foresti*, a term that has nothing to do with trees and probably comes from the Latin *fera statio* = abode of wild things). These reserves became the equivalent of the *paradises* of the Persians or *temene/templa* of the Greeks/Romans, but more exactly the Crown/public lands of Canada/United States. The forests were leased for firewood, grazing, thatch, and posts. Although small game was hunted by local people, royal game was reserved for the monarch.

At first, the system was an effective conservation tool. The laws were enforced fairly and humanely. The royal hunting prerogative was increasingly granted to princes and nobles. But as Charlemagne's empire began to fragment under provincial sovereigns, the Forest Laws became more oppressive.

Although this system was already in place in Britain under King Canute, William of Normandy, by right of conquest, greatly expanded the network of deer forests and imposed harsh penalties for violation of the Forest Laws. By 1200, royal forests covered approximately 20% of England and these were guarded by an army of royal game keepers who increasingly abused their privilege and power.

This abuse of power was finally curbed in 1225 with the signing of the Forest Charter. This charter, actually a supplement to the Magna Charta (Main Charter), protected citizens from capital and corporal punishment for breaking game laws.

This was the beginning of the end of the royal prerogative. The Forest Laws became obsolete during the reign of the Tudors, who had to be more concerned about the loyalty of their subjects rather than exercising such privileges. Briefly after 1603 the House of Stuart attempted to reassert the royal prerogative and to establish enlightened programs of wildlife conservation that included captive management propagation (Kirby and Kirby 1931). But this initiative was arrested by civil war.

Permission to maintain a chase, park, or free-warren on private land that was once awarded by royal grant became considered a right rather than an honor or privilege. Political patronage was replaced with rank and property qualifications with the Game Act of 1671. But even these qualifications were relaxed with time and eventually abolished in 1831.

The democratization of hunting opened new opportunities for fee hunting. With industrialism, urban people had both the means and inclination to participate. Particularly in the Scottish Highlands, hunting became so profitable and popular that deer forests increased from 1 975 209 acres in 1884 to 2 878 342 in 1911, creating considerable hardship for the crofters employed by the sheep industry (Orr 1982). At some social cost, landscape conservation was achieved.

Recapitulation in America

A similar story to that in the ancient Mediterranean world and historical Europe is being replayed in America and other former European colonies. Democratization of access to game led to disastrous depletion, which was finally curbed by transferring responsibility (read ownership) to the Crown. Although we acknowledge that wildlife is held in trust for the public by the state, recognize that Charlemagne used similar conservation rhetoric.

In the United States, central authority was established by the Lacey Act (1900), which restricted interstate movement of game products in response to the emergency created by uncontrolled market hunting. As an emergency measure, this was desperately needed but it established a course that seems unable to adapt to changing pressures on wildlife.

Two of the most vocal critics of market hunting, William Hornaday and Gordon Hewitt, endorsed private wildlife husbandry. Hornaday (1931) claimed to have invented a game fence manufactured by a Mr. Page. He saw the Lacey Act as an emergency measure and called the situation around 1910 "absurd and cannot long endure." Hewitt (1921), despite his determination to stamp out market hunting, urged the Dominion Department of Agriculture to launch their bison project and endorsed game farming, arguing that: "The sale of such surplus and propagated game is an entirely different matter from the sale of wild game as it now exists in our woods."

Part of the reason these men distinguished market hunting and game farming probably was the role of game breeders in the conservation of the bison.[1] But their position probably reflected a general view of rational exploitation as part of national progress.

History of Game Husbandry in America

Interest in the agricultural potential of wildlife in western Canada can be traced at least as far back as Samuel Hearne (1778) who advocated domestication of caribou for meat and an alternative to dogs for transportation in the north. A variety of animals were shipped to Britain,

---

1 We cannot judge what Samuel Walking Coyote thought when he herded a few of the last wild bison calves and sold them as foundation stock for the famous Pablo-Allard herd. I suspect he wondered "how much they were worth" as well as "how would they survive."

including black bears that were raised to provide grease for the treatment of baldness. Later, as the fur trade moved inland, a few bison were kept at some trading posts as a hedge against an interruption of supplies of wild meat for whatever reason.

Although native people certainly knew that wildlife could be tamed, they made no concerted effort to domesticate them, probably because they had no need to. However, the parkland and prairie tribes quickly seized the opportunity to supply the fur posts. Their burning programs seem to have been motivated at least partly to improve their marketing position. In general, had it not been for the massive Red River hunts and subsequently the robe trade, this system of communal tribal may have been sustainable.

The first serious attempts at game production were conducted at the Red River settlement *ca.* 1820. A bison herd was established, cross-breeding with cattle was attempted, and a Buffalo Wool Company was formed. However, bison were difficult to fence with materials available to the settlers and the project was disbanded with the widespread availability of cattle from Missouri (Moody and Kaaye 1976).

A number of private bison herds appeared throughout North America as settlement advanced and herds of wild bison dwindled. These were to play an important part in the rehabilitation of the species.

Beginning with the stock from these private herds, the Dominion Department of Agriculture launched a 50-year project in 1917 to explore the potential for cross-breeding bison and cattle. Although results of cross-breeding were disappointing, something was learned about the agricultural potential of pure bison. Despite an apparent potential, few bison were in private hands until 1968 when the federal government allowed the transfer of breeding stock and several provinces de-gazetted bison as wild animals. This has allowed the firm establishment of a modest but significant industry.

Interest in game domestication was not limited to bison. In 1917, Stephansson reported on the work of his Royal Commission on Reindeer and Musk oxen Domestication. The American Breeders Association formed an *ad hoc* committee to explore the agricultural potential of a variety of species. Although a number of exotics were considered, bison and wapiti were considered to offer the greatest potential.

In 1908, D.E. Lantz prepared a handbook for deer farmers that drew heavily on J.D. Caton's (1877) book on the deer and antelope of America and their suitability for domestication. Judge Caton considered the wapiti to be:

much better adapted to domestication than any of the other deer with which I have experimented. . . . They manifest dispositions not altogether lovely nor yet desperately wicked.

Everyone seemed to agree that the only obstacle was inimical legislation designed to curb market hunters. Most had faith that these were necessary emergency measures that would be relaxed once the crisis was averted. I suppose they are still waiting.

Hope was further dashed by two World Wars and an intervening Depression that limited the specialty markets necessary during the difficult first years of a fledgling industry. Thus, the current wave of interest should be seen as simply the continuation of a long-term trend rather than a brand new opportunity or threat.

Conclusions

What are we to make of all of this? Although Voltaire called history "tricks we play upon the dead," I hope I have drawn a valid historical conclusion that wildlife administration evolves in predictable ways presumably in response to similar needs. Far from being a brilliant bureaucratic invention, centralized management is a logical and rather unremarkable response to curb unregulated use in a frontier economy. Step-wise franchising of responsibilities for management to landowners or the public is an adaptive response when pressures on land replace unregulated hunting as the main threat to wildlife.

There is nothing inherently aristocratic about franchising with the North American system of land ownership. Many of the things North Americans dislike about European systems of management have more to do with the necessary limited access to wildlife where pressures are many times greater than in Alberta. Germany, for example, is about one-third the area of Alberta but it supports twice the Canadian population and more than twice Canada's industry. They have little alternative to a territorial hunting system and unusually intensive wildlife husbandry. The North American management system could no more be adopted there than the German system could be adopted here.

Problems with Public Wildlife Management

There is no question that wildlife populations have improved since the turn of the century in the aftermath of unbridled subsistence and market hunting. White-tailed deer have extended their ranges and are much more abundant now than in historic times. Wapiti and bison have been repatriated to some of their former ranges. Predators are now being seen as components of ecosystems and are managed rather than controlled. Many people are proud of these achievements and place great faith in the future.

Yet, compared with the abundance at the time of exploration and with what could still be, there are serious shortfalls. Canada still has a long list of species listed in CITES schedules, most of which live in rich prairie and parkland habitats now used for agriculture. Clearly, much remains to be done, but it is not simply a matter of doing more of the same.

This modest progress has been achieved simply by partially regulating harvests (perhaps 50% of the kill is unregulated), certainly the most important threat when North American wildlife policy was formulated. However, the much more formidable challenge of land-use control lies ahead. Frankly, this is a challenge that our system is not prepared to meet.

Although wildlife management has broadened emphasis from game to wildlife (that is, hunting to non-consumptive use) in response to a changing clientèle, it has not broadened administrative approaches. I am encouraged that we have started to explore co-management of resources with native people and to provide full compensation for wildlife damage, but I am embarassed that it has taken 80 years to do so.

Decentralization of Wildlife Administration

I see game ranching and farming as only one aspect of an overdue decentralization of wildlife administration. I would like to see many of the responsibilities for wildlife in the White Zone passed to regional management boards. I would like to see conservation education passed to public groups. I would like to see land (owned or leased) managed by wildlife management associations. And I would like to see individual landowners, or better yet, groups of neighboring landowners, form private nature reserves on which wildlife-related revenue could be generated. What we need is a diversity of approaches and, above all, the involvement of the public as participants rather than as spectators; as managers rather than as lobbyists. People are a creative force to be harnessed, not a problem to be controlled.

References

Benson, D. E. 1992. Commercialization of wildlife: A value-added incentive for conservation. pp. 539-553 in Brown, R. D. (ed.), *The Biology of Deer.* Springer-Verlag, New York.

Caton, J. D. 1877. *Antelope and Deer of North America: A Comprehensive Scientific Treaties upon the Natural History, Including the Characteristics, Habitats, Affinities and Capacity for Domestication of the Antilocapra and Cervidae of North America.* Hurd and Houghton, New York.

Forester, E. S. and Heffner, E. H. (trans.) 1068. *Lucius Janius Moderatus Columella on Agriculture.* Vol II Loeb Classical Library No. 407, Heinemann, London.

Geist, V. 1992. Deer ranching for products and paid hunting: Threat to conservation and biodiversity by luxury markets. pp. 554-561 in Brown, R. D. (ed.), *The Biology of Deer.* Springer-Verlag, New York.

Hawley, A. W. L. (ed.) 1993. *Commercialization and Wildlife Management: Dancing with the Devil.* Kreiger Publ. Co. Malabar, FL, 124 pp.

Hewitt, C. G. 1921. *Conservation of Wildlife in Canada.* Scribner, New York.

Hooper, W. D., (trans.) 1934. *Marcus Porcius Cato on Agriculture and Marcus Terentius Varro on Agriculture.* Harvard University Press, Cambridge.

Hornaday, W. T. 1931. *Thirty Year War for Wild Life: Gains and Losses in the Thankless Task.* Scribner, New York.

Hudson, R. J. 1993. Origins of wildlife management in the western world. pp. 5-21 in Hawley, A. W. L. (ed.), *Commercialization and Wildlife Management: Dancing with the Devil.* Kreiger Publ. Co. Malabar, FL.

Kirby, C. and Kirby, E. 1931. The Stuart game prerogative. *Engl. Hist. Rev.* 46: 239-254.

Moody, D. W. and Kaaye, B. 1976. Taming and domesticating native animals of Rupert's Land. *Beaver* 307(winter): 10-19.

Orr, W. 1982. *Deer Forests, Landlords and Crofters.* John Donald, Edinburgh.

Whittuck, E. A. 1904. *Institutes of Roman Law by Gaius.* Oxford University Press, Oxford.

Editor's Note: Exotic Animals: Conservation Implications

Texas wildlife management is dominated by *de facto* private control over wildlife via strong trespass laws with a nominal involvement by the state, and a long-standing tradition by land owners leasing their land for hunting or charging hunters by the day or the kill. There is little public land in the state. The focus on allodial rights brought with it a wide introduction of exotic ungulates on private lands, be it for private pleasure or for business. Professor Teer's paper gives a current evaluation of this, as the populations of exotics are increasing and spreading. There is little doubt that more attention will be given to these exotics in the future, and that policies pertaining to their shipment and use will be re-examined.

Exotic Animals

Conservation Implications

James G. Teer

Introduction

As humans entered new areas, so too did plants and animals they brought with them, or sent for later. Introductions were made for several purposes, generally to satisfy fundamental needs. Most cereal grains, fibre and ornamental plants, food and work animals, pets, and animals of sport hunting were moved from one place to another – often between continents – to provide food, shelter, clothing, and recreation. Out of nostalgia for the natal area or for former times, familiar forms of life were brought or sent for to provide mental links to the past (Teer 1979).

Translocation of native birds and mammals is important to re-establish species that have been extirpated from former ranges, to increase heterogeneity in gene pools, and to augment populations that are threatened by low reproductive viability. Griffith et al. (1989) reported that at least 93 species of native birds and mammals were translocated between 1973 and 1986 in Australia, Canada, Hawaii, New Zealand, and the United States. Most (90%) were game species, but threatened and endangered species also were translocated. Of the average 700 translocations made annually, 98% occurred in the United States and Canada. I suspect these data probably do not include the trade and movement of exotic animals in the United States; numbers would no doubt double if these were included (Teer 1991).

Despite the reasons why introductions are made, most are ill advised and there is little knowledge of their outcomes. Some have initially succeeded, but the introduced animals and plants have failed to become established. Through careful husbandry, selective breeding, and even evolutionary processes, many species of plants and animals have adapted to their new environments. Not all translocations, however, have ended happily or met human interests. Many translocated species have become pests or noxious to human health and agronomic and industrial pursuits. Some have transmitted or harbored other organisms that were inimical to human interests. A few, but only a few, have met expectations, and those few have stimulated further interest in these endeavors.

Importation and quarantine laws for wildlife are lax for most countries (Teer 1991). Laws and regulations governing introductions of livestock are stricter than those for wildlife. Although the private sector has been the primary importer and translocator of exotic animals, some government organizations have been active in searching for and stocking animals, especially game animals, for their constituencies. The U. S. Fish and Wildlife Service and some of the states formerly sent biologists abroad to find candidate species, especially game birds, for release in the United States.

Illegal traffic is widespread in many less-developed nations. The more affluent ones provide the markets. Illegal traffic is not usually in animals for transplanting purposes. Rather, contraband animals are the objects of the pet trade and may, in some cases, find their way to zoological parks. Some animals such as elephants and rhinos are threatened by their commercial value. However, commercial value may promote conservation of animals. The system of fee hunting in some parts of the world, which takes many forms including guided hunts, has promoted conservation of many large mammals.

I will now discuss my own region, Texas, where the introductions of large herbivores have had a significant impact on native habitats and fauna. Texas is a primary target for introductions of large herbivores. Many large Texas ranches can afford the cost of buying and stocking large ungulates, but motives go beyond wealth. Texans enjoy animals, want them in their presence in zoos if not at large, and can accommodate them along with their domestic livestock on large ranches. Although affordable cost and open rangelands are among the reasons Texas has been deluged with exotics, the primary interest has been generated by commercial interests in using animals for sport hunting.

The semi-arid regions of the world and the brush-invaded grasslands and savannas of Texas are similar habitats. Especially similar are Texas west of meridian 100, and the great ranges of eastern and southern Africa and Asia between latitudes 30$S and 30$N. Low precipitation that falls in a bimodal pattern and warm temperatures characterize the sub-tropical and semi-desert ecosystems in Texas. In addition, vegetation such as the brush species, *Acacia, Prosopis, Euphorbia, Disopyros, Zizyphus,* and many genera of grasses are common to the savannas, woodlands, and grasslands of Africa, Asia, and Latin America. These similarities have not been lost on the private sector in the New World. Many persons who have seen these distant ecosystems yearn to add the animals to their own ranches and regions.

Most transplants have been "trials," which succeed or fail in a hit-or-miss fashion, not planned translocations. Studies of the suitability of an exotic animal for a particular habitat, or of the requirements of the species, either ecologically or ethologically, are seldom made prior to moving the animals.

Some Ecological Principles to Consider in Introductions

A number of ecological principles are important in the success or failure of translocations (Teer 1979). Briefly stated, they are:

(1) Few if any vacant niches occur in the wild; every habitat tends to be occupied by a native form. Some argue the validity of this point for large mammals, because of vacant niches alleged to have been created by the extinction of Pleistocene herbivores (Martin 1984).

(2) Each species has a set of ecological requirements or tolerances that must be met if the animal is to succeed. Organisms or widespread distribution in a number of habitats are genetically plastic and have higher probabilities of success.

(3) Competition will occur between two species with similar requirements; that is, two tigers cannot occupy the same ant hill. Native species have the advantage because they have evolved in place.

(4) Animals taken from complex to simple habitats are more likely to succeed than reverse translocations.

A great many species of deer, antelope, camelids, and bovids from every continent have been introduced from abroad and from one place to another within their new locations. Curiously, the ones that have escaped from pens, as many have done, and have become established in free-ranging, reproducing populations, are almost entirely from Asia and particularly from the Indian subcontinent. In fact, all successful translocations in Texas, except the aoudad (Barbary sheep) came from Asia.

Perhaps there is something special in the physiology or behavior of Asian and Indian species that permits them to succeed where so many others from other continents have failed. One would expect successes with plains game from the great savanna ecosystems of East Africa, but not so. Despite many introductions, not one has been established in free-ranging, but is usually penned or herded, fed, and protected. Some other species occur in sparse and precarious numbers in escaped populations.

Many exotics are susceptible to low temperatures. Enormous numbers have died when ice and snow covered food supplies. Those from temperate and sub-tropical climates do not exhibit behavior patterns such as pawing through the ice and snow to get at food. Losses of blackbuck antelope occur frequently in the Edwards Plateau of Texas due to freezing rain. Many other species are affected. One example with which I am personally familiar involved the nilgai antelope on the Norias Division of King Ranch. Many succumbed in January 1973 after two successive episodes of cold and freezing rain coated the already sparse food supply. One of my students, Ben Brown, estimated 1400 animals of a total population of 3300 were lost (Sheffield et al. 1983).

Predation limits the success of some introduced species. Nilgai antelope, for example, seem to be especially vulnerable to coyotes, which are suspected of having kept nilgai numbers very low for many years when they were first introduced on King Ranch in south Texas. Coyotes, hunting by sight and smell, kill a naive prey with ease.

There are no known examples of failure of transplants of exotics or native herbivores caused by indigenous parasites or pathogens in Texas. Most have been remarkably free of infestations as they came in. But various parasites and diseases of domestic and native wildlife do infect exotics with debilitating effects on their populations, although none has been responsible for failures. Screw-worms, now virtually eradicated from Texas, at one time were a serious cause of death to newborn herbivores and their dams. It is suspected that this parasite had profound effects on initial attempts to establish nilgai antelope and other exotic herbivores in Texas.

Kind, Number, and Distribution of Exotic Herbivores in Texas

The number of exotic animals introduced into Texas has steadily increased since records have been kept (Table 1). The first estimate of exotics in Texas, made in 1963 by Jackson (1964), recorded 13 species totalling about 13 000 head. Thirty-three percent of the 1979 population of axis, sika, and fallow deer (36 938 head) were free-ranging in 17 of 35 counties of the Edwards Plateau of Texas (Baccus et al. 1983). By 1988, the number of exotic animals had increased to 123 species totalling 164 257 individuals on 486 ranches (Traweek 1989). Of the total, 73 857 were free-ranging in populations of unhusbanded animals.

Three cervids and three bovids make up most of the species successfully established in the wild: axis deer or chital, sika deer, fallow deer, nilgai antelope, blackbuck antelope, and aoudad or Barbary sheep (Table 2). Most of the exotics, both penned and free-ranging, are in the Edwards Plateau of west-central Texas, and in the Rio Grande Plains and Coastal Bend regions of south Texas.

Of the six species listed above, the nilgai antelope is arguably the most abundant of all the Artiodactyls in free-ranging herds in Texas.

Table 1: Number of principal exotic animals in Texas[1]

Species	1963	1966	1971	1979	1984	1988
Axis deer	2196	6450	11 171	22 799	38 035	39 040
Sika deer	634	875	2036	6217	7956	11 879
Fallow deer	220	445	2617	7922	10 507	14 163
Blackbuck antelope	3693	4125	5470	9639	18 798	21 232
Mouflon sheep	1846	10 000	16 169	9563	3817	4022
Aoudad sheep	1588	1300	3217	8451	14 651	20 402
Nilgai antelope	3334	4000	4120	2241	15 394	36 756

[1]All data were obtained by personnel of the Texas Parks and Wildlife Department using questionnaires to ranch owners and managers and from information provided by State Game Wardens. Inconsistencies in the data result from differences in survey methods and likely from mixing of species by respondents. (From Ramsey 1969; Young 1973; Armstrong and Wardroup 1980).

Table 2: Principal confined and free-ranging exotic ungulates in Texas in 1988[1].

Species	# confined	# free-ranging	Total	Principal vegetation area
Nilgai antelope	294	36 462	36 756	South Texas plains; coastal plains and marshes.
Axis deer (chital)	22 045	16 995	39 040	Edwards Plateau
Aoudad or Barbary sheep	10 927	9475	20 402	Edwards Plateau and rolling plains
Fallow deer	9433	4730	14 163	Edwards Plateau
Sika deer	6225	5654	11 879	Edwards Plateau
Total	48 924	73 316	122 240,	

[1]From Traweek (1989).

The nilgai's life and times in Texas will serve to illustrate some of the problems with introduced herbivores.

The Nilgai Antelope in South Texas

Nilgai were first introduced into Texas on the King Ranch in Kenedy County, Texas in about 1926. No more than a dozen were purchased from the San Diego Zoological Garden and released in lots of three to five head on the Norias Division. Another dozen (eight cows and four bulls) were released on the same division in 1941 (Sheffield et al. 1983). Numbers remained very low for many years. Lehman (1948) estimated only 100 were present on Norias in 1948. As could be expected, the growth rate began to accelerate as increasing numbers of adult females entered the population (the exponential stage of growth) in the middle to late 1950's. Twin calving is an attribute of nilgai not shared by many other bovids. The population peaked in the 1970s. Nilgai spread to neighboring ranches to the north and south of the transplant site.

In February 1989, when the most recent estimates were made by helicopter census, some 6500 were located on the 180 000 acre Norias Division (W. H. Kiel, personal communication). The original transplant has spread to the Arroyo Colorado, which is about the southern limit of the rangelands habitat in the Coastal Bend, and to north of Baffin Bay, primarily east of U.S. Highway 77. Stragglers have been reported as far north as San Patricio and Refugio counties, about 150 miles from the original transplant site.

The survey by Traweek (1989) of exotics listed 36 361 free-ranging nilgai in five south Texas counties: Kenedy, Willacy, Brooks, Hidalgo, and Jim Hogg. Most (33 340) remain in Kenedy County on the ranch where the original transplants were made.

These population data were obtained from interviews of ranchers and conservation officers. Although numbers are likely overestimated, it is not beyond reason for at least two-thirds of that number to be presently free-ranging, mainly in five very large ranches: the King, Kenedy, Armstrong, Yturria, and Pennell. Protection afforded them on these large ranches has ensured their increase and spread.

Competitive Relationships Among Nilgai, White-tailed Deer, and Cattle

During the years 1981-1993, studies of the relationships among white-tailed deer, nilgai antelope, and cattle were conducted on Haciendo Campo Alegre, a cattle ranch in Willacy County, Texas. The 5300-acre ranch adjoins the Norias Division of King Ranch where nilgai antelope were first released. Counts of nilgai, deer, and cattle were made from a helicopter each October or November. Counts were made on 200-metre wide transects from a height of about 30 metres, at a ground speed of about 35 mph. Transects for the census were established in 1981 and were used every year. Each transect was counted twice in the annual census. The area of the transects in the sample comprises 20% of the total ranch area. An average of the two censuses was used as the density of each class of ungulate.

Aerial censuses of large mammals in south Texas vary a great deal with weather, time of day, season of the year, and experience of the observers. Censuses made in this study were conducted by the author in all years, and in October or November when temperatures were beginning to decrease with the onset of fall. Despite standard conditions the differences in census results occasionally were larger than could be expected from the previous year's population parameters. Nonetheless, the trends were apparent and within reason in most years.

During the first 10 years of the study, 1981-1989, cattle numbers, and especially cattle with calves at side, varied, but averaged about 150 cows and bulls or about seven adult animals/km^2 (Table 3).

Table 3: Density of white-tailed deer, nilgai antelope, and cattle on a 5300 acre ranch in south Texas, 1981-89, in numbers per k^2.

Year	Deer	Nilgai	Cattle	Total
1981	11.8	6.6	7.0	25.4
1982	22.1	8.6	7.0	37.7
1983	10.7	9.7	7.0	27.4
1984	9.7	2.6	7.0	19.3
1985	15.4	6.6	7.0	29.0
1986	12.0	10.8	7.0	29.8
1987	18.9	9.2	7.0	35.1
1988	12.5	9.3	7.0	28.8
1989	11.0	10.0	7.0	28.0
1981-89 average	13.8	8.1	7.0	28.9

A change in the cattle operation was instituted in 1989, when the ranch was destocked and pastures rested for the three years. In 1992, 200 steers weighing about 220 kg each were pastured for six months, a stocking rate of a cow/2.3 km^2. Two lots of 300 steers, each weighing about 200 kg, were pastured in 1993, each lot being pastured successively for six months. Thus in 1993, the stocking rate of cattle was 3.5 animals/km^2. Although nilgai are present on Campo Alegre throughout the year, their numbers varied seasonally. Movements of nilgai occurred between adjacent ranches and Campo Alegre. They were most abundant on Campo Alegre in the cooler months, October through February or March. Causes for the seasonal movement were not clear; however, we suspected that nilgai were attracted to more abundant and preferred food sources on Campo Alegre.

Table 4: Average weight, in kilograms, of adult white-tailed deer, nilgai antelope, and cattle on Campo Alegre[1]

Age and sex	White-tailed deer	Nilgai antelope	Domestic cow
Adult male	64	240,	
Adult female	50	170	454
Average	57	205	454

[1]Adapted from Shefield et al. (1983)

Table 5: Animal unit equivalencies of white-tailed deer, nilgai antelope, and cattle in terms of live weight (biomass), in kilograms.

Class of animal	Average weight	Animal unit equivalent[1]
Domestic cow	454	1.0
Nilgai antelope	204	2.2
White-tailed deer	57	8.0

[1]Animal unit equivalent of deer and nilfai is obtained by dividing the weight of the nilgai (or deer) into the weight of a 1000 pound (454 kg) cow; for example, 454/204 = 2.2

Densities of white-tailed deer and nilgai antelope averaged 13.2 and 10.6 animals/km^2 respectively, from 1981 through 1993 (Table 3). During the 13 years, nilgai slowly increased until their numbers were essentially equal to those of white-tailed deer (13.2 deer/km^2 vs 10.6 nilgai/km^2). However, due to differences in average body weight, the relative importance of deer, nilgai, and cattle on food resources was quite different from their relative densities (Table 4 and 5). When densities of the three species on the 5300-acre ranch are adjusted for their weights, nilgai biomass was twice that of white-tailed deer and about one-third that of cattle. In terms of forage use, the relative impacts of deer and nilgai on forage resources were reversed.

The total stocking rate of all herbivores on the ranch has averaged 10.8 animal units/km^2 (Table 6), or one animal unit to about 9.2 hectares. Stocking rate or carrying capacity has been determined over the long term on a trial and error basis by ranchers of the region. According to the conventional wisdom of the ranching community, carrying capacity of rangelands in the sandy soils of the region is about one cow/11.2 kg. Thus the rate of stocking of the three herbivores has about equalled the long-term carrying capacity of the range.

Table 6: Stocking rates (in animal unit [AU] equivalents) on a 5300 acre (21.4 km^2) ranch in south Texas, 1981-88

Class of animal	Average # of animals on ranch, 1981-88	Animal unit equivalent (AU)	Number of AUs on ranch	AUs per km^2
Cattle	150	1.0	150	7.0
White-tailed deer	295	8.0	37	1.7
Nilgai antelope	173	2.2	79	3.7
Total	618	11.2	266	12.4

Table 7: Forage classes consumed by deer, nilgai antelope, and cattle[1] (in percent)

Class of animal	Grasses	Forbs	Browse	Mesquite beans
White-tailed deer	23	60	13	1
Nilgai antelope	60	25	6	9
Steer	95	3	1	1

[1]Adapted from Sheffield et al. (1983)

The three herbivores have quite similar food preferences, especially seasonally and for certain items (Table 7). With drought, as has occurred periodically in the region, competition for forage becomes severe. All herbivores are affected by the food shortages because all are reduced to feeding on whatever forage is available. White-tailed deer, the species favored by the ranch owners, are especially affected, with losses in body condition, productivity, and at times increases in mortality.

To accommodate wildlife during drought conditions in 1989, Campo Alegre took all cattle off the ranch. Even though the ranch owners are more interested in wildlife than livestock, they are finding nilgai a problem in management of the rangelands. The nilgai is not a particularly attractive trophy for hunting and the owners of the ranch do not wish to engage in any kind of commercial or sport hunting programs other than for themselves. Although these ranch owners are not particularly interested in cattle for profit, most are. To give forage and other resources over to animals not utilized for economic gain or significant recreational purposes can represent a serious loss to ranch owners.

Until recently, little use was being made of the transplanted species. Many ranches in the region have nilgai whether they want them or not; in fairness, most smaller ranches do desire some nilgai. The very large King and Kenedy ranches have begun to crop nilgai for sale of the meat to the restaurant and exotic meat trades. About 1500 nilgai of both sexes were harvested for sale of the meat in one 18 month period (Mike Hughes, personal communication). Sport hunting for deer and nilgai is also practiced on King Ranch, a matter causing some difficulty for meeting harvest quotas set by the meat-producing company.

The nilgai case history is a specific example of a generic problem with introduced animals. More striking successes and failures of transplants and translocations of animals and plants are available. New Zealand is, of course, the prime example. It and many of the oceanic islands have lost much of their indigenous fauna to exotics. Some of the native bovids on public lands in the western United States are threatened by releases of near-relatives with similar requirements and perhaps with burdens of parasites and pathogens that affect indigenous stocks; for example, bighorn sheep in the mountainous states, where ibex and aoudad have been released by well-meaning sportsmen and ranchers.

Competition for resources, and transfer of diseases and parasites from one region to another and between major land masses have frequently occurred. The probability of exotics becoming pests in significant.

What Can Be Done?

Considering the potential impact of exotics on indigenous fauna and flora, laws in the United States and elsewhere in the New World that govern the release of animals into wild environments are surprisingly lax. If one has the resources, practically any mammal can be brought in. Frequently, arrangements are made with a zoological park or some such holding agency for display of animals, in return for the offspring. Ultimately, progeny of the penned animals are released into wild environments. Birds may be trapped and transported to the United States. After about three weeks of quarantine, they may be released directly into the wild.

With 121 species already in the hands of the private sector in Texas and with no restrictions on their movement within the state and between most other states, one might say that all of this is only an exercise in reporting. Obviously, regulations governing intra-state and intra-regional translocations of animals should be strengthened.

The United States, and other countries for that matter, may be a melting pot of all nationalities of humans, but it should not be so for the world's animals as well. Every area possesses a specific environment in which a small subset of the world's fauna and flora have co-existed. The uniqueness of this environment should not be compromised for the permanent establishment of exotics.

Where we have free-ranging herds of exotics from several continents we have a large zoo without boundaries. Few people in today's society realize this. The lure of exotics is as the name implies: because they are . . . exotic. What needs to be impressed upon the public is that communities of native animals and plants are just as exotic to those who have not experienced them, as exotics are to those who have. Even though we may not be able to return to "ecological purity," circumspection and responsibility by those who control the land, by animal dealers, and by the public are called for in regards to introductions and translocations.

It is our responsibility, any of us who have an interest in conservation, to educate these individuals that the natural world is not just any kind of animal populating fields, forests, and ranges, but a subset of fauna depending on the characteristics of the present environment. We have an obligation to this natural world.

References

Armstrong, W. E. and Wardroup, S. 1980. *Statewide Census of Exotic Big Game Animals.* Fed. Aid Project W-109-R-3, Job 21, Texas Parks and Wildlife Department, Austin, 33 pp.

Baccus, J. T., Harvel, D. E. and Armstrong, W. E. 1983. Management of exotic deer in conjunction with white-tailed deer. pp. 213-226 in Beasom, S. L. and Roberson, S. F. (eds.), *Game Harvest Management*, Proc., Third Int. Symp., Caesar Kleberg Wildl. Res. Inst., Texas A&M Univ., Kingsville.

Griffith, B., Scott, J.M., Carpenter, J. W. and Reed, C. 1989. Translocation as a species conservation tool: Status and strategy. *Science* 245: 477-480.

Jackson, A. 1964. Texotics. *Texas Game and Fish* 22(4): 7-11.

Lehmann, V. W. 1948. Restocking on King Ranch. *Transactions North American Wildlife Conference* 13: 236-242.

Martin, P. S. 1984. Prehistoric overkill: The global model. pp. 354-403 in *Quaternary Extinctions: A Prehistoric Revolution.* University of Arizona Press, Tucson.

Ramsey, C. 1969. *Texotics.* Texas Parks and Wildlife Dept., Bulletin 49, 46 pp.

Sheffield, W. J., Fall, B. A., and Brown, B. A. 1983. *The Nilgai Antelope in Texas.* KS5, Caesar Kleberg Res. Prog. in Wildl. Ecol., Texas A&M University, College Station, 100 pp.

Teer, J. G. 1979. Introduction to exotic animals. pp. 172-177 in Teague, R. D. and Decker, E. (eds.), *Wildlife Conservation, Principles and Practices*, Wildlife Society, Washington, D.C.

Teer, J. G. 1991. Non-native large ungulates in North America. pp. 55-66 in Renecker, L. A. and Hudson, R. J. (eds.), *Wildlife Production: Conservation and Sustainable Development.* Agric. and Forestry Exp. Sta. misc. pub. 91-6, Univ. of Alaska, Fairbanks.

Traweek, M. S. 1985. *Statewide Census of Exotic Big Game Animals.* Fed. Aid Project W-109-R-8, Job 21, Texas Parks and Wildlife Dept., Austin, 40 pp.

Traweek, J. S. 1989. *Statewide Census of Exotic Big Game Animals.* Fed. Aid Project W-109-R-12, Job 21, Texas Parks and Wildlife Dept., Austin, 52 pp.

Young, E. L. 1973. Exotics. *Texas Parks and Wildlife* 31(8): 2-9.

Editor's Note:
Law Enforcement: A Wildlife Management Tool of the Future

Law enforcement, the monitoring and compliance check on laws and policies, is the subject least understood by wildlife biologists – unless investigations become part of their professional work. With the increase in conservation legislation and treaties this is a likely consequence. Moreover, luxury markets in dead wildlife in affluent states such as the U.S., Germany, and Japan, aided by rapid international air traffic and containerized shipments, have spawned organized criminal activity that is now plundering our wildlife resources. Add to this the breakdown of conservation legislation such as via game ranching and the legal markets they demand, and the difficulties supporting free-ranging public wildlife may prove to be insurmountable.

At the very least society requires a national investigating arm to simply stay informed about the dimensions of the wildlife crime problem. In this regard the U.S. Fish & Wildlife Service has done outstanding work; there is no comparable agency in Canada, one reason this nation's legislators and leaders are but scantily informed about the national problem of illegal wildlife destruction. Were it not for the U.S. Fish and Wildlife Service law enforcement efforts, many nations would be poorer informed still. The increase in conservation and environmental legislation, the development of the professions of Environmental Science and Professional Biology, increase the likelihood of wildlife managers and biologists working closely with law enforcement agencies and the courts. This makes wildlife law enforcement a very important topic.

Law Enforcement

A Wildlife Management Tool of the Future

Thomas L. Striegler[1]

Abstract

Dwindling wildlife populations coupled with an increasing human population have created an economic incentive to the illegal commercial trade in wildlife and wildlife products. In order to effectively address the problem of organized criminal activity involved in commercial wildlife trade, environmental pollution, and other modern wildlife crime, wildlife managers must ensure that law enforcement remains an effective tool of wildlife management. It is the responsibility of wildlife managers to ensure that law enforcement activities under their control have goals and priorities that address the most significant law enforcement problems facing the wildlife resource. Wildlife law enforcement must be properly organized, trained, and equipped to deal with the sophisticated problems of wildlife crime in the future. Wildlife managers must ensure that appropriate control of law enforcement activities is exercised and that adequate funding and staff resources are provided to ensure that wildlife law enforcement is capable of addressing the problems of wildlife crime in the future.

Introduction

Current Problems Facing Wildlife Law Enforcement

Over the past 20 years, wildlife law enforcement has changed dramatically. Today, the world's human population is approaching a level at which it will eventually exceed the planet's capacity to feed, clothe, and house it. Global destruction of forests and other wild areas to provide food, fibre, and building materials is destroying wildlife habitat at alarming rates. Pollution of air, water, and soil is approaching a point where some people believe the very existence of life on this planet is threatened. All of these factors have combined to create unprecedented threats to wildlife populations.

[1] Special Agent in Charge, Branch of Investigations, Division of Law Enforcement, United States Fish and Wildlife Service.

Unless otherwise noted, all figures are for fiscal year 1992.

Dwindling wildlife populations coupled with an ever-expanding human population have created an economic incentive to poaching and illegal commercial exploitation of wildlife resources that was unknown only a few years ago. Prior to the late 1960s, wildlife law enforcement officers were primarily involved in the enforcement of laws designed to regulate the sport hunter and fisherman. Wildlife officers enforced game bag and creel limits, checked hunting and fishing licenses, and conducted other law enforcement duties that society has traditionally associated with the job of "Game Warden." However, since the early 1970s, the job of the wildlife law enforcement officer has become more complex than previous generations could ever have imagined.

Wildlife crime is no longer limited to nighttime deer hunting or fishing out of season. Today, wildlife officers must deal with major international cartels trading in millions of dollars worth of illegally taken wildlife and wildlife products. Illegal commercial markets in ivory, parrots, furs and hides, live reptiles, deer and elk antlers, and numerous other products abound. It is not uncommon to find these same criminal elements dealing in narcotics, illegal firearms, and other contraband. Frequently, wildlife law enforcement officers are being asked to enforce laws against environmental pollution and toxic wastes. Looking into the future, it does not appear that things are going to improve. In fact, it is almost certain that global problems of pollution, habitat loss, and overcrowding will only get worse. The resulting loss of wildlife populations will escalate the competition for the resource. This increased competition for a dwindling resource will require wildlife criminals to become even more sophisticated.

The nature of wildlife crime today is more complex than at any time in history. The most serious threat to the wildlife resource is not from the individual poacher who kills an animal illegally for his own consumption. Today, many species are threatened by criminal organizations that include poachers who kill animals illegally for the commercial market. These poachers then sell their kill to middlemen, who in turn sell the animals or their products to processors. Processors manufacture the animals into products that are then sold to the consumer. This chain of illegal commerce may be confined to a small rural community and involve a half dozen or fewer individuals, or it may involve hundreds of conspirators and a worldwide consumer market. To effectively attack this type of criminal activity, wildlife law enforcement must be able to identify all levels of the criminal organization. To attack only the poacher or only the end retailer ignores the people in the middle, who are the ones making the enormous profits.

Added to these problems is a continuing public perception that wildlife violations are not really criminal activities. For the most part, the public still seems to think of wildlife crime as about the level of seriousness as a traffic violation. Because of this public attitude toward wildlife crime, law enforcement techniques that are considered acceptable for anti-drug enforcement or white collar crime are criticized as outrageous government conduct when used by wildlife law enforcement officers.

Present Systems of Wildlife Law Enforcement

In the past 20 years, significant improvements have been made in the field of wildlife law enforcement. Officers are better educated, trained, and equipped than ever before. In many areas, however, wildlife law enforcement still lags behind other law enforcement specialties. If wildlife law enforcement is to be a useful tool for wildlife managers in the future, it must be brought on par with other law enforcement activities in terms of organization, control, resources, and techniques.

Most modern wildlife managers have a background in biology. Many universities throughout the world offer excellent curricula in wildlife management. The graduates of these schools are the leaders in wildlife management today. However, because few of these schools include law enforcement as part of their wildlife management curriculum, many wildlife managers may have little knowledge of, or experience in, law enforcement. Therefore, an examination of current wildlife law enforcement practices may be helpful in determining how wildlife law enforcement can be improved in the future.

Generally, wildlife law enforcement activities are administered by the wildlife management agency of government. There are some notable exceptions to this, however. In Alaska and Oregon in the United States, wildlife law enforcement is the responsibility of the state police, whereas wildlife management responsibilities are carried out by the respective state game and fish departments. In most countries, the enforcement of the Convention on International Trade in Endangered Species of Wild Fauna and Flora (CITES) is the responsibility of customs, although in the United States, primary authority for CITES enforcement rests with the U.S. Fish and Wildlife Service. For the most part, however, wildlife law enforcement is a responsibility of the government's wildlife management agency.

Regardless of the various systems of wildlife management practised around the world, wildlife law enforcement programs are often surprisingly similar. In Zimbabwe, for example, the Chief of Law Enforcement is responsible to the Director of Wildlife. In each region, there is a Regional Supervisor for law enforcement who supervises a number of Game Scouts. These Game Scouts perform the field law enforcement activities.

This organization is not unlike that found in the United States Fish and Wildlife Service or in game and fish departments of many of the states. In the U.S. Fish and Wildlife Service, the Chief of the Division of Law Enforcement serves as staff to the Director. Field law enforcement activities are supervised by an Assistant Regional Director for Law Enforcement assigned to each of the seven regional offices. Actual field law enforcement is performed by Special Agents.

Despite the similarities in organization, field enforcement activities may vary significantly. In Zimbabwe, wildlife law enforcement activities involve paramilitary patrols. Game Scouts engage in what is essentially counter-guerilla warfare. Both poachers and Game Scouts may be heavily armed and a confrontation between the two may result in a full-scale fire fight. In the United States, Fish and Wildlife Service Special Agents are trained as criminal investigators and use sophisticated investigative techniques to uncover wildlife crime. These officers function more along the lines of the agents of the Federal Bureau of Investigation or of the U.S. Customs Service. In each case, however, the wildlife law enforcement agency is responding to the particular circumstances under which it is required to do its job.

Regardless of the system of wildlife management employed by a government, there are certain basic concepts that must be considered if law enforcement is to be an effective part of that system. These include goals and objectives for law enforcement, the organization and control of the law enforcement program, the techniques and procedures used by law enforcement officers, and the provision of sufficient funding for effective operations.

Goals and Objectives

The basic goal of law enforcement is to create a deterrent to crime. In wildlife law enforcement, the goal is to create a deterrent to the violation of wildlife laws. Modern wildlife laws can generally be classed as one of two types. Laws are designed either to protect wildlife from illegal taking, or to accomplish management or administrative goals such as collecting of management information or raising revenue. Wildlife laws that are intended to protect wildlife from illegal taking may prohibit or regulate many other kinds of activities including hunting, killing, trapping, selling, purchasing, importing, exporting, and transporting wildlife. However, the basic objective of these laws is to prevent the illegal taking of wildlife from the wild. Laws that are designed to accomplish management or administrative goals generally require the purchase of a license or permit before a person can legally hunt, trap, fish, or engage in some other activity that would otherwise be prohibited by the laws designed to protect wildlife from illegal taking. Often these laws also require the submission of information by licensees. This information is often a primary source of management data to the agency.

If wildlife law enforcement is to meet its objectives, it must serve the needs of wildlife managers. Although this statement appears obvious on its face, it implies an underlying responsibility on the part of wildlife managers to identify those needs. This identification of management needs goes beyond the establishment of law enforcement priorities and annual objectives, although these are important. It goes to the heart of the basic fabric of the society itself. Good law enforcement requires good laws. It is incumbent that wildlife managers work with the legislative body of government to ensure that the laws designed to protect wildlife are fair, understandable, and enforceable. Wildlife laws must be based upon identifiable needs to protect the resource.

Laws must be flexible enough to allow fair and just application without permitting preferential treatment of the politically or financially favored. If laws are too complex, neither the public not the agency itself can clearly understand the need or intent. On the other hand, if laws are too simplistic, they often lack the flexibility needed by wildlife managers to effectively adjust management practices to changing biological trends.

In addition to serving the needs of wildlife managers, wildlife law enforcement must be perceived as necessary and fair by the public. Without public support, wildlife law enforcement, like any other government function, becomes a liability of the government rather than an asset. If the public believes that wildlife law enforcement is arrogant, abusive, or overzealous, the objectives of wildlife protection may well be jeopardized. Voluntary compliance with the law is based upon public support of the law and its enforcement, and on public belief that violators will be caught and punished.

Organization and Control

Wildlife Agency Versus Police Agency Control

The organization and control of law enforcement is a major factor that must be considered by wildlife managers. In a democratic society, civilian control over the military and law enforcement is essential. Both of these functions of government should be maintained to serve society, not to control society. However, within the basic concept of civilian control, there is a wide range of options available to the wildlife manager.

In most of the United States and Canada, as well as around the world, wildlife law enforcement is a function of the wildlife management agency. As mentioned earlier, two notable exceptions are the states of Alaska and Oregon, in which wildlife law enforcement is the responsibility of the state police. Even in these states, however, the wildlife law enforcement officers are assigned to a separate division within the state police organization. In Alaska, wildlife officers of the state police even wear a different uniform.

The issue of whether wildlife law enforcement should be the responsibility of the wildlife management agency or part of the general police agency of government has proponents on both sides. There are good arguments for each system. Those who believe that wildlife law enforcement should be the responsibility of the wildlife management agency argue that if law enforcement is, in fact, a tool of wildlife management, then control of that tool must rest with the wildlife manager. The wildlife manager must be in the position to establish law enforcement priorities that are consistent with the management needs of the resource. Proponents of this option also argue that in a general police organization, wildlife law enforcement cannot compete for budget and staff resources with law enforcement activities directed toward crimes against people such as robbery, rape, homicide, or drugs.

As an example of how wildlife managers can change the priorities of law enforcement to meet the needs of the resource, the U.S. Fish and Wildlife Service has, during the late 1980s, increased its priority for the protection of migrating and wintering waterfowl because of the sharp decline in populations of these species. The Service's Division of Law Enforcement quickly responded to this priority by sending task forces of Special Agents into principle waterfowl concentration areas along the migration routes and into the wintering areas. These task forces were instructed to concentrate their efforts on apprehending hunters who exceeded the daily bag limit and who hunted over bait (feed placed in the hunting area to attract birds). Of the various hunting violations encountered, these are believed to have the greatest adverse impact on the waterfowl population in North America. This increased law enforcement activity produced a remarkable decline in these violations within just one year.

Because wildlife law enforcement is an integral part of the U.S. Fish and Wildlife Service, this shift in priorities was accomplished quickly and efficiently. The result was a significant decrease in the violations most closely associated with illegal taking of migratory waterfowl.

Advocates of placing the responsibility for wildlife law enforcement within the government's police agency argue that, however specialized it may be, wildlife law enforcement is essentially a police activity. Wildlife managers, they argue, do not have the knowledge or experience to manage a police organization. Modern-day law enforcement is too complex to be managed by anyone who is not a law enforcement professional. Further, in times of tight budgets, wildlife managers tend to place lower priority on law enforcement than on biologically based management practices. Therefore, the law enforcement budget is the last to be raised and the first to be cut.

Both sides of this issue raise valid arguments to support their position. Wildlife law enforcement is much more complex than it was even 20 years ago. Notwithstanding the fact that the wildlife laws passed by the United States Congress in the past 20 years are some of the most complex statutes in the country, the entire area of law enforcement in the United States has been complicated by countless laws and court decisions upholding the civil rights of private citizens to be free of unreasonable government intrusion. Certainly, the vast majority of people, including the law enforcement community, support this emphasis on individual rights. However, the restraints that these court decisions and laws have placed on law enforcement have significantly increased the complexity of law enforcement. To be effective in today's society, a law enforcement officer must be a highly trained professional.

For years, wildlife managers and wildlife law enforcement officials argued that since law enforcement benefited the wildlife resource, it was somehow exempt from the restrictions placed upon the law enforcement community in general. One might term this the theory of the "higher call." Such is clearly not the case, at least in the United States. Wildlife law enforcement is subject to the same constitutional constraints that restrict the actions of other law enforcement activities. Hunters, fishermen, trappers, importers, and other consumptive users of wildlife have the same constitutional protection as do other citizens. Violation of this basic constitutional protection can subject the officer and the agency to civil liability and result in enormous monetary damages being awarded to the plaintif. In addition, the concept of vicarious liability can place supervisors and managers of law enforcement officers at risk of civil action if it can be shown that they were negligent in providing proper supervision or training.

Certainly, the increasing complexity of law enforcement and the need to ensure the protection of the rights of individual citizens are strong arguments for placing responsibility for wildlife law enforcement under professional police management. However, this does not necessarily preclude wildlife law enforcement from being a part of the government's wildlife management agency. Actually, a stronger argument can be made that the world's increasing human population and decreasing wildlife populations and habitat have increased the complexity of wildlife management at least as much as the emphasis on individual rights has increased the complexity of law enforcement. Therefore, it is essential that wildlife managers be provided with control of all the tools available to them, including law enforcement. With appropriate organization and proper controls, a wildlife management agency can effectively manage its law enforcement responsibilities to ensure protection of individual rights, while at the same time providing wildlife managers control of this valuable management tool.

Systems of Organization Currently in Use

There is a continuing debate over the most effective organization for wildlife law enforcement. This debate essentially focuses on two separate issues. First is the issue of centralized authority versus decentralized authority for law enforcement activities. In many wildlife management agencies, the chief law enforcement officer at the central headquarters exercises direct supervisory authority over all law enforcement activities within the agency. Even if the general agency organization is one of regionalization, law enforcement does not fall under the regional organization. Most law enforcement professionals tend to favor this type of organization. This "paramilitary" style of authority is the type used by most law enforcement agencies.

In agencies that exercise decentralized authority over law enforcement, the chief law enforcement officer at the central headquarters functions as staff to the agency director. Line authority over law enforcement is delegated from the director to a regional director, who is usually a wildlife management professional. Actual supervision of regional law enforcement activities is the responsibility of a regional law enforcement supervisor who is usually a wildlife law enforcement professional. This form of law enforcement organization is generally favored by professional wildlife managers.

It is difficult to state categorically whether centralized or de-centralized control of law enforcement is more effective. To a large extent, the decision was made so long ago that it is now a matter of agency tradition. Certainly, enough examples of each type of organization can be shown to operate effectively and efficiently to indicate that this is not a major factor in the overall effectiveness of an agency's wildlife law enforcement program.

The second issue involves the type of wildlife law enforcement officer employed by the agency. This issue is somewhat more complex because there are really two major issues involved. The first is the debate over full-time law enforcement officers versus dual-purpose wildlife manager/law enforcement officers. Proponents of full-time law enforcement officers argue that the complexity of modern law enforcement requires that wildlife officers be full-time professional law enforcement officers, whereas advocates of dual-purpose wildlife manager/law enforcement officers believe that the cost effectiveness of the dual-purpose officer outweighs any shortcomings.

Again, the decision between full-time law enforcement officers and dual-purpose officers is often a matter of agency tradition. In this case, however, a strong argument can be made that both wildlife management and law enforcement have become so complex that it is difficult, if not impossible, for one individual to maintain proficiency in both disciplines. Another disadvantage to the dual-purpose officer is that generally these employees joined the agency following graduation from college with a degree in wildlife management. Many of these officers never considered law enforcement to be a duty that they would be required to perform, and often they have little interest in law enforcement. Therefore, these officers may neglect their law enforcement duties to concentrate on the wildlife management responsibilities of their job. On the other hand, many dual-purpose officers may find the challenge and excitement of law enforcement exceeds that of wildlife management. When this occurs, wildlife management duties may be neglected in favor of law enforcement. In either case, it is difficult for a dual-purpose officer to truly master both disciplines.

In addition to this debate, there is another debate over uniformed patrol officers versus criminal investigators. In the United States, state wildlife conservation agencies primarily employ uniformed patrol officers although some state agencies maintain a limited investigative staff. The U.S. Fish and Wildlife Service, on the other hand, depends primarily on plain clothes criminal investigators to fulfill its major law enforcement responsibilities. The Service does employ uniformed officers, but most of these officers are generally assigned to law enforcement as an incidental responsibility an addition to their primary management duties. Generally, uniformed officers of the Service are responsible for law enforcement within the boundaries of the National Wildlife Refuge System, although they may engage in limited enforcement activities in adjacent areas. This difference in the use of uniformed officers versus plainclothes investigators is more a function of the law enforcement priorities of the various agencies rather than a major difference in law enforcement philosophy. An examination of any mid-size or larger police department reveals that both uniformed patrol officers and plainclothes investigators, usually called detectives, are needed to effectively accomplish the objectives of the department. The same is true of most wildlife law enforcement programs.

The enforcement of CITES presents special organizational problems to wildlife law enforcement agencies. As stated previously, most of the approximately 110 party nations use their customs services to enforce CITES restrictions on the import and export of wildlife and wildlife products. However, CITES is primarily a wildlife management agreement. Generally, customs officers have neither the training nor the experience to effectively enforce the complicated provisions of CITES. In addition, the use of customs officers to enforce CITES is equivalent to using state police to enforce other wildlife laws. It takes control of this phase of wildlife law enforcement out of the hands of wildlife managers.

An alternative is to give responsibility for the enforcement of CITES to the wildlife management agency of the government. Because it is not generally necessary for CITES enforcement officers to have full law enforcement authority, CITES enforcement officers do not need the full police training that is required for uniformed patrol officers or for criminal investigators. For example, in the United States CITES enforcement is primarily the responsibility of the U.S. Fish and Wildlife Service. Using a group of officers known as Wildlife Inspectors who are stationed at designated customs ports of entry, the Fish and Wildlife Service inspects and clears approximately 72 000 importations and exportations annually. Because their law enforcement duties are limited to the inspection of wildlife shipments in the controlled environment of a customs port of entry, wildlife inspectors are not authorized to carry firearms or to make arrests.

All except perhaps the smallest wildlife law enforcement programs need both uniformed patrol officers to perform what can be called compliance enforcement, and plainclothes criminal investigators to conduct investigations into more complex wildlife criminal activity. Uniformed officers provide a level of presence that is readily recognizable by the public, and are responsible for field law enforcement activities as well as overt compliance duties, such as facilities and records inspections of license and permit holders. Criminal investigations can uncover complex criminal conspiracies and illegal commercialization of wildlife, which often represent a far greater threat to wildlife populations than the opportunistic violator. As with a police department, it is only through an appropriate mix of patrol officers and investigators that a wildlife law enforcement program can be fully capable of addressing the law enforcement problems of the future. If a wildlife agency has responsibility for the enforcement of CITES, then consideration should also be given to the inclusion of uniformed wildlife inspectors into the agency organization.

Control of Law Enforcement Activities

Although organization is important to the effectiveness of any wildlife law enforcement program, proper control of the law enforcement activity is essential. The primary elements of control of law enforcement, which are described in detail below, include development of adequate law enforcement policies and priorities, ensuring compliance with those policies and priorities, providing adequate law enforcement training, providing effective supervision of law enforcement personnel, and developing adequate procedures to deal with allegations of misconduct.

Development of Law Enforcement Policy

The first step in ensuring adequate control of law enforcement is to develop a comprehensive set of law enforcement policies. Law enforcement policy is defined as the basic guidelines for how the agency conducts its law enforcement activities. Policies are relatively stable. They do not change based upon changes in wildlife resource populations, agency budgets, or priorities. Examples of the types of activities for which policies must be developed to effectively manage a wildlife law enforcement organization include qualification with, and use of, firearms, investigative and crime-reporting procedures, conduct of undercover activities, handling of evidence, and limitations on the types of enforcement or investigative activity in which officers are to engage. Other areas in which policies are needed include accountability and use of undercover funds (if authorized); procedures for establishing and running an undercover business; use of agency owned or leased motor vehicles; and conditions under which vehicle emergency equipment such as lights and siren may be used. Certainly this is not a comprehensive list, but it serves to give an idea of the variety of policies that are necessary.

Within each policy, the agency must establish specific guidelines for its officers to follow. For example, if wildlife law enforcement officers are authorized to carry firearms, agency policy should establish the circumstances under which officers are expected to be armed, the types of firearms authorized, the type of ammunition permitted, the procedures for requalification and the frequency with which an officer must requalify with each type of weapon authorized, and the conditions under which an officer is permitted to use deadly force. An agency's firearms policy should also include procedures for reporting and investigating any use of deadly force by an officer and procedures for addressing an officer's failure to requalify or otherwise comply with the policy.

In developing policy, an agency should develop a system that codifies all agency law enforcement policy into a single manual. To be effective, policy must be disseminated to the field officer. Therefore, the agency must ensure that policy is distributed in a timely manner. The agency must also have a mechanism for periodic review of existing policy to ensure that revisions are made as necessary.

Establishing Priorities

Priorities should be flexible agency guidelines that tell law enforcement officers where and how they should be spending their time. As opposed to policies, which are relatively stable, priorities should change to reflect the most serious problems facing the wildlife resource. The agency should have an established procedure for developing and disseminating priorities to the field. In many agencies this is done through some kind of annual work plan document that is developed by headquarters based upon input from the field. For example, if a review of reports from field biologists indicates that deer populations are declining, an agency may want to have law enforcement officers spend more time in apprehending nighttime deer poachers.

Ensuring Policy and Priority Compliance

Once an agency establishes policies and priorities, it must also develop procedures to ensure compliance with those policies and priorities. There is a distinction between failure to comply with policies and priorities, and employee misconduct, although the two may be closely related and in fact one may be an indication of the other. Ensuring compliance with policies and priorities should be a routine agency activity. Dealing with employee misconduct should always be an extraordinary occurrence.

One of the most effective ways to ensure policy and priority compliance is to develop a standard program of inspections of subordinate offices. Under such a system, each supervisory office has responsibility for conducting periodic compliance inspections of the next lower level of the organization. Such a system would require the central headquarters office to conduct periodic inspections of each region within the agency. Regional offices would be responsible for inspecting the field offices under their supervision. Following each inspection a report should be submitted that would recommend areas in which improvements could be made. In addition, it is helpful if inspection reports also point out areas in which an office excels. Generally, the office that has been inspected should be required to take corrective action based upon the recommendations of the inspecting team and to report those corrections to the next higher headquarters.

For an inspection program to be effective, it must be fair and objective. If employees perceive that the primary purpose of inspections is to find fault, then morale will suffer and the result of the program may be counterproductive. On the other hand, if the inspection program is designed to help subordinate offices manage their operations more effectively, then the results of the inspection will benefit both the employees and the agency. One of the simplest ways to ensure fairness and objectivity in an inspection is to prepare an inspection check list that outlines each area that an inspection team will examine. Acceptable levels of compliance should also be documented. Each office to be inspected should be notified well in advance of the dates of the inspection and should be provided a copy of the check list as a guide for preparing for the inspection. This procedure provides an incentive for the office being inspected to correct any deficiencies before the inspection, thereby making the employees a part of the inspection process.

Training Requirements

Wildlife law enforcement officers must be as fully professional as any other law enforcement officers. Proper training is one of the best methods of ensuring professionalism among wildlife law enforcement officers. If a government is going to give its wildlife law enforcement officers the authority to deprive citizens of liberty through the process of arrest, to seize private property with or without a search warrant, and to carry firearms, then it is incumbent upon that government to ensure that those officers are as well trained as any other law enforcement officers having the same authority.

Law enforcement training is generally divided into three categories: basic, advanced, and continuing. Basic training is the training that new law enforcement officers receive when they are first hired by a law enforcement agency. This training is designed to provide the basic skills that are needed by a law enforcement officer as he or she first starts out in his or her career. Advanced training is usually specialized training that an officer may receive at any time during his or her career. Advanced training is generally given to an officer when the need for a particular law enforcement skill has been identified by the agency. Continuing training, often called "in-service training," is refresher training, usually given at regular intervals to all law enforcement officers.

In all but six states in the United States, wildlife law enforcement officers have full peace officer status. This means that they have the same authority as state police or county sheriffs to enforce all criminal laws of the state. Generally, the laws of the various states require that state peace officers meet certain minimum training requirements. Therefore, most state wildlife officers in the United States receive the same basic training as state or city police officers. Following this basic police training, new wildlife officers receive training in the basic skills that are unique to wildlife law enforcement.

Special Agents of the U.S. Fish and Wildlife Service have full federal law enforcement authority, equivalent to their counterparts in the Federal Bureau of Investigation or the U.S. Customs Service. Newly hired Special Agents must complete an eight-week criminal investigators training course at the Federal Law Enforcement Training Center in Glynco, Georgia. This is the same course required of all federal criminal investigators except FBI agents and Drug Enforcement Administration agents, who are trained at the FBI Academy at Quantico, Virginia. In criminal investigators school, Wildlife Service Special Agents learn alongside other federal investigators, including agents of the U.S. Secret Service, the U.S. Customs Service, and the Bureau of Alcohol, Tobacco and Firearms. Included in the curriculum of the criminal investigators course are training on the laws of arrest, the rules for criminal court procedure, handling of evidence, testifying in court, basic firearms training, unarmed defensive tactics, photography, fingerprinting, report writing, raid planning and execution, interviewing of witnesses, and law enforcement ethics.

Following this eight-week course, new Special Agents must complete a five-week Special Agent Basic Course provided by the Fish and Wildlife Service. This course includes training in the various laws and regulations enforced by the Service, wildlife identification, report writing and case management, ethics, small boat operation, four-wheel drive vehicle operation, and Service firearms policy. Upon successful completion of these 13 weeks of formal classroom training, new Special Agents are assigned to one of several training assignments where they undergo 12 to 18 months of on-the-job training under the close supervision of a senior Special Agent.

Because law enforcement is a constantly changing profession, it is imperative that wildlife law enforcement officers be provided periodic in-service training. In the United States, 40 hours of in-service training annually is generally considered necessary to maintain proficiency. Subjects normally taught at in-service training include review of policies, updates on laws and recent court decisions, firearms requalification and defensive tactics, officer health and safety issues, review of recent significant investigations, and instruction in new investigative techniques.

In addition to basic and periodic in-service training, wildlife officers may require specialized advanced training. Such training may include advanced law enforcement photography, white collar crime investigation, undercover operations, or the use of specialized equipment such as polygraph, electronic surveillance devices, or radio-tracking equipment.

Ensuring Effective Supervision

If wildlife managers are going to maintain a successful law enforcement program, they must ensure that field officers are properly supervised. Because wildlife officers are often widely dispersed and many times assigned to single officer duty stations, supervision is especially difficult. However, effective supervision is the key to meeting the priorities of wildlife law enforcement.

Like the non-commissioned officer in the military, the first line supervisor is the key to effective supervision. The first line supervisor must provide guidance and leadership. Although field officers are expected to exercise resourcefulness and ingenuity in performing their duties, the first line supervisor must ensure that agency policies and priorities are followed. Supervisors must know what their employees are doing and ensure that employee efforts are directed toward the highest priorities of the agency.

There are a number of measures that an agency can take to assist first line supervisors. First, it is essential that basic supervisory training be provided to all newly selected supervisors. This supervisor training should encompass the practical aspects of supervision as well as the theoretical. For example, in addition to teaching techniques for motivating employees, new supervisors must be taught how to deal effectively with employee misconduct and poor employee performance. New supervisors must be taught that their primary duty is supervision. Supervisors should clearly understand the goals, policies, and priorities of the agency, and they should also be taught communication skills.

Secondly, the agency should establish specific responsibilities for which supervisors will be held accountable. Each level of supervision must ensure that it accomplishes its responsibilities without interfering in the duties and responsibilities of subordinate supervisors. Upper levels of supervision and management should establish clear policy to prevent employees from going over the head of their immediate supervisor. This does not mean that an agency should not have appropriate grievance procedures, but management should insist that employees follow the procedures that are established and work through their immediate supervisors.

Care must be taken that the span of control of any supervisor is not excessive. As the distance between employees and their supervisor increases, so does the difficulty for a supervisor to maintain control. While a first line supervisor may be able to effectively supervise eight to ten employees who are all assigned to the same duty station, that same supervisor may only be able to effectively supervise half that number if each employee is assigned to a single officer station 100 to 200 miles from the supervisor.

Finally, supervisors should be held accountable for how well they supervise. The rating of supervisory ability should not be directly related to the performance of subordinate employees, although it cannot be entirely divorced from it either. However, it should be recognized that a unit that has a number of good, self-motivated employees and a poor supervisor may outperform a unit that has an outstanding supervisor but a number of poorly performing employees. It is easy to supervise good employees and difficult to supervise poor employees. The true test of a supervisor is how he or she is able to deal with problem employees.

While good supervision is important in any organization, its importance in law enforcement cannot be overemphasized. Employees who are chronic problems are generally a result of poor current or past supervision. An officer who is allowed to continually make trivial or petty cases or to abuse the public can undermine public support for the agency's law enforcement program. Law enforcement is unpopular enough without contributing to its unpopularity by allowing an officer to abuse his or her authority. Eventually, such conduct will undermine public trust in the agency and can result in a reduction of funding available for the law enforcement program. It is the responsibility of both management and supervisors to ensure that this does not happen.

Handling Employee Misconduct

No matter how well organized, no matter how adequate its policies, no matter how well trained and supervised a law enforcement agency is, it will at some point become subject to allegations of misconduct on the part of one or more of its officers. Allegations may include charges of excessive force, violations of civil rights, harassment, criminal activity, or even personal misconduct on the part of an officer. It is imperative that wildlife law enforcement agencies have established procedures for investigating such allegations, and if the charges prove valid, for taking firm disciplinary action. Many police departments have internal affairs units that handle investigations of misconduct against their officers. Other law enforcement agencies are part of a larger organization that has an independent internal investigative staff, such as the Office of the Inspector General for the Department of the Interior, which investigates allegations of misconduct on the part of the U.S. Fish and Wildlife employees as well as employees of other bureaus within the Department.

Once an allegation of misconduct is received, it is essential that a fair and independent investigation be conducted as quickly as possible. If the investigation clears the officer of the charges of wrongdoing, then that fact should be made public. If, on the other hand, the investigation substantiates misconduct on the part of an officer, then swift and appropriate disciplinary action should be taken.

Techniques of Wildlife Law Enforcement

Patrol Versus Investigative Techniques

As wildlife crime has become more complex, so have the techniques used by wildlife law enforcement officers to apprehend wildlife criminals. The wildlife law enforcement officers of today may use law enforcement procedures that range from routine patrol to complex undercover operations. The key for proper management of wildlife law enforcement programs is to ensure that the appropriate technique is used in the appropriate circumstances.

To a large extent, the techniques used by wildlife law enforcement officers are a function of the organization of the agency. Those agencies that primarily employ uniformed officers generally rely on police-type, patrol-related enforcement techniques. On the other hand, agencies that primarily employ plainclothes criminal investigators generally rely on investigative techniques. Virtually no modern wildlife law enforcement agency maintains an adequate mix of uniformed patrol officers and plainclothes criminal investigators. Therefore, almost all wildlife law enforcement agencies have handicapped themselves by limiting their ability to use the full range of law enforcement techniques effectively.

To some extent, agencies have tried to overcome this problem through inter-agency cooperation. For example, the U.S. Fish and Wildlife Service often conducts joint investigations with state wildlife law enforcement agencies. This type of cooperation provides the state agency, which may have little experience or expertise in complex investigations, with the investigative experience of the Fish and Wildlife Service. At the same time, the Fish and Wildlife Service often requests assistance of state wildlife agencies for uniformed officers to assist in situations where a uniformed presence is preferred to plainclothes officers. There are, however, limitations to this type of cooperation. Each agency has its own priorities and often is unable to provide assistance to the other agency because of limitations of funding, staff, or operational mandates.

Selection of Appropriate Techniques

One of the most difficult management decisions in wildlife law enforcement involves the selection of the appropriate technique for a particular case. If patrol procedures are used in a case that requires an undercover operation, then it may not be possible to gather sufficient evidence to prosecute. On the other hand, if undercover tactics are initiated in a case that could be successfully handled through routine law enforcement techniques, then valuable funds and staff time will have been wasted. There is no single best law enforcement procedure. Effective wildlife law enforcement depends upon an agency being able to determine the appropriate techniques for a given situation and having the resources within its own organization to carry out those techniques effectively.

Use of Undercover Operations

Perhaps the most controversial investigative technique used by law enforcement agencies today is the undercover operation. Wildlife managers should clearly understand that an undercover operation is one of many investigative techniques that are available. However, because of the sensitivity and the controversial nature of undercover operations in today's society, a separate discussion of this investigative technique seems advisable.

Undercover operations pose both special problems and special risks for any law enforcement agency. Where the use of undercover operations is authorized, this technique can be particularly effective in cases involving illegal commercial activity. Undercover operations have been used successfully by a number of wildlife law enforcement agencies. However, undercover activities must be closely monitored and supervised. In addition to the inherent risks to the safety of the undercover operative, there are substantial risks that civil rights violations may occur, as well as the potential for adverse public reaction.

Before an agency approves the use of undercover operations, it should develop a comprehensive policy to govern the approval and conduct of such activities. This policy should include circumstances in which undercover operations are warranted, procedures for approval of an undercover operation, levels of review and approval of undercover operations, controls on the types of activities in which an undercover operative may or may not engage, procedures for periodic review of the undercover operation, policy for accounting for the use of undercover funds, and steps that must be taken to prevent undercover operatives from engaging in outrageous government conduct. Once such a policy is adopted, no undercover operation should be initiated or continued unless it complies with all aspects of the policy.

Undercover operations should be the investigative technique of last resort. Almost always, undercover operations are more expensive, more time consuming, and require a greater investment in staff than conventional investigative procedures. Therefore, such activities should be used with discretion. Often a careful review of the investigative options will reveal that the same results can be achieved more quickly and economically through the use of conventional investigative activities. However, there is an aura about undercover operations that often leads law enforcement officers to request approval of such techniques when it is obvious to the objective observer that it is not appropriate. For this reason it is essential that each request for approval of an undercover operation be closely reviewed. Approval should only be granted when it is clear that conventional techniques will not work.

In reviewing an application for approval of an undercover operation, an agency should evaluate the investigation against its current priorities. All too often, law enforcement officers request approval to conduct expensive, time consuming undercover operations against activities that are considered low priority by the agency. In these cases, the time and expense may not be worth the result, no matter how successful the operation. Agencies should also evaluate the risks involved in an undercover operation versus the potential benefits.

Once an undercover operation is initiated, the agency should review the progress of the operation periodically. At each review, the agency should make a conscious decision to continue, modify, or discontinue the operation. The conduct of the operation should be evaluated against the undercover policy of the agency to ensure compliance.

Scientific Investigative Support

The increased sophistication of wildlife crime and the complexity of modern wildlife laws require that wildlife managers provide wildlife law enforcement with up-to-date scientific investigative support. There are over 600 species and subspecies listed in the appendices to CITES. Often products manufactured from products of these species or subspecies can only be identified through the use of the most modern scientific equipment. Identification of the source of hair, blood, bone, hide, feathers, and other material is often crucial to a successful wildlife investigation. Successful prosecution of a wildlife criminal is often dependent upon the identification of a species or subspecies from which these samples derived. The wildlife law enforcement officer also needs the capability of submitting for scientific examination other items of evidence such as bullets and shell casings, soil samples, paint chips, fingerprints, hair and fibre samples, pesticide samples, and any other items of evidence that may be discovered.

For decades, police departments have used the modern crime laboratory to augment other investigative procedures. Beginning in the mid-1970s, a few police crime labs began research designed to assist wildlife law enforcement officers with their investigations. However, most of this work was considered low priority when compared to lab work involving crimes against people. It was not until 1989 that the first crime lab dedicated to wildlife law enforcement became operational. The U.S. Fish and Wildlife Service's National Fish and Wildlife Forensics Laboratory in Ashland, Oregon, is a modern, fully equipped crime laboratory. Scientists there are currently engaged in research that may one day revolutionize wildlife law enforcement.

Financing a Wildlife Law Enforcement Program

Wildlife law enforcement programs are expensive. The U.S. Fish and Wildlife Service currently estimates that it spends about U.S. $100 000 to operate each Special Agent per year. The average cost per Wildlife Inspector is currently U.S. $55 000 annually. These costs include salary and benefits, travel, equipment, training, and administrative and clerical support. The U.S. Fish and Wildlife Service employs an average of 220 Special Agents and 80 Wildlife Inspectors. Added to these costs are the costs of maintaining a headquarters staff, computer support, and other administrative and support costs. The total annual budget for law enforcement in the Service exceeds U.S. $33 250 000 annually. An additional U.S. $2 000 000 is needed to fund the operation of the National Fish and Wildlife Forensics Laboratory.

Today there are generally two primary methods used to fund wildlife management programs. The first is through the use of funds appropriated from the government's general tax collection process. This is the primary source of funds for the U.S. Fish and Wildlife Service. The second is to fund the program from the funds derived by the agency from the sales of hunting and fishing licenses and other revenues collected by the agency. Many state wildlife agencies in the United States are funded through this method. Wildlife law enforcement programs that are the responsibility of the government's wildlife management agency receive their funding through the agency's budgetary process and are, therefore, either funded from appropriated funds or self-funded, depending on the system used by the parent agency.

In the past ten years, the United States government has relied increasingly on a concept of user fees to help fund services that are provided for the benefit of a limited number of citizens. Using this user fee concept, the Fish and Wildlife Service charges inspection fees to most commercial importers of wildlife and wildlife products. The Fish and Wildlife Service also charges user fees for processing most of the wildlife permits issued annually. These fees, which total more than $2 000 000 annually, are used to offset the cost of providing these services.

Another source of revenue available to the law enforcement program of the U.S. Fish and Wildlife Service is money collected from criminal fines and civil penalties assessed to wildlife violators. These funds are placed in a special account and may be used to pay rewards for information leading to the arrest or conviction of wildlife criminals and to pay for the costs of storing wildlife and wildlife products seized as evidence in wildlife crimes.

A final source of funding available to the law enforcement program is the Fish and Wildlife Foundation. The Foundation is a semi-public organization established by the United States Congress to accept private donations and provide these funds to assist the Service in accomplishing projects for which public funds are not available. Primarily, Foundation funds are used to finance wildlife management projects. However, some funds have been used to assist in the purchase of law enforcement equipment and to fund law enforcement operations.

As the world's population increases and the public's demand for more and better government services escalates, the competition among the various functions of government tax revenues will increase. Wildlife managers will have to be innovative in their efforts to provide adequate funding for wildlife law enforcement. Appropriated funds, user fees, fines and penalties, and private donations are all viable sources of funding that may be used to finance wildlife law enforcement and other wildlife management programs.

Looking to the Future

No one can predict the future with complete accuracy. However, although conservation efforts may slow current patterns of habitat loss and reductions in wildlife populations, it is unlikely that these trends will be reversed in the foreseeable future. The deterioration of the environment will further complicate the already complex problems facing wildlife managers. As the supply of wildlife and wildlife products diminishes, demand for these products will increase. The basic laws of supply and demand will drive already high prices even higher. As the populations of more and more species become threatened by commercial exploitation, restrictions on trade in those species will increase. The result will be huge profit incentives for those who are willing to engage in illegal trade in wildlife and wildlife products.

As profits from illegal wildlife trade increase, those engaged in such trade will become more sophisticated and dangerous. If wildlife managers are to effectively curtail this illegal trade, they must use all the modern law enforcement techniques available. The concept of the monolithic wildlife law enforcement organization is rapidly becoming obsolete. The wildlife law enforcement agency of the future must incorporate uniformed patrol officers and plainclothes criminal investigators. If the agency has responsibility for enforcement of CITES or domestic legislation that restricts the importation or exportation of wildlife, then some form of wildlife port inspector should be included in the agency's organization. To support their wildlife law enforcement, wildlife managers must ensure that adequate forensics laboratory capabilities are available.

Wildlife managers must ensure that their wildlife law enforcement program is fully as professional as other law enforcement agencies. The public will no longer support inadequate or poorly trained law enforcement efforts. To ensure the level of professionalism that will be required, wildlife managers must develop adequate policies and priorities to properly manage and control law enforcement activities. Wildlife law enforcement officers must receive professional training compatible with other law enforcement professionals. Wildlife law enforcement must be professionally managed and efficiently supervised. Supervisors and managers must be properly trained and held accountable for achieving the law enforcement goals and objectives of the agency.

Wildlife law enforcement agencies must be capable of using the most modern law enforcement techniques and procedures. The future of effective wildlife law enforcement depends upon wildlife managers and wildlife law enforcement officers being able to adapt to an ever-changing world. As wildlife and environmental crime become more sophisticated, so must the techniques and procedures used by wildlife law enforcement officers. The days of the field game warden are not gone, but to this traditional wildlife law enforcement officer must be added the skills and talents of the trained criminal investigator, the undercover officer, the wildlife port inspector, and the forensic scientist. It is only through a multi-disciplinary team approach to law enforcement that the wildlife manager of the future will be able to effectively utilize this valuable management tool to prevent the criminal exploitation of the world's wildlife resources.

Editor's Note: Alternative Forms of Wildlife Management and Their Consequences

This is the voice of a practitioner, of a manager of wildlife, of one who served in the rough and tumble of state politics in Wyoming, in the halls of power of Washington, and the distant abode of Africa. And he served effectively. These thoughts and propositions are not from the halls of academia, but spring from a life of service to the public and to the wildlife resource most North Americans cherish. That is why the words of Doug Crowe are so important. The arise from the grass roots of practising wildlife management – and they need to be heeded.

Alternative Forms of Wildlife Management and Their Consequences

Douglas M. Crowe[1]

Wildlife resources in America are held in common by all the people. No one person is more endowed than any other with rights or privileges concerning their use. Because wildlife belongs to all, public agencies are entrusted with the responsibility to manage this resource in our common interest.

These basic tenets of wildlife management and conservation are being questioned. There are private interests now seeking special privileges not enjoyed by the common citizen. Further, these interests desire, for themselves, management prerogatives superseding those currently vested with public agencies. The objective of this movement to "privatize" wildlife is to grant to commercial interests the right to determine hunting seasons and bag limits, and to designate who may participate in the hunting experience and who may not.

Some view this movement as a good thing. Others view it as an anathema. Conflicting viewpoints are the "stuff" of argument and politics, so the debate rages as both sides of the issue vie for the hearts and minds of the people. The fires of this debate are fanned by wildlife managers themselves. We, as a profession, seem unable to decide whether we are in the business of wildlife conservation or animal husbandry. Perhaps this should come as no surprise, since the very term by which we define our profession is an oxymoron – a combination of contradictory words. My dictionary defines "wild" as "free of control and direction," and "management" as "the act of controlling and directing." We are, therefore, involved in the business of controlling and directing a resource that is, by definition, free of control and direction. Is it any wonder the profession is schizophrenic?

Despite this apparent enigma, wildlife is routinely managed. The question is, should the emphasis be on "wild" or on "manage?" There are those in the profession who lean toward the "manage" side of the ledger. Others favor the "wild" side. My own personal bias is that wildlife managers should, first and foremost, be responsible for the

---

[1]U.S. Fish and Wildlife Service.

maintenance and perpetuation of free-ranging populations of wild animals. In attending to this charge, the orderly and equitable distribution of wildlife-related benefits to the general public is the primary consideration. In other words, one can manage people and one can manage habitats, and in so doing one can manage animal populations. But, when one actually controls and manipulates the animals themselves, they are by definition no longer wild, and it is animal husbandry, not wildlife conservation, that is being practised.

If the premise that wildlife management should be directed at the maintenance of wild populations, and not individual animals, is to be accepted, then a practical definition of a population is in order. The gist of most textbook definitions is that populations are "collective groups of organisms of the same species occupying a particular space." This concept may be useful in an academic context, but inadequate from a management perspective. A population might be a dozen deer feeding in a meadow, or all the caribou in the western hemisphere. The definition can, however, be expanded to provide the precision necessary for application to wildlife conservation efforts. In this regard, and for purposes of wildlife management, a population can be defined as a "naturally self-maintaining group of organisms of the same species occupying a geographic area that will sustain it for the foreseeable future." Three phrases are key to this definition.

(1) *A naturally self-maintaining group*: a wild population is a self-contained entity requiring no artificial supports for its maintenance. Another characteristic of a naturally self-maintaining group is that the members are actually or potentially interbreeding. That is, the individuals making up the group are distributed such that the opportunity for mating with each other occurs in each reproductive cycle. Patterns of dispersal and/or behavioral characteristics may prevent some members of the population from contributing to the reproductive process during any given cycle, but the potential exists. Therefore, a population is a relatively closed system, genetically. Immigration is not necessary to maintain viability, and emigration usually occurs to the extent that it has little impact on the population dynamics.

(2) *A geographic area that will sustain it*: wild animals have demonstrated for many million years that they are capable of taking care of themselves. All they require is a place in which to do so. From a population perspective this means that suitable habitat, and free access to it, must be available within a framework of seasonal habitats. In this context, a population of wild animals is inseparable from the area it occupies. Occupancy may vary seasonally and involve a number of jurisdictions over the land occupied, but the manger must take a broader view than that offered by individual seasonal ranges or land ownership.

(3) *For the foreseeable future*: this final qualifier connotes that for a population to exist it must be subject to the evolutionary processes that shaped it. No wild population can be maintained long if insulated from the forces of natural selection. Without the effects of meteorological extremes, predation, disease, accidents, and inter/intraspecific competition, a population will undergo behavioral and genetic drift. For wild animals to retain those characteristics for which we value them, they must coexist with the forces that made them what they are.

This definition of a population leads to a practical and operable description of management as it applies to the long-term maintenance and perpetuation of wildlife resources: "Wildlife management is the process of maintaining populations of wild animals at levels consistent with the social, economic, and cultural desires of the people." To maintain populations at levels consistent with the social, economic, and cultural desires of the people is a complex issue. To begin with, these desires quite often are at odds with one another within any one culture. When this is expanded to include the global community, the immensity of the problem comes into focus. The fact is that on a global scale no such consistent level exists. The people have no such common desires. What is acceptable in one country will not be acceptable in another. The only common denominator is that for a wildlife conservation strategy to be successful it must benefit the people, for without public support the maintenance of viable wildlife resources cannot occur. These benefits may be social in one country, economic in another, and cultural in a third – or occur in various combinations. But the central paradigm remains. The public will not support a wildlife conservation effort from which they perceive no benefits.

This brings me to what it was I was supposed to discuss in the first place – alternative forms of wildlife management. In recent years much has been made of various approaches to wildlife management, with a great deal of rhetoric expended on the relative merits of the European versus the African versus the North American approaches to hunting. My observations on this debate are within the definition of wildlife management offered earlier.

Throughout much of Europe, wildlife is a commodity of the landed gentry, managed for monied interests by techniques of animal husbandry. That this form of management is considered a viable North American alternative by anyone strikes me as curious. Our founding fathers left Europe to escape this sort of "privileged class" oppression and created a system on this continent that reserved wildlife to the people. All the people!

Although the European system did not make it to North America, it did migrate to Africa. Consequently, for the average African, wildlife represents no social, economic, or cultural benefit. That much of Africa's wildlife has been decimated during this century is testimony to the fact that when benefits do not accrue to the people, wildlife is inevitably the loser. Recently, the African country of Zimbabwe has moved to reverse this trend by assuring that benefits do accrue to the general public. They have given wildlife back to the tribes in the sense that money derived from hunting is returned directly to the people. The results have been remarkable. No longer are wild animals a symbol of the rich and powerful. Instead, they are seen as a valuable benefit to the "rank and file" native. Dramatic increases of wildlife on tribal trust lands have been the result. Unfortunately, this has been misinterpreted by some. Those who would "privatize" North America's wildlife point to this success as a model for this continent. But North America is not Africa! The people here have not been disenfranchised from their wildlife. Hunting is part of our cultural heritage. It is the benefit the average hunter receives from wildlife, and the reason conservation programs are supported. To remove the opportunity for this experience from the common man removes the cultural benefits derived by the many in exchange for economic benefits flowing to the hands of a few. History has shown us all too clearly that wild things and wild places are the loser when this happens.

The North American conservation movement arose in reaction to commercial exploitation, and with it came the notion that the cultural benefits associated with wildlife were for everyone. Theodore Roosevelt perhaps said it best when he wrote:

> *Above all, we should realize that the effort toward this end is essentially a democratic movement. It is in our power . . . to preserve game . . . for . . . all lovers of nature, and to give reasonable opportunities to the exercise of the hunter, whether he is or is not a man of means.*

Man, Wildlife, and Conservation in North America

Status and Change

Ian McTaggart-Cowan

The first Europeans reaching the Atlantic Coast of North America looked out from their ships at an endless sweep of wilderness. To the horizon in all directions stretched a sea of forest; no recognizable villages, no smoking chimneys, no roads, no fields with grazing livestock, nothing that reminded them of the land they had departed. This first impression was confirmed on landing; still no roads, no carriages or carts – nothing with wheels, no beasts of burden or people on horseback. The small number of people they saw dressed strangely, occupied dwellings that seemed inadequate to the newcomers and lacked even the simple furnishings that were essential for comfort.

These settlers brought with them the basics for survival European style: metal tools, household furnishings, domestic animals, a start-up supply of seeds and roots, gunpowder, and weapons. They also brought an urgency for land clearing, the concept of land as a commodity, an economic philosophy based upon money, a militant theistic religion, and a fear of wilderness and all it connoted. This was a wild, strange, and untamed land seen as a challenge to be conquered and converted to some semblance of what they had left. At the same time most of them were escaping intolerable conditions in the 'old land.' They were here to stay.

The native North Americans who watched them land were at home. They and their ancestors had occupied this continent for some 12 000 years and had learned to knit together the widely diversified resources into a life that satisfied them. They had no concept of wilderness. What to the new arrivals was, in large part, an uninhabited land free for the taking, was to them the source of their existence, the burial place of their ancestors, and the residence of the spiritual concepts around which their lives were organized. They tilled the land with simple tools, grew crops of corn, beans, artichoke, pumpkin, squash, and melons. They gathered and stored fruits, nuts, roots, and mushrooms. They fished, used a great variety of marine and fresh water invertebrates, hunted birds and mammals for meat, pelts, hides, sinew, and bone. They had dogs for the hunt and to carry burdens; they had an effective technology for making fire, for converting materials to their use, for manufacturing functional tools of wood, bone, antler, and stone; they had weapons for distant killing, for offence and defence, and a substantial *materia medica*. They used the great rivers and lakes of the continent and the near-shore seas as transportation corridors via canoes of many ingenious designs. Their spirituality embodied the forces of the environment and the creatures that assured their survival. Ritual gave order to their lives through the passing seasons.

Through the 12 000 or more years since the first people crossed from northeastern Asia into this uninhabited continent, they had steadily increased in numbers to an estimated North American maximum of some 3.6 million people (Denevan 1992). They had extended their range from the high arctic of North America to the southernmost tip of South America. In so doing they had evolved great cultures as well as cultural specialists in the use of many ecosystems. On the way, also, they had greatly changed the character of the land they first entered, modifying it to their purposes. So the landscape that to the arriving Europeans was a frightening wilderness actually bore the imprint of man in every direction.

Recent research has revealed that the 19th century concept of the American continent at the time of Columbus as an almost uninhabited land, with barely perceptible evidence of human disturbance, was largely a myth invented by 19th century primitivist writers such as W. H. Hudson, Cooper, Thoreau, Longfellow, and Parkman (Denevan 1992). "To the contrary, the Indian impact was neither benign nor localized and ephemeral, nor were resources always used in a sound ecological way (Denevan 1992)." There is convincing evidence that throughout New England, the midwest, and southeast, much of the landscape had been considerably altered by Indian industry well before the end of the 15th century. Even as far north as what is now southern Ontario agriculture made an important contribution to the food resource and increasingly to the south much of the forest had been altered by frequent burning. It was no longer a dense tangle of trees difficult to pass through, but a forest of widely spaced trees, few shrubs, and large areas of grass and other herbage (Williams 1989), a very different biotic community from the original state. Not only did Indian burning maintain a mult-iaged and restructured forest but, looked at from the harvester of natural food products, it favored fire resistant species, many of them mast producing,[1] and it greatly increased the amount of forest edge where berry producing plants and small game flourished. It is evident that the extensive agricultural clearing and repetitive burning had led to the creation of forests in many different

[1] trees producing primarily acorns of the many species of oak found in the U.S., but also beech nuts, pine nuts, filberts, walnuts, chestnuts, etc.

successional stages and interspersed with glades, meadows, savannas, and prairies.

Unavoidably the details of the impact of long continued burning on forests is best known from eastern North America. Contemporary accounts are available from there prior to the time that European infectious diseases decimated the Indian populations and advancing European-style land clearing for agriculture began to obscure evidence of precolumbian conditions. Along the Mississippi Valley the indigenous people (the Choctaws) were described as living primarily on the products of their cultivated land which extended many miles along the fertile river valleys (White 1983). These cultivators also transplanted American chestnut, Canada plum, Kentucky coffee tree and groundnut, and other food plants (Day 1953).

The many different ecological regions of North America differed greatly in their capacity to provide for a hunter/gatherer society. They differed also in their potential to support the cultivation of food crops, but almost throughout the continent the early inhabitants used fire to alter their surroundings to better suit their wants (Day 1953).

The most detailed accounts of the purposeful use of fire to accomplish predetermined changes in the ecosystem are available from the research of Henry T. Lewis of the University of Alberta. While his studies relate to California and Australia as well as the boreal forest of northern Canada the latter are of special significance. Using evidence derived from 50 older Native people from 30 communities across the forested areas of northern Alberta, a picture emerges of "a remarkably sophisticated approach to and understanding of the dynamics of fire for the management of plant and animal resources in a boreal forest environment" (Lewis 1977). It is true that the accounts he derives refer to practices of the late 19th and early 20th centuries and involve a cultural approach to forest resources heavily oriented to the fur trade and the use of horses for transportation. Burning practices may have evolved to become ever more specialized during the 400 years of Indian contact with European ideas, but there is little reason to doubt that the understanding of ecology he attributes to the Native people and the burning practices they demonstrated were other than ancient. The unanimity apparent from his informants from widely separated communities belonging to different linguistic groups is significant in this regard.

These were people who had survived for centuries hunting and gathering in some of the most inhospitable landscapes of the continent. They had gained a detailed understanding of the relative productivity of different stages of forest succession and had developed considerable skill in manipulating them, using the only tool they had – fire. They burned to produce and maintain openings in the forest that made travelling easier, that attracted moose, and made hunting more productive. They created and maintained meadows varying in size from a few hectares to as much as 90 square kilometres or more (Lewis 1977). They had learned that removal of the accumulated dry vegetation made for earlier green-up in the spring and that this attracted wildlife. They used fire to set back streamside succession[2] for the benefit of their beaver colonies and to improve marshes for muskrats and waterfowl. And the burning was done at seasons and under local circumstances that usually permitted control of the fire.

The extent to which the North American landscapes were altered by man depended in part on their capacity to support people and the advantage gained by the inhabitants through changing the environment. The "nations" inhabiting the coast from Alaska to Washington State probably had the lightest touch on the environment. The exceptional productivity of the northern Pacific Ocean provided most of their food requirements. The forests of huge coniferous trees in a generally humid climate resisted burning as an easy way of altering their surroundings. The durable and easily worked western red-cedar provided building materials and the source of canoes. The sea was the only needed highway.

In the extensive delta of the Fraser River and along the southeastern shores of Vancouver Island there is evidence that fire was used much as it was along the Atlantic Coast and that deer and elk were important creatures as food and for material products. North of Vancouver Island there were no elk, moose, or caribou and the small black-tailed deer were scarce and generally stayed close to the seashore with its fringe of deciduous vegetation. The mountain goat, though localized, scarce, and demanding of skill and courage in the hunt, was the most important ungulate largely as a source of wool for ceremonial costumes. Large runs of spawning salmon to all rivers and most streams attracted grizzly and black bears in numbers. There was little to be gained by gross modification of the environment. Here the signs of 10 000 years or more of occupation by early man are almost confined to the revegetating clearings that once held villages, the mounds of clam shells holding the residue of uncounted meals, the canoe haulways cleared of rocks, and giant cedar trees, still living, but bearing the scars where bark was removed by people long departed. It was a region where the abundance of resources gave scope for the development of a culture extraordinarily rich in social organization and artistic and ceremonial expression but that changed the environment little and had no discernible impact on the wildlife.

---

[2] the succession of plant (ecological) communities that follow on the deposits of silt and gravel laid down by a stream as it changes its course in a valley.

Aboriginal Man and Wildlife in North America

It is unfortunate that the Europeans who first had the opportunity to describe in detail the ecological circumstances in which the Indians of the early 16th century lived, almost totally ignored the topic. There are fanciful reports of the lands along the eastern seaboard rich in all forms of wildlife and edible plants, reports that read like those of land promoters to this day. Other writers give accounts of wars fought over hunting grounds, of hunger and starvation (White 1983). Strife over hunting grounds is a certain indication of populations no longer able to meet their needs on the lands available to them. If this occurs over any considerable area the inference can be made that population has exceeded resources and overkill of the food animals is almost certain.

In the literature there is a tendency to overgeneralize as to wildlife abundance and failure. North America is a land of immense environmental diversity and was inhabited by societies just as diverse in their specialization for survival. The environmental diversity to a large extent reflected variations in climate. We know from present experience the magnitude of even very local changes from year to year that heavily impact stocks of native wildlife as well as crops of berries and mast. Thus it would be surprising if wildlife and user groups were so synchronized that they ebbed and flowed in unison over large geographic areas. What was true of the wildlife stocks available to the native agricultural societies of the American southeast is unlikely to have been so for the hunters of the Canadian boreal forest areas.

In the northern regions of the continent, where hunting and gathering were the survival mode, the limitation on human population was almost certainly failure of the food supply. However, Cronon (op cit.) gives his opinion that "the low Indian populations of the precolonial northern forests had relatively little impact on the ecosystems they inhabited." He implies an equilibrium situation and invokes unstated ways in which Indian populations restrained their fertility to maintain a low density, and thus to avoid the otherwise inevitable confrontation between the availability of animal prey, and the number of mouths to be fed. Usher (1981) warns against the acceptance of such a predator\prey paradigm in considering the interaction of subsistence hunters and the food sources they depended on. He suggests that cultural mechanisms for control or management should be assumed to be at work. This is probably correct where alternative external food sources are available, but without these the room for cultural responses is very limited.

Generalized hunters, such as those of much of pre-Columbian Canada, appear to present the most exacting constraints upon the development of a model that will reveal the environmental factors and biological responses that can lead to a sensitive equilibrium between man the hunter and the hunted. The testing time in northern North America is winter and there starvation has probably always been an important cause of death (Dunn 1968).

Even if some demographers are correct in their view that populations of hunter/gatherers, other than small groups trapped by unusual circumstances, in some unknown way usually escaped the food imposed limits on population size, there seems to be no unanimity on alternatives. The loose category of social mortality including infanticide (Birdsell 1968), geronticide, homicide, warfare etc. have been identified by Dunn (1968) as significant in the population equation. More recently a searching examination of the "myth of population self regulation" has led to the conclusion that "While the human population of the earth may indeed have been regulated for much of its existence, it has rarely, if ever, been established for the particular groups that ecological anthropologists study, that population regulation existed or was brought about by any particular social practice" (Bates and Lees 1979). Under such circumstances it is logical to conclude that the most ready source of ultimate population control on the numbers of predators was operative also for man.

The impact of the availability of animals for food on the size of human populations is but one side of the equation. The other is the impact of man the predator on the numbers of the species used as food.

Two lines of evidence appear to link historical predation by man with decline in wildlife numbers and distribution. The first can be found in rapid increase in the numbers of some food-resource animals after epidemic disease decimated the hunter populations. Pandemics of small pox, and possibly chicken pox, and other diseases of European origin, devastated the Indian peoples of the Atlantic coast beginning in 1616 and recurring in one part of the region after another until at least 1633. It is stated that in some regions as much as 95% of the population died (Cronon 1983:87). Contemporary accounts refer to rapid increases in the numbers of deer and elk subsequent to the pandemics. Such wildlife increases would be fuelled by the reduction of the kill along with the availability of many acres of revegetating fields now left fallow with the deaths of their cultivators.

The advance of the American bison east of the Mississippi took place at the same time and it may have been facilitated by the presence of the clearings formerly tilled or burned by the resident Indians (Roe 1971).

A second example is from the other side of the continent. When, in 1793, Alexander Mackenzie made his historic transit from a winter camp on the Peace River to the Pacific Coast and back, he travelled a land almost devoid of large eatable wildlife. His journal records the sighting of just 2 large animals on the entire journey, 2 deer on an island in the Fraser River south of the present town of Quesnel. In the area he travelled in northeastern British Columbia, moose were so scarce as to be of no consequence as a food animal, and from there on west to the coast they were absent. Moose began to enter the region some 70 years after Mackenzie's journey (Hatter 1950). It has been suggested (McCabe 1928) that this "break out" of the moose population in western Canada began when the populations of subsistence hunters declined from epidemic disease.

Another source of evidence of the interaction between early man and wildlife on the North American continent comes from the apparent occurrence of overkill of some vertebrate species by precolumbian hunters (Martin 1979; Kay 1994).

Martin (1967) first called attention to the possible role of man in the extinction of many species from the megafauna of the late Pleistocene of North America. He pointed to the coincidental occurrence of the emergence of man as a significantly numerous predator and the disappearance of several genera and species of large late Pleistocene mammals. He also adduced evidence from the association of the remains of these species with cultural evidence of human hunters on site. His conclusion that these early hunters had contributed to, or were responsible for, the surge of Pleistocene extinctions sparked a spate of research exploring his contention alongside the competing climatic change theory. This theory maintained that extinction arose as an indirect consequence of climatic change that led to the development of new ecosystems. These were so different from those of the late Pleistocene that many of the large species of mammals were unable to adapt. The debate has continued (Martin and Wright 1979; Martin and Klein 1984) and has done much to enlarge understanding of that dramatic period in biological and human history. Several appraisals of the state of present knowledge of the event appear in Martin and Klein. It is obvious that both the climatic and the consequent environmental changes and the arrival of man as a major player had an effect on the ecosystems of the day. What effect one would have had in the absence of the other cannot be tested and therefore their relative importance must remain unknown. "Did one set up the punch which the other delivered or vice versa. In any event their combined effect was devastating and the world is much poorer" (Guilday 1984).

The most recent evidence on the details of the late Pleistocene extinction pattern suggests a relationship between the activities of man and these prehistoric events. The model of overkill and its special case, termed "blitzkrieg" by Martin (1984), offer a viable alternative to other explanations of the catastrophic disappearance of many genera and species of large mammals that terminated the Pleistocene epoch in North America.

Examining a more localized event, a strong case has been made that aboriginal man exercised an intensity of use on elk, mule deer, and buffalo that prevented them from reaching substantial numbers in the Colorado – Wyoming Rockies during the late Pleistocene (Kay 1994). It is reasoned that the potential then for abundant elk and buffalo was much as it is today. However the remains of these species are infrequently found in the contemporary middens. Both species became abundant in the region years later after disease had decimated the aboriginal populations. Earlier use by man at a level which prevented the build-up of large populations would satisfy the known facts and has not been refuted.

Even admitting the many survival strategies available to people, but not to social animals, and, in the absence of convincing alternatives, it is reasonable to conclude that in the northern regions of North America the availability of food, that determines populations of such companion carnivores and omnivores as wolves and bears (Jonkel and Cowan 1971; Peterson 1994), has been a controlling influence also on human populations. This might be by restricting conception rates or increasing postnatal mortality.

As a general rule the simpler the ecosystem and the narrower the resource base in terms of alternatives, the more vulnerable the user population. But this is complicated by the relative frequency of environmentally induced perturbations in the abundance and availability of the important food species. In both these areas the users of far northern ecosystems are under threat. The general picture of life of the original populations north of the Arctic Circle in North America is of small numbers of people living at approximate carrying capacity and, despite extraordinary skills and environmental understanding, at the mercy of chance perturbations in weather, climate, and the food resource.

The number of polar Eskimos at the time of discovery by Europeans is believed to have been between 250 and 300 individuals (Laughlin 1968) and it is difficult to conceive of them having an important impact on the populations of marine mammals that were their main food source or on the Peary caribou and musk ox that were available to them. The Eskimo of the central arctic of Canada were believed to number about 7000 at discovery. Their food base was broader and included reasonably predictable access to the large herds of migratory barren ground caribou, anadromous[3] fish, migratory waterfowl, cranes, ptarmigan, hares, musk ox (locally), and marine mammals as well as an assortment of

[3] organisms which move between salt and fresh water.

plant food. Their problem was the annual distribution of the animal populations within the vast area the people occupied. When caribou, walrus, beluga, seals, bears, and other resource animals could not be found, even though they were not scarce in the population sense, the people of the central arctic faced final starvation, as witness the Sadlermiut Eskimos (Laughlin 1968). Here also it is unlikely that before the arrival of firearms the people had significant impact on the wildlife.

Further south on the continent, where the alternative food sources were numerous, the situation was different. While meat was important as a supplement to the diet drawn from agriculture and gathering, it was not essential. The record, however, speaks of the scarcity of game animals within the hunting radius of the agricultural settlements in the American southeast (Cronon 1983)

In summary, any population of predators has its preferred prey as well as its alternative sources and there is no evidence that man did not follow this pattern. This can lead to a burgeoning population of the predator, deriving its main support from an abundant prey animal, but inflicting serious losses on a prey species that is preferred but scarce. Where several predators, as for instance wolves, bears, and man, are opportunistically drawing on the same scarce species, the result can be extirpation or perhaps even extinction.

Conservation Practices by Early American Hunters

The practice of wildlife conservation involves the exercise of various forms of restraint by the hunter, or imposed on the hunter. These are directed to reducing the kill in the interest of maintaining or increasing the numbers of the wildlife species available for the future. These practices may involve confining the human take to ages or sexes of the prey animal to the end that a harvest can be taken without impairing the productive capacity of the remaining population. They may involve restricting hunting to selected seasons that are likely to reduce a kill or to improve the quality or yield from the individuals taken. They may also involve adoption by the hunter of a limit on the harvest to be taken. This limit is estimated to maintain the remaining population at a level at which it can continue to produce a surplus large enough to meet the needs of the human population. At the extreme they may involve periodic abstinence from killing or the setting aside of areas in which all the hunters agree no killing will take place. A special application of this category concerns species identified as scarce and vulnerable to extinction and in need of total protection.

Conservation also includes purposeful alteration of the environment to make it more favorable for the production of the desired species. A third area of conservation activity rests on the identification of competitors for the animals desired by man and the reduction of this competition, i.e. predator control.

Conservation from the perspective of an anthropologist with a lifetime of experience with northern Indians and Inuit is defined in different terms by Freeman (1988) when he says "The second caution is in respect to the notion of 'conservation' which in contemporary usage by environmentalists and scientists implies a deliberate knowledgeable act, and a full understanding of the consequences of that act for long-term sustainable use of the resource. It may well be that in societies whose intellectual culture is directed to and by other concerns, these understandings and goals may not apply. So the question becomes first, does this particular observed behavior or set of values or proscriptions in respect of animal-human interactions contribute to conservation or sustainable use of the resources? A second, and quite separate, question is: are the hunters seeking these conservation objectives?" The question is an interesting one as it implies broadening the definition of conservation to include an unspoken societal imperative to maintain itself and thus to include within the definition any ritualistic, religious, or socially ingrained behaviors, related to the hunting practices of early aboriginal hunters, that have the effect of preserving the integrity and productivity of the animal population. These would be included whether or not the hunter intended that outcome or even understood the background or consequence of the behavior. There is a danger in broadening the definition of conservation until the diagnostic evidence is the long term survival of man and his prey species. Conservation thus defined might equally apply to the wolf.

At the same time it is important to understand the approach of companion cultures to their long term dependence upon the creatures that provided them with food and other products critical to the maintenance of a satisfactory way of life. As described by those who have striven for this understanding, the traditional attitude of the hunter in North American Indian and Inuit societies included the other living creatures as fellow residents of the earth. It was understood and accepted that they too survived by using many of the same resources as man. Thus they did not see the wolf or polar bear as a competitor to be destroyed so that the food it used could be transferred to man.

Another basic belief, at least in the few North American cultures that have been described in detail, was that an animal could not be killed unless it had offered itself to that end. It was appropriate for the hunter to offer proper thanks to his quarry or to in other ways propitiate the creature's spirit. In this way the dependency relationship was acknowledged in order to insure the continuing success of the hunter as a provider. It also follows that the remains of the animal should be used wisely and treated appropriately.

It appears also that the definition of waste would not include abandoning parts or most of a carcass to be used by other wild creatures.

These few references, while inadequate to convey the complex relationship, with at times religious overtones, that is understood to have characterized the man/animal relationship, will serve to indicate the great differences in attitude between the early hunters and more recent cultures of European origin referred to by Freeman (above).

Asking the general question of whether or not aboriginal hunters applied conservation practices in their day to day hunting for food is inadequate. It has been demonstrated that they did so, at least with some species at some times. It is more useful to ask what species under what circumstances were the beneficiaries of conservation practices. Sufficiently detailed information on wildlife harvesting practices in early historic periods is meagre. Most contemporary accounts assume an idealized relationship between early hunters and their prey that is not supported by evidence. It is unlikely that any of these early writers on the lifestyles of the aboriginal North Americans were sufficiently knowledgeable about the environmental relationships within any hunting based culture, or indeed their own culture, to view intelligently the situation in which they were strangers. It is unfortunate that we know nothing of these early American environmental relationships from the people themselves.

Most of what has been reported in detail refers to studies undertaken in the 20th century. Inevitably these refer to practices that existed after the cultures had been through two centuries of the fur trade. During this period all the native cultures had been seduced into expanding their demands on the native animal resources in order to trade for many European artifacts that made their lives easier. It is important to remember that the hunting practices reported of today's hunters and gatherers represent an amalgam of traditions inherited from ancient generations and ideas gleaned from frequent contact with practitioners of science based conservation.

The studies of the Waswanapi Cree of northwestern Quebec by H. A. Feit (1973, 1986, 1987), and those of the use of fire as a habitat management tool by H. Lewis (1977, 1985, 1988) are unique in the detail they provide, and the authenticity of their sources. Still other studies by Berkes (1982) and Winterhalder (1981) of other northern hunting people provide a basis for understanding their resource use strategies. Whether or not the excellent accounts of habitat manipulation, conservation, or resource management practices of these hunters of northern Canada today, describe practices that have persisted from the 17th century, they are probably in large measure indigenous inventions and important in the consideration of present and future conservation of the wildlife resources of the continent.

Specific references to animals presently managed by the Cree of northern Quebec are largely confined to moose (Feit 1987), beaver (Berkes 1982 and Feit 1986), and fur bearers. There are references to the management of the goose harvest (Craik 1975; Berkes 1982) but the details given concern managing the hunt and techniques to assure that each hunting party is effective. The only instance where reducing the kill of a species to favor a declining stock was requested it did not occur. The species involved was the brant.

It is interesting also that while tribal rules aim at the control of the take of moose and beaver, it was apparently recognized that the same techniques were not applicable to the management of the harvest of such cyclical species as grouse, ptarmigan, and hares (Feit 1987).

Among the northern people that have cooperated in studies of their use of wildlife it is evident that a central theme is the identification of hunting areas, each under the direction or guidance of a leader (Feit 1987, uses the term steward). This individual has long experience of the area and is aware of the quantities of wildlife on it. He also attempts to keep up to date on the changes in abundance. He advises the other hunters that are assigned to use the area as to the approximate numbers of different game species he thinks may be taken. The quantitative knowledge is much the same as that known by most wilderness trappers or hunting guides. It is not recorded. Guidance on the kill is permissive. However, many if not most hunters were able to kill more than they and their families required and made the surplus available to others in the community (Feit 1986).

The most important response to an apparent decline in the stock of moose, or in the numbers killed, is to agree to leave an area unhunted for a year or two. Few of the subregions within a hunting area were hunted for two successive years. There is no reference to selectively sparing females or females with calves.

The exercise of constraint in killing was also applied in the harvesting of beaver, where the hunters are reported to have elected to forego the use of the technique that involved opening the lodge, even while it was known that it provided the largest kill for the effort. Presumably they have found, as have others, that this technique damages the colony.

The ungulate mammals have always been the most important source of wild meat to North Americans, aboriginal and recent, but as a group they were poor candidates for conservation practice by the early hunters. Indeed it has been stated that it has not been possible to find any evidence that Native Americans effectively conserved ungulates (Kay 1994, Presnall 1943). Some present day exceptions to this generalization have been documented and the knowledge and ability may be more widespread than has been noticed. Its antiquity is unknown.

It was impossible for any group of early hunters to manage their kill of migratory species such as the barren ground caribou or buffalo. To design conservation of these species requires knowledge of widely distributed events. There was no way for a hunting society to know where and how many of the herd had already been taken by other hunters and to relate this to a reasonable kill for their group. When caribou or buffalo were present it was frequently in such numbers that overkill was not a perceived problem. Biological mathematics was yet to be invented. It was equally impossible for the early hunter to form the concept of an endangered species and to modify his activities so as to give it special advantages. Indeed the concept of extinction was probably impossible to formulate.

For the aboriginal hunter hunting was a very serious activity involving hard and often dangerous work and this is thought to have led to conservative killing. Among the Inuit and forest Indians of northern Canada the tradition of sharing was also a force in reducing waste.

As would be expected with any human endeavor the checks and balances did not work perfectly; local populations have been extirpated and there were in the past, and still are, instances of actual or apparent killing beyond need. There are many references in the literature from the late 19th and 20th centuries to apparently wanton killing, most of them referring to buffalo which when available existed in such large numbers that waste of some meat and hides was not seen as important (Roe 1971, Presnall 1943). The driving of herds of buffalo over cliffs is a case in point. It must be commented also that it is easy for the person unfamiliar with Arctic conditions to misjudge situations. After a large herd of caribou has passed by a hunter group, there may be many carcasses apparently unused. Often these are taken as an insurance of available food when the hunter passes that way in the winter. No special preservation techniques need be used except protection from other predators.

This discussion of subsistence hunting has dealt in the main with conditions past, but the way of life is not an abandoned lifestyle. Indeed in northern Canada today wildlife remains of critical importance to a large part of the population both as a source of income and as a staple in the diet. The annual harvest of game and fish in the Northwest Territories in 1981 was estimated at 3881 tonnes, and the fur harvest, including seals, brought about 1.5 million dollars into the community annually (Fuller and Hubert 1981).

Six years later Usher (1987) stated that the domestic harvest of meat in the Northwest Territories of Canada was about 2.5 million kg annually, with an estimated value of $25 million. Ninety five percent of all red meat and half the fish harvested were consumed by the Native people.

The Waswanipi Cree of north western Quebec have cooperated in a number of studies of their use of wildlife. In the 1968-69 hunting season, among the several hunting groups, beaver contributed between 20 and 45% of total calories available for human consumption, moose 15 to 40%, fish 1 to 13%; approximately 20% of total calories was purchased foods (Cox 1973).

As further evidence of the continuing role of game meat to the Indians of northern Canada, the Cree-speaking Métis of northern Saskatchewan recently cooperated in a study of the importance of wildlife to the annual food supply (Tobias and Kay 1994). It reveals that 80% of the 151 males of hunting age in the community were successful participants in harvesting 8232 waterfowl, 3305 grouse and ptarmigan, 931 snowshoe hares, 31 lynx, 296 beavers, 2813 muskrat, 52 moose and woodland caribou, 10 white-tailed deer, and 72 black bear, plus large amounts of fish. The total harvest by this small community amounted to 84.5 tons, or .342 kg of meat per day for each of the 676 residents. However, today it is most difficult for the most skilled and industrious individual wishing to live off the land to do so without calling upon back-up resources. The technical changes now deemed essential to the way of life: the snowmobile, rifle, telescope rifle sight, radio, and so many other new essentials inflict a heavy annual cost on the hunter that can only infrequently be met from the sale of furs or other products of the land (Smith 1981).

It is important to remember that the food species of post Pleistocene days and of today are the distillate of millennia of testing for survivability. They have survived centuries of use as the primary food source of the native people of this continent. They have been exploited for meat and hides by both cultures during the colonial period and experienced massive overkill during the early post colonial period of North American history (see below). Despite this, once the Pleistocene shake-out had occurred, all species of North American large mammals survived into the present. Some subspecies have been exterminated. Several of the ungulate mammals are probably more numerous now than at any time since precolumbian days. The American moose, white-tailed deer, coast black-tailed deer, barren-ground caribou, and musk ox are in this category.

The majority of the Indians and all the Inuit of North America who still depend heavily on the wildlife resource occupy northern Canada and Alaska. Here they are in the forefront of the most important sociopolitical development since colonial times. This is the recognition that many of the descendants of aboriginal cultures have a right to control their own destinies within the framework of the continental political philosophy. For many it is seen as essential that they regain an effective land base and a say in the management and use of the land-based resources.

One of the facts of wildlife and fisheries resource management in the largely unsettled north of North America is that it is most effectively managed with the cooperation of the subsistence users. Those that still live on the land bring a body of personal and cultural experience to their use of wildlife which can complement the scientific, data based approach to modern conservation. Various degrees of joint management are emerging as an effective way of conserving these resources of the North to the long term benefit of the subsistence users while maintaining the National interest in the preservation of biodiversity and thriving biological resources in all parts of Canada.

The establishment of the principle of joint management and its implementation in the northern regions of Canada is the most significant development in wildlife management since the introduction of science-based management half a century ago. This new experiment was inaugurated in 1984 with the signing of the Inuvialuit Final Agreement and its subsequent enactment into Canadian Federal Law. The formal details are available in Bailey et al (in press) but some informal details are relevant to this review. The Inuvialuit number about 4000 people, about 3000 of whom live in six settlements adjacent to and east of the estuary of the Mackenzie River and the Beaufort Sea in the western Northwest Territories. The residents of three communities, Sachs Harbour, Holman, and Paulatuk lead a life centred around subsistence hunting and fishing while many Inuvialuit, those living in Aklavik, Inuvik, and Tuktoyaktuk in the Mackenzie delta, are wage earners, though most of them continue to hunt, fish, and trap as a fundamental aspect of their lifestyle and culture.

The management agreement covers about 1.092 million km sq.; within that region the Inuvialuit have surface title to 72 000 km sq. and subsurface title to another 18 000 km. sq. The arrangements for wildlife and fisheries management include recognition that, on constitutional grounds, the ownership of the wildlife is maintained by the Crown and ultimate authority rests with the Minister of the appropriate department. The Inuvialuit have significant involvement in all decision making respecting the land and wildlife. This is implemented by the creation of 5 Renewable Resources Committees: 1. The Fisheries Joint Management Committee; 2. The Wildlife Management Advisory Council, North West Territories; 3. The Wildlife Management Advisory Council, North

Slope; 4. The Environmental Impact Screening Committee; and 5. The Environmental Impact Review Board.

Each of these is equally made up of Inuvialuit and government members. Each has an impartial chairman who must be mutually acceptable and plays an impartial role.

Within the region in each community exists a Hunters' and Trappers' Committee; these develop to advise on all local renewable resource matters. An Inuvialuit Game Council receives the matters brought to it by the Hunters' and Trappers' Committees. The memberships of all these regional committees is exclusively drawn from the beneficiaries of the land claims agreement.

The novel feature of this co-management process is that it brings together government fish and wildlife managers with the Inuvialuit to develop, together, recommendations on management actions. In this way the decisions benefit from the technical, political, and administrative information the government appointees have available and the practical and personal knowledge which the Inuvialuit members bring to the discussions.

Each of the Communities is developing a Conservation Plan applicable to the lands it uses. The co-management agreement has been in place for ten years. The procedures are still evolving but there are already many achievements to point to that indicate the breadth of the conservation issues being addressed. These include the establishing of a harvest quota for the barren-ground grizzly; development and approval of a Beaufort Sea Beluga Management Plan; the negotiation of An International Agreement on the Conservation of Polar Bears and Their Habitat, and the closure of the arctic char fishery on the Big Fish River. In each instance the emphasis has been wise use required to maintain the long term viability of an element in their living resources.

While co-management is certainly a most important innovation in the management of wildlife where indigenous subsistence users are concerned, it has limited applicability outside the special situation described. It is essential that there be a community of hunters with special legislated rights to the wildlife resource on designated land areas; that the community be involved in the harvesting as a major component of their time and survival. Only in this situation can they build the special knowledge that they can bring to the partnership. It is essential also that there exist an internal discipline within the group such that agreed-upon actions will be undertaken.

Two elements in the agreement are of fundamental importance:

1. Priority right to the allowable kill belongs to the indigenous users of the resource; in this case the Inuvialuit.

2. Conservation requirements are the only acceptable reason for denying them the harvest they see to be needed by them. It is at this point that the Minister's veto can be applied if required.

Already, in parts of the North, there are signs that the wildlife will not indefinitely provide for all who wish to use it, in the rapidly expanding population.

Two principles of general application emerge once again:

1. The determination of the allowable harvest is primarily an exercise in applied science and must be based as much as possible on biological reality.

2. The allocation of the permitted harvest (i.e. the details of where, when, how, and by whom the harvest is taken) can have a large component of small "p" politics.

Failure to recognize and apply the differences between these two processes has been the root of many failures in the management of fish and wildlife resources elsewhere on the continent.

From Colonizing to Commercialism

The establishment of European settlement on this continent introduced forces which were to dramatically alter the numbers and the lives of the indigenous people and the wildlife that supported them. With Europeans came human diseases to which the local people had little resistance. For two centuries epidemics decimated the Indians nations of the continent, beginning on the Atlantic coast in the early 17th century (Cronon 1983) and finishing on the Pacific Coast in the late 19th century (Boyd 1994). Commercialization of wildlife for meat, hides, fur, and feathers along with the introduction of the firearm as a hunting weapon, the steel trap for taking fur bearers, and a host of other devices that made life easier for the native people, provided the incentive for them to participate in the destruction of the resources that had supported their survival.

Through the first century of European occupation of the continent, while the new diseases decimated the indigenous people, the impact of the newcomers on the wildlife was relatively benign. The colonists, excluding the Spanish in the West, numbered only 300 000 people by 1700 (Mulhall 1899, Govt of Canada 1931), a number that probably did not replace the indigenous population of two centuries earlier. However, the slaughter of wildlife that occurred through the subsequent 200 years remains as a dramatic example of the "Tragedy of the Commons" in action, driven by ignorance, thoughtlessness, greed, and sometimes necessity. The engine driving the disaster was commercialization of wildlife.

It began quite innocently with colonists hunting edible wildlife to support a tenuous survival. But as agriculture took hold, community hunters assumed the task of supplying meat to the communities for a price. Entrepreneurs emerged to organize the markets for fur, hides, bird plumage, elk tusks, buffalo tongues, meat, or for the opportunity to slaughter large mammals for no reason at all. Wolves, cougars, coyotes, foxes, and golden eagles were seen as threats to man's livestock and organized killing under public subsidy became an approved pattern of behavior. Burrows dug by badgers and prairie dogs were seen as a hazard to men on horseback and added to the list for destruction. The course and the consequences have been documented in dozens of publications and need not be repeated here (Allen 1877, Hornaday 1913, Roe 1972).

By early in the 20th century, the plains and wood bison, musk ox, bighorn sheep, pronghorn antelope, wapiti, Newfoundland caribou, plains grizzly, grey wolf, swift fox, black-footed ferret, sea otter, beaver, trumpeter swan, whooping crane, eskimo curlew, great auk, Labrador duck, passenger pigeon, snowy egret, and great egret had been reduced to endangered remnants, extirpated from large areas of their former range, or exterminated.

A combination of forces contributed to the destruction, but paramount were commercial exploitation, conflict with a burgeoning agriculture, and political purpose. The destruction of each of these species presents a story from which conservation lessons have been learned. Brief allusion to three of them will illustrate.

The destruction of the vast herds of American bison has been well documented by Allen (1877), Roe (1971), and by Seton (1937), though Seton's arithmetic will not stand much scrutiny. The purposeful overkill that reduced bison to a tiny remnant of the millions that once occupied North America from the Rocky Mountains to the Atlantic seaboard and from Great Slave Lake to the Gulf of Mexico took only 25 years (Seton 937). The assault was driven by a commercial market for hides and meat, and by the expansion of European settlers onto the Great Plains where cattle raising came into conflict with the wild herds of bison. The final assault came when it became public purpose to dispossess the nations of Indians that made their homes on the Great Plains and in the foothills of the Rockies. Their culture was dependant on the bison (buffalo) for its survival. Destruction of the buffalo became a military purpose as part of a strategy to confine the Indians to reservations.

The extirpation began in the 18th century and by the beginning of the 19th century the species had been eliminated east of the Mississippi River. The speed with which the elimination proceeded is hard to believe. In the 60 years between 1830 and 1890 one of the greatest concentrations of a single species of large mammal in the world, estimated variously as upward of 15 million animals, was destroyed (Seton 1937).

Since early in the colonization period, the wolf had been in conflict with the newcomers as a constant drain on their livestock. The conflict was greatly exacerbated by the increase of free ranging cattle on the western plains. With the wapiti and buffalo gone from east of the Mississippi and greatly reduced in the West, the grey wolf that depended on them turned to alternative food. Range cattle were the right size and easier to kill than the prey they were used to. Half a century of off and on local bounties proved futile and the destruction of the wolf became a political priority. If cattle ranching and sheep raising were to prosper in the west a well organized and widespread wolf reduction program was imperative.

The complaints of the ranchers were heard clearly in Washington and the United States Bureau of the Biological Survey was instructed to take action. Its first contribution was to bring research and professional advice to assist the locally organized predator control campaigns. But in 1914, by act of Congress, the Bureau of biological Survey was given a mandate to destroy "wolves, prairie dogs and other animals injurious to agriculture." (Young 1944). An early addition to the kill list was the coyote. The campaign became focused on extermination of the wolf in the cattle country and was conducted with professional zeal primarily with the use of traps, poison, and den hunting.

So far as the wolf was concerned, the task was completed in about two decades, but as with so many bureaucratic endeavors the extermination program gained alternative focus and continued with emphasis on the coyote until, in 1932, the American Society of Mammalogists called attention to the large numbers of small carnivores and scavenging birds that were being killed by the traps and poison baits set for the coyotes. At the same time they exposed the selective reporting that was concealing the bycatch (Hall 1930, Adams 1930, Howell 1930). Howell, then President of the American Society of Mammalogists, stated "Among the tens of thousands of carnivores killed in 1928 by federal hunters there were only 10 grey wolves. The rest have gone from the far west. In 1926 the Biological Survey said that there were no wolves known to occur in Arizona, and a few years ago that there were no more than 5 adult wolves were known to occur in Wyoming . . . since 1916, about 416,000 predatory mammals, with an additional estimated kill of 696,000 coyotes poisoned but not found at a cost of nearly $10,000,000." (Howell 1930).

Howell went on to say "There are strong indications that we are now at a crisis – at the crossroads of conservation as concerns treatment of our wildlife. Conditions have been growing intolerable, but there is clearly evident a gathering storm of resentment that should accomplish many reforms . . . the Biological Survey is potentially the most powerful single factor, for good or evil, that we have in this field. For many years it was the respected and trusted public guardian of our fauna, but whether we will or no, conditions are now such that we are forced to label it not our federal wildlife warden, but the guardian of the sheep men and other powerful interests." So was a bureaucracy gone astray brought back to its proper purpose – research and action toward what we would now term conservation and the maintenance of biodiversity.

The fur industry was a major player in the commercialization of North American wildlife. With formal beginnings in 1670 with the establishment of the Hudson's Bay Company, and the North-West Company in the 1776, the trading posts and transportation routes were established widely over a huge area of the continent roughly north of a line connecting Lake Superior with the lower Columbia River. Statistic abound on the pelts, largely of the smaller carnivores, traded over the years, however, from the standpoint of the conservation of wildlife species only the musk ox and the beaver suffered long term damage. The major impact of the fur trade was certainly a revolution of many of the native cultures. It provided access, for the first time, to the mechanical conveniences of a more advanced society, in exchange for some of their own resources. The indigenous people would have been more than human to resist the temptation to abandon some of the community customs that had regulated their use of wildlife. The result was overkill of some species, notably musk ox and beaver.

Hudson's Bay Company records reveal that between 1864 and 1878 the number of musk ox skins traded did not exceed 200 annually. From that year numbers increased until over 600 were traded in 1881. The highest annual kill was in 1892 when nearly 2000 skins reached the Hudson's Bay Company. After that there was steady decline to 1907 when only 100 hides were brought to the traders (Hewitt 1921). While these numbers were being taken by the Indians and Eskimos and a few European trappers, large numbers also were being killed for food by exploring expeditions to the northern Arctic islands. In 1921 Hewitt wrote that "the extermination of the musk-ox is only a matter of a few years, unless prompt and adequate steps are taken to put an end to the killing of the animal for the sake of its skin.

Hewitt was successful in having conservation legislation established including an important provision that musk ox could be killed only by Eskimo and Indians or Métis who were bona fide residents of the Northwest Territories and only when they were in actual need of the meat to avert starvation. With the cooperation of the people the tide was turned and the musk ox recolonized most of its former range.

The decimation of the beaver population was driven by the same commercial forces that threatened the musk ox but it covered most of the continent. The collapse of the population of North American beavers probably reached its nadir in the United States between 1895 and 1900 (Seton 1937), and in Canada about 1913 (Hewitt 1921). There were nucleus populations remaining of all the subspecies and under wise management the recovery required about 70 years.

Science Based Management

The plight of North American wildlife was recognized before widespread exterminations had occurred and a handful of resourceful, determined, and politically influential individuals persuaded the governments and the public to support a series of protective measures that we today identify as the birth of wildlife conservation of this continent.

It is useful to remind ourselves of the principles that have underlain the philosophy of wildlife conservation in North America. Theodore Roosevelt is credited with synthesizing them into three simple statements, the "Roosevelt doctrine," which (1) recognized all these outdoor resources as one integral whole; (2) recognized their conservation through wise use as a public responsibility, and their private ownership as a public trust; (3) recognized science as a tool for discharging this responsibility.

Geist (this volume, and 1988, 1991a, 1991b, 1994) has restated some of these principles in the wisdom of hindsight. He recognizes four as of paramount importance:

1. Wildlife is public property and the responsibility of the state; if in private ownership it shall be held in trust for the public.

2. There shall be no trafficking in vulnerable wildlife (big game, upland game, waterfowl, and songbirds).

3. Wildlife surplus to healthy populations shall be allocated by law (not by market, land ownership, special privilege, or birthright, excepting aboriginal people).

4. Wildlife shall not be killed frivolously, but only for cause (food, fur, to prevent crop and property damage.

He also states that the last two policies of the Roosevelt doctrine have not been fully integrated into operational management.

It is important that, 80 years ago as now, most wild land in North America was under public ownership, and that all wildlife was under the ownership and care of the state. Ownership of land did not subsume any right to wildlife living on that land. Nor was there any misunderstanding as to the goals of wildlife conservation: first, to encourage as many individuals of the useable species of wildlife as could be supported by the habitat, and second, that no species of wildlife was to be reduced to extinction, if it was possible to prevent it.

In 1933, when Leopold's classic volume on game management was published almost every state and province in North America had a Game Department, or a Department of Game and Fisheries entrusted with the management of the huntable or fishable species of birds, mammals, and fish. No legislative jurisdiction had a Department of the Environment. Sixty years later these state and provincial administrations are Wildlife Departments and are frequently immersed in an overriding Ministry of Environment.

The change reflects an important revolution in philosophy. While in many regions the financial resources may still be going predominantly to the huntable species, there is an increasing focus on the management of ecosystems and the preservation of biodiversity. This is a change being driven by rising public concern for the integrity of the world we occupy and a reluctance to accept unchallenged the policies of governments and large corporations where they appear to compromise the future of aspects of the environment we enjoy.

The highly successful programs of conservation are built upon the application to wildlife conservation of scientifically gained data, the elimination of commercial exploitation, regulation of harvest, manipulation of environment, and nurturing of individual species. Most of the large mammals that were so severely reduced in numbers during the 18th and 19th centuries, most of the so-called game birds, and many of the raptors have been returned to healthy populations. Several of them are once again among the useable resources.

However, success has not been uniform across the species or across the continent. Both in Canada and the United States, there are growing lists of species of all orders of vertebrates that are endangered or vulnerable. These are the red and blue lists that motivate special conservation status for the species concerned. Species of birds that pass through from two to many countries during their annual migrations are particularly susceptible to hazards. Not only must they find a suitable nesting habitat at the northern end of their annual movement and a hospitable wintering area at the other end, but often they are dependent upon the persistence of traditional feeding and resting areas at suitable distances en route. Good examples are to be found among the shorebirds that travel between breeding areas on the North American Arctic tundra to wintering areas in Central and South America (see Butler and Campbell 1987). Habitat loss and degradation of habitat anywhere along the annual routes are recognized as the most important factors in the declines of these species (Flather and Hockstra 1989). The red and blue listed species are not confined to migrants.

There are several species where the plight of the creature is of our own making and the redress in our own hands. These include, in Canada, such species as the Burrowing Owl, the Spotted Owl, the Whooping Crane, the Piping Plover, the Greater Prairie Chicken, and the Peary Caribou (Muir, 1980).

It is also true that for 90% or so of the birds and mammals of the continent, we are ignorant of the details of their biology and of their habitat requirements, which would permit us to intercede on their behalf. Basic data on the relative status of numbers of wintering birds are available from the Christmas bird counts, a remarkable effort involving many hundreds of people coordinated by the National Audubon Society, and from the breeding bird census conducted both in Canada and the United States. But most of the biota is left to its own resources in coping with naturally occurring or imposed changes in the environment. However, biota that is of concern to hundreds of thousands of people from bird watchers to professional biologists, or the detection of major changes in the number of a species, elicits biological enquiry and subsequent action. Projects are in place that are summarizing the state of knowledge on amphibians, reptiles, birds, and mammals of North America that will provide the starting point for more intensive studies as they become necessary, but for most species, their continuing well being must rest on the identification and protection of the environmental essentials.

A specially noteworthy change in the public interest in and concern for wildlife in North America is the explosive interest in bird-watching that has occurred since the early 1940s. A 1980 survey of the American public found that 55% of them (93 million individuals) took part in some form of non consumptive use of wildlife. Of these, 26 million maintained bird feeders and more than 2 million put out 100 lbs or more of bird food a year. This interest is the basis of a very considerable industry that is estimated to spend some 600 million dollars a year on bird houses, bird feed, field guides etc. Bird seed alone accounts for some 500 million dollars a year. A collateral issue arises, in that most of the funding for wildlife conservation in North America is provided by those who hunt or fish, a number far below that of the non consumptive users who do not contribute directly (Shaw and Mangun 1980).

Another group of species requires special comment. The carnivorous fur bearers and the muskrat and beaver have been taken for their furs for nearly 400 years, and all species, except for the fisher, wolverine, black-footed ferret, and swift fox have maintained healthy populations over much of the habitat still available to them.

Many technical developments and new techniques now exist for learning the details of the biology of wildlife species and for monitoring their numbers. Specific deficiencies in the environment of many species can now be identified, and for some, mitigative procedures are in use. But we have little information on the processes within entire ecosystems. This deficiency becomes progressively more serious as profligate resource extraction, misuse of natural habitats for agriculture, and the pestilence of widespread pollution degrade ecosystems to the detriment of wildlife.

An allied problem is that in most instances the agency responsible for the conservation of wildlife does not have effective influence over the other uses imposed on the land and water areas upon which wildlife depend.

The specific, highly successful programs (referred to earlier) in the conservation of North American wildlife species have led to the opinion that, in general, we have been successful in protecting wildlife from over exploitation and have been resourceful and resolute in restoring depleted species. At the same time, there have been growing stresses on the systems. These have primarily arisen from actions over which wildlife conservators had no control.

A few of the perturbations confronting wildlife conservators as they move toward the 21st century are discussed below.

People Problems with Habitat

Habitat change by man has been part of North American history since long before the arrival of Europeans. Extensive alterations to some environments were made by the Indian populations that spread over the continent. This was accomplished primarily by use of fire and by land clearing for cultivation with all its consequences.

During the first three centuries of European occupation, native wildlife had to cope with the draining of wetlands, destruction of the prairie ecosystems, devastating overuse of native grasslands, forest removal in ecologically unsound ways, flooding of river valleys, and the pollution of lakes and rivers. Collectively, these actions have materially altered the mix of wildlife species and the numbers of some. An increasing body of species are being recognized as threatened or in danger of extinction.

The consequences of these alterations to the natural environment cannot be measured, but are seen to be very great. The gross changes are obvious in certain ecosystems that have been greatly altered as the needs of our society for agricultural land, for minerals, timber, transportation, space in which to live, and places to get rid of the bewildering complex of waste products. It is beyond the scope of this review to even highlight the most altered ecosystems, or the consequences to even major elements in the biota. Many species have proven highly resilient and able to adapt to greatly altered habitats; one need only mention the racoon, coyote, grey squirrel, white-tailed deer, Columbian black-tailed deer, cottontail rabbit, mallard duck, Canada goose, American robin, American crow, several species of gulls, and the black-capped chickadee as examples. Other species adapt with difficulty or have lifestyles that do not mesh with those of man. Notable are several of the larger species of carnivorous mammals whose distribution in North America has been shrinking.

Endangered Spaces

Recently the World Wildlife Fund of Canada has publicized the plight of the larger predators of Canada as part of the well chosen title "Endangered Spaces" (Hummel 1989). At issue is the fate of such species as the grizzly bear, grey wolf, mountain lion, and wolverine. Each of these now occupies only a small fragment of its original range on this continent. Each of them is inseparable from what North America has been and is. Each, over time, has been marked for extinction by some special interest in our society. But all are still present in viable populations largely restricted to the remaining 'undeveloped' areas of the continent. An increasing number of people treasure the knowledge of their existence.

It is evident that none of these species will maintain its present numbers and distribution unless it becomes public policy that it shall. Each of them requires large areas upon which their requirements will have primacy. Their presence will require some accommodation by various groups in society. National park users will have to be prepared to adjust their travels to give way to grizzly bears, and must accept the element of danger their presence introduces. Wildlife users need to understand the food requirements of wolves and mountain lions. Raising of domestic stock will have an additional hazard in areas adjacent to the carnivore reserves.

In the other direction any thriving population of these large predators will give rise to emigrants that will come into collision with other human interests in areas beyond the orbit of acceptance. So those dedicated to the well being of the large carnivores will require tolerance that will not compromise the conservation purpose.

Several genetically different races of grizzly bear, wolf, and mountain lion survive and the thrust for biodiversity dictates that viable populations of each should be identified and become the focus of survival priorities. The areas required for designation are large (McTaggart-Cowan 1989), but still available. But each year unplanned and uncoordinated actions press in on the land and make action to conserve the large carnivores more urgent.

Commercialization of Wildlife

For centuries the fur bearing mammals of North America have been the basis of a thriving industry that has contributed greatly to the income of Indians, Inuit, and a few thousand trappers of other backgrounds. After the early exploitive period during which itinerant groups of trappers, often in the employ of fur companies, devastated some of the species, government directed management has successfully restored the populations, while allowing the annual harvests to proceed. Various approaches to management have been successful. Many of the communities of Indians and Inuit prefer community trapping grounds within which trapping rights are assigned, by common consent, to individuals or families. This works thanks to the authority of those who "manage" the areas and the community of interest of the trappers.

A system of registered trap lines has proven most effective in other parts of the continent. The essential component is providing a situation in which it is obvious to the trapper that it is to his/her benefit to conserve the resources of the trapline.

Since the development of government responsibility for the wildlife resource, fur trapping has been the sole direct commercialization of wildlife. Benign products such as eider down have had a small market. The only exception has been commercial whaling which occurred off and on in both Canada and the United States until the 1970s.

In the last three decades, however, there has been a resurgence of attempts to convert wildlife products into a saleable resource. Three directions are being taken: 1. Game ranching: This was explored half a century ago in South Africa, New Zealand, and the USSR, but has only recently attracted much attention in North America. Members of the deer family have been the animals of choice and in all jurisdictions the responsible authority has been province or state. In order to avoid problems of law enforcement where native deer have a legal harvest, some provinces have insisted that only exotic species may be raised. The animal of choice is the European fallow deer. In other provinces or states it is legal to farm native deer, primarily elk. In neither case is profitability a foregone conclusion.

Wildlife conservation interests have raised important concerns, among which are, where native species are involved, the danger of importing exotic diseases that may be transmitted to wild stock, and the dangers of genetic pollution where domestically raised stock escapes (See Geist 1988, 1991a, 1991b, 1994 and this volume; Hudson, this volume)

2. In a few regions of the continent there have been experiments with the raising of exotic wildlife in very large enclosures within which the species are essentially wild and more or less self supporting. These animals are available for hunting for a fee.

Many of the same arguments raised about game farming have arisen also with wildlife ranching. In addition there are questions as to whether or not this type of hunting should be regarded as the equivalent of 'fair chase' sport hunting.

3. In recent years the population of musk ox on Banks Island has increased to the point where the range is judged to be overstocked. Under the joint management of Inuit and Government, an attempt is being made to create a successful market for the meat of the surplus animals. There is a logic in this but also a hazard. The hazard arises from building an infrastructure and a cadre of entrepreneurs based upon a marketable surplus that may have a short lifespan. Income once enjoyed is difficult to put aside when the surplus ceases to exist and wisdom calls for more conservative management. Time will tell whether the management team is substantial enough to handle the situation when it arises.

There is a widespread concern that the spread of commercialization of wildlife, including the private ownership that is involved, will prove harmful to the successful system that has restored the numbers of native game species and maintained the principle of access to all.

The clouding of boundaries between the conservation of wildlife as the basis of a subsistence or recreational resource, rather than of a commercial enterprise, has created threats to the survival of some species that are not yet fully appreciated by governments.

Already in Canada the traditional commercial harvest of fur pelts has burgeoned into a flourishing market for a wide variety of wild animal parts. For example, there is an industry based on narwhal and walrus tusks, a small but lucrative trade in bear paws and gallbladders, a growing underground trade in trophy heads of most ungulate mammals, as well as the highly profitable market for velvet antlers of the deer family. Some perceive that the potential illegal market as growing out of control.

Genetic Pollution

Escapes from game farms are a potential threat to the genetic integrity of locally adapted genotypes of wildlife. The threat is already reality with us as a consequence of unwise actions by past and present wildlife administrations.

The transplanting of wildlife into unoccupied or depleted areas has become increasingly popular with the availability of new techniques for capture and transport of large mammals. Sometimes these transplants have been made with little concern for the potential impact on the remnant or adjacent populations of the same species. The plains/wood bison fiasco is too well known and too immediate to require further comment but other moves with the potential to be equally damaging are taking place. In British Columbia, we have transplanted Manitoba elk into an area already inhabited by the most northerly adapted stock of the species in North America, a survivor of the great winter-kill of the late 1800s.

We have placed Rocky Mountain bighorn sheep where interbreeding with the indigenous California bighorn is almost certain.

At this time the coastal, salt-water-adapted race of the river otter from Vancouver Island is being released into depleted habitat in one of the north-central states of the United States. The cottontail rabbit, a species with many regionally adapted subspecies, has been transported widely over much of the United States without any thought for the genetic consequences. The list could be greatly extended.

Philip (1990:10) states, "Protection of genetic diversity is an essential component of sound conservation programs." Referring to his experimental examination of genetic diversity between different stocks of largemouth bass, he summarizes "Each experiment confirmed that local stocks do become genetically tailored for their environment," a result that has significant implications for many management policies.

Animal Rights

The most recent introduction in the area of human dimensions is the challenge to the basic objectives of wildlife management under the general banner of animal rights. At its most extreme, the proponents of this philosophy maintain that it is unethical for humans to use animals for any purpose (Rollin 1981).

This movement is well financed and has been effective in establishing its views in some instances. The widely publicized and effective campaign against the taking of harp seals is well known, much better known than the consequences to the atlantic cod industry or devastating impact on the livelihood of many Inuit who depended upon the sale of the pelts of ringed seals that were a byproduct of their meat harvest.

Other well publicized endeavors include the current attack on the fur industry and attempts to prevent the application of predatory animal control, where it has been judged to be necessary in order to achieve management objectives that involve some of the wolf's prey species.

It is impossible to predict the outcome of this challenge to wildlife conservation and its consequences to many species. But it is essential that serious consideration be given to its potential for destroying the existing system without thought for the future of our native vertebrates.

Conclusion

In this review of the interaction of people and wildlife in North America one can identify a sequence of events involving people that had major impact upon many species of wildlife over large areas:

1. The arrival of man on this continent and its sequel, the elimination of a number of large species unable to adapt to the new circumstances.

2. The invasion of Europeans with its consequences of pandemic disease that decimated the native North Americans, and the widespread reductions and extermination of wildlife through commercialization and uncontrolled killing.

3. The introduction of the concept of wildlife as public property separated from the ownership of land; and the legislated responsibility of government to manage wildlife for the long term benefit of all citizens.

4. The introduction and evolution of science-based wildlife management and the emergence of Wildlife Biology and Conservation as a profession.

5. The emergence of non-consumptive wildlife use as a major avocation in North America.

6. The legal recognition of the special relationships existing between the aboriginal people and their use of certain species of wildlife. Arising from this the invention of the co-management relationship involving government and those Inuit, Indian, and Métis groups that could bring to a partnership responsibility, special knowledge of local wildlife gained through their long term use, and management of wildlife as a major element in their survival.

7. The threat to wildlife arising from the burgeoning human population on the continent and the accompanying technical and chemical complexity of North American culture that threatens the habitats essential to wildlife survival in full diversity.

References

Adams, C. C. 1930. Rational Predatory Animal Control. *Jour. Mammalogy* 11: 353-357.

Allen. J. A. 1877. *History of the American Bison.* U.S. Geological Survey for 1875. Part III. Zoology.

Bailey, J. L., Snow, N. B., Carpenter, A. and Carpenter, L. In Press. Cooperative Wildlife Management under Western Arctic Inuvialuit Land Claim. 16 pp typewritten.

Bates, D. G. and Lee, S. H. 1979. The myth of population regulation. pp. 244-288 in Chapman, N.A. and Irons, W. (eds.), *Evolutionary Biology and Human Social Development*. Dunsbury Press, North Scitulate, MA.

Birdsell, J. B. 1968. Some predictions for the pleistocene based on equilibrium systems among recent hunter gatherers. pp. 229-242 in Lee, R. B. and DeVore, I. (eds.), *Recent Hunter-Gatherers.* Chicago, IL, University of Chicago Press, 415 pp.

Boyd, R. 1994. Smallpox in the Pacific Northwest: The first epidemics. *British Columbia Studies* #101: 15-41.

Butler, R. W. and Campbell, R. W. 1987. *The Birds of the Fraser River Delta: Populations, Ecology and International Significance.* Occ. Papers #65. Canadian Wildlife Serv. 71pp.

Carpenter, A., Hanbidge, B. M. V. and Richard, M. B. 1994. *Co-management of Wildlife in the Western Canadian Arctic an Inuvialuit Perspective.* 13 pp typescript.

Cronon, W. 1983. *Challenges in the Land: Indians, Colonists, and the Ecology of New England.* Hill and Wang, New York, 261 pp.

Day, G. M. 1953. The Indian as an ecological factor in the northeast forest. *Ecology* 34: 329-346.

Denevan, W. M. 1992. The pristine myth: The landscape of the Americas in 1492. *Annal. Assoc. of Amer Geographers* 82: 369-385.

Diamond, J. M. 1984. Historic extinctions: A Rosetta Stone for understanding prehistoric extinctions. pp. 824-962 in Martin and Klein, *Quaternary Extinctions: A Prehistoric Revolution*. Univ. Arizona Press.

Feit, H. A. 1973. The ethnoecology of the Waswanapi Cree: Or how hunters can manage their resources. pp. 115-125 in Cox, B. (ed.), *Cultural Ecology: Readings in Canadian Indians and Eskimos.* McLelland & Stewart, Toronto.

———. 1986. James Bay Cree Indian management and moral considerations of fur bearers. pp. 49-65 in *Native People and Renewable Resources Management.* Alberta Soc. Prof. Biologists, Edmonton.

———. 1987. North American Native hunting and management of moose populations. *Swedish Wildlife Research.* Supple. 1: 25-42.

Flather, C. H. and Hockstra, T. W. 1989. *An Analysis of the Wildlife and Fish Situation in the United States 1989-2040.* U.S. Dept. Agric., Forest Service. Gen. Tech Bull. R.M. #178. 147pp.

Freeman, M. M. R. 1986. Renewable Resources, Economics and Native Communities. pp. 29-37 in *Native People and Renewable Resource Management*. Alberta Soc. Prof. Biol. Edmonton.

———. 1985. Appeal to tradition: Different perspectives in arctic wildlife management. pp. 265-280 in Brosted, J. et al. (eds.), *Native Power: The*

Quest for Autonomy and Nationhood of Indian Peoples. Universitets vorlagetus, Bergen.

———. 1988. The significance of animals in the life of northern foraging peoples and its relevance today. pp. 5-12 in *International Symposium on Human and Animal Relationships in the North.* Hokkaido, Japan.

Fuller, W. A. and Hubert, B. A. 1981. Fish, fur and game in the Northwest Territories: Some problems of and prospects for increased harvests. pp. in *Renewable Resources and the Economy of the North.* Assoc. of Canadian Universities for Northern Studies, Ottawa.

Geist, V. 1988. How markets in meat and parts, and the sale of hunting priviliges, jeopardize wildlife conservation. *Conservation Biology* 2(1): 1-12.

Geist, V. 1991a. Deer ranching for products and paid hunting: Threat to conservation and biodiversity by luxury markets. pp. 554-561 in Brown, R. T., *The Biology of Deer.* Springer Verlag, New York.

Geist, V. 1991b. Some lessons from North American wildlife management. pp. 7-10 in *Present Trends and Perspectives for the 21st Century: Wildlife Conservation.*

Geist, V. 1994. Wildlife conservation as wealth. Commentary. *Nature* (London) 368: 491-492.

Government of Canada. 1931. Seventh Census of Canada. Ottawa. 1. 1522 pp.

Guilday, J. E. 1984. Pleistocene extinctions and environmental change: A case study of the Appalachians. pp. 250-258 in Martin, P. S. and Klein, R. G. (eds.), *Quaternary Extinctions: A Prehistoric Revolution.* Univ. Arizona Press.

Hall, E. R. 1930. Predatory mammal destruction. *Journ. Mammalogy* 11: 362-369.

Hatter, J. 1950. *The Moose of Central British Columbia.* PhD. thesis, State Coll. of Washington, 356 pp. unpublished.

Hewett, C. G. 1921. *The Conservation of Wildlife in Canada.* Scribners, New York, 344 pp.

Hornaday, W. T. 1913. *Our Vanishing Wildlife.* New York Zool. Soc., New York, 411 pp.

Howell, A. B. 1930. At the crossroads. *Journ. Mammalogy* 11: 377-389.

Hummel, M. 1989. *Endangered Spaces.* W. W. F. Canada. Key Porter, Toronto, 288 pp.

Jonkel, C. J. and McTaggart-Cowan, I. 1971. *The Black Bear in the Spruce-fir Forest.* Wildl. Monogr. #27, 53pp.

Kay, C. E. 1994. Aboriginal overkill: The role of Native Americans in structuring western ecosystems. *Human Nature.*

Laughlin, W. S. 1968. The demography of hunters: An Eskimo example. pp. 241-243 in Lee, R. B. and DeVore, I. (eds.), *Man the Hunter.* Aldine Publications Co., Chicago.

Leopold, A. 1933. *Game Management.* Scribners, New York, 481 pp.

Lewis, H. T. 1977. Maskuta: The ecology of Indian fires in northern Alberta. *Western Canadian Jour. of Anthropology* 7: 15-52.

Lewis, H. T. 1985. Why Indians burned: Specific versus general reasons. pp. 75-80 in *Proc. Symposium and Workshop on Wilderness Fire*. Intermaountain Forest and Range Exp. Sta. U.S.D.A., Forest Service, Ogden, Utah.

Lewis, H. T. and Ferguson, T. 1988. Yards, corridors, and mosaics: How to burn a boreal forest. *Human Ecology* 16: 57-77.

Martin, P. S. 1979. Prehistoric overkill. pp. 75-129. in Martin, P. S. and Wright, H. E. (eds.), *Pleistocene Extinctions – the Search for a Cause.* Yale Univ. Press, New Haven.

Martin, P. S. and Klein, R. G. 1984. *Quaternary Extinctions: A Prehistoric Revolution.* Univ. Arizona Press, 892 pp.

McCabe, T. T. and McCabe, E. B. 1928. The Bowron Lake moose; Their history and status. *Murrelet* 9: 1-9.

McTaggart-Cowan, I. 1989. Room at The Top? pp. 249-260 in Hummel, M., *Endangered Spaces.* Key Porter Books, Toronto, 288 pp.

Muir, R. D. 1980. Committee on the status of endangered wildlife in Canada – COSEWIC. pp. 285-288 in *Threatened and Endangered Species and Habitats in British Columbia and the Yukon.* British Columbia Ministry of Environment, Victoria.

Mulhall, M. G. 1899. *The Dictionary of Statistics.* 843 pp.

Peterson, R. O. 1994. *Ecological Studies of Wolves on Isle Royale.* Ann. Rep. 1993-94. 16 pp.

Philipp, D. 1990. Fish introductions: When do good intentions go bad? *Canadian Society of Zoologists Bulletin* 21(1): 10.

Roe, F. G. 1971. *The North American Buffalo.* Univ. Toronto, 991 pp.

Rollins, B. E. 1981. *Animal Rights and Human Morality.* Preometheus Books, Buffalo, N.Y., 182 pp.

Seton, E. T. 1937. *Lives of Game Animals* 1: 258-268; 3: 641-702. Literary Guild of America, New York.

Shaw, W. W. and Mangun, W. R. 1980. *Non Consumptive Use of Wildlife in the United States.* Fish and Wildlife Service. U.S.D.I. Resource Bull 154: 1-20.

Tobias, T. N. and Kay, J. J. 1994. The bush harvest in Pinehouse Saskatchewan, Canada. *Arctic* 47: 207-221.

Usher, P. 1987. Indigenous management systems and the conservation of wildlife in the Canadian North. *Alternatives* 14: 3-9.

White, R. 1983. *The Roots of Dependency: Subsistence, Environment, and Social Change Among Choctaws, Pawnees and Navajos.* Univ. Nebraska, 433 pp.

Achevé d'imprimer en octobre 1995 chez
VEILLEUX
IMPRESSION À DEMANDE INC.
à Boucherville, Québec